Change and Innovation in Elementary and Secondary Organization

Change and Innovation in Elementary and Secondary Organization

SECOND EDITION

EDITED BY

Maurie Hillson
Rutgers—The State University of New Jersey

AND

Ronald T. Hyman
Rutgers—The State University of New Jersey

HOLT, RINEHART AND WINSTON, INC.
NEW YORK   CHICAGO   SAN FRANCISCO   ATLANTA
DALLAS   MONTREAL   TORONTO   LONDON   SYDNEY

PREFACE

The title to this edition delineates rather dramatically what has happened in the whole realm of educational innovation since the publication of the original set of readings of 1965 entitled *Change and Innovation in Elementary School Organization.* This revised and expanded edition indicates the basic understanding that to discuss the elementary school as an exclusive entity misrepresents what is actually happening in American education concerning the full range of articulation and integration of educational purposes. The orientation toward organization in the elementary school has been replaced by a much broader one: it is the *whole educative process* and the changes and innovations in that process, including organization, that is marked by ferment on the American educational scene today.

In the preface to the first edition we observed that in the decade of the 1950s some stirrings in American education were taking place. We indicated that in the 1960s intensive activities and experimentation started to challenge the concept of the graded school and the organization of the self-contained classroom. The 1970s promise rather clearly, we think, to be a decade that will see major implementations of many of the themes that started in the fifties and sixties.

There are now on the American educational scene (including Canada) some distinguishable trends in the elementary and secondary school process and organization. Each of the particular

themes that is being presented, developed, and implemented very frequently overlaps other themes that could be isolated and identified. However, if one were to pick some of the more intense activities and try to
synthesize and categorize them, the following ideas would seem to represent what is the present climate in American educational change and
innovation.

The main trend seems to be in the direction of the individualization
or personalization of instruction. In addition, and coincidental with this,
attempts to create programs that develop limitless opportunities for unhampered and continuous progress-oriented growth on the part of the
learner mark the educational scene quite heavily. Also current are the
programs that create collaborative or team endeavors in education. This
collaboration is seen both in the planning and execution of programs and
involves both teachers and students. This also brings into focus the whole
concept of enlarging opportunities for teachers to become decision-makers
through the cooperative planning process. Finally, another major theme
that is now developing in education reflects movement on the part of
students toward greater involvement in determining the meaningful, relevant aspects of both the content and the educative process of school.

In the preface to the first edition we also noted that it was a formidable task to set up a collection of readings dealing exclusively with the
reorganization of the elementary school. No less a formidable task faced
the editors in trying to select a broadly based set of germane readings
that deal with the changes and innovations in elementary and secondary
education. The eight parts of this collection of readings are an editorial
attempt to categorize with some precision the major themes mentioned
above. For obvious reasons various readings overlap and could be placed
in several sections. For example, along with the development of continuous
progress-oriented schools, educators desire to create collaborative endeavors,
especially in the teacher planning area, and also to develop approaches
that lead to heightened individualization. All of these coalesce to become
a total program. Hence, to compile readings on the concepts of independent study and personalization of instruction, continuous progress education, or collaboration in education as separate categories becomes difficult without alluding to the other features that make up the total educational program. However, this is healthy because the integration of various innovative components could lead to great gains in the educational
process.

By examining the eight parts of this expanded and revised edition,
the reader will become immediately aware of the fact that what has
happened in the last five years has been a rather remarkable change in
some quarters of American education. It can be pointed out that there
are categories identified that not only did not exist but could not have

existed ten years ago, because the very concepts on which they are based were not in existence. It should also be noted that material included in this collection of readings has been taken, in some instances, from journals that did not even exist five years ago. Certainly, the recognition of historical landmarks of progress in American education is not in need of defense.

The articles in this collection of readings were chosen by applying several criteria. Recency was one criterion. But in addition we asked ourselves, "What is the relative impact of this idea on the educational scene?" To collect only esoteric, speculative, or romantic notions that could not be translated into action by the reader would not have fulfilled our purpose, namely, to show what is and can be accomplished in changing and innovating educational processes. The articles largely reflect in their scheme of presentation the criteria for which the parts were selected. Each part, with the exception of the summary approach found in Part One, contains articles that are, first, readable narratives or statements on the ideas or concepts developed. Second, each section carries a research-oriented article. If it is not an original piece of research or fundamental research article, it is one that summarizes, refers to, or is taken from a fundamental research statement. Third, we also selected an article (or articles) that is implementation-oriented for each part. These recount what people in the field have done or present a description of programs in action. In addition, we were guided both by the manner in which the article treats the essential idea or activity under consideration and the stylistic and literary presentation made by the writer. We felt that innovations themselves, though exciting, could critically "tune" the reader out if dully presented. Our objective was to select articles on innovation that were written in stylistically adept prose so that readers would become engaged. Learning about change and innovation in written form, we hope, may lead them to attempt such ideas within their own educational contexts.

Each part is preceded by a critical introductory statement relevant to the concept under consideration. The index of authors and their affiliations will give readers a readily usable list of people to whom they can write for additional information or insight into the particular innovation or change with which the author is identified.

These selected readings comprise what is felt by the editors to be a cohesive collection that can be used in many ways. The text has relevance for those who are in the field of educational administration. It will serve those who are in the area of teacher education, both inservice and preservice. Its basic intent is to give the reader a collection of materials beyond the superficial that produces insight into the whole range of innovations that presently mark the educational scene.

The editors are grateful to all those who gave permission to reprint materials included in this book. The willingness of both the journals and the authors of the articles to share their material attests to the kinds of individuals who represent the leadership of American education.

New Brunswick, N.J.   Maurie Hillson
October 1970   Ronald T. Hyman

CONTENTS

PREFACE   v

**PART
ONE**   **CHANGE AND INNOVATION IN EDUCATION:
         AN HISTORICAL AND PRESENT-DAY
         PERSPECTIVE**   1

         INTRODUCTORY STATEMENT   1

         1. HOW WOULD YOU RATE YOUR SCHOOL?
            Margaret Gayfer   7

         2. GUIDELINES FOR REORGANIZING THE SCHOOL AND
            THE CLASSROOM   *Glen Heathers*   12

**PART
TWO**   **THE CONTINUOUS PROGRESS EDUCATION
         MOVEMENT**   33

         INTRODUCTORY STATEMENT   33

         3. GRADED SCHOOLS   from the *Cyclopaedia of
            Education*   41

         4. PROMOTION OR NONPROMOTION?   *Walter H. Worth*   44

         5. CONTINUOUS PROGRESS EDUCATION
            Maurie Hillson   55

         6. THE NONGRADED ELEMENTARY SCHOOL: SELECTED
            PROBLEMS   *B. E. J. Housego*   68

         7. A CONTROLLED EXPERIMENT EVALUATING THE
            EFFECTS OF A NONGRADED ORGANIZATION ON PUPIL
            ACHIEVEMENT   *Maurie Hillson, J. Charles Jones,
            J. William Moore, and Frank Van Devender*   79

         8. THE NONGRADED SECONDARY SCHOOL
            Walter Baden and David Maurer   85

ix

PART THREE   **TEAM TEACHING**   107

INTRODUCTORY STATEMENT   107

9. TEAM TEACHING IN AN ELEMENTARY SCHOOL
   *Robert Anderson, Ellis A. Hagstrom, and
   Wade M. Robinson*   111

10. TEAM PLANNING: HEART TRANSPLANT IN TEACHING
    William Goldstein   122

11. TOWARDS A DIFFERENTIATED TEACHING STAFF
    M. John Rand and Fenwick English   127

12. EVALUATION OF ENGLISH ACHIEVEMENT IN A
    NINTH-GRADE, THREE-PERIOD, TEAM-TEACHING CLASS
    William Georgiades and Joan Bjelke   136

13. AN ANALYSIS OF THE EFFECTIVENESS OF TEAM
    TEACHING COMPARED TO TRADITIONAL TEACHING OF
    HEALTH TO HIGH SCHOOL SOPHOMORE STUDENTS
    Richard G. Schlaadt   149

14. WHY TEACHING TEAMS FAIL   *Carl O.–Olson, Jr.*   154

PART FOUR   **VARIOUS ASPECTS OF GROUPING PUPILS**   161

INTRODUCTORY STATEMENT   161

15. THE EFFICACY OF TWO ORGANIZATIONAL PLANS FOR
    UNDERACHIEVING INTELLECTUALLY GIFTED CHILDREN
    *Merle B. Karnes, George McCoy, Richard Reid
    Zehrbach, Janet P. Wollersheim, and Harvey F.
    Clarizio*   166

16. SHOULD WE GROUP BY ABILITY?   *Jim Olsen*   179

17. HOMOGENEOUS ABILITY GROUPING—BRITISH STYLE
    Earl Ogletree   184

18. TEACHING IN ABILITY GROUPED ENGLISH CLASSES:
    A STUDY OF VERBAL INTERACTION AND COGNITIVE
    GOALS   *Isobel L. Pfeiffer*   191

19. ABILITY GROUPING   from the *NEA Research
    Bulletin*   200

20. AN ANNOTATED LIST OF 40 GROUPING PLANS
    Harold G. Shane   204

PART
FIVE   INDIVIDUALIZED INSTRUCTION   213

              INTRODUCTORY STATEMENT   213
              21. INDIVIDUALIZED INSTRUCTION   *Alexander Frazier*   217
              22. WHAT IS INDIVIDUALIZED INSTRUCTION?
                  William Hedges   229
              23. INDIVIDUALIZING INSTRUCTION: EDUCATIONAL FAD
                  OR EDUCATIONAL FULFILLMENT?   *Maurie Hillson*   236
              24. INDIVIDUALLY PRESCRIBED INSTRUCTION
                  John O. Bolvin   241
              25. INDEPENDENT STUDY: WHAT DIFFERENCE DOES IT
                  MAKE? *Don H. Richardson*   246
              26. INDIVIDUAL INSTRUCTION AND GROUP INSTRUCTION:
                  A CASE STUDY *John A. Zahorik*   256

PART
SIX   FLEXIBLE SCHEDULING   263

              INTRODUCTORY STATEMENT   263
              27. FLEXIBILITY IN THE SECONDARY SCHOOL
                  Howard M. Johnson   266
              28. AN APPROACH TO FLEXIBILITY   *Arnold J. Moore*   276
              29. NANCY DRAWS UP HER OWN DAILY SCHEDULE AT
                  THURSTON   *Kenneth G. Gehret*   283
              30. FLEXIBLE SCHEDULING—ADVANTAGES AND DISAD-
                  VANTAGES *Nicholas C. Polos*   286

PART
SEVEN   EDUCATIONAL TECHNOLOGY   293

              INTRODUCTORY STATEMENT   293
              31. TECHNOLOGY MAKES INSTRUCTION VISIBLE
                  Robert Heinich   298
              32. THE RISE OF PROGRAMMED INSTRUCTION
                  Paul Saettler   305
              33. COMPUTER-ASSISTED INSTRUCTION
                  Patrick Suppes and Max Jerman   324
              34. AN INSTRUCTIONAL MANAGEMENT SYSTEM FOR
                  CLASSROOM TEACHERS   *Cleone L. Geddes
                  and Beverly Y. Kooi*   336

35. THE EFFECTS OF COMPUTER-BASED RESOURCE UNITS
UPON INSTRUCTIONAL BEHAVIOR   *George S. Holden*   345

36. STUDENT FILMMAKING: WHY AND HOW
Paul Carrico   352

37. THE MYTHS OF EDUCATIONAL TECHNOLOGY
Anthony G. Oettinger   365

PART EIGHT   THE TOTAL SCENE CONCERNING CHANGE AND INNOVATION IN THE EDUCATIVE PROCESS   373

INTRODUCTORY STATEMENT   373

38. SCHOOLS FOR YOUNG CHILDREN: ORGANIZATIONAL
AND ADMINISTRATIVE CONSIDERATIONS
Robert H. Anderson   377

39. A SCHOOL DESIGNED FOR KIDS   *James Cass*   386

40. HIGH SCHOOL WITH NO WALLS—IT'S A HAPPENING
IN PHILADELPHIA   *Henry S. Resnik*   391

41. THE CONGENIAL SCHOOL   *Harold B. Gores*   398

42. FRAMEWORKS FOR OBSERVING TEACHING
Ronald T. Hyman   406

43. "OPENNESS" IN THE ORGANIZATIONAL CLIMATE OF
"HUMANISTIC" AND "CUSTODIAL" ELEMENTARY
SCHOOLS   *Wayne K. Hoy and James Appleberry*   415

44. SUGGESTIONS FOR INVOLVING TEACHERS IN INNOVA-
TION   *Richard W. Burns*   421

45. LAG ON MAKING IDEAS WORK   *John I. Goodlad*   424

INDEX   427

PART ONE

Change
and Innovation
in Education

AN HISTORICAL
AND PRESENT-DAY
PERSPECTIVE

The two words "change" and "innovation" have interesting meanings, and they mean interestingly different things. The word change is related to the word "exchange." It connotes the idea of making something different in one or maybe two particulars, but not really the activity of converting to something wholly new. Innovation, on the other hand, does mean the introduction of something new. It takes its meaning from the root for "new." To innovate is to create something new, something that deviates from standard practice. The American educational scene today is marked both by changes in programs and by innovations that are creating totally new programs and directions. They are based on themes and ideas that are not yet consummately attained, but are certainly inspirational and serve as goals to be achieved.

James Cass observed that, "Education reporting today is very much like snapping a photo of a moving object—by the time the shutter has clicked the picture has changed. Not many years ago it was possible to forecast with reasonable accuracy what the schools would be like a decade hence by looking closely at contemporary classrooms. Action for change was directed primarily toward improving and expanding what already existed—an effort to achieve more of the same. But today the education scene is changing so rapidly that no man can predict with certainty what the schools of 1976 will be like. We do know the direction the change is likely to take, and we can identify many of the ingredients, but we do not know how fast they will come, and in what combinations they will appear—or what innovations will develop as spinoffs of the changes already taking place." [1]

We are in an era of accelerating change in elementary and secondary education. We are in a period of marked changes at the college level as well. One small aspect of the change process is seen in the activity that broadens the base of educational decision making. We have moved from developing programs based on simple applications of psychologically based findings to the more generalized applications of findings that are undergirded by research from sociology and anthropology. We are developing and moving toward newer educational activities based on the heightened knowledge of the technocracy that has developed in the past several years. It can be said that we are entering a new phase in education that will involve basic attempts to create some totally new theories of instruction by the use and evaluation of all the extant research. These new theories may create, when applied, wholly different settings for learning and schooling, and education will be seen in a fundamentally new light. It is accurate to report that there are powerful forces both in and out of education which compel those of us in the field to create innovation and reform, in order that our young charges might share, in a more realistic way, the largess of an innovated and technologically oriented society.

Title III of the *Elementary and Secondary Education Act of 1965* was specifically set up to underpin some of these inno-

[1] James Cass, *Saturday Review*, October 15, 1966.

vative directions in education. Many of their documents refer to their philosophy of innovation. The magazine entitled *PACE* is an acronym for the words "*P*rojects to *A*dvance *C*reativity in *E*ducation." Various reports generally carried titles such as "Pace-setters in Innovation." Whereas change, innovation, and creativity may have been frighteningly dangerous concepts in the past, they have now become rallying cries and will continue to be so for the decade of the 1970s. The innovative and exemplary thrust of Title III is only one example. The whole force of the United States Office of Education, supported by an education-oriented Congress of the United States, is but one indication of the strong movement for change and innovation in education.

Why is this national behavior somewhat different from what had historically reflected change and innovation in education? Why have we had such a confluence of innovative intensity that has literally moved us from an ebb and flow and sometimes moribund program of educational change to a vital arena of implementation and dialogue concerning the needs for educational innovation and change? There may be three reasons why our present-day perspective is different from the historical movements that in comparison seemed to limp along rather than rush forward with some impact.

First, the scientific study of behavior and of learners—how they learn and the styles attendant upon that learning drawn from the psycho-socio-anthropological context—has made a telling impact on educators. We know more about perception and learning, more about the intuitive forces that have to do with learning and the styles of learning, and more about the affective aspects related to learning, as well as the effective applications of what is learned, than we have ever known before. Second, the great resource of research on how to organize the setting for learning so we can capitalize on these findings is more readily available now than it has ever been before. We now know how to move pupils around in many ways which are quite different from the present self-contained classroom. We have many studies and ongoing programs that reflect much better ways of making teacher-pupil assignments to create greater opportunities for learning than we have ever had before. Third, we now have and are continuing to create materials for instruction that are so excitingly original and superior compared to what we have had in the past, that not to get maximum value out of these materials by changing their context is almost a denial of our own educational calling. Some materials and their use insist on a change of setting and approach.

These three conditions were not extant for those who attempted changes or innovations in the years past. Earlier innovations did not have what we have: a knowledge of technology, organization, and process that combine to give us depth of insight into better ways of achieving some of the higher purposes and aims of education never available in the history of education prior to 1970. We have new media that were never within the scope of the imagination of our educational ancestors. We have new teaching strategies, approaches, and methodological and educational activities from all levels —preschool through the twelfth year—that are much more fruitful in gaining adequate responses from our students than we have ever had in the past. And, we are a society that has put a man on the moon. This has allowed for an acceleration of educational change and a sympathy for it, although one must hasten to indicate that we do not move as fast in education from research-proven ideas to implementation as they do in other fields of endeavor.

So rapid is change that Glen Heathers (the author of the second article in this section) in another context wrote, "Writing an epitaph for grouping may well be the task of the reviewer of research on grouping for the 1980 edition of this encyclopedia. Even today it appears that grouping as a central theme of organization for instruction has nearly run its course and is in the process of being replaced by a familiar theme— individualized instruction—that becomes a focus of educational reform in the mid-1960s.

"The concept of individualization has acquired such potency that it is reducing to subordinate status even those grouping arrangements being promoted under the banners of nongrading and team teaching." [2]

The manifold aspects of change and innovation in education certainly reflect this point of view. Couple this observation with the circumstance that the critics, both in and out of education, are posing rather intense questions concerning the present status of education. The questions and criticisms are hard to ignore. Social crisis does abound in the land and schools are a focal institution of critical concern.

The whole period from classical antiquity to the present

---

[2] Glen Heathers, "Grouping," *Encyclopedia of Educational Research*, 4th ed., Robert L. Ebel, editor, The Macmillan Company, 1969, p. 568.

day may not have had anywhere near the number, nor in any-way faced, the problems that our society faces at the moment. American education in the twentieth century has consolidated the growth that it has made since the middle 1800s. Now it must turn to face the criticisms that have been made of it from the middle 1940s through the 1960s. The changes that took place and are still in flux because of the vast economic and social reverberations brought on by two world wars and a third undeclared war now must be presented as *implemented* innovations to prepare a nation that must face problems hith-erto unknown to man. That is the reason for the need for change and innovation in the elementary and secondary edu-cative process to a degree of intensity never before realized.

The two articles that make up Part I enunciate the ma-jor themes of change and innovation in education that will be pursued in the decade of the 1970s. The short article by Margaret Gayfer summarizes another article from *Chatelaine* magazine that was entitled "65 Best Schools in Canada." These 65 schools were singled out as the best by a variety of people throughout the Canadian Provinces. There are approx-imately 18,000 schools in Canada. Out of that 18,000 a list of 65 was extracted. The questionnaire reported on in the article was developed by a team of graduate students at the Ontario Institute for Studies in Education, Toronto. The important point of this article is that the questionnaire reflects distinc-tively the themes of (1) individualization of instruction, (2) unlimited and unhampered education for continuous progress, and (3) collaboration in education—all basic and germane ed-ucational movements of the present day. This questionnaire can serve as a checklist concerning the extent to which innova-tions and changes are being implemented in any given school district. By coupling it with the much more definitive discus-sion by Glen Heathers in his article, we can start to get the picture of the whole spectrum of educational innovation and change.

Heathers offers the reader "six facts of life" facing the inno-vative school leader that denote a challenge in the develop-ment and implementation of change and innovation in the schools. He goes on to create a framework for decision making related to educational innovation. Heathers sees organiza-tional changes as being highly related to the instructional aims and indicates that if the aims bring with them certain valid emphases, then organizational arrangements must be de-veloped to achieve the realization of these aims. Using examples of selected aims, Heathers faces the problem of how organization and changes in organization can improve the teaching of theory and inquiry, and how organizing instruction may help develop ways for students to learn how to learn. He discusses the way we can organize instruction to foster excellence or mastery, as he defines it, and some of the organizational arrangements that foster the individualization of instruction. The second part of Heathers' article deals with the development of local capabilities for making organizational change and some steps that a school system needs to take in preparing itself to design and conduct educational change programs. This discussion and the design he suggests for local programs to reorganize instruction round out a very adequate statement concerning the way a system-wide change program can be developed—one that will focus on independent study, standards of excellence for mastery, and individualized instruction.

1 | How Would You Rate Your School?

MARGARET GAYFER

Reprinted with permission from the supplement "Trends and Innovations" of *School Progress*, September 1969, pp. 56–57.

Be prepared to see more of the questionnaire on these pages. It's likely to bring reactions from education-conscious readers of *Chatelaine*, a homemakers' magazine with 1¼ million readers across Canada.

Whether this reaction comes to you via a letter dropped into your basket or through conversations with associates, the article is bound to raise questions about the excellence of your school system in comparison with the schools cited in the survey.

Prepared by a team of graduate students at the Ontario Institute for Studies in Education, the questionnaire was sent to 65 school principals across Canada. These schools were nominated by education departments, school board officials, teachers, and other qualified observers as the best in the country. The results of this survey, plus comments from some of the principals who answered, are featured in the September [1969] *Chatelaine*.

Near the end of the article, the suggestion is made that readers should ask the principals of the schools their children attend to complete the survey. Further, if parents are unhappy with the answers, the questionnaire could be used as "a basis for pressure on school boards, superintendents and principals," who, the article suggests, "may be waiting for a sign that parents will back them." Be forewarned. Rate the schools in your jurisdiction and see how they stack up against the schools cited by *Chatelaine*.

According to the article, all nominations for the best schools were progressive schools that "value a child's unique personal development higher than the marks he gets on a history exam." For some principals,

The Chatelaine Questionnaire
HOW WOULD YOU RANK YOUR SCHOOL?

Please assign a number 0, 1, 2, 3, according to the degree of success of your school in meeting each of the following criteria. (For instance, if your school is not oriented that way at all, mark it 0; if it is moving in that direction, 1; if a program like that is under way, 2; if it is succeeding, 3.)

(1) THE PRIMARY AIMS OF THE SCHOOL ARE

a. to develop a feeling of self-adequacy in the child ____

b. to develop socialization: the ability to get along with others ____

c. to encourage self-direction in the student so that he sets his own goals and knows how well he's doing ____

d. to develop a spirit and skills of enquiry: he looks for reasons rather than ready-made explanations ____

(2) MOTIVATION, THE CHILD IS ENCOURAGED TO LEARN BY

a. emphasis on inner satisfaction rather than outside rewards and punishments (i.e., marks, prizes, detentions) ____

b. use of a variety of teaching materials, including visual and audio-visual aids ____

c. a generally warm, mutually respectful relationship between teachers and pupils ____

d. an adequate pupil-teacher ratio (no more than 30 to 1) ____

(3) CURRICULUM CONTENT

a. suits the stages of child development (social, physical, conceptual) ____

b. is developed by the staff of the school appropriate to local needs ____

c. includes option subjects ____

(4) PUPIL PROGRESSION

a. is by subject rather than by entire grade so that each student can go forward at his own rate ____

b. depends on the evaluation of his work by more than one teacher ____

c. self-evaluation by the student is considered ____

d. students progressing to higher schools but failing in a subject can take makeup programs (evenings, summer, spare periods) ____

e. there is a school guidance department to assist teachers in compiling school records, especially anecdotal report cards ____

(5) ORGANIZATIONAL STRUCTURE
a. the school is not graded ____
b. there is some team teaching ____
c. the size of learning groups varies ____

(6) CHILD GROWTH AND DEVELOPMENT
a. differences between children are recognized and allowed for ____
b. children are free to move around ____
c. the school provides facilities for "letting off steam," e.g.,
   games, wrestling, clay molding, etc. ____

(7) PHYSICAL SCHOOL STRUCTURE
a. the school has flexible spaces which can be enlarged or made
   smaller for quiet solitary work, small groups or large team
   teaching ____
b. it has comfortable furniture ____
c. temperature, ventilation, humidity, light, color, texture and
   noise are geared to help learning ____

(8) EVALUATION AND HOME-SCHOOL COMMUNICATION
a. the school uses parent-teacher interviews as well as report
   cards ____
b. students are present at parent-teacher interviews ____
c. anecdotal report cards (describing a student's achievement,
   not ranking it) are directed at students as well as parents ____

(9) LIBRARY RESOURCES
a. students always have free access to the library ____
b. the library contains films, film strips, video and audio tapes,
   slides and records as well as books ____
c. it has magazines, newspapers, pamphlets ____
d. the materials incorporate many points of view on various
   subjects ____
e. there are individual study carrels ____
f. the library can accommodate a large proportion of the
   student body at one time (about one fifth) ____
g. there is one full-time librarian and one clerk for each five
   hundred students ____

(10) SERVICES FOR EXCEPTIONAL CHILDREN
a. a child with special needs, either gifted or handicapped, can
   stay in his own area school rather than go to a special school ____
b. a handicapped child spends part of the day with his peer
   group but also receives extra help ____
c. specially trained teachers assist regular teachers with
   handicapped children ____
d. there is extramural teaching for students who are ill at home
   for a prolonged period (i.e., three months)

however, marks still rate higher in importance than inner satisfaction and other intangible (and unmeasurable) benefits of a loosely structured, no-failure program. So far, it appears few schools have completely discarded the punishment-reward approach to student motivation although many principals profess a dislike of the examination syndrome. "All I can say," wrote one principal, "is that any teacher who needs such a motivation as the threat of failure should hand in his resignation today."

Centralized control of curriculum is another headache for principals, who seek more local control and freedom to experiment with the strict regulations emanating from provincial departments of education. Generalized John Young, the vociferous principal of now-famous Campbell River Secondary School in British Columbia, "the curriculum in schools across Canada is universally poor. There is needless and irrational division into very specific subject areas." And, he adds, "it seems that most of what we do is organized according to the age of the student or the size of the room or the calendar or some other stupid arrangement having nothing to do with how the child learns."

In keeping with their "progressive" outlook, almost all of the nominated schools are trying innovations in organization, programs, and use of facilities. Only three of the 65 schools continue to promote by grade rather than by subject, for example. However, it must be noted that the term nongraded is an ambiguous term, interpreted in a wide variety of ways by different principals. Similarly, various forms of team teaching are practised by many of the surveyed schools.

The section dealing with the physical school structure reveals dissatisfaction by many principals, who generally find they must cope with an inflexible building not particularly suited to its modern educational role. The schools nominated were housed in buildings ranging in age from the 40-year-old Central School in Queen's County, N.S., to Calgary's brand-new Memorial High School, less than a year old. Age of the building, of course, is not a prime indicator of the school's worth. Says one principal, "Fine facilities provide fine opportunities, but they do not guarantee fine education."

The gulf separating the *have-not* provinces from the *haves* is depressingly obvious when it comes to school library resources. The survey indicates that even in the "best" Maritime schools, the library, if the school has one at all, is still no more than a repository for books. Lacking are the glittering array of AV hardware and all the accompanying tapes, filmstrips, records, magazines, and other learning aids commonly found in schools in the richer provinces. In one New Brunswick school, opened without one library book, the students collected money for books and AV equipment and now are raising funds to buy a videotape recorder.

Comments from principals surveyed indicate that the spirit of innovation and discovery is more rampant in elementary schools than at the secondary level. This is especially evident in the answers given in the first section under aims. According to *Chatelaine* "most elementary schools maintain they are succeeding with all the aims, whereas the senior schools more often feel they are just under way." However, it is encouraging to discover that many principals would like to achieve the enlightened aims listed in the questionnaire, and are only prevented from doing so by lack of funds for equipment, and worse, opposition from the establishment. As a member of that establishment, the school business official has an obligation to encourage improvement and the introduction of imaginative programs. A first step toward improvement is identification of problem areas, and this could be done by giving principals and teachers a questionnaire similar to the one shown here.

2 | Guidelines for Reorganizing the School and the Classroom

GLEN HEATHERS

Reprinted with permission from *Rational Planning in Curriculum and Instruction,* Washington, D.C., Center for the Study of Instruction, National Education Association, 1967, pp. 63–86.

"Next year, we'll reorganize" has become a wry joke in many fields—but seldom as close to the bone as when school administrators attempt to strengthen the instructional program. The organizational changes most popular lately are some version of nongrading or cooperative teaching. Schedule modifications may be adopted as part of a program of cooperative teaching, for example, or a version of the Trump Plan may be introduced at the secondary level.[1] Some schools have replaced the self-contained classroom in the upper grades of the elementary school with a departmental or semidepartmental plan.

Instead of involving changes at the school-wide level, some new programs reorganize instruction at the classroom level. The Durrell pupil-team learning plan calls for dividing a class into groups made up of from two to five pupils who study together in a team fashion.[2] Another

[1] J. Lloyd Trump and Dorsey Baynham, *Focus on Change: Guide to Better Schools.* Rand McNally, 1961. 147 pp.

[2] Donald D. Durrell, editor, "Adapting Instruction to the Learning Needs of Children in the Intermediate Grades." *Boston University Journal of Education,* 142; December 1959.

approach to reorganizing the classroom is individually prescribed instruction, as in the program at the University Elementary School at UCLA under the direction of John I. Goodlad, and in the elementary program at Oakleaf School in suburban Pittsburgh under the leadership of Robert Glaser.[3]

Numerous innovative programs involve changes in curriculum organization. In many nongraded programs, grade-level division lines in such areas as reading and mathematics have been erased, and continuous, vertical curriculum sequences have been introduced.[4] Some innovations in curriculum involve establishing a spiral progression in which the learner encounters the same topic two or more times at successively higher levels of advancement in the curriculum area. There are curricula that introduce students to certain topics—algebraic equations, for example—at much earlier ages than is conventional. A radical departure in curriculum building is the experimental program in elementary science being developed under the auspices of the American Association for the Advancement of Science, entitled *Science, a Process Approach*. In this program, the curriculum units that are placed in sequence represent different areas and levels of competence in conducting scientific inquiry (the *processes* of science) rather than areas and levels of scientific knowledge (the *content* of science).[5]

Faced with a bewildering array of innovations in the organization of the school, the classroom, and the curriculum, how should the school leader set about selecting the innovations he wishes to introduce in the schools? How should he proceed to provide leadership in implementing and evaluating the changes being introduced?

At the outset, it is recommended that the local school leader, as agent of change, should give attention to some major "facts of life" concerning the development and use of educational innovations.

Few of the educational innovations currently being marketed have been fully developed, implemented, and evaluated. Most of the innovations that are being brought forward are still in the pilot phase of development. This applies to the various new approaches to school organization—nongrading, team teaching, the Trump Plan, the Stoddard dual progress plan, and so on. It applies to new approaches to organizing the classroom—the Durrell pupil-team learning plan and the programs

[3] John I. Goodlad, "Nongraded Schools: Meeting Children Where They Are." *Saturday Review*, 48: 57–59ff.; March 20, 1965; *Newsletter*, No. 11, University of Pittsburgh, Learning Research and Development Center, February 1966.

[4] Frank R. Dufay, *Ungrading the Elementary School*. West Nyack, N.Y.: Parker Publishing Co., 1966. 230 pp.

[5] American Association for the Advancement of Science, Commission on Science Education, *Science, a Progress Approach*. Parts I–VII for Kindergarten through Grade 6. Washington, D.C.: the Association, 1965 and 1966.

employing individually prescribed instruction. The new approaches to curriculum organization also are in early stages of development and are relatively untested.

Many innovations exist in a variety of forms rather than having a standard form. Nongraded programs, for example, vary in terms of the age levels covered, the curricular areas placed on a nongraded basis, the procedures used in grouping pupils, and the ways in which curriculum organization is modified to suit the purposes of the plan. There are as many varieties of team teaching or cooperative teaching as there are centers that spearheaded the development of this type of school organization. There is the Lexington Plan, the Norwalk Plan, the Pittsburgh Plan, and so on. It is noteworthy that the organization of team teaching in the elementary school ordinarily is radically different from that used in the secondary school.

An innovation ordinarily must be modified somewhat to meet the requirements of a local situation. This is true almost always when a school or school system adopts any type of organizational change. Such factors as school philosophy, size of school, composition of the student body, makeup of the local staff, space and equipment at hand, and available help from consultants play a role in shaping the innovation to the local schools.

Implementing an innovation effectively always calls for a system of interrelated changes in the local situation. In the case of making changes in school organization, the system of changes required includes among others schedule modifications, reassignments of staff, curriculum changes, changes in uses made of space and equipment, changes in communication patterns, and staff reeducation. Unless all of these types of changes occur together, the innovation is likely to be implemented in form but not in substance.

The most crucial factor in making an innovation function at the instructional level is staff reeducation. The great majority of local change programs in schools fall short of success in large part because of a failure to provide school leaders and teachers with the education that would enable them to conduct instruction that meets the purposes of the innovation. Many nongraded programs, for example, are ineffective because the teachers involved lack sufficient knowledge of how to individualize instruction to organize and conduct instruction in terms of nongraded advancement. Team-teaching programs also require for their success that team members have in common a set of competencies in planning and conducting instruction to meet the learning needs and characteristics of individual pupils in the team. The staff reeducation called for by an innovation cannot ordinarily be provided through occasional classroom visits by a curriculum consultant, by taking an in-service course that meets a dozen times at the end of the school day, or in a short-term summer workshop. The reeducation called for must be carried on intensively and continuously over a considerable period, seldom less than one year.

In most instances, local leadership must be relied on to plan and implement the school system's innovative programs. The nationwide dissemination of new developments in education will not, in the foreseeable future, have the services of a sufficient number of educational change agents from outside the schools to offer more than a small fraction of the leadership that the many thousands of school systems will require in planning and conducting their change programs. The education of local school leaders for their roles as key agents of change thus becomes a matter of high priority.

Taken together, these six facts place the innovative school leader at the center of a complex and challenging process of change. Adopting an innovation in the instructional program is a very different matter from replacing worn-out furniture. It calls for creative planning, for designing and launching an appropriate program of staff education, and for skillful leadership in orchestrating the numerous aspects of the process of implementing the innovation.

ORGANIZATIONAL CHANGES AS RELATED TO INSTRUCTIONAL AIMS

School leaders often start the process of developing a local change program by considering the desirability of introducing some new organizational arrangements in school, classroom, or curriculum. For example, they ask: Should the school system adopt a nongraded program in the primary school, team teaching in the upper elementary grades, a version of the Trump Plan in the high school? This is one way to get started in thinking about introducing changes in the local program. However, very early in the process, it is essential that the school leader give systematic attention to determining what improvements he hopes to accomplish in the *instructional* program, and to what extent the innovations being considered can be expected to accomplish such improvements.

It is true that school leaders sometimes introduce organizational changes for reasons other than the improvement of instruction. Thus the use of teacher aides has sometimes been justified as a way of maintaining the current instructional standards with fewer certified teachers. Team teaching has been recommended at times as a way to keep superior teachers in the classroom through giving them improved status, salary increments, and better working conditions. In the great majority of cases, however, organizational changes are introduced to improve instruction, and local administrators ordinarily present the proposed changes to the school staff and the community in this light.

I would concur with [my colleague] that the surest route to improving instruction starts with an analysis of the school system's aims and an appraisal of how well these aims are being accomplished. Perhaps the aims previously adopted will be found adequate. Perhaps it will be decided that they should be changed or that the relative emphasis placed on different aims should be modified. It may be decided to eliminate driver education, to offer all pupils French in the elementary school, to teach all pupils scientists' methods of inquiry, to place greater stress on teaching all pupils to read well or to place less stress on instruction in foreign language.

Once the school's aims have been determined, a logical next step is to take stock of the instructional program in relation to accomplishing these aims. How successful is the reading program considering the school system's aims and the abilities of different children? Is the science program accomplishing its purposes with all pupils, regardless of their ages or levels of ability? Are the pupils of different ability levels learning skills in independent study or are such skills being developed only in pupils of relatively high ability?

When this stocktaking has been completed, the proper next step is for the school's leaders to consider possible organizational changes, to accommodate other changes. Considerations in this step are not specific innovations but *organizational* themes. To illustrate, the school system's leaders should examine the theme of teacher cooperation in general before singling out specific approaches to team teaching such as the Norwalk or Lexington Plan, or, they should examine the general theme of continuous progress before looking into the nongraded program in the elementary schools at Appleton, Wisconsin, or in the high school at Melbourne, Florida.

At this point, it will be valuable for us to examine the relations between certain organizational themes and certain instructional aims that are being emphasized in today's educational reform movement. At least five major aims of instruction are emphasized in the speeches and writings of leading reform spokesmen. If the reform spokesmen and the many innovators who are developing means of bringing these aims into the classroom have their way, any school system that does not pursue these aims energetically will soon become out of date.

Stress teaching the structure of a discipline rather than facts in the content areas of the curriculum, at all levels of instruction, and to all students. This calls for focusing teaching upon the general ideas or principles that enable one to explain or predict phenomena dealt with in the curricular area.[6]

Teach methods of inquiry or problem-solving thinking as those methods are employed in gaining new knowledge within a given curricular

---

[6] "Innovations in Instruction." *The National Elementary Principal*, 43: 8–60; September 1963. See also John I. Goodlad and others. *The Changing School Curriculum.* New York: The Fund for the Advancement of Education, 1966. 122 pp.

area. Thus, pupils should learn scientists' methods of inquiry, and should learn science by following the intellectual pathways that scientists followed in gaining the knowledge the pupil is studying. Similarly, pupils should learn to think like mathematicians, and should learn the methods of inquiry used by social scientists in such areas as sociology and history.[7]

Teach competencies in independent study so that all pupils become capable of planning and conducting their own learning activities much if not most of the time. Independent study, or self-instruction, requires among other things that the pupil possess skills in the uses of English, arithmetic, and instruments of measurement.[8]

Set standards of excellence or mastery and hold all students to levels of accomplishment corresponding to those standards in whatever they study.[9] The notion here is that the instructional program is at fault when a student fails to learn well what he studies. The problem is to suit the learning task, the methods of instruction, and the pace of advancement to the student's characteristics as a learner.

Individualize instruction by providing each student with a program of studies that is tailored to his learning needs and capabilities.[10] An appropriate program for a student will sometimes call for independent study, sometimes for a tutorial relation with a teacher, sometimes for working cooperatively with other students, and sometimes for studying in groups of various sizes with lectures or discussions conducted by a teacher.

Assuming these aims to be valid emphases in the school's program, how do different organizational arrangements relate to their realization? Let us consider first the ways in which organizational arrangements might contribute to achieving the first two aims listed above—teaching theory and teaching methods of inquiry.

CAN ORGANIZATIONAL CHANGES IMPROVE THE TEACHING OF THEORY AND INQUIRY?

In the opinion of many spokesmen for educational reform, the most fundamental changes that should be made in the instructional program

[7] Jerome S. Bruner, *The Process of Education.* Cambridge, Mass.: Harvard University Press, 1960. 97 pp.; Joseph J. Schwab, "The Teaching of Science as Enquiry." *The Teaching of Science.* Cambridge, Mass.: Harvard University Press, 1962. pp. 3–103.

[8] Glen Heathers, *The Strategy of Educational Reform.* New York: New York University, School of Education, November 1961 (Mimeo.)

[9] John W. Gardner, *Excellence.* New York: Harper & Row, 1961. 171 pp.

[10] Ronald C. Doll, editor, *Individualizing Instruction.* 1964 Yearbook. Washington, D.C.: Association for Supervision and Curriculum Development, a department of the National Education Association, 1964. 174 pp.; Nelson B. Henry, editor. *Individualizing Instruction.* Sixty-First Yearbook of the National Society for the Study of Education, Part I. Chicago: University of Chicago Press, 1962. 337 pp.

are related to teaching students to understand ideas rather than merely to memorize facts, and teaching them problem-solving thinking so that they can conduct their own inquiries instead of simply accepting what they read or what they are told. How can such changes of emphasis in the instructional program be brought about?

The most basic way for a school system to accomplish changes in the instructional objectives it emphasizes is by changing the contents of the curriculum and the instructional methods teachers use. For example, the PSSC physics course that one-half of the nation's high school students are taking today places stress on teaching the student physical theory and the methods of inquiry used by physicists in conducting experiments. Teaching the course effectively requires that physics teachers in the high school learn instructional methods that are appropriate for an emphasis on teaching theory and inquiry.

How can organizational arrangements help a school system strengthen the teaching of theory and methods of inquiry? At the elementary level, introducing specialist teachers of mathematics and science within a team-teaching or departmental plan would seem to be a way to accomplish this purpose. But specialist teachers in these areas will not do a better job of teaching theory and inquiry than the general elementary teachers they replace unless they have special preparation for teaching in relation to these aims. In selecting specialist teachers of these fields, the school administrator needs to be sure that they have an appropriate background of courses and that they take special in-service work to meet the new requirements of their specialities. As far as in-service preparation is concerned, an important advantage of specialist teaching is that teachers can concentrate their work in just one subject area.

Other organizational arrangements have a less direct relation to the teaching of theory and methods of inquiry than does specialist teaching. Team teaching offers increased opportunities for teachers to share ideas and to plan together. If some members of the team are versed in the requirements for teaching theory and inquiry, they have numerous opportunities in team teaching to help other members of the team to strengthen the emphasis they place on these goals. Flexible arrangements for scheduling and grouping can offer various individual and small-group settings that are better suited for planning and conducting inquiries and for studying theory than are conventional classroom groups. This is because the learning of theory and inquiry occurs best when the student has a great deal of freedom to chart his own course and when he has many opportunities to share his ideas and experiences with other students and with his teachers. The Durrell pupil-team learning plan, through setting up small work groups within the classroom, can provide excellent arrangements for planning and conducting group inquiries.

ORGANIZING INSTRUCTION TO HELP
STUDENTS "LEARN HOW TO LEARN"

Some leading educators believe that the most important of the school's objectives should be to teach all students the learning skills, attitudes, and habits that will enable them to study independently. These educators reason that during much of his time at school, and nearly all of his time after he leaves school, the individual is responsible for planning and conducting his own learning activities. Since most of his life, then, the student will need to take responsibility for what he learns, a vital task of the school is to prepare him to be a self-educating person. Another important reason for teaching all students skills in independent study is that the types of thinking called for in the study of theory and the conduct of inquiries must largely be one's own thinking. While a teacher can guide a student's thinking, thinking by its very nature is largely an individual matter.

Presently, teaching the student the basic learning skills is the chief purpose of the elementary school, particularly in the primary grades. Reading, writing, listening, and speaking are taught to enable the student to acquire and communicate knowledge through the uses of language. Also, a certain amount of attention is given to teaching so-called study skills so that the student can use an alphabetical index, read maps, and interpret charts and graphs. Two other sorts of learning skills are given emphasis in the elementary program: one is in the area of arithmetic where the effort is made to teach the four fundamental operations; the other is in the use of measuring instruments, especially rulers, thermometers, weight scales, and timepieces.

The failure of the schools to teach the basic learning skills effectively to all students is today a matter of national concern, with reading retardation receiving the greatest amount of attention. As one evidence of the severity of the problem in the area of reading, the public schools of New York City recently announced the policy of requiring for graduation from high school that the student read at least at the level of the average beginning eighth grader.[11] Programs for the educationally disadvantaged, notably Head Start, have as their chief purpose improving instruction in basic learning skills.

It is a remarkable fact that, as students in American schools advance year by year toward graduation from high school, less and less attention is given to teaching them the basic learning skills that are required for independent study. The program becomes increasingly concentrated on subject matter. In junior and senior high school, some attention is paid

[11] *New York Times,* June 30, 1966.

to remedial instruction in reading and arithmetic, but only with those students who are severely retarded. Also, during these years, many schools have programs that permit some superior students to learn part of the time on an independent basis. However, no systematic efforts are made to *teach* competencies in independent study.

How can organizational arrangements contribute toward teaching students basic learning skills? Nongrading the school program to provide "continuous progress" that is suited to the student's advancement in a subject and his learning rate is an important approach to strengthening instruction in basic skills. Virtually all nongraded programs in the country, especially those set up in the primary school, focus on skills in reading and arithmetic. A continuous progress plan, when installed in a school, permits the staff to depart from the usual grade-level arrangements and teach each pupil reading and arithmetic at the level and at the pace that suit his needs. The purpose is to ensure that the pupil learns each unit in the curricular sequence well before moving on to the next. Through permitting less mature or slower learners to stay an additional year at the primary level, continuous progress plans can ensure that these pupils will be better prepared for the program of the intermediate years than if they had been promoted from the primary school at the usual time. Nongrading, it should be noted, is an organizational approach to doing away with the necessity for remedial instruction. Also, it is a way to ensure that the pupil is prepared to learn the succeeding unit in the curricular sequence.

Nongrading, remedial programs, and special programs for the educationally disadvantaged appear to be the only organizational provisions that are being used to strengthen the teaching of basic learning skills. Instead of strengthening such skills, most school systems simply take cognizance of the fact that students differ greatly in their competencies as learners and provide different learning settings for gifted, average, and slow learners. Ability grouping, or tracking, is the most frequent approach that schools use to permit teachers to use different instructional materials and methods with students of different levels of competence in basic learning skills. Usually, no serious efforts are made to teach learning skills to students who lack command of them. Organizational arrangements, in this case, tend to be used to avoid, or even prevent, improving the teaching of basic learning skills.

B. Frank Brown, in *The Nongraded High School,* devotes a chapter to independent study and calls for encouraging students to elect this type of learning setting.[12] Similarly, Trump calls for using independent study a major share of the time in the secondary school.[13] However, merely of-

[12] B. Frank Brown, *The Nongraded High School.* Englewood Cliffs, N.J.: Prentice-Hall, 1963. 223 pp.
[13] Trump and Baynham, *op. cit.*

fering organizational settings in which independent study can take place means little unless the school makes provision for teaching the majority of students skills in studying independently. A swimming pool is fine if you know how to swim. Correspondingly, arrangements for independent study are fine if you know how to learn on your own.

ORGANIZING INSTRUCTION TO FOSTER EXCELLENCE

Most people in education evidently believe that excellence is a fine thing and that we should have more of it in our schools. However, they appear to believe also that only a small percentage of students are capable of achieving excellence. The research of psychologists and test makers concerning differences in native ability have led many principals and teachers to insist upon "grading on the curve." In their view, only a few students should receive *A* as the mark of excellence, while the greatest number should receive *C* as the mark of so-so learning, and a moderate number should receive failing marks as proof that the test was fair and the grading honest. This is a thoroughly absurd and irrational conception of what the schools should accomplish. Anytime a student fails to learn well what he studies, something serious is wrong with his instructional program or the way it is being conducted. Either the student is being taught the wrong thing, or it is being taught him in the wrong way. The task of the school is to suit the learning task, the learning materials, the methods of learning, and the pacing of study to the needs, capabilities, and interests of the student. If these requirements are met, almost any student can achieve mastery of the learning task. Compared to the superior student, the less capable learner will need to tackle less complicated or less advanced tasks, will need different learning materials, will require more guidance from the teacher, and will need more time. When these requirements are satisfied, and only then, is the "slow learner" given a fair chance to show what he can do, or learn to do.

Mastery, as the term is used here, does not mean complete and final command of the learning task. The school, it is proposed, should satisfy four criteria of mastery with every student as much of the time as possible. The four criteria are these: (a) the task is learned well enough so that what was learned is remembered for a considerable period of time; (b) the student can apply what he learned to topics or situations that are appropriate; (c) the student can use what he learned as a building block toward higher learnings in the subject; and (d) the student can take pride in his learning.

How can organizational changes in the school foster the attainment of excellence? Nongrading, as was noted above, is one way of changing the organization of instruction so that slower learners are given the extra time and help they need to master learning tasks, especially in the skills areas. Nongrading arrangements, of course, should be supported by appropriate curriculum organization, appropriate tests to measure achievement of learning goals, and appropriate instructional methods if mastery is to result.

Beginning with Winnetka, a series of plans for organizing instruction in the elementary school have shown that students of less-than-average ability can master skills in reading, spelling, and arithmetic.[14] The requirements for achieving such mastery are three: (a) the pupil accepts that he must continue studying the unit until he can pass the qualifying test for that unit with a high score (usually 90 percent or better); (b) he is supplied with study materials and, in some plans, with practice tests to help him determine whether he is ready to go to the teacher for the qualifying test; and (c) he is given as much time as he needs to master the unit. In addition to the Winnetka program, this approach is used in the Durrell pupil-team learning plan where several pupils study a unit together. A comparable approach to mastering skill learnings is employed in the individualized program at the Oakleaf School, which is located in the Baldwin-Whitehall School District in suburban Pittsburgh.

In the secondary school, a type of organizational arrangement that could foster excellence is making provisions for independent study. Once again, this will not result in excellence unless students are capable of planning and conducting their own learning and unless they commit themselves to achieving excellence. In short, organizational arrangements alone will not produce excellence; they simply improve the opportunities the student has to master the learning task.

ORGANIZATIONAL ARRANGEMENTS
AND INDIVIDUALIZING INSTRUCTION

Changing the organization of the school, classroom, or curriculum most often is justified as a route toward better adapting instruction to differences among individual learners. Thus nongrading, or continuous progress, is an approach that is based on the assumption that learning will be improved if the rate of advancement is geared to each individual student's learning rate. The Stoddard dual progress plan, a semidepartmental organization of the elementary school, provides for nongraded advancement and differential grouping, subject by subject, to meet individ-

---

[14] Carleton W. Washburne and Sidney P. Marland, Jr., *Winnetka: The History and Significance of an Educational Experiment.* Englewood Cliffs, N.J.: Prentice-Hall, 1963. 402 pp.

ual differences better. Team-teaching plans stress provisions for meeting individual differences through flexible grouping and flexible uses of personnel, time, space, and equipment. The Trump Plan resembles team teaching in offering various provisions for small-group and independent study to take account of differences among learners.

Many school leaders believe that the best practicable approach to individualizing instruction is some form of achievement or ability grouping. Such grouping, whether at the school level or within the classroom, has the purpose of sorting students into relatively homogeneous groups. The assumption is that all members of such a group can be taught the same units with the same instructional methods and at the same pace. A difficulty with this approach to meeting individual differences is that no group of students is truly homogeneous. Teaching the group on the assumption that all its members are similar actually works against the individualization of instruction. Indeed, some schools insist on heterogeneous grouping so that the teacher will be required by the sheer range of differences in the class to use different instructional approaches with different children.

Probably the greatest fault of ability grouping is that teachers are prone to teach high-ability and low-ability groups very differently. They tend to emphasize drill and memorization with the low groups, while they turn to conceptual approaches with the top groups and offer the students opportunities to do individual projects. In short, ability grouping tends to result in inferior teaching of low-ability groups. Also, the stigma associated with being in a low-ability group leads to feelings of inadequacy and tends to lessen motivation to study.[15]

The most thoroughgoing approaches to individualization call for planning and conducting, with each student, a program of studies that is specifically suited to him. This approach calls for pretesting each student to determine the extent to which he already has learned the unit in question. Also, it calls for diagnosing the student's characteristics as a learner as a basis for planning his learning unit. Depending on the nature of the learning task and the characteristics of the learner, as well as on available instructional resources, the plan for the student may call for independent study, for a tutorial relation with the teacher, for studying in a small group, or for studying in a normal-sized class group. The feasibility of this type of individualization is being demonstrated in the University Elementary School at UCLA under John Goodlad's direction, and at the Oakleaf School outside Pittsburgh under Robert Glaser's leadership. Both programs are described by the term *individually prescribed instruction* (IPI).

---

[15] Walter R. Borg, *Ability Grouping in the Public Schools*. Madison, Wis.: Dembar Educational Research Services, 1966. 97 pp.

The analysis offered in the preceding pages indicates that various organizational arrangements can improve opportunities for achieving instructional aims. However, the analysis has emphasized that no improvements are likely to result unless appropriate learning materials are available and unless teachers have the competencies required to plan and conduct instruction in relation to the aims. School leaders, for this reason, should not expect to improve the instructional program merely by installing a new oganizational plan. Instead, organizational changes should simply be a part of a system of changes related to an instructional aim. The system of changes often will need to include modifications in curriculum, tests, and the in-service education of teachers.

The major themes of school or classroom organization—continuous progress, flexibility in instructional arrangements, teacher specialization, and teacher cooperation—simply offer improved opportunities for teachers to use the competencies they possess in planning and conducting lessons that are directed toward certain learning goals and designed to meet the learning needs of the pupils they are teaching. For example, consider continuous progress plans that are designed to permit pupils to advance in a curricular sequence at whatever rate they can master successive units in the sequence. Such plans cannot be implemented unless teachers know how to use tests to determine the level in the curricular sequence each pupil has reached, unless they can plan lessons suited to the learning needs of different children, and unless they can conduct instruction in ways that take into account differences in pupils' rates and methods of learning. In short, teachers must be competent in planning and conducting individualized instruction before they can make a continuous progress plan work.

To take another example, teacher teamwork depends especially on teachers' speaking an explicit, common educational language about the behavioral objectives of instruction and about measures of pupils' achievements and characteristics as learners. Also, they need to have a common understanding of lesson planning for individualized instruction that employs flexible arrangements in scheduling, grouping, staff assignments, and the uses of learning materials. Since most teachers, like most others in education, lack this common language and these common understandings, teacher teamwork generally falls considerably short of its potential.

DEVELOPING LOCAL CAPABILITIES
FOR MAKING ORGANIZATIONAL CHANGES

This section is intended to sketch out the steps a school system should take in preparing itself to design and conduct its own educational change programs with little outside assistance. The assumption basic to this section, as stated near the beginning of this paper, is that local programs to adopt innovations depend for their success largely on whether a school system's leaders and teachers develop professional capabilities in deciding the directions local change projects are to take, in planning appropriate change programs, and in carrying these programs out effectively. Frequently a school system's staff will be too small to develop these competencies fully; in such cases, an association of neighboring school systems, perhaps at the county level, would be an appropriate agency for leading the change programs of its members.

The approach recommended here, it should be noted, rejects the current basis on which most school administrators, according to Brickell's analysis, decide about adopting innovations and go about planning and conducting programs to implement innovations they have decided to adopt.[16] What are being rejected are the prevailing superficial and piecemeal approach to change in which innovations tend to be tacked onto the ongoing program; the selection of innovations largely on the basis of seeing them demonstrated in schools very like one's own, with smiles on children's faces used as the chief evidence of success of the demonstration; and the failure in local change projects to provide the fundamental training needed by school leaders and teachers if they are to realize the purposes of the innovation in the actual conduct of instruction.

How should a school system go about developing capabilities in introducing changes in organization for instruction? As was proposed earlier in this paper, the system's leaders should not start out with a concern about making organizational changes, but rather with an examination of instructional aims and an appraisal of current successes and failures on the part of the instructional program to realize those aims.

In developing their capabilities in working toward the school system's aims, staff members must first acquire an explicit and detailed working definition of each aim. *Without operational definitions of instructional aims, the staff lacks a basis for making independent professional decisions about instruction.* When staff members possess such definitions of the school's aims, they are in a position to begin working together in designing and implementing changes in the content, organization, and procedures of the instructional program.

Explicit definitions of aims lead directly into selecting or developing ways of measuring the degree to which each aim is being accomplished. The school's staff should formally take this step as part of the process of developing a functional understanding of the objectives of the instructional program.

[16] Henry M. Brickell, *Organizing New York State for Educational Change*. Albany: New York State Education Department, 1961. 106 pp.

At this point, the consideration of curriculum content and organization is appropriate since the curriculum translates definitions of learning goals into the working materials of instruction.

Logically the next step is the analysis of instructional procedures and techniques that will bring pupils and curriculum into effective relation. This step calls for a local study of teaching: pretesting pupils' achievement of lesson goals, diagnosing pupils' learning needs, lesson planning, techniques of individualizing instruction, and so on. Also it calls for finding ways of providing the school system's teachers with the requisite professional skills for guiding all pupils' learning toward the school's learning goals.

Thus far, the recommended approach has concerned the fundamentals of instruction that underlie any type of organization for instruction. In general, it is held that a school system's staff should not consider any new plan for organizing the school until these fundamentals (instructional aims, curriculum content and organization, tests, and methods of teaching) have been given systematic attention. An exception to this rule might be to introduce teacher specialization in the elementary school to make it easier for teachers to learn to teach theory and inquiry in their fields by permitting each of them to concentrate on his chosen field. Another exception might be to introduce provisions for teacher teamwork to facilitate the training of beginning teachers in relation to the school system's aims.

When a school system's staff members have made sufficient progress in acquiring sophistication and competence in the fundamentals of instruction, it is time for them to consider new patterns of school or classroom organization. The approach recommended is to select those organizational themes that are judged to be important in relation to one or more instructional aims, work out a design for an organizational scheme that incorporates the themes selected, then undertake an intensive program of study and training to prepare staff members to install the new plan as efficiently as possible.

The approach to local staff development proposed here may seem unnecessary or unrealistic. It calls for at least a year of intensive study of instruction on the part of all, or a major proportion of, the school system's staff. Where is the time to be found for such an undertaking? Doubtless most school systems would have to find ways and means (including money) for releasing many staff members from regular instructional duties several hours each week during the school year. If school leaders and teachers were placed on a full-year basis, full-time staff training workshops could be held each summer for a period as long as six weeks. Any less investment of time and resources in staff development would prove to be inadequate for achieving the purposes outlined above.

Where would the leadership be found for conducting the recommended program to prepare school leaders and teachers for designing and conducting local change programs? Clearly, this need places the onus on universities, on state education departments, on federal educational agencies, and on agencies such as the NEA Center for the Study of Instruction, to develop guidelines and materials for local programs of staff development, and training programs to help school leaders organize and guide staff development projects.[17]

A central part of the problem of achieving adequate local leadership for change programs concerns the selection, training, and assignments of members of the school system's staff who are responsible for leading those programs. There are a number of key functions that must be performed by local personnel if the school system is to be effective with its innovative programs. These functions concern curriculum, diagnostic and achievement testing, teacher education, administrative planning, and program evaluation. Perhaps new positions in school systems should be established to serve these functions. Perhaps, however, they can be assumed as part of existing positions such as curriculum coordinator, director of instruction, guidance counselor, school psychologist, and research director. Whatever decision is reached on this issue, there will be a need for clarifying the functions of local change agents, for selecting and training persons to fill these functions, and for making organizational arrangements in school systems that permit these functions to be carried out effectively.

DESIGNING A LOCAL PROGRAM
TO REORGANIZE INSTRUCTION

The recommendations made above would have the school leader launch his planning of a school improvement program by selecting one or more instructional aims to be the focus of the program. Preferably, he would select a set of two or more aims since the aims of instruction interact to reinforce each other.

Consider the five types of instructional aims discussed earlier in this paper: teaching of theory, teaching of inquiry, teaching of independent study, requiring standards of excellence or mastery, and individualizing instruction. The learning of theory and of inquiry methods goes hand in hand. One aim should not be selected as a focus of instructional improvement without the other. (Note that the new curricula in mathematics and science focus about equally on theory and inquiry.) To teach theory and

[17] National Education Association, Project on Instruction, *Schools for the Sixties: A Report of the Project on Instruction.* New York: McGraw-Hill Inc., 1963. 146 pp.; National Education Association, Center for the Study of Instruction, *From Bookshelves to Action.* Washington, D.C.: the Association, 1964. 32 pp.

inquiry methods well, mastery should be required and instruction should be individualized (using the definition of individualization offered earlier in this paper).

An alternative set of aims to select as foci for a school improvement program would be independent study, standards of excellence or mastery, and individualizing instruction. While there is a considerable overlap of inquiry skills and skills required for effective study, the two aims represent different emphases in the instructional program. Inquiry places stress on analytic and creative thinking. Study skills place the emphasis on basic competencies in communication (notably, reading and writing, and preparing reports), on uses of source materials, and uses of various instruments (rulers, thermometers, microscopes, and so on). It is clear that effective instruction in independent study calls for applying standards of excellence or mastery and for individualizing instruction.

Let us suppose that a school system adopted the latter set of aims—independent study, standards of excellence or mastery, and individualization—as the foci for a system-wide project to improve instruction. What changes in the instructional program might be introduced? In arriving at an answer to this question, the first task would be to decide which study skills the program would be designed to improve. Reading? Spelling? Essay writing? Library skills? Interpreting tables, graphs, and charts? Preparing tables and graphs? Specifying the learning goals of a unit of study? Planning one's approach to a learning task? Evaluating one's progress and locating points of difficulty? and so on. In addition, it would be important for the school leadership to decide whether the study skills selected for attention would be dealt with on a K-12 basis, with all the students, and in all relevant curricular areas. Decisions on these matters would reflect views as to which study skills were most important, which skills especially required additional emphasis in the local program, and which students required better instruction in study skills than they were receiving.

Changes in the study skills to be emphasized in the school system's instructional program would require examining the curriculum and associated learning materials to determine whether changes were required in curricular sequences or in the types of learning materials made available to students. It would be very important to determine whether new procedures and instruments were required to measure students' attainment of the study skills called for in the school improvement project. In all probability, it would be found that teachers possessed very inadequate means of testing students' achievement in study skills.

An analysis would be needed of instructional methods required to teach the skills included in the project. The facts that instruction would be individualized and that students would be required to master the skills being taught would demand extraordinary changes in instructional procedures over conventional ways of teaching students how to study.

Changes in organizational arrangements should be considered in this point with the purposes especially of adapting instruction to individual differences and of enabling each student to attain mastery of the learning tasks. To accomplish these purposes, several *organizational themes* are germane: continuous progress; flexibility in scheduling, grouping, and the uses made of space and equipment; new patterns of staff specialization; the employment of teacher aides; and teacher teamwork.

The theme of continuous progress (nongrading) would offer approaches to assigning different learning tasks to different students dependent on differences in what they had attained. Also, arrangements for continuous progress would allow for differences in the length of time students required to learn particular skills. Flexibility in scheduling, grouping, and so on, would be required to accommodate the varied uses of instructional resources called for by continuous progress. Sometimes a student would study a task alone, sometimes as a member of a small group, and sometimes as a member of a large group. The times different students spent on a task would vary considerably. Also, the materials and equipment used with a given learning task would vary from student to student.

To achieve excellence in individualized learning of basic study skills, it is essential to make the best use possible of instructional personnel. New patterns of staff specialization may be required. For example, specialists in reading instruction might be assigned in both elementary and secondary schools. Other specializations might involve teaching quantitative skills (measuring, computing, and so on) or skills in preparing reports. To free teachers to devote more time to actual teaching, paraprofessional teacher aides might be hired to relieve teachers of various chores (taking attendance, duplicating learning materials, grading objective exams, and so on).

New patterns of teacher teamwork should be considered as a route toward ensuring that each student's total program (shared by different teachers) placed proper emphases on different learning tasks and yet was a unified whole. Such teacher cooperation might occur in a formally structured teaching team, or it might occur through less formidable arrangements for teachers to plan and work in unison.

In selecting organizational changes that were intended to improve the teaching of study skills, the school system's staff would gain from a careful reading of the literature on nongrading and team teaching (Goodlad and Anderson, Dufay, Brown, Shaplin and Olds, Bair and Woodward, and others). Especially valuable also would be the approaches to individualized instruction (with mastery) represented by the Winnetka plan and the pupil-team learning plan (see references by Durrell, and by Washburne and Marland). Finally, and of greatest value, staff representatives should seek detailed information about the methods used to achieve individually prescribed instruction at the UCLA University Elementary School and the Oakleaf School.

The critical role of staff education in preparing for conducting a change program must not be overlooked. Teaching study skills with mastery and individualization cannot be successfully conducted unless teachers have an expert knowledge of methods of assessing students' learning, of diagnosing their learning needs and capabilities, and of planning individual programs of study. In their turn, effective leadership in designing and conducting change programs of the type that has been sketched above requires that school administrators and supervisors acquire a detailed knowledge of the requirements of such programs and of how to organize and lead them.

This section has employed as an illustration of a change program one that focuses on independent study, standards of excellence or mastery, and individualized instruction.

Another type of system-wide change program that might equally well have been used would have as its aims learning theory and methods of inquiry, also with mastery and individualization as reference points. The essential points in the recommendations offered in this paper are the same, whatever the change program that a school system undertakes. These points are listed below:

1. Begin planning a change program by deciding which learning goals, in which curricular areas, and with which students, are to be the focus of the program.

2. Make sure that staff members involved in planning the new program have an explicit understanding of the learning goals selected.

3. Analyze what the learning goals require by way of curricula, materials, test, and instructional methods.

4. Analyze requirements for instruction that is conducted with individualization, and in ways to ensure that students achieve mastery of the learning tasks they undertake.

5. Examine organizational themes that can be employed to improve the extent to which individual students attain mastery of learning tasks in the program.

6. Make provisions for staff education that will enable teachers and other professionals to foster the purposes of the program.

7. Give due attention to the fact that any change program, to be effective in accomplishing its instructional aims, must be made up of a system of changes. Such a system normally must include changes in curriculum, tests, diagnostic procedures and instruments,

instructional methods, organization of school and classroom, and continuing staff education.

That these suggestions may seem obvious to many educators, we readily acknowledge. We submit that this may be so because they have been often honored but seldom observed. None of the steps can be glossed over, nor is any very simple to put into practice. They are emphasized here because, in desperation or zeal, they can be given scant attention or attempted superficially.

PART TWO

The Continuous Progress Education Movement

In the first edition of this book a large section was devoted to "nongrading" and the "nongraded school." These terms are still very much abroad in the land. However, the confusion that the term "nongraded education" has created has often proved more harmful than helpful in attempting to develop programs and activities calculated to focus on the individual child and his continuous progress. Very frequently the terms "nongraded education" referred more to administrative tinkering and grouping procedures than to the more broadly based attempts to develop programs of value that relate to the individual growth and development of learners. As it is now being defined, continuous progress education as a concept aims at developing an approach to provide much more flexibility in the education of the child, while at the same time employing the maximum capabilities of teachers. Continuous progress education is thought to be, and in fact is, much more than organizational redefinition. It represents attempts to create programs that are made up of components that not only create flexibility in the organizational structure of the school, but develop flexibility in the curriculum and the child's relation to it as he pursues his educational career.

Changing the lock-step in education, opening the system, and moving toward innovative forms that embrace continuous progress education is really an attempt to maximize opportunities for children by developing their capacities to the fullest. The acceptance of individual difference is basic to the success of such a program. Curricula are tailored to the needs of the child. The child becomes the baseline from which to measure growth and the focus of the program. Continuous progress oriented education is more than merely creating a series of levels through which youngsters are programmed. It engenders a much greater insight into the whole area of what the educational process entails.

The term "nongraded" and the identification of something as a nongraded school have served their time on the educational scene. However, there is a history, short though it may be, of what is called the nongraded movement. It is (or was) a movement that developed from the conventional graded school toward the newer innovative forms where grades were eliminated and continuous progress was substituted and based on diagnostic and prescriptive approaches to learning.

One has to pick out various historical threads and try to weave them into meaningful patterns in order to satisfy the desire to know where and when it all began. Nongrading was not wholly a positive activity during this history. It was, at times, rather a reactive one to the constraints and strictures that were imposed upon the learner by the graded program. Although it was positive because it was child-oriented, the evils of nonpromotion continued to exist and still exist today. The Quincy Grammar School in Quincy, Massachusetts, set up a graded program in 1848. Immediately, counteractive movements were established. In 1865 in St. Louis, pupils were part of a graded school plan that insisted on reclassification every six weeks. The brighter ones were placed into advanced sections. Superintendent Francis W. Parker, who introduced the graded school in Quincy himself, also introduced the counteractive coaching scheme that was to keep the less able pupils in step with the grade level. The Batavia Plan which used two teachers per classroom was another reactive movement that attempted to deal with the constraints of the graded organization. Rarely did these educators attack the grade concept as such. Rather they resorted to plans that would vary the material to be studied by the fast, average, or slow learners. Many attempts to break the grade-bind were used. Extra-help activities, differentiation of assigned materials, half-term promotions, nonpromotion, and acceleration—all were used, but the grade generally remained. It was in the late 1930s in Milwaukee that nongrading as a "modern" educational concept started to take root. It was during the decade of the sixties, however, that nongrading became an increasingly intense educational movement. The term "nongraded" is giving way to the term "continuous progress," which connotes a broadened concept of education. Also, the concepts of vertical growth, or continuous progress, and horizontal approaches to education, defined as cooperative or collaborative endeavors, are frequently combined.

In 1970, we find ourselves in probably a resurgent period aimed at developing continuous progress oriented education so that each child can savor growth in keeping with his whole potential. The readings in this part have been selected to give a clearer insight into what continuous progress education attempts to do. There are many clear and distinct advantages to continuous progress education, especially when the added aspects of collaboration, differentiated teacher staffing and use, and multiage grouping procedures are used. A nonexhaustive list would represent some of the following:

- Learning skill sequences that are operationally defined and developed to meet the needs of the learner population involved generally reflects better teaching opportunities as well as learning opportunities.
- Children are taught skills from learning sequences ranging from readiness to competency or mastery, and the development of skills is more carefully attended to.
- The elimination of promotion or nonpromotion eliminates much of the threat that brings about unhappiness in school.
- Children who are deliberate learners, but no less intelligent than their faster counterparts, can move at their own pace without the penalty of being nonpromoted simply because necessary coverage over a given year is defined as a grade. When multiaging is used in skill development programs, older children frequently

become leaders when working with slower or younger children and teach them how to use manipulative and mechanical materials.

• When multiaging is used, children who would not make a contribution because of their peer critics now tend to do so in a group where they are at a relevant, problem-solving level.

• There are no gaps in instruction because there is no grade to skip.

• There is no repetition of material that the child already knows since he begins each year where he left off.

• There is a greater opportunity for flexibility in grouping procedures and this allows for appropriate and pertinent placement of youngsters.

• Because of the problem-solving nature of the program attendant to the need of the child, the reduction in behavior problems is great.

• There is much more teamwork on the part of faculty members when they are involved in a collaborative planning program that allows them to evaluate and to deal with the needs of the individual youngsters.

• There is increased awareness of pupil individuality since individual differences are the very core of continuous progress.

• Where multi-adult exposure (through team teaching) takes place, a greater opportunity for real evaluation of the quality of the learner is made.

• There is no fear of encroachment on materials supposedly reserved for a particular grade.

• There is no ceiling on learning in a continuous progress program.

• The pressures normally found in graded education to achieve end-of-term goals and to maintain standards that may be clearly outside the attained abilities of pupils are eliminated since the norm in continuous progress is the child. His placement and work are always appropriate to his capacity, readiness, or competence.

This list could be extended considerably to attest to the perceived as well as the empirically established advantages that proponents of continuous progress education set forth.

However, as in any program, there are certain disadvantages. Many of the disadvantages that are purported concerning continuous progress education, interestingly enough, are not cited by those who are involved in programs of continuous progress education, but rather by those who have some stake in maintaining the present conventional programs that have marked the educational scene for so many years. Those who have been involved have made certain points that could be seen as problems to be dealt with in a program. The reader will notice, however, that each of these problems or disadvantages under the proper kind of administration may never endanger what essentially seems to be one of the more realistic approaches to better growth in teaching and learning in our schools. The disadvantages that have been mentioned are as follows:

- Parents and teachers have been brought up in a graded atmosphere, therefore the tendency to continue grade-mindedness is still very pervasive.
- Establishing continuous progress educational programs without establishing new curricula to support them may simply result in developing minuscule grades called levels which would be worse than the grades that were replaced.
- Unless there is a strong movement from the top down (high school) as well as from the bottom up (kindergarten), the child involved in continuous progress education may suffer discontinuity as a result of going from an open system into a closed, graded upper elementary, junior, or senior high school.
- Many school curricula today are still generally organized around graded topics and depend heavily on graded textbooks. There is a need to create curriculum material that is based on a continuum of growing educational skills and concepts that are sequential in nature. This requires a great deal of effort and time on the part of the faculty who must reorganize curricula to serve the needs of a continuous progress orientation.
- The teaching in continuous progress education is more difficult, but may be more challenging, and is probably more rewarding.
- Without careful teacher preparation, the development of continuous progress educational programs and attendant flexibility in organization may find the teacher

imposing his own constraints and being just as "graded" in what should be a new, liberating situation.

- There must be significant differences in the teacher's practices if continuous progress is to be successful.

- Continuous progress education always brings into focus the need for new record-keeping and reporting practices because the traditional or conventional marking systems are no longer consistent with the aims of continuous progress education. These new activities take time. They also are in an educationally sensitive arena that can make many faculties and parents unhappy.

There is a vast body of material now available on the whole movement of continuous progress education. The wholesome idea of providing more flexibility in the education of the child and creating maximum opportunity for teachers to make significant contributions to that education is a healthy sign. The interplay of factors and components which eventuate in programs that further these goals can help shape the direction of education for the seventies as it faces the many crises so well-known to all of us. Continuous progress programs can serve as directions toward better education.

With the exception of the first article, those selected for this part represent an up-to-date status report of continuous progress education—its genesis, its directions, and some of its problems at all levels of schooling.

The first article is taken from the *Cyclopaedia of Education* (1877), the first published in the English language in education. This alerts the reader to some of the historical background and problems of progress, gradedness, and educational change. This publication is only slightly less than a hundred years old; yet in it one can find a discussion on whether "phrenology affords a reliable means of discerning the mental peculiarities of different individuals, or how far such peculiarities are manifested in cerebral structures." Haven't we come a long way! Much of the article reprinted here contends that "many objections have been urged against the system of graded schools, chief among which is, the interests of the individual pupil are often sacrificed to those of the many, the individual being merged in the mass." It has a very interesting discussion of educational promotion and nonpromotion and makes an allusion to Harris and his program in St. Louis, referred to above in the history of educational change and innovation.

The second article by Walter Worth is retained from the first edition. The reason for this is simple. Very little that is new has been presented to the field and reported on concerning nonpromotion that is not found here. His article replicates much of what has been done. It restates much of what is known about the attendant problems of nonpromotion that have been extant for many years. His conclusions reiterate what now are classic findings, and the implications of his study lead one toward the creation of basic educational programs that are continuous progress oriented. Nonpromotion, and the attendant evils, undergird the desire to change graded education.

Hillson in his article on "Continuous Progress Education: Some Theoretical Aspects, Philosophical Backgrounds, and Sociological and Psychological Correlates" clarifies various components that are indigenous to continuous progress education. It is interesting that Worth is a Canadian educator, that Hillson's statement was made to a Canadian audience, and that the third article by Dr. Housego is also from a Canadian journal. By juxtaposing the articles by Hillson and Housego, the reader can see that if the components called for in the Hillson article are generally well worked out or adapted to meet the needs of particular systems which are innovating continuous progress education, then the problems that Housego identifies and discusses may never become extant, or at least may only be momentary, as educators work out programs of value and critical worth. Housego perceptibly discusses the problems and recounts rather clearly some of the items that have for many years been critical points in developing first-rate programs of continuous progress education. Taken together, the Hillson and Housego articles may serve as a two-fold base from which one can measure what ought to be and what should not be done, and, additionally, what guidelines have to be adhered to in order to avoid pitfalls that engender problems.

The second of the two articles by Hillson is retained from the first edition. It was the first empirical study of continuous progress education. The completion of the program and experimental period from which the article was drawn was reported by the coauthors of the original Hillson article in a followup in the *Journal of Educational Research,* "A Comparison of Pupil Achievement after One and One-half and Three Years in a Nongraded Program," Vol. 61, No. 2, October 1967, pp. 75–77. It is almost an exact replication of the original one that is herein reprinted and that was published in 1964 in the same journal. The design of the study was maintained, the data collected, and evaluations made in the same manner. The researchers who continued the original study concluded, "Pupils participating in a nongraded primary organization achieved at a significantly higher level on measures of reading ability at the end of one and one-half academic years than did pupils enrolled in a conventional graded program. However, these results were not stable; at the end of the third academic year while differences which favor the nongraded group still existed, none of the differences were statistically significant." There may be many reasons for this: the initial superiority of pupils in the continuous progress organization in the earlier study may have been due to factors such as teacher enthusiasm, the fact that it was continuous progress and thereby more suitable for very young and beginning students, or a combination of a host of other factors. But is continuous progress only for the very young?

The last article in this part on the nongraded secondary school consists of three dialogues between Walter Baden and David Maurer, both active practitioners of nongraded education at the secondary level. The ideas and material that they discuss is drawn from their experiences at the Wheatland-Chili School, Scottsville, New York. Their definitions, as one can see, relate well to the concepts found in the articles above. This should lead the reader to the understanding that at all levels of continuous progress the concepts are similar. The translation for various age groups may require some alterations of degree, but not of kind. Here too we see the concept of continuous progress replacing the less open idea of nongradedness. From a definition ("What It Is—and Isn't"), to a discussion of grouping, and finally to a discussion of a tripartite approach (cycling, open electives, continuous progress) to content acquisition, we get from Baden and Maurer a clear and concise picture that completes the range from school entry to school completion in a continuous progress fashion. The six articles combine history, theory, research, and practice related to the continuous progress education movement.

3 | Graded Schools

From *The Cyclopaedia of Education: A Dictionary of Information for the Use of Teachers, School Officers, Parents, and Others,* edited by Henry Kiddle and Alexander J. Schem (New York: E. Steiger, 1877), pp. 375–377.

Graded schools are usually defined as schools in which the pupils are classified according to their progress in scholarship as compared with a course of study divided into grades, pupils of the same or a similar degree of proficiency being placed in the same class. An ungraded school, on the other hand, is one in which the pupils are taught individually, each one being advanced as far, and as fast, as circumstances permit, without regard to the progress of other pupils. The *graded system* is thus based upon classification; and its efficacy as a system must depend very greatly upon the accuracy with which the classification has been made. Grades, however, are not to be confounded with classes; the former are divisions of the course of study based upon various considerations, the latter are divisions of the school based upon uniformity of attainments. In a small school, the same number of grades may be needed as in a large school, the course of study being the same, and the promotions being made with equal frequency; hence, as the number of classes must be smaller, it will be necessary that each class should pursue two or more grades simultaneously or in succession; that is to say, the promotions from grade to grade will be more frequent than from class to class. On the other hand, in a large school, the number of classes may be greater than that of the grades, which will necessitate the forming of two or more classes, under separate teachers, in the same grade. In the management of a large school, this will be found to be better than a subdivision of the grades, requiring either an extension of the time for completing the course, or greater frequency in the promotions. In the small district schools of the United States, the ungraded system prevails, because each school is taught by a single teacher, and sometimes there is a want of uniformity in text-books; but in the cities the graded system prevails. The advantages of the graded system have been thus enumerated: (1) They economize the labor of instruction; (2) They reduce the cost of instruction, since a smaller number of teachers are required for effective work in a classified or graded school; (3) They make the instruction more effective, inasmuch as the teacher can more readily hear the lessons of an entire class than of the pupils separately, and thus there will be better opportunity for actual teaching, explanation, drill, etc.; (4) They facilitate good government and discipline, because all the pupils are kept constantly under the direct control and instruction of the teacher, and, besides, are kept constantly busy; (5) They afford a better means of inciting pupils to industry, by promoting their ambition to excel, inasmuch as there is a constant competition among the pupils of a class, which cannot exist when the pupils are instructed separately. On the other hand, many objections have been urged against the system of graded schools, chief among which is, that the interests of the individual pupil are often sacrificed to those of the many, the individual being merged in the mass. "As a mechanism," says E. E. White, in *Problems in Graded School Management*, a paper read before the National Educational Association, Aug. 4, 1874, "it [the graded system] demands that pupils of the same grade attend school with regularity, and that they possess equal attainments, equal mental capacity, equal vigor, equal home assistance and opportunity, and that they be instructed by teachers possessing equal ability and skill. But this uniformity does not exist. Teachers possess unequal skill and power. Pupils do not enter school at the same age; some attend only a portion of each year; others attend irregularly; and the members of the same class possess unequal ability, and have unequal assistance and opportunity. This want of uniformity in *conditions* makes the mechanical operation of the system imperfect, and hence, its tendency is to force uniformity, thus sacrificing its true function as a means of education to its perfect action as a mechanism." There is no doubt that this difficulty is inherent in the system, and that no administration, however excellent, can wholly eliminate it. Various methods of procedure have, however, been suggested to diminish its injurious effects. That proposed by Superintendent W. T. Harris, of St. Louis, and carried out in the public schools of that city is frequent discriminative promotions. The following are the points on which the system is based: (1) The different rate of progress in study on the part of pupils of the same class, due to a difference in age, capacity, regularity of attendance, and opportunity; and (2) The continual diminution of the size of classes, particularly of the higher grades. "Provision," he says, "must be made for this difference in rates of progress by frequent reclassification; otherwise the school will become a lifeless machine." This arrangement, however, was a reaction against the system of annual promotions, which necessarily require wide grades and unfrequent changes in classification. The other extreme, according to the views of many educators experienced in school management and supervision, was approached in the recommendation by Superintendent Harris to require promotions as often as every ten weeks, and, besides that, to permit pupils "to move forward as fast as their abilities might permit." The objections to incidental discriminative promotion are the following: (1) It encourages precocity in the pupils; (2) It produces a tendency in the teacher to give an exclusive attention to the bright, intelligent pupils to the neglect of the dull ones, because in this way promotions are secured, which redound to the teacher's credit; (3) It deprives the pupils thus promoted out of the regular course, of the means of properly pursuing certain grades or parts of grades, inasmuch as, if placed from a lower grade into a class of pupils already advanced in the next higher one, they must take up the studies of that grade at the advanced point, without acquaintance with the preceding part of the grade, thus confusing the classification and embarrassing the teacher. Semi-annual promotions seem to be approved by the majority of educators, with such an adjustment of the number of the grades of the course of study and the requirements of each, as will enable pupils of an average capacity to complete the amount of study prescribed in the half year. There is another danger connected with the graded-school system, as sometimes administered, to which allusion is often made. It *prescribes* too much, leaving to the teacher too little scope for the exercise of individual skill, judgment, and intelligence. "It is not important," says Mr. White, "that the several teachers accomplish the same result day by day, or week by week. Nothing is more ridiculous than the attempt to parcel out primary instruction, and tie it up in daily or weekly prescriptions, like a doctor's doses. This week the class is to take certain facts in geography; to count by twos to fifty (to sixty would be a fearful sin!); to draw the vertical lines of a cube; to learn to respect the aged, etc.!" This, however, with many other objections which are urged against the system of graded schools, is only a fault in administration. A system of this kind requires intelligent, earnest, and judicious direction and supervision; with this, ably seconded by well-trained and experienced teachers, it will approximate to individual teaching, and, in the powerful and wholesome stimulus which it constantly applies to the pupil, prove much more effective.

Graded schools are far more numerous in the United States than in England, or in most of the countries of continental Europe. The system is, however, beginning to be introduced. "The plan of teaching classes or grades in separate schoolrooms has been adopted," says Adams (*Free School System of the United States*, 1875), "in some of the Birmingham Board schools, and also in London, I believe, and has given great satisfaction." So essential has it been considered in the United States to the efficiency of a school that it should be graded, that no aid is given from the Peabody Fund except to graded schools.—See Wells, *The Graded School* (N.Y., 1862); Wickersham, *School Economy* (Phil., 1868); Kiddle, etc., *How to Teach* (N.Y., 1874).

4 | Promotion or Nonpromotion?

WALTER H. WORTH

Reprinted from *Educational Administration and Supervision*, Vol. 46 (January 1960), pp. 16–26, by permission of the publisher.

Promotion practices are still a controversial issue in many school systems (6, 7). The incidence of nonpromotion is apparently increasing (9) even though existing research evidence (7, 18) indicates that few benefits accrue to pupil achievement and social-personal development from nonpromotion. This disparity between theory and practice suggests the need to test the continuing applicability of earlier research findings. The present study (19) seeks to do this. It also aims at some measure of control over variables not considered in previous research. The findings may be of assistance to school workers in understanding and eventually solving the promotion problem.

PROBLEM

This study [1] sought to determine the effect of promotion and nonpromotion on the school achievement and social-personal development of matched groups of third and fourth grade pupils ordinarily categorized as low-achievers in a large urban school system.

Decisions were made among the following three kinds of hypotheses with reference to those aspects of school achievement and social-personal development which were observed:

[1] The writer wishes to acknowledge the advice and assistance of his doctoral advisor, Dr. J. Harlan Shores of the University of Illinois, in the conduct of this investigation.

44

1. There is a difference between promoted and nonpromoted low-achievers, and this difference is in favor of promoted low-achievers.

2. There is a difference between promoted and nonpromoted low-achievers, and this difference is in favor of nonpromoted low-achievers.

3. There is no difference between promoted and nonpromoted low-achievers.

PROCEDURE

Subjects

The subjects of the investigation were two groups of 66 children each matched with respect to sex, IQ, chronological age, total achievement (California), and located in similar schools. One group consisted of low-achievers who had been promoted to the fourth grade, the other was made up of low-achievers who were nonpromoted and repeated the third grade. Each group contained twenty girls and forty-six boys. This sort of sex ratio was a reflection of the higher nonpromotion rate among boys than girls in the population sampled. Table I shows the characteristics of the groups with regard to IQ, chronological age, and achievement.

TABLE I
Comparison of Promoted and Nonpromoted Groups with Regard to IQ, Chronological Age, and Total Achievement

Characteristic	IQ	Chronological Age in Months	Total Achievement Grade Score
Mean for promoted group	94.53	108.71	3.79
Mean for nonpromoted group	94.68	107.89	3.91
Standard deviation for promoted group	12.24	6.77	.34
Standard deviation for nonpromoted group	12.17	6.47	.34
Correlation between the promoted and nonpromoted groups	+.99	+.70	+.52

Experimental Conditions

During the experimental year the pupils were enrolled in eighty different classrooms in more than thirty schools. No attempt was made to influence the treatment accorded them by school workers. However, information was secured by means of a questionnaire completed by each pupil's teacher about selected environmental and instructional factors judged to be influential in determining school progress. A statistical analysis [2] of these data did not detect differences in teacher experience, training, or continuity; pupil attendance, health, home or family conditions; small-group and individual instruction; provision of supplementary learning materials in reading, arithmetic, and language; and special treatment (e.g., referral to auxiliary services) for the populations of which the two groups were samples. The nonpromoted were, however, enrolled in larger size classes. The teachers of the promoted, on the other hand, provided more supplementary learning materials in spelling, and made greater use of special incentives, rewards, and punishments. For a large number of pupils in both groups, there appeared to be few provisions made for adapting instruction to individual needs.

Measures of Achievement
and Social-Personal Development

The measures of achievement were gain scores in twelve areas derived from the California Achievement Test, Primary, and the Gates Advanced Primary Reading Tests administered prior to the promotional decision and at the end of the experimental year. Teacher ratings on the following seven personality traits: emotional control, creativeness, judgment, cooperation, dependability, courtesy, and work habits, as defined and used in the school system's reporting procedures; and choice by classmates on a sociometric test as desirable and undesirable work and play companions served as measures of social-personal development. An attempt was made to observe the effect of promotion and nonpromotion through a comparison of the groups on these data.

Statistical Treatment

A three-decision procedure (3, 5), employing a t or sign test, was used to decide (a) in favor of the promoted group, (b) in favor of the nonpromoted group, or, (c) in favor of the (null) hypothesis of no difference between the promoted and nonpromoted groups on each of the achievement, social-personal development, and experimental conditions variables observed. This procedure is equivalent to two one-sided tests being carried out simultaneously (2), thereby permitting the detection of directional differences in favor of either group, or a retention of the hypothesis of no difference.

The statistical tests were so constructed that the probability of deciding upon a difference in favor of the promoted group when the hypothesis of no difference is true was set at the conventional value of .05. The probability of deciding in favor of the nonpromoted group when the hypothesis of no difference is true was also set at .05. Thus the probability of falsely rejecting the hypothesis of no difference is .10.

[2] This analysis is explained in the section entitled "Statistical Treatment."

FINDINGS

Achievement

In the twelve areas of achievement observed, as is shown in Table II, the decision was in favor of the promoted group with regard to gain in

TABLE II

Comparison of Promoted and Nonpromoted Groups with Regard to Gains in Twelve Achievement Areas As Measured by the California and Gates Tests Expressed in Grade Scores

Achievement Area	Promoted Group		Nonpromoted Group		Differ- ence	Ob- served value of t	‡ P value
	Mean Gain	S.D. of Gain	Mean Gain	S.D. of Gain			
CALIFORNIA							
Reading vocabulary	.78	.58	.51	.53	+.27	+2.76	.004***
Reading comprehension	.69	.49	.55	.53	+.14	+1.46	.07*
Total reading	.71	.40	.51	.37	+.20	+2.80	.004***
Arithmetic reasoning	.71	.41	.72	.49	−.01	− .10	.46*
Arithmetic fundamentals	.82	.59	.55	.50	+.27	+2.75	.004***
Total arithmetic	.74	.38	.63	.41	+.11	+1.63	.054*
Mechanics of English	.23	.76	.23	.87	+.00	+ .00	.50*
Spelling	.59	.52	.51	.40	+.08	+1.01	.16*
Total language	.42	.44	.36	.47	+.06	+ .76	.23*
Total achievement	.59	.45	.53	.30	+.06	+ .92	.18*
GATES							
Paragraph reading	.54	.75	.76	.77	−.22	−1.76	.04**
Word recognition	.55	.65	.67	.46	−.12	−.125	.11*

(Critical value of t with 65 degrees of freedom ± 1.67)
* Decision in favor of hypothesis of no difference.
** Decision in favor of nonpromoted group.
*** Decision in favor of promoted group.
‡ The P value is the probability, if the null hypothesis is true, of observing a value of t greater than or equal to (or less than or equal to) the observed value of t depending on the direction of the difference between the means. Its derivation is explained in Wallis and Roberts (17).

reading vocabulary, total reading, and arithmetic fundamentals. In paragraph reading the decision favored the nonpromoted. The decision was in favor of the hypothesis of no difference in reading comprehension, word recognition, arithmetic reasoning, total arithmetic, mechanics of English, spelling, total language, and total achievement. In the eight achievement areas for which the hypothesis of no difference was not rejected, the majority of the differences in the sample means were in the direction of the promoted pupils. The gains in all twelve areas for the pupils of both groups were less than the ten-month gains normally expected of typical pupils on the standardized tests used.

Social-Personal Development

When the groups were compared on eleven aspects of social-personal development, as indicated in Table III, the decision was in favor of the

TABLE III

Sign Test Comparison of Promoted and Nonpromoted Groups with Regard to Teachers' Ratings on Seven Personality Traits and Frequency of Choice by Classmates as Desirable and Undesirable Work and Play Companions

Trait or Choice	$P<NP$ —	$P=NP$ 0	$P>NP$ +	N	Critical Value of x	Ob- served Value of x	‡ P Value
Emotional control	15	42	9	24	7	9	.15*
Creativeness	25	26	15	40	14	15	.08*
Judgment	13	39	14	27	8	13	.50*
Cooperation	22	27	17	39	13	17	.26*
Dependability	27	25	14	41	14	14	.03**
Courtesy	18	34	14	32	10	14	.30*
Work habits	22	29	15	37	13	15	.16*
Desirable work companion	38	8	20	58	22	20	.01**
Undesirable work companion	24	12	30	54	20	24	.25*
Desirable play companion	31	6	29	60	23	29	.45*
Undesirable play companion	39	6	21	60	23	29	.45*

* Decision in favor of hypothesis of no difference.
** Decision in favor of nonpromoted group.
‡ The P value is the probability, if the null hypothesis is true, of observing a value of x less than or equal to the observed value of x (1).

nonpromoted group with regard to desirability as a work companion, and dependability. The decision was in favor of the hypothesis of no difference in emotional control, creativeness, judgment, cooperation, courtesy, work habits, undesirability as a work companion, desirability as a play companion, and undesirability as a play companion. On the nine aspects of social-personal development for which the hypothesis of no difference was not rejected, the bulk of the differences in the sample medians were in the direction of the nonpromoted pupils.

Influence of Observed Differences
in Experimental Conditions

It is possible that these findings may reflect, to some degree, the difference in class size noted earlier. However, research on the effects of class size strongly suggests that class size in itself bears little relationship to pupils achievement, and is inconclusive concerning the effect of class size on social-personal development (4, 10, 11, 12, 13). It is also possible that differences in teachers' uses of incentives, rewards, or punishments may have played a part in influencing the results of the experiment. Psychological research has amply demonstrated the significance of incentives, rewards, and punishments for all aspects of learning (14, 15, 16). But the kinds of incentives, rewards, and punishments that the teachers reported using, such as progress charts, detentions, and special privileges may not have been as effective in changing behavior as those described in the psychological literature. If this were so, it would tend to limit the importance to be attached to this factor in interpreting the findings of this study. Gain in spelling did not appear to be greatly affected by the difference between the groups in the provision of supplementary spelling materials.

DISCUSSION

Normal school progress is commonly considered to be one grade each year. Nonpromotion is usually advocated only when it can be demonstrated to be in the best interest of the child concerned. An argument often used to justify nonpromotion is that it improves school achievement. The findings of this study, however, do not support the view that nonpromotion improves school achievement. Low-achieving pupils who are nonpromoted appear to make no greater, and often less, gain in achievement than they do when promoted.

A possible explanation for the apparent inability of low-achievers to profit academically from nonpromotion may lie in the fact that teachers in this investigation reported using few, if any, supplementary learning materials in an effort to adapt instruction to the individual needs of the pupils concerned. It might therefore be inferred that, in large measure, the nonpromoted pupils repeated the regular third-grade program, while the promoted pupils were exposed to the regular fourth-grade program. If this were the case, and assuming that the repetition of partially learned material is less stimulating than the challenge of new material, then the repetitive nature of the treatment accorded the nonpromoted pupils may account for these low-achievers not exhibiting greater gains in achievement. The lack of special provisions for the nonpromoted suggests the need for teachers to individualize instruction at the point of error for pupils so classified, in an effort to overcome the boredom and wastefulness that may result from mere repetition of the regular program. Such individualization of instruction may well require the development and utilization of special curricula, methods, and materials. The fact that few teachers reported individualizing instruction for the subjects of this study also suggests that existing programs of teacher education, both of a preservice and in-service nature, may not be as helpful in preparing teachers for this responsibility as they might be.

Another way to meet the instructional problem posed by the low-achievers could be to develop a form of school organization in which promotion and nonpromotion would not occur. Such a form of school organization would eliminate traditional grade level lines, and the curriculum rigidity that tends to result, and would substitute a flexible method of pupil classification permitting the continuous progress of pupils from one school term to the next. If this were done, and at the same time provisions made for individualized instruction, it might be possible to bring about greater gains in achievement for low-achievers than those observed in this experiment.

There was some inconsistency in the gain scores in reading. The promoted gained more than the nonpromoted on the California measures. The nonpromoted, on the other hand, gained more than the promoted on the Gates measures. The disparity of these results is difficult to explain. It could be that errors in measurement occurred, or that these tests do measure different aspects of reading ability. It also could be that the Gates tests more closely resemble in content and format the exercise materials commonly used in primary reading programs than do the California tests. If this is the case, then the higher gain scores made by the nonpromoted pupils in paragraph reading and word recognition may reflect, to some degree, the nonpromoted pupils' more recent and frequent practice with similar materials occasioned by their repetition of the third grade. Furthermore, it may be that while tasks not challenging in level and at a low level of expectation lead to a low level of achievement, continued practice with these low-level tasks develops a high level of proficiency with them when proficiency is measured by amount accomplished correctly in a given period of time. If this is so, and assuming that repetition of the third grade reading program and the Gates tests both emphasize reading tasks which are at a relatively low level of challenge and expectation, it may afford another possible explanation for the higher gain scores of the nonpromoted pupils in paragraph reading and word recognition as measured by the Gates tests. Conversely, the greater gain of the promoted pupils in reading vocabulary, reading comprehension, and total reading, as measured by the California tests, may reflect the influence of practice with reading tasks at a relatively higher level of challenge and expectation. Regardless of the reason, the conflicting nature of the gain scores in reading points up the need for school workers to exercise special caution in generalizing about pupil achievement on the basis of performance on a single standardized test.

The findings of this study concerning the effect of promotion and nonpromotion on social-personal development seem to run counter to those reported in the bulk of previous research (7, 18) on this problem.

Nonpromotion does not appear to have an adverse effect on the social-personal development of low-achievers. On the contrary, low-achievers who are nonpromoted tend to be rated as high or higher on personality traits, and be accorded the same, and sometimes better, sociometric status than those who are promoted. This suggests the possibility that the greater gain in achievement made by the promoted pupils may have been at the expense of their social-personal development.

Obviously, however, the promotion factor is not the only influence which was reflected in these results. It may be that as members of larger-size classes the nonpromoted pupils' general behavior was less often drawn to the attention of their teachers and classmates, thereby increasing the likelihood of somewhat favorable, or at least rather neutral reactions. It may also be that the nonpromoted pupils, though they experienced less gain in achievement than did the promoted pupils, were better able to match the academic performance of the other pupils in their classes. If this were so, then this factor may also have led to more favorable reactions from their teachers and classmates. In addition, the extent to which the teachers of the nonpromoted pupils may have deliberately sought social acceptance for these pupils in an effort to aid them in accepting the fact of nonpromotion is not known. Likewise unknown, is the effect of the age differential between the nonpromoted pupils and their classmates. Moreover, since no measure of social-personal development was obtained prior to the promotional decision, it is not known what differences existed in this respect at the beginning of the experiment. It is conceivable, therefore, that the findings with regard to social-personal development were conditioned by earlier differences and thus do not accurately reflect the effect of the promotion factor. And, finally, the limitations of the measures or social-personal development which were employed also need to be recognized.

A further explanation for the disparity between the results of this investigation and those conducted earlier may be that the effect of the promotion factor on social-personal development varies with age or grade level. This fact, plus the likelihood of some contamination of the results of this experiment by other factors, serves to emphasize the need for further study of the effect of promotion and nonpromotion on social-personal development.

It is interesting to note that almost seventy percent of the subjects of this investigation were boys. This was a reflection of the higher nonpromotion rate among boys than girls in the population from which the nonpromoted sample was drawn. While each pair of pupils studied was of the same sex, the larger proportion of boys in both groups raises the question, however, as to whether some sort of sex difference may still be mirrored in the results of this experiment. Moreover, the fact that more boys than girls tend to be nonpromoted, as has been shown in this and other studies (8), is in itself a matter which merits further consideration by those concerned with promotional decisions.

In total, this study may be viewed as one bit of evidence that challenges the whole structure of the present elementary school. The findings strongly suggest that, as long as the relatively rigid grade placement of both pupils and content persists, neither promotion nor nonpromotion will adequately meet the needs of the low-achiever. It appears that, until school workers develop more flexible instructional and organizational policies and practices, the problems associated with promotion and non-promotion will be slow to diminish, and the low-achiever, as well as many of his classmates, are unlikely to be provided with the educational program they require.

CONCLUSIONS

1. Continued reliance upon nonpromotion in itself to improve school achievement is unwarranted. Low-achieving pupils who are nonpromoted appear to make no greater, and often less, gain in achievement than they do when promoted. If the practice of non-promotion is to continue it must be justified on grounds other than improved achievement.

2. Nonpromotion does not appear to have as adverse an effect on social-personal development as previous research might lead one to expect. The social-personal adjustment of low-achievers when they are nonpromoted appears to be as good, if not better, than it is when they are promoted. However, further research is needed to facilitate a more clear-cut interpretation of the differences in the social-personal development of promoted and nonpromoted pupils.

IMPLICATIONS

1. Existing promotion policies and practices need to be carefully re-examined with a view to clarifying the bases for promotional decisions, and reducing the incidence of nonpromotion for the purpose of improving achievement.

2. Attempts need to be made to ascertain why more boys than girls are nonpromoted so that administrative and curricular policies may be modified to account for this sex difference.

3. Experimentation needs to be undertaken to develop a type of school organization which will permit continuous pupil progress, thereby eliminating many of the problems associated with promotion and nonpromotion.

4. Attention needs to be given to the development of special curricula, methods, and materials designed to facilitate individualized instruction so that the educational needs of the low-achievers may be more effectively met under conditions of promotion and nonpromotion, or in continuous progress plans wherein promotional decisions are not required.

REFERENCES

1. Harvard University. "Tables of the Cumulative Binomial Probability Distribution." *The Annals of the Computation Laboratory of Harvard University,* 35, 1955, pp. 407–23.
2. J. L. Hodges and E. L. Lehman, "Testing the Approximate Validity of Statistical Hypotheses." *Journal of the Royal Statistical Society,* Series B (Methodological), 26, No. 2, 1954, pp. 261–68.
3. H. F. Kaiser, "Directional Statistical Decisions." Bureau of Educational Research, University of Illinois. Unpublished manuscript.
4. L. C. D. Kemp, "Environmental and other Characteristics Determining Attainment in Primary Schools." *British Journal of Educational Psychology,* 25, June, 1955, pp. 67–77.
5. E. L. Lehman, "Some Principles of the Theory of Testing Hypotheses." *Annals of Mathematical Statistics,* 21, March, 1950, pp. 10–26.
6. National Education Association. *Ten Criticisms of Public Education,* Research Bulletin 35, Washington: Research Division, 1957, pp. 148–52.
7. National Education Association. *Pupil Failure and Nonpromotion,* Research Memo 2. Washington: Research Division, 1959.
8. National Education Association. *Pupil Promotion Policies and Rates of Promotion,* Educational Research Service Circular 5. Washington: American Association of School Administrators and Research Division, 1958, p. 4.
9. *Newsweek,* September 1, 1958, p. 55.
10. H. J. Otto, M. L. Condon, E. W. James, W. Olson, and R. A. Weber, *Class Size Factors in Elementary Schools,* Bureau of Laboratory Schools, Publication 4. Austin: University of Texas Press, 1954.
11. H. J. Otto, and F. Von Bergersrode, "Class Size," *Encyclopedia of Educational Research,* Revised Edition, 1950, pp. 213–15.
12. H. J. Spitzer, "Class Size and Pupil Achievement in Elementary Schools." *Elementary School Journal,* 54, October, 1954, pp. 82–86.
13. J. P. Steffensen, "The Relationship Between Class Organization in the Elementary School and Achievement in Certain Subject Matter Areas." Unpublished Doctoral dissertation, University of Illinois, 1958.
14. P. M. Symonds, "What Education Has to Learn from Psychology." *Teachers College Record,* 56, February, 1955, pp. 277–85.
15. P. M. Symonds, "What Education Has to Learn from Psychology: II. Reward." *Teachers College Record,* 57, October, 1955, pp. 15–25.
16. P. M. Symonds, "What Education Has to Learn from Psychology: III. Punishment." *Teachers College Record,* 57, April, 1956, pp. 449–62.
17. W. A. Wallis, and H. V. Roberts, *Statistics: A New Approach.* Glencoe: The Free Press, 1956, p. 436.
18. H. W. Worth, "Promotion vs. Nonpromotion: I. The Earlier Research

Evidence." *Alberta Journal of Educational Research,* 5, June, 1959, pp. 77–86.

19. W. H. Worth, "The Effect of Promotion and Nonpromotion on Pupil Achievement and Social-Personal Development in the Elementary School." Unpublished Doctoral dissertation, University of Illinois, 1959.

5 | Continuous Progress Education

MAURIE HILLSON

Reprinted with permission from *A Report of an Invitational Conference on Continuous Progress Sponsored by the British Columbia Teachers' Federation,* February 24–25, 1967. Also printed in The PACT Magazine (Provincial Association of Catholic Teachers of Quebec), Vol. 7, No. 4 (December 1968), pp. 12–20.

The term "nongraded" is purposely left out of the title of this paper. Nongraded is a reactive term. It indicates the absence of something; the reverse of something. In this case, it means the absence of grades. When one speaks about a nongraded school, it is about a school that has done away with some of the strictures that are reflected in the customarily graded organization. The term nongraded (an antiseptic term intended to neutralize a situation that has prevailed in education for over 100 years), really needs to be eliminated from the vocabulary of school organization. It should be used historically to mark the first thrust of a comprehensive movement to change the elementary schools of the United States and Canada. As one visits and reads about schools of the United States and Canada and the programs that they operate, it becomes clear that there is no one single or classic model "nongraded" school. A model for nongraded education is much more aspirational than real. This is desirable because the raising of trenchant questions and the continuous search for better ways of doing things may allow us to achieve much more flexibility.

What actually needs to be discussed in elementary education today is something quite different from what the term "nongraded" connotes. We need to think about the kinds of organization and approaches to education that will serve functions quite different from those of the graded school. The reason for this is obvious.

The scientific knowledge that we now have attendant to learning was not extant when the graded school was proposed, created, and crystallized by a hundred years of practice. Unfortunately, graded education in too many areas of our countries is quite venerated. For that reason in my comparisons of graded education with different kinds of educational setting I refer to the *customarily* graded school rather than the traditionally graded school. The word "traditional" seems to give the graded school some veneration. The word "customary" seems only to indicate it as a habitual pattern. And, it should be noted that it has continued because of habit—not because of research. The graded school has never been a proven nor a tested plan of education or of organization. It has never been clearly assessed, evaluated, or compared with other clearly established models that serve different educational functions. Presently, where different kinds of models have been achieved and compared to graded schools, we are beginning to get some new insights. They indicate that there are some very marked and indeed statistically significant differences among children in the newer and different kinds of organizations. A concrete definition, therefore, of the nongraded school is certainly hard to find. For that reason it seems wise for the remainder of this paper to eliminate the term "nongraded." In its place I shall use other terms that are more accurate and appropriate to the activities that mark a school that is different from the graded school and which has inherently built into its fabric the elimination of the strictures that seem to militate against sound learning principles.

It seems reasonable to assume that a school that is different from the graded school and which attempts to build a program of continuous progress education and which attempts to create a program that actually explores and exploits the individual abilities and differences found in children, is more readily identifiable in terms of the philosophical correlates that underpin it. In the activities throughout our nations that presently aim at eliminating the graded school, there is in almost every attempt a conscious desire on the part of the educators to deal more effectively with the individual differences found in children. This is not only the case today. Any reading of the history of the elementary school in America leads immediately to the conclusion that all of the attempted basic circumventions of the graded idea that are cited were honest attempts to eliminate the strictures that graded education insinuated on its users.

The philosophy of continuous progress education, or education aimed at fully expanding on the individual differences resident in groups of children, as well as within the single child, was born in the heat of reaction. The philosophy is a pragmatic one. It is one which is inextricably bound up in the great scientific and child-centered movements of the immediate past three decades. Before one can truly probe the totality of that philosophy, one must look very carefully at some broadly defined, and necessary theoretical generalities.

Any attempt at continuous progress education or any plan aimed at fully probing the activities by which one can enhance the individual learning capabilities of all children, must be generally and broadly defined as one that necessarily embraces the scientific knowledge about that learner and how he learns. Any continuous progress organization inherently embraces in its curricular designs and formats the flexibility that allows for the placement of pupils irrespective of their so-called "grade" or chronological years of school attendance.

Pupil placement in a continuous progress organization must be appropriate not only to the rate and the gait of learning, but to the many other factors which attend learning ability. The curriculum as it is enunciated for a "graded" school becomes immediately obsolete and unrelated to the different goals that should be sought when one attempts to fulfill the individual learning capabilities and aspirations of all learners.

A basic generalization seems to be that in order to create a continuous progress school there needs to be the prerequisite of a general commitment to the idea of a curriculum that is without restriction in terms of the height that one can achieve. It has to be a curriculum that is carefully planned out. It must be sequential in its growth from the most simplistic to the most complex in terms of accomplishment. It needs to be one which reflects the idea of true individual progress. It emphasizes the attitude that each learner can become all that he is capable of becoming irrespective of the age or the number of years in school or the particular classroom that he is assigned to.

Probably the most important theoretical generalization that one need subscribe to is that individual continuous progress education refers to a concept rather than a thing. Continuous progress education is *concept* oriented. *It deals with the way learning and growth take place in relation to the knowledge about how children learn and grow.* It is in philosophical consonance with the concept that all individuals, and especially elementary school individuals, do differ profoundly in all areas of their endeavors. It embraces the concept that there are very many learning styles as well as teaching styles that are fruitful. It rejects the idea that there is one single way of doing things. And, it certainly is in keeping with the concept that there still remain some untapped individual aspects of life and learning that should go in to making up a wholesome and fruitful educative experience. It can be added that the major concept about the way true learning takes place is the basic generalization that must be embraced by all who endeavor to create a continuous progress education program. Simply stated, that concept is: true learning takes place only when the learner himself becomes ultimately committed to participating in such a way that he involves his own applications of learning skills and experiences in ways that create successful opportunities to achieve the goals that he seeks according to his abilities, to do so.

Basically then these are the theoretical generalizations that undergird the creation of a different kind of education. These generalizations immediately lead to the point that continuous progress education, wherever found, is not a discreet entity. Many of the continuous progress programs do have similar features, as Gail M. Inlow points out (Gail M. Inlow, *The Emergent in Curriculum,* New York: John Wiley and Sons, Inc., 1966, p. 311):

> Even though the many instances of implementation have much in common both in terms of theoretical rationale and practical manifestations, the nongraded pattern is basically a lengthened shadow of the philosophies and experiences of those doing the implementing.

The theoretical aspects of continuous progress education differ somewhat from system to system, program to program, and educator to educator. However, there are some core fundamental theoretical aspects that must be noted.

First continuous progress education insists that each pupil be involved fundamentally in a program wherein he will actually savor benefits of continuous progress. The pupil himself is the baseline and the yardstick of true accomplishment. In a continuous progress plan, therefore, one of the theoretical aspects is that each pupil starts his program at a different point.

A second and very important theoretical aspect of continuous progress education is that it eliminates the whole area of pupil retardation, promotion, and nonpromotion. The school, involved in a continuous progress plan, commits itself to a program of actual continuous progress. The realities that exist in every group of learners concerning their needs are capitalized on and fruitfully used.

A third theoretical aspect has to do with the whole area of readiness. John E. Horrocks (John E. Horrocks, *Assessment of Behavior: The Methodology and Content of Psychological Measurement,* Columbus, Ohio: Charles E. Merrill Books, Inc., 1964, p. 418) states:

> An individual's readiness to participate in a new school learning experience, and to profit to any extent from his exposure to it, depends upon the extent to which he has the information and skills basic to the new learning, upon his level of intelligence and his possession of appropriate special abilities and aptitudes, and upon his desire to learn the new material.
>
> *A continuing concern of the schools lies in the readiness to learn of the children placed in their care.* When children lack such readiness it is recognized that they will either fail to learn at all or that at best their

learning will be slow and insufficient. Moreover, children who are encouraged to learn before they are ready are likely to meet discouraging failure, build work or study habits which must later be painfully unlearned, and they even endanger normal physical and social development. Readiness to learn the various kinds and levels of subject matter taught in school has many facets but may generally be defined as a capacity to learn accompanied by the wish and the skills and the proper background to do so. (Italics are mine. M.H.)

Continuous progress education with no established ceiling for learning housed in a school that can create an extended readiness program, and wherein no one faces the fear of encroachment of the grades of the higher years, all represent ancillary theoretical aspects. It can be stated almost categorically that these support a much more defensible educational plan than that of the hitherto graded school.

A fourth major theoretical aspect is the concept of flexibility. This creates the opportunity for teachers as they deal with the problems of their young charges to collaborate in their educational behalf. In a continuous progress education program, by establishing the various sequences that youngsters will participate in, by the alteration and rethinking of those sequences, by juxtaposing them with other sequences and by bringing together specific groups as needs arise, and by having teachers assigned to various groups as they show desire, one truly moves to a point of realizing that the theoretical aspects of a continuous progress program certainly do have value when measured against most situations offered by a customary graded program.

The theoretical aspects, then, that ally themselves with continuous progress education enunciated above are plausible, and seemingly result in better education for all youngsters. They are not meant to be an exhaustive listing. They are merely indications of the kinds of thing that one addresses when creating a new form of organization in education in an attempt to better realize the basic goals of education in general.

The psychological and sociological correlates interestingly become confluent as they support a program of continuous progress education. It is from the sociological and psychological correlates that one draws the pragmatic philosophy of the different kind of school that is alluded to above.

By investigating the philosophy of the continuous progress school, one may arrive at a definition that shows the philosophical, psychological, and sociological realities of continuous progress education in an integrated matrix.

The psychological and sociological studies now extant seem to repudiate many of the activities of the customarily organized graded school. These findings seem to suggest the essential need for a rethinking and a recasting of the educational framework as well as the curriculum and the approaches to it as necessary for greater success on the part of our students. The psychological and sociological findings tend to reject most of the features that are found in a graded school. By necessity then, if these are rejected one must seek an alternative approach in which educational growth can take place.

By glancing at what seem to be accepted educational principles drawn from the areas of psychology and sociology, one can establish, with some degree of surety, a basic posture for the creation of a different kind of school which serves a different kind of function. This different kind of school embraces the concept of continuous progress education because the research findings point to a greater insistence on dealing with the individual needs of individual learners.

The following represent a categorization of some broadly accepted tenets that serve as background upon which one can establish approaches to the organization, curriculum, and learning activities attendant to better education for youngsters in the elementary school years. In addition, when taken as a whole these seem to tend to support a continuous progress educational program. It can, therefore, be stated that these represent in some measure the philosophical backgrounds for continuous progress education. By reflecting on them momentarily, one can almost see that the psychology, sociology, and philosophy of continuous progress education become orchestrated in an integrated fashion. This orchestration in turn creates the situation and the setting for learning that bring about behavioral integration within the learned which is, indeed, real learning.

Much research indicates that there exist in every group of learners, without exception, wide differences in the quality, desire, and intent as it concerns learning. For example, one need only reflect on the insights of Edgar A. Doll. He observed that in reality four IQ's must be recognized as factors which are involved in achievement. These four IQ's are: "the intelligence quotient, the inner quest, the ideal qualities, and the innate quirks," and may be operative in any individual at any given time. (Edgar A. Doll," "The Four IQ's," *Exceptional Children,* Vol. 24 [October 1957], pp. 56–58.) These insights alone should create the impetus in education to find a concept of organization, curricula, and teaching and learning approaches quite different from the customary graded school.

The most consistently conclusive body of research presently in the literature relates to the problem of nonpromotion. It indicates that the undesirable growth characteristic, unfair school programs, and poor progress in school are closely associated more often with nonpromoted children than with their slower learning counterparts who have been promoted. Those who are promoted usually do better, make better progress, indicate better mental health habits and adjustments than to their peers who are retained. Repeating a grade rarely yields any advantage it is reported. This seems to relegate the concept of nonpromotion as an academic practice to a vestigial position of disrepute in the whole area of educational growth and progress. Retention and failure with all of the frustrations attendant to both are still widely practiced in the graded schools of the United States and, I do believe, still applied frequently in Canada. But, the collection of empirical evidence indicates that nonpromotion as an educational practice is unequivocally indefensible. It is by far one of the most intense traumas in the educational career of any given youngster. In fact, we have evidence that indicates a one-to-one relationship between nonpromotion and leaving school. This does not mean to suggest, however, that we could eliminate the problem of leaving school by eliminating nonpromotion. Conversely, however, it does suggest that nonpromotion, a result of an organizationally enforced idea, may be an attempt to support a continued dropout rate. This is lamentable but the school operates as a sorting agency and "squeezes out" students. Nonpromotion is a device to assure the "squeeze-out" process. To adduce a small portion of the evidence on nonpromotion would indeed represent a small volume in itself.

A bold philosophy of education for many years has been embraced verbally and mythologically by the people of my country, even if not applied totally. It operates on the assumption that every pupil in the elementary school is judged by the best that he can do. It contends that if a child works to his capacity and makes strides according to his intellectual growth pattern and becomes an ultimate learner, he has in a personal sense accomplished the full measure of existence in this area of his life and, therefore, has met the needs of his own life situation and will progress successfully.

Coupled with this and leading from it is the idea that no child should ever be judged by the median performance of a nonselected group. In the literature there is ample evidence to support this. Many of the textbooks concerned with the methods of teaching the various areas of the curriculum importune their readers to try to group in a reflective manner, taking into consideration the various ranges which reside in their classroom due to the schoolwide nonselective assignments and grouping. This problem is not very different even if schoolwide practice attempts a program of homogeneity. One need only ponder what John Goodlad (John I. Goodlad and Robert T. Anderson, *Nongraded Elementary School*, New York: Harcourt, Brace and World, Inc., 1963, p. 20), felt to be the case when he once found himself in a teaching situation which offered the promise of considerable homogeneity.

> The institution was a specialized one in that it received only boys committed for delinquent acts. The pupils were relatively homogeneous on a criterion supposedly related to learning in that almost all of them fell in a IQ range of 70 to 110, with a mean of 85.

It did not take long for the obvious to happen. It took only six weeks in fact and Goodlad reports that he "found himself wishing for a specialized school down the road that might receive those who deviated most markedly from the others on various significant traits."

I think that it is equally worthy of consideration that no child be judged on the basis of his chronological age as the single factor as it concerns his placement or his learning parameter. This should be the case even though chronological age does play a part in many endeavors during our daily life. We all know people who in my country are 21 years of age or over and therefore able to vote, but who should not be allowed to exercise the franchise essentially because they are immature in every aspect of the requirements needed to make a sound and rational judgment. Nonetheless, sometimes chronology must be involved in the endeavors of our ongoing, day-to-day lifetime activities. However, I would suggest that Cronbach makes a germane point when he indicates that, "age-grading is inconsistent with the facts about pupil differences, and allocating pupils to grades according to their overall ability in one subject does little to improve the situation." (Lee J. Cronbach, *Educational Psychology*, New York: Harcourt, Brace & World, Inc., 1963, p. 263.)

Finally, I think it can be stated with rather consistent security, because of the congeries of evidence which have been amassed in the studies made by the psychologists, that age-grading is inconsistent with what we know about the way children grow and develop. It is inconsistent because grade standards, as a matter of fact, and certainly as a matter of measurement of educational progress, are untenable in light of the new studies being made in the areas of intuition, cognition, learning, and mental age. Jerome S. Bruner (Jerome S. Bruner, *The Process of Education*, Cambridge: Harvard University Press, 1962, p. 33), hypothesized, "that any subject can be taught effectively in some intellectually honest form to any child at any stage of development . . . No evidence exists to contradict it: considerable evidence is being amassed that supports it." There are, of course, many qualifications to this statement, but the concept of the grade standard is eroded by what is a very plausible hypothesis. Even thirty-five years ago, Louella Cole, without today's sophisticated techniques of scientific research, observed that "in no grade . . . are the children sufficiently similar in their mental capacity to permit individual differences to be ignored. The basic fact of wide individual differences per grade persists in spite of the school's constant effort to adapt itself to them." (Louella Cole, *Psychology of Elementary School Subjects*, New York: Farrar and Rinehart, Inc., 1934, pp. 6–7.) For years the educational literature has carried similar statements, some based on perceptions of day-to-day educational practitioners and others as a result of carefully documented and controlled studies. The late William S. Gray summed up the conclusions found in this vast body of research when he wrote, "Research has shown conclusively that children differ widely in capacity to learn and other basic characteristics. The need is urgent, therefore, of organizing instructions to provide adequately for the needs of all." (William S. Gray, The Teaching of Reading, *Encyclopedia of Educational Research* [Third Edition], New York: The Macmillan Company, 1960, p. 1118.) These findings are primarily psychological in nature. It becomes equally impressive if one looks at the sociological correlates that combine with these to build a philosophical case for a program of continuous progress education.

The sociological correlates of differentiated instruction and differentiated approaches to the needs of youngsters in order to insure the greatest opportunity for entré into the mainstream of our society, are just at this moment in the United States making an impact on education. It was only twelve years ago, in 1954, that our Supreme Court declared and ordered that "separate but equal" had no place in American education if all youth were to participate fully in the larges of free public education *(Brown et al. v. Board of Education of Topeka et al.,* Supreme Court of the United States, May 17, 1954). The actual decision of the court was a mere reflection of what had long been known by some first-rate educators and social scientists for many years. The problem that faces the United States in this area is far from solution, because the imponderables that make up the sociological aspects attendant to school success are not yet fully known. However, the very plausible ideas and insights that have been given to us by the sociologists are not only worthy but are far more meaningful in the analysis of behavior. They are far more exciting when one realizes that probably greater changes in education will take place when we deal with the problems in a structural way rather than according to the etymology of the psychologists. The sociologists, therefore, have given us a sound basis for much more action than has been taken to date.

Because of their research, we understand now the situation of discontinuity which is attendant to the educational programs and problems of the United States. We are aware of the cultural shock that discontinuity creates. We know that the patterns of public school education, the organization and curricula based on the accepted and broadly defined middle-class goal orientations that make up the mainstream of our existence, create a conflict in the school. We know that the cultural distance between the aspirations of a middle-class defined curriculum and the needs of youngsters from ghettos and slums is great. Unfortunately, teacher behavior and the application of values attuned to meeting the needs of children who by their up-bringing are ready for this kind of work, put other youngsters who are not so attuned at a disadvantage. Educational differentials created to meet the needs of the disadvantaged learners are hard to find in the public schools of the United States.

The concept that the inability to cover prescribed material in a given amount of time marks one as a slow learner, hence a dull learner, is widespread in the United States. Children who come from different cultures approach various kinds of prescribed materials in different ways. Some do not approach it at all. Some violently reject it. Some attempt it deliberately or slowly but not necessarily dully. Knowing this, it is obvious that the concept of continuous progress education, backed by a deep probing of individual needs, is in essence a program necessary for success. It now becomes increasingly apparent that to base a curriculum on the middle-class population's desires only, is to create a whole series of sociological discontinuities. To expect all children in school to approach, assay, attempt, and achieve the same curriculum offered to everyone in the same manner, at the same time, and with the same enthusiasm, is foolhardy. To maintain a system of educational progress based on these notions in the face of the collective research concerning the whole concept of the typologies of modes of adaptation, based on the theories of success and opportunity, social stratification and mobility, social class attitudes, behaviors, and values, limits the chances of our success in educating all of the children of all of the people. It is a matter of reality that differing approaches to the learner, the curricula, and the organizational patterns of the school are necessary.

A whole series of sociological correlates insist on creating the kind of school that is more consistent with the varying and various environments of society as a whole. It insists on the creation of a school in which success can be attained when a wholesome and reasonable effort is made by the student regardless of his class or culturally different background. It insists on a school that is different from the one that operates a prescribed graded normative standard that is value laden and made unattainable and alien to the learner of the moment. This does not imply that the different kind of school will not be as strong in terms of quality or quantity of educational content as the other kind of school. Indeed, in many cases it will be more worthwhile. It means, in fact, that it will observe the incoming population in terms of the realities of profound individual differences. It will establish those kinds of programs that probe deeply into these differences. It will explore them and prescribe learning activities to meet these particular needs. Intensive attention must be given to this area of the sociological correlates or else curricula and school progressions based on the concept that all youngsters in the United States and Canada should have the same kind of education applied willy-nilly will prevail and will continue to create frustration for many. The infinite variations, and differentiations, and dimensions that we may need in a different kind of school are not yet fully known. But one thing is quite certain. Much more attention should be given to the *needs and realistic opportunities of the youngsters* in order to create the kind of school and program that will have value for them.

With all of the above variables coalescing to create an extensive set of rubrics, we have what is, seemingly, a new theory or different theory of grouping and instruction than has hitherto been embraced. It means that we now need a school that establishes a program of continuous progress education but this does not answer all of the problems which confront the schools in general. Continuous progress is not a method of teaching. It is not an administrative or teaching panacea. Rather it is something that allows us to create a matrix in which better methods can be used, in which teacher and pupil vistas can be expanded, and in which a flexibility will allow for a greater exploitation of all of the activities that one needs to explore in order to further learning. It is not a simple reorganizational shuffling.

Continuous progress education that embraces the theoretical aspects, the philosophical, sociological and psychological correlates that underpin it means that the school will now be a place wherein all attempts will be made to deal with the problems of inflexibility that frequently mark the education of the child. It will be a school wherein continuous opportunity for continuous academic progress takes place. All the grades of the school will be removed as designators. A child will learn to grow and acquire insights and knowledge at his own speed in terms of his own learning style and intensity. The child may be grouped with other children of a similar nature at times where they display similar or comfortable learning rates. The child will have an opportunity to be flexibly, appropriately, and pertinently placed at a given moment in time. This school will be a place wherein the imprecise and unrealistic aspects of year-end norms are removed. And just because the winter snows pass into the warmth of the June of the year the child will not by some magical experience turn into a "second grader" or a "third grader" or some other indefensible category.

Education is not a foot race; rather it is an activity in which the aspects of the program and institutions need to be tailored to fit the students. Nonpromotion and promotion and the attendant fears of both will be completely eliminated. How can there ever be failure if a child works to his ultimate capacity? The continuous progress school that arises from these correlates will be the school in which there exists a concentration on the individual pupil and his needs. It will be a school in which activities, grouping, teaching, and learning reflect more precisely the research in sociology, psychology, human growth, and development. And, it will be a school represented by collocation in which fruitful and educative experience is constantly realized by each of the individual learners. Finally, it will be a school in which there is offered to the teachers limitless possibilities to move into other kinds of activities that were hitherto unapproachable because of the constrictions and circumspections of the customarily graded program.

SUMMARY AND SOME CONCLUSIONS

It is impossible within the purview of this paper to adduce all of the evidence which now seems to be unequivocally pointing favorably toward a program of continuous progress education. Both empirical and descriptive research data are beginning to indicate strongly that when a serious effort has been given to creating a well developed and well conceived form of continuous progress education and it is measured against its graded counterpart, the youngsters do, in fact, in the continuous progress program, achieve significantly better in all measures of school work. Other collected evidence shows a very interesting by-product of continuous progress education: common agreement among the teachers of a whole list of values that have accrued to them and to the school administration because of a new approach to the youngster in the school that must now serve a different function. The literature of education with its growing discussions about the approach to the organization and teaching of youngsters at the elementary school age has turned the continuous progress education school movement in the United States into a ubiquitous one. But, a caution must be sounded. Educational change cannot be and should not be sustained by mere enthusiasm. By necessity it must rest on the evidence that clearly indicates continuous progress education to be a better way of doing things. As of this moment everything points to this being the case.

The impact, the direction, and the intensity of the movement of continuous progress education insist that all interested educators involve their staffs and faculties in the study and reflection of the manifold aspects and variations of this type of activity. The graded school can now be classified as a very static reference being imposed on a dynamic, evolving process: the process of education. The organization, curricula, approaches to teaching and learning, must emanate from the elementary school's many-faceted activities. These activities will serve the needs of all children. They will be established on the basis of clearly thought out experimentation shown to be worthy and germane to the vast education endeavors of a free society. To simply accept the graded school organization as the environment to nurture this endeavor without fundamentally attempting to seek more efficient and scientifically proven ways of achieving our goals is to achieve only a limited acceptance of limited ideas as well as a set of very limited vistas. We can ill afford that. It would seem from what we now know about continuous progress education and its attendant features that it more realistically fits the Space Age. At this time of protean growth and change in educational history, the newer designs and aspects of a different kind of school are necessary in order to achieve the wholesome aims required in a rapidly changing and much harrassed world.

6 | The Nongraded Elementary School: Selected Problems

B. E. J. HOUSEGO

Reprinted with permission from *Canadian Education and Research Digest*, Vol. 8, No. 4 (September 1968), pp. 245–257.

Making a decision, accepting the responsibility for having made it, and abiding by that decision—these are things we expect of the persons who control our educational system. These expectations may be idealistic; however, trustees, superintendents, supervisors of instruction, principals, and teachers must, in one phase or another of their work, do just these things. They must make choices, accept responsibility for them, and make further decisions in keeping with the initial choices.

The decision to implement nongrading appears to be an example of such a choice. More careful analysis would lead one to believe that the implementation of nongrading is perhaps the outgrowth of a still more basic choice of direction or position, that of viewing the school as child-centered rather than subject-centered. Goodlad (1962, p. 211) states that the ideal function of the subject-centered school is to impart facts, principles, and ways of doing; whereas, the prime purpose of the child-centered school is to develop the unique potentialities of the children therein. One might protest that these are not discrete aims, and therefore no choice between the two need be made. Still, it is a matter of priorities. Which is more important, the child or the subject matter? Which should be subordinated, if one need be? If nongrading is a committal to the view that the development of the individual child is the school's primary aim, then future decisions must be made to achieve this aim. The teacher must make this goal central.

A system, then, espouses nongrading because it is a possible means of meeting the needs of the individual child, a way of providing him with success and thereby developing within him a positive view of himself, so that he might meet future problems with this initial advantage. If nongrading is implemented as a more efficient means of ensuring that learners progress through a sequential body of subject matter, it is being "sold short" or underrated.

Dufay (1967, p. 111) tells us that nongrading is not a handy way to make the tasks of teachers and administrators easier, not a magic lantern to rub three times in September to ensure June miracles, and is not necessarily team teaching, complex scheduling, sophisticated grouping, inter-age classes or the elimination of grade designations. Moreover, it is not new. Plato recognized the existence of differing capacities and advocated in the ideal state an educational system which would make it possible for each child to develop his capacities and capabilities. We are still struggling to establish such schools.

In this paper several problems associated with nongrading are discussed: first, the provision of flexibility; second, the use of grouping procedures; third, the reporting of progress; and fourth, the effects of acceleration and deceleration on pupils.

PROVIDING FLEXIBILITY

The most essential prerequisite to successful nongrading or the individualization of instruction is the provision of flexibility; that is, if individual needs and interests assume priority, rigid structures like a firmly established timetable or a body of material to be taught in a set sequence must become secondary. How can flexibility be provided?

First, it is time to question the notion that every pupil must be exposed to the same sequence and body of subject matter during the first six years of school or in any predetermined period. This notion results in the prescription of topics for a class or a grade with no determination of what is already known. It results in the use of the same texts for all, in the pupil's memorizing extensively, and in the use of group norms rather than individual standards, all of which are rigid and inflexible practices. In the graded school, of course, an additional result of this expectation is nonpromotion. What might replace this point of view? Goodlad (1966, p. 9) suggests that,

> The concept of common coverage for all at relatively equal rates of speed confounds the intellect. The school's function increasingly is being recognized as that of teaching students processes of inquiry through guided practice in them. They (pupils) must learn how to learn.

Not the specifics learned, but rather the process of learning should receive emphasis. Some pupils might be exposed to minimal factual content, some too much more, depending on need to experience the techniques used in dealing with a certain kind of material or on acquaintance with the central concepts involved. Educators must identify the fundamental concepts around which the specifics of instruction are organized and deal with these rather than the customary mass of facts. This will provide greater flexibility in the classroom.

The promotion of discovery learning will also lend flexibility to classroom proceedings; as it is by nature an individualized procedure with the teacher serving as a co-worker, a source of data and an aid in the pupil's efforts to chart his own progress. Pupils who encounter the same difficulties in their work might form small, probably temporary, groups—but the greater part of discovering is individual.

The use of supplementary books, workbooks, films, records, programmed material and study guides as well as the usual texts is the most common means of providing flexibility. Pupils who need practice or on the other hand have made rapid progress might use such resources to pace their studies more individually. A variety of available materials makes it possible for the teacher to prescribe a suitable activity without extensive preparation; hence different children may at the same time be engaged in varying activities in small groups or as individuals.

It is also suggested that the establishment of priorities for each phase of education as well as generalized expectations for the whole process promotes flexibility. (Goodlad, 1966) For example, some believe that in elementary school the major aim should be to have children learn to read, write, and compute. Miel (1967) suggests the major concerns of elementary education are the development of strategic concepts, ways of processing information, and ways of feeling about and relating to people. These aims might guide the teacher and at the same time simplify and make less rigid the proceedings of the classroom.

Cooperative teaching is a frequently mentioned means of attaining greater flexibility in the classroom. While one teacher instructs a large group, others might work with small groups or individual pupils. Pupils thus devote more time to independent study. It is important that they learn to work independently, and surprising is the extent to which they can progress in this direction, if encouraged to do so. Pupils need to do more planning, make more decisions, and more often select the material they are to study.

Some more specific suggestions as to how flexibility might be attained are made by Dufay (1966). He notes that the use of several series of readers will permit smoother progress in learning to read. A child might progress from one level of series A (average difficulty) to the second level of series B (less than average difficulty) and thus move forward a partial step, if he is not ready to move a full step. He suggests that in schools where mornings are devoted to reading and the language arts, pupils might disperse and be regrouped in the afternoons for mathematics, depending on their present levels of skill, and for science or social studies, depending on previous exposure. If pupils remain in the same classrooms during the afternoons, they might be grouped for ability in subject areas. If all work on the unit, assignments might be made at different levels of sophistication. Pupils might be grouped for interest or in learning teams which work at projects for a time and then jointly present themselves for testing. A tutorial approach in which one student aids another is a further possibility.

Dufay (1966) describes an attempt to individualize the science program through recognizing major categories of content, each of which is encountered each year on one or another of seven levels of complexity, and a multitext approach in social studies, the major aims of which are the development of critical thinking, skills of observation, methods of inquiry and intelligent response to social happenings. Individualization in spelling is possible through the use of placement tests and the practice of adding the few incorrectly spelled words from one list to the next one undertaken. Pupils might test one another and thus the teacher becomes involved only in mastery tests and in periodic supervision.

In conclusion, it should be emphasized that the most important means of gaining flexibility in a classroom is simply to *determine* to have it. Given liberation, teachers who cannot function in such a setting invent their own complicated rules and restrictions. Those without freedom, who nevertheless genuinely desire it, manage to achieve a degree of this freedom despite the rules which prove a hindrance. (Wolfson, 1967)

GROUPING

Recognition of the need for flexibility in our schools dictates a point of view concerning grouping, a point of view well expressed by Goodlad. (1965, p. 159) He states,

> The potentiality of grouping patterns fades and the crucial significance of individualized instruction looms large. Needed is a system of such flexibility that it is scarcely a system at all. Such a system must reveal individuality not disguise or obscure it.

Briefly, no matter what the criteria for establishing a permanent group of pupils for joint instruction in all subjects, the situation in which pupils either cannot meet group standards or, more likely, could work far beyond them, is bound to develop. As Wolfson (1966, p. 33) observes:

Most nongraded schools, as they exist today, are in fact graded by reading achievement. Children are grouped for likeness and put through essentially the same curriculum.

In a later article (1967, p. 354) she again registers this complaint:

Most observations and descriptions of the nongraded school, however, reveal a structured-leveled rather than graded-organization that provides only for different rates of learning the same content or for various subgroupings of children who learn the same content.

Stating the same problem in other terms, Goldberg, Passow and Justman (1966, p.v.) speak of "the dark possibility that ability grouping functions not as 'individualized instruction' but as selective deprivation."

The graded (leveled) school is patterned on certain assumptions (Wolfson, 1967) that curriculum can be meaningfully sequenced year by year, that children develop and progress in a step-by-step manner paralleling the curriculum sequence, and that there is special content to be covered and evaluated at each grade level. When we homogeneously group children as it is usually done on the basis of achievement, a measure said to indicate ability, and perhaps teacher judgment, we assume that we *can* identify children achieving at the same level, that they *will* all profit from the same instruction and that their achievement levels, once determined, will remain relatively the same for some time, perhaps a month, a semester, a year or even longer. Are these assumptions irrefutable? Many think not.

Suppose we make the reverse assumptions, as Wolfson (1967) does in defending multiage grouping of children; that is, why not assume that there is no logical or inherent sequence in the various curriculum areas, that every child's development can't be matched with the same curricular sequence, and that there is no special content to be covered and evaluated at any particular grade level? Miel (1967) reinforces Wolfson's thinking in challenging the belief that all children necessarily progress through the same sequence to arrive at a similar point in learning. She also questions the assumption that coverage of a topic is a guarantee of any particular level of intellectual activity or any progress in understanding basic concepts. If there is no predetermined sequence appropriate for all learners, if individual levels of competence and interest are constantly in flux, and if the pattern of learning differs from one child to another, then the need is for individualized instruction and the setting up of workable, homogeneous groups to remain constant in all subject areas is an impossibility.

Grouping must be of a temporary or at most semipermanent character. Current interests, similar problems, or the degree to date, might bring children into groups for limited periods of time.

We must recognize ". . . that no matter how precise the selection of [pupils] becomes or how varied by themselves the [pupil] deployment may be, grouping arrangements by themselves serve little educational purpose." (Goldberg, Passow, and Justman, 1966, p. 169). We must plan for flexibility in grouping to ensure maximum pupil growth.

REPORTING

The current curricular and organizational reforms in education have changed the setting in which the individual's progress is evaluated and reported; they have made the old-fashioned, competitive, comparative marking schemes obsolete, yet many "reformed schools" continue to try to report in the traditional manner. They see no alternative and are reinforced in their unwillingness to change by parents who complain loudly about any change introduced in the reporting procedure.

First, it should be made clear that reporting in itself is of less consequence than evaluation, of which it is a logical outgrowth. Ideally the teacher does not evaluate for the purpose of reporting, but rather, he evaluates in order to discover whether or not progress is being made toward his and the pupils' goals and objectives. Anderson (1966) suggests that the teacher would review and summarize the child's progress for his own information, and, having a useful summary, make it at least partially available to parents. He also discusses the usefulness of evaluation and reporting to teachers, parents and children. Through evaluating and reporting, teachers are enabled to see children as individuals, reconsider their placement in one group or another, and discuss their progress with other teachers. Parents need evaluative information in their immediate relationships with children and for long-range planning. Information concerning their own progress is helpful to children in coming to know and accept themselves.

The goals of traditional reporting (Chadwick, Durham and Morse, 1966) entail evaluation of the child's progress in terms of his own ability, in comparison with his peers, and in relation to provincial or national sampling. Traditional reporting has tended to be subjective, for in most instances teachers do not know precisely what a child should be able to achieve, whether his position in class is fifteenth or eighteenth, or what the degree of his achievement is by national standards. Adequate, that is reliable, valid, and suitable, tests in the various subject areas are not always available, not always used. Instead, the teacher guesses at a mark or reports a percentage computed on teacher-made tests. Judgment is in relation to pupils of past years and others at present in class, and as such, it is subject to extreme halo effects. Such procedures ensure that those pupils who are more able always receive the praise and those pupils who are less able are always criticized.

In reporting the progress of pupils in the nongraded school, teachers should state what a child has achieved and whether or not this achievement is satisfactory. Chadwick, Durham and Morse (1966) describe a rather complicated reporting system. They advocate the use of three terms to be applied to accomplishment: Commendable, indicating outstanding work in terms of ability; adequate, signifying average performance with average effort; and, need for improvement, implying the child has more to give and more territory to cover. Each subject area has a separate page and each is broken into components featuring a further breakdown to the level of subskills and explanatory items, the checklist —commendable, adequate and need for improvement—being applied to all. Bar graphs and written comments are also featured. In every subject but music, art and physical education a charting of basic concepts, understandings, skills and attitudes occurs, hence the need for careful analysis and breakdown of the aims and objectives for the particular period of schooling in each subject area and the development of refined tests and other measuring devices.

Anderson (1966, p. 9) emphasizes the value of parent-teacher conferences, describing them as ". . . the most effective and fruitful of several alternatives available at the elementary school level." Initiated by teacher or parent, these meetings provide a time when reports might be interpreted, work samples shown, and questions answered. A parent may find out how he can most effectively help his child; a teacher may gain new understanding of a pupil. Parent-teacher conferences require foundation and support. Teacher education should include conference techniques and dictating equipment, secretarial assistance and substitutes should be part of the budget for an effective conference program.

There may be no *best* system of reporting, but there are some useful guidelines in keeping with which changes might be made:

1. Movement in the direction of dichotomies rather than toward wide rating scales is desirable. A child's performance is satisfactory, not so, or perhaps outstanding.

2. Evaluation of study skills and work habits should be included.

3. Noncognitive aspects of development like emotional and social growth, self-acceptance, relations with others, and self direction should be treated separately.

4. More specificity in verbal comment is required. Why say, "Johnny is a delight in the classroom"?

5. A positive rather than a negative focus is desirable so that evaluation reinforce and enhance learning. This concern has led in some areas to dual reports, one section of which discloses the extent of the child's progress in relation to his own standards, and the other of which charts the child's progress in contrast to that of others in the group.

Reporting must keep pace with change in the schools. Success in individualizing instruction is somewhat dependent on the refinement of evaluative techniques and a good report is simply an offshoot of adequate evaluation.

EFFECTS OF ACCELERATION
AND DECELERATION OF PUPILS

Making any definite statement about the effects of acceleration and deceleration on pupils is most difficult. Surely, being allowed to progress at his individual rate, neither being unduly pressured nor held back, should have nothing but beneficial effects on the pupil. Adverse effects of either acceleration or deceleration are likely to be the product of the manner in which the procedure is carried out and the attitudes of parents, peers and teachers themselves.

One of the most frequently mentioned undesirable effects of acceleration is advancement beyond one's age level and subsequent difficulty in adjusting socially; that is, if a child is accelerated so that he is maybe two or three years younger than his fellow pupils, he may not be accepted socially, probably because he is smaller and younger and does not have the same social interests as his classmates. At the same time, he will lack contact with those whose social interests parallel his own, and as a result, he might be "left out". Barnickle and Lindberg (1967) describe four children, each of whom was capable of attempting an accelerated program but none of whom was permitted to do so. In each case the parents refused to let the boy (all were boys) progress more quickly than the average group. Reasons, in addition to possible social maladjustment, included small physical stature, lack of a nongraded program beyond elementary school, being faced with vocational choice too early, emotional immaturity and the feeling that it is better for a pupil to be top of an average class than bottom of an accelerated group.

An excellent study related to the question at hand was carried out by Goldberg, Passow and Justman (1966), who attempted to assess the effects of ability grouping on the academic, social, and personal attainment of fifth and six grade children. Children were classified as follows:

A—IQ   130+   —gifted
B—IQ   120 – 129—very bright
C—IQ   110 – 119—bright
D—IQ   100 – 109—average
E—IQ   below 99 —low and below average

They were located according to all possible combinations of ability levels and ranges of ability in 86 different classes.

The findings of the Goldberg, Passow and Justman study concerning achievement are complex and varied. Children of different ability level are affected differently and in only some subjects by being in narrow or broad range classes and by the presence or absence of gifted or slow pupils. For example, the presence of gifted pupils in science classes was consistently related to greater achievement increments in pupils of the other four ability levels. In social studies, the presence of gifted pupils had upgrading effects only on the very bright and bright student and only in counteraction to the presence of slower students (D's and E's). The presence of low and below average students had an upgrading effect on the arithmetic achievement of all other pupils. Most important, and contrary to expectation, there were no downgrading effects in any subject from the presence of gifted pupils.

The ability range in the classroom had effects on achievement in some areas (social studies, reading comprehension, vocabulary, arithmetic, and total average) and not in others (science, language arts, and work-study skills). The total population, generally, showed greater gains in broad range classes as compared with medium or narrow range ones. These findings are further complicated by taking note that very bright pupils in either broad or narrow range classes exceeded those in medium range classes in social studies and arithmetic comprehension, gifted pupils were unaffected by range, average pupils in the broad range achieved more in social studies and arithmetic comprehension, and low and below average pupils in the broad range were superior to those in medium and narrow ranges only in vocabulary. Of the one hundred five possible comparisons (five ability levels, three ranges and seven test areas) only eleven reached significance and ten of these were in favour of broad range classes. The following summary is worthy of note:

> The effects of the teachers on the work of the class were at least as potent as the effects of the pupils' intelligence, and ability range in the classroom, or the position held within the range. (Goldberg, Passow, and Justman 1966, p. 71)

Achievement is but one area in which acceleration and deceleration might affect pupils. Self-attitudes compose another. In the Goldberg, Passow and Justman study (1966), self-attitudes were measured through self-ratings on 50 traits both from the point of view of present status (I am) and ideal self (I wish). The difference between ideal and present status, a negative discrepancy score, showed the extent to which the subject felt he did not meet his ideal. Expected achievement or level of aspiration was measured in terms of the expected number of items correct out of a possible 100. Satisfaction on receiving the expected score was measured as well. These ratings on all but the discrepancy score were initially related directly to ability and continued to be so, except in the case of very bright students who rated themselves lower than bright ones at the end of the two year period of the study. It is apparent in this study that "ability grouping had more significant and more consistent effects on self attitudes than on achievement." (Goldberg, Passow and Justman, 1966, p. 105) Briefly, range has a significant effect on the self-attitude of the slow student. In competition with brighter students, he produces a lower self-estimate (I am) and a lower ideal (I wish). The finding that a narrow range deflates the self-image of the gifted pupil, and being in broad range raises even higher an initially high self-image, coupled with the findings concerning slow students, lead the authors to state,

> . . . to the extent that a pupil's view of himself plays a significant role in school achievement, the . . . findings would argue for classes in the narrow range at least for the gifted (A) and for the low and below average (E) pupils. (Goldberg, Passow and Justman, 1966, p. 105)

However, from the achievement perspective, low average pupils did better in broad range classes and the gifted pupils did no worse in such a pattern. Decisions depend on what the educator desires most for the student, a positive and realistic self-image or maximum achievement. Again, however, the teacher's role is prime. What the child experiences in the classroom makes more difference in how he views himself than the organizational pattern does.

Interests and attitudes toward school were investigated and found not significantly related to grouping. The overall conclusion is that ability grouping, which can mean acceleration or deceleration, is neither good nor bad. The manner in which it is used determines its worth. (Goldberg, Passow and Justman, 1966, p. 168)

CONCLUSION

The nongraded school is based on the fact that children are different and on the belief that the teacher's task is to make provision for these differences through locating and defining them and subsequently planning appropriate activities. This is a matter of educational diagnosis and prescription. (Goodlad, 1965). There must be choices so that prescription be possible. Evaluative techniques must change, hopefully in the direction of comparing the pupil's performance with his own standard rather than a group one.

The questions raised in this article are but a small sample of the problems associated with establishing a truly individualized approach to instruction. Nongrading is, in a sense, a philosophy of teaching and learning, and as such it pervades every aspect of the classroom, grouping, the nature of pupil progress, curriculum planning and emphases, and the role of the teacher. How much progress has been made toward genuinely individualizing instruction?

REFERENCES

Anderson, R. H., "The Importance and Purpose of Reporting," *National Elementary School Principal,* 1966, 50, 6–11.

Barnickle, D. W., and R. T. Lindberg, "A Problem of the Ungraded School: The Unwilling Accelerate," *The Education Digest,* 1967, 32, 41–43.

Chadwick, R. E., R. Durham, and M. Morse, "The Report Card in Nongraded School," *National Elementary Principal,* 1966, 50, 22–28.

Dufay, F. R., *Ungrading the Elementary School,* West Nyack, N.Y.: Parker Publishing Co., 1966.

Dufay, F. R., "When Nongrading Fails," *School Management,* 1967, 11, 110–113.

Goldberg, M. L., A. H. Passow, and J. Justman, *The Effects of Ability Grouping,* New York: Teachers' College Press, Columbia University, 1966.

Goodlad, J. I., "Diagnosis and Prescription in Educational Practice," *The Education Digest,* 1966, 31, 8–11.

Goodlad, J. I., "Meeting Children Where They Are," *Saturday Review,* March 20, 1965, 57–59, 72–74.

Kingston, A. J., and J. A. Walsh, Jr., "Research on Reporting Systems," *National Elementary Principal,* 1966, 50, 36–39.

Miel, Alice, "Sequence in Learning," *The Education Digest,* 1967, 32, 35–39.

Wolfson, B., "Individualizing Instruction," *N.E.A. Journal,* 1966, 55, 31–35.

Wolfson, B., "The Promise of Multi-age Grouping for Individualizing Instruction," *The Elementary School Journal,* 1967, 67, 354–362.

7 | A Controlled Experiment Evaluating the Effects of a Nongraded Organization on Pupil Achievement*

MAURIE HILLSON

J. CHARLES JONES

J. WILLIAM MOORE

FRANK VAN DEVENDER

Reprinted from *The Journal of Educational Research,*
Vol. 57 (July–August 1964), pp. 548–550, with the permission of the authors.

A recurrent criticism of the educational system of this country has been that many programs and procedures have been put into large scale operation in the schools on the basis of the subjective impressions or the evangelistic zeal of their proponents and, once instituted, have been continued, in some cases for many years, with little or no effort being made at systematic evaluation. Hilgard (4) and others (1) have pointed out the tendency of educators to force psychological principles, without regard to their relevancy, into educational theory, using psychological labels as justification or support for existing educational practices.

* This work was supported in part by the Susquehanna Valley Program, Bucknell University, through a grant from the Ford Foundation.

In recent years the public elementary schools have shown increasing interest in nongrading as a possible solution to many of the academic problems encountered in the primary grades. In addition to an interest in improving achievement, there has been an understandable concern over the effects of academic failure on young children, estimates of the failure rate under the present grades system running as high as 18 percent on a national basis. The nongraded system has been promoted, not as a change in instructional method, but as a *reorganization* of the primary levels of instruction whereby children may progress at a rate appropriate to their abilities and without the disorganizing effects of the threat of failure. Other specific advantages claimed for the nongraded system in addition to improved achievement and reduction of tensions and anxieties for both pupils and teachers have been: instruction can be adjusted to individual spurts and lags in development; children will compete with their own records rather than with each other; teachers need not fear encroaching on "materials for the next grade" or be required to bring all children up to the same levels of achievement without regard to the ability of some children to achieve these norms; and children, after absence from school, may resume at the point where they left off. Moreover, those who attest to the worth of nongrading, state that a unique outcome of this procedure is that achievement is increased at all levels of pupil ability.

A procedure which promises so many benefits, with few if any drawbacks, is worth careful evaluation. To date, such evaluation as exists is largely subjective, anecdotal, and at the level of demonstration rather than experimentation.

Typical are results reported for a nongraded program in the Elmira Heights, New York, elementary schools which indicate that it is not uncommon for 90 percent to 95 percent of the nongraded pupils to be reading at a fourth-grade level at the end of three years, this in contrast with the 60 percent typical of the pupils in a conventional graded program (5). Similar results are reported for the Linda School District, Marysville, California by R. A. Anderson (6). Other nongraded programs make comparable claims. However, some critics question the reliability of such evidence. *The Third Edition of the Encyclopedia of Educational Research* notes that "nongrading is supported by some plausible sounding claims and theories rather than by research" (2). It could be suggested that the apparent success of nongraded programs might be attributable to a number of uncontrolled variables, e.g., selection of the most able teachers for the nongraded groups, establishing in-service training programs for teachers and administrators prior to and during the program, development of special materials for use in the program and improved parent orientation and interest. The possibility is thus raised that demonstrated gains may result from the operation of one or more of these variables rather than from the change from a graded to a nongraded organization. The purpose of this investigation was to assess in a controlled experimental situation, the effects of a nongraded program on the reading achievement of a group of elementary school pupils. This is a preliminary report covering the first one and one-half years of the experimental period; the complete experiment will extend over three years.

METHOD

Subjects

All first-grade students entering the Washington Elementary School (2) for the academic year 1960–61 were randomly assigned to either experimental ($N=26$) or control groups ($N=26$). Subjects remained in their respective groups for the academic years 1960–61 and 1961–62 and continued into 1962–63. Subjects identified as a part of the experimental program included only those initially assigned to these groups. Transfers or new entries were randomly assigned to experimental or control groups but were not included in the evaluation. Reading readiness levels for all children in both experimental and control groups were determined during the first two weeks of the school year and three levels of reading ability were established for each group.

TEACHERS

All teachers, whether assigned to experimental or control groups, were selected for participation on the basis of their excellence in teaching. Selection was made by the administration and an attempt was made to match the teachers on the basis of their past effectiveness. They were then randomly assigned to experimental or control groups. All teachers, whether experimental or control, participated in workshops in preparation for the nongraded program; all received the assistance of a reading consultant in selecting materials, carrying on their programs, and the observation and assessment of pupils for placement in reading groups.

PROCEDURE

Nongrading for the experimental group proceeded on a year-by-year basis; children were permitted to move from reading level to reading level as their level of performance dictated, there being a total of nine possible reading levels through which a pupil might progress during a three-year period. By the third year nongrading for grades one through three will be completed and the designations of first, second or third grade eliminated.

Pupils in the control group were placed in one of three reading level groups within a conventional graded program and instruction was adapted to the ability levels of the groups. At the end of each school year the entire class, with the exception of those classified as failures, was promoted to the next grade and again subdivided into three reading level groups. No child was assigned to a reading group except those contained within his own grade level, e.g., no child was assigned to a second grade reading group who was not in his second year of school and only those second year children who had failed first grade were assigned to reading groups below the three contained within the second grade.

RESULTS

The effects of the nongraded organization on pupil achievement were evaluated at the end of the third semester of the experimental period by use of three achievement tests. The first was the Lee Clark Reading Test, the second and third were the Paragraph Meaning and Word Meaning tests of the Primary Battery of the Standard Achievement Test.

The results of the comparisons of the mean grade placement using the t-test analysis (two-tailed test), for the experimental and control groups for the Lee Clark Reading Test, Word Meaning, and Paragraph Meaning tests are presented in Table 1.

TABLE I

A Comparison of Mean Grade Placement on Reading, Word Meaning and Paragraph Meaning Achievement Tests

Test	Experimental Group N=26	Control Group N=26	t	p
Lee Clark Reading	3.19	2.81	2.71	.01
Word Meaning	3.33	2.86	3.13	.01
Paragraph Meaning	3.27	2.90	1.95	.06

It can be observed in Table 1 that the E group for grade placement was significantly higher than the control group on all three measures of achievement.

DISCUSSION

Since it was the primary purpose of this investigation to provide more reliable data covering the effects of the nongraded primary organization on reading achievement, any conclusions which are drawn must be evaluated in terms of the soundness of the design of the experiment as well as the statistical analysis of the data. From this point of view, an evaluation of the design indicates that in general the variables were sufficiently controlled so that data resulting from the experimental situation were reliable. The only portion of the design in which greater control seemed desirable and was not possible within the limits of this investigation was teacher variability. Although care was exercised in the matching and the random assignment of teachers, because of the small number ($N=6$), it is possible that some systematic differences still existed.

Turning to the statistical analysis of the scores obtained by the students on the related measures of reading achievement, it was found that the nongraded pupils performed at a higher academic level on all three measures. Specifically, a comparison of mean grade levels for reading as measured by the Lee Clark Reading test was significantly (.01 level) in favor of the nongraded primary organization. Comparison results were obtained when mean grade levels for related measures of reading (word meaning and paragraph meaning tests) were compared statistically. As observed in Table 1, the mean grade level on the word meaning test was significantly greater for the nongraded group at the .01 level of significance, and the paragraph meaning was greater in the same direction at the .06 level. These results are in keeping with a number of previous research findings supporting the use of the nongraded primary organization (6).

Since confidence can be placed in the design of the study and the resulting empirical evidence is strongly in favor of the nongraded group, it can be inferred that the superior achievement in reading of pupils in the nongraded group in this experiment was attributable to the organizational structure rather than to either superior pupil ability and/or teaching methods.

CONCLUSIONS

Generally it can be concluded that pupils participating in a nongraded primary organization (all other things being equal) will achieve at a significantly higher level on measures of reading ability and related measures of reading than will pupils participating in a graded organization. Specifically, it may be stated that pupils of all levels of ability achieved at a higher level than pupils in a graded situation. Further, it is concluded that the increased achievement of the participants in the nongraded primary program is primarily related to organizational structure when methods of teaching are held constant.*

* See the Introduction to this Part for a comment on the results of the follow-up to this study. MH and RTH, editors.

SUMMARY

Ss ($N=52$) were taught reading in one of two public school organizational structures (graded versus nongraded). At the end of one and one-half years of the three-year experimental period, analyses of grade level achievement for three measures related to reading achievement favored the nongraded organization at a level which was statistically significant.

REFERENCES

1. Davis, Robert A. "Applicability of Applications of Psychology with Particular Reference to Schoolroom Learning," *Journal of Educational Research,* XXXVII (1943), pp. 19–30.
2. *Encyclopedia of Educational Research, 3rd Ed.* The American Educational Research Association (New York: The Macmillan Company, 1960), p. 22.
3. Goodlad, John I., and Anderson, Robert H. *The Nongraded Elementary School* (New York: Harcourt, Brace & World, Inc., 1959).
4. Hilgard, Ernest R. "The Relation of Schools of Psychology to Educational Practices," *The California Journal of Elementary Education,* VII (1939), pp. 17–26.
5. "Non-Graded Primary Unit Plan," unpublished report, The Elmira Heights Control Schools, Elmira Heights, New York, December 1959.
6. Personal communication from Dr. Anderson as reported in a speech to the American Association of School Administrators, Atlantic City, New Jersey, February 1960.

8 | The Nongraded Secondary School

WALTER BADEN
DAVID MAURER

Reprinted by permission of the publisher from Baden-Maurer Letters, *Secondary Trends and Issues,* Numbers Three, Four, and Five, © 1967, Science Research Associates, Inc.

WHAT IT IS—AND ISN'T

WALT: What kind of problems were you trying to solve when you began looking at the nongraded secondary school?

DAVE: We had a track system. The problem with our track was little consideration for the rails. If youngsters were good English students, their schedules put them in track one for everything. Subject teachers were critical of the Guidance Department. The reply of Guidance: scheduling conflicts!

WALT: The nongraded organizational pattern can help increase flexibility, particularly in the area of pupil scheduling and grouping requirements. I would suggest that grouping flexibility, in some cases, can be more than doubled. The implications of this, especially for the smaller school, are enormous.

DAVE: There's another implication here. I'm sure a few English teachers have wondered what crystal ball put some of those pupils in their classes, forcing them to teach "down the middle."

WALT: I think every veteran of the classroom has experienced the same thing. Shortly after a school year began I used to feel like I was on the stern of a ship sailing away from an island and waving a fond farewell to a few forlorn souls who were left behind. These were the two or three that I knew I couldn't wait for anymore, and once left behind they were doomed to stay behind forever.

DAVE: We have summer school to solve that problem.

WALT: That's one of the three R's of the graded school: repetition, retention, and remediation. The major impetus to the consideration of the nongraded school comes from practicing classroom teachers who have come to realize there are built-in contradictions in the graded school.

DAVE: There are few secondary schools without varsity athletic teams. I wonder how a coach would feel if he were forced to use only individuals from a specific grade level.

WALT: We talk about pupil achievement and pupil attitude, but within the graded framework we have built-in impediments to learning —the usual 65 or 75 percent passing grade is not high enough. With grading we build in our own problems. For years teachers have said that a pupil cannot be expected to do well in a sequential subject without a sound foundation. A graded system may slavishly insist upon a predetermined course of study in an area such as mathematics. A student in junior high who has a history of minimum passing grades should have substantial gaps in knowledge of foundation material.

DAVE: I believe that substantial gap is at least one-third. Consider a foreign language class. If a student accomplishes two-thirds of the work, he can take the second year's course. At this rate he would be lucky to pass the second year. Lack of accomplishment is a geometric progression, not an arithmetic one. This arbitrary means of passing dooms that student to future failure.

WALT: It does, not only because of lack of skill, but also for attitudinal reasons. I am sure that we arbitrarily set standards of achievement in a given classroom that are purely accidents of geography. I have seen sophomore courses in English in an affluent suburban community that are much more difficult and sophisticated than a so-called course in senior year English in a less affluent community.

DAVE: There's another factor that deserves consideration. A look at a so-called sophomore English class would bring out an age range variable as much as three or four years.

WALT: In all the districts I have served as a consultant our research has borne this out. When we see the age-grade distribution figures we find that in a graded system there is as much age differential as in a nongraded one. Regarding attitude, the student sees he is unable to measure up to a preconceived course of study. I think if I were a student who was forced to attend a school that often reminded me of my academic inferi-

ority, and whose system almost doomed me to failure before I started, I'd
be pretty hostile when I was twelve or thirteen.

DAVE: These considerations encouraged us to survey our own situation. I spoke earlier of the ambiguity in our former tracking system. Age
and prerequisites are not necessarily the only factors. We knew you were
erasing your blackboard of grade levels and came over to take a look.
You drew some conclusions for us about traditional grouping patterns.

WALT: Traditional grouping practices in most secondary schools are
based, *in fact,* on the assumption that the primary grouping criteria is
the number of years a pupil has been in school. The idea of the grade
level is so ingrained in our thinking that we hardly realize that it is a
prime factor in our grouping. Consider a six-year secondary school with
an enrollment of six hundred. Usually pupils are sorted out considering
each grade level as a separate group. Only then do we make further
subgroups based on achievement, ability, reading level, motivation, etc.

DAVE: We had a system whereby a student had to pass certain
courses before moving on to the next grade homeroom. His position in
school was as much determined by his particular homeroom as it was by
his accomplishment in school.

WALT: This type of policy is philosophically indefensible unless one
really believes that the so-called grade level is a major factor in grouping.
Grade level standards vary enough from teacher to teacher to be a myth.

DAVE: We were trying to escape the contradictions of our trackless
tracking system. Numbers were needed. I can remember you drawing a
diagram that quickly shed light on our problem.

Graded Pattern		*Nongraded Pattern*	
Seventh Grade English:		Junior High English:	
Group A—1 section of 25	25	Group A—1 section of 25	25
Group B—2 sections of 25	50	Group B—2 sections of 25	50
Group C—1 section of 25	25	Group C—6 sections of 25	150
total	100	Group D—2 sections of 25	50
Eighth Grade English:		Group E—1 section of 25	25
Repeat as above	100	total	300
Ninth Grade English:			
Repeat as above	100		
total	300		

WALT: By sorting out pupils by grade level in the case referred to
the school would have about one hundred pupils at each grade level. Assuming that the staff wanted to group pupils in English according to
demonstrated achievement in that subject, it would probably end up
with one top group, one bottom group, and two middles, each of about

twenty-five pupils in "seventh grade" English. The master schedule could allocate two periods for middle group seventh grade English. Pupil scheduling would be limited to one of those two periods.

DAVE: In other words, this is just as true for eight, nine, or ten.

WALT: Right! But if the school felt that pupils achieving at the same level should be grouped together even though they may have been in school for a different number of years, a very different pattern emerges. It can now consider all junior high pupils as a single group of three hundred, and forget the arbitrary distinctions of grade level. Pupils may then be grouped according to what is really considered the most important criterion. If it applies the criterion of achievement in English for grouping in that subject, it might now end up with one top group, one bottom, and ten groups in between. Since the school is now grouping three hundred pupils instead of one hundred, it might have six middle groups of junior high English instead of two each at the seventh, eighth, and ninth grades. Then the school can distribute the middle group over six different time slots in the master schedule. In addition, the school can group on five levels if it wishes.

DAVE: I think it's also a matter of sheer economics. With your hundred students per grade level it's questionable to provide a teacher for those who really need remedial help or enrichment. In any grade level there are talented youngsters. If there are only six or seven of them, few schools could provide a class for them. But if you are referring to a total of three hundred there's no problem! Automatically those six per grade level provide an eighteen pupil class, putting us on economically sounder ground.

WALT: The illustration shows all groups with an enrollment of twenty-five. Actually schools vary in their grouping patterns. Since we believe that the more extraordinary the learning needs of a pupil, the more extraordinary should be the learning setting, our grouping distribution and class sizes look like this:

Group A—one section, 16 pupils	16
Group B—two sections, 22 pupils	44
Group C—six sections, 30 pupils	180
Group D—two sections, 22 pupils	44
Group E—one section, 16 pupils	16
	total 300

DAVE: Here's the back of that old envelope again. I remember asking what you would do with that increased middle reservoir. It was good economy to serve those sixteen individuals on the top and bottom. But you also wanted to provide for the needs of what we call too often the average student. I like groups B and D.

WALT: For the first time, a school with a small number of students can design a schedule that allows an individual to be in a top group in one subject, and in a different group in another.

DAVE: This automatically gave us more students with which to work. We saw that we could have more class sections geared to specific groups. Our old track idea seemed rather outmoded next to this more individualized program. As much as it is a must for the smaller school, I can see just as many possibilities for it in larger ones.

WALT: For one thing, the larger school can match pupils with particular teachers to a larger extent. This matching looms as a very large factor in giving pupils a chance to learn. Students vary considerably in the extent to which they are ready for more independence and responsibility for their own learning. Teachers also vary significantly in their ability to adopt different modes of teaching. Some teachers are more adept at working with students in a highly independent type of learning setting, while others operate best in a more teacher-directed one.

DAVE: Thousands of smaller secondary schools in this country are searching for a way out of the vertigo. Nongrading their curriculum can flexibly individualize student programs. It gave us the framework to make a small school big. The severity of grade lines was eased, creating pools of students. I know you feel that much more is involved.

WALT: This raises some fundamental issues. *The nongraded secondary school is both an organizational structure and an institutional frame of mind.* It isn't an organizational scheme only, and it isn't a system of replacing three or four grade levels with four or five phases or steps or groups. It is also important to keep in mind that there is a substantial difference between existing nongraded practices and the ideals of nongraded schools. The graded school has been evolving for over a hundred years in this country. The nongraded pattern is much newer, and we're a long way from an ideal.

DAVE: But Walt, it's still a structure. It offers the opportunity to do things that couldn't be done before. What more is in this box created by accepting the principle of a nongraded secondary school?

WALT: You pointed out that this is a simple idea. It is essentially simple in one respect, or to the degree we have discussed. But we have only talked about organization. The point should be made very clear that while all roads do not lead to Rome, there are many that do. There are many schools throughout the country not known as nongraded, developing policies and practices that are much like those of some of the highly publicized nongraded schools. The target that the nongraded school is aiming for is also the target of many other schools, though the approach may differ. Actually, of all the innovations now being introduced into schools, nongradedness is the most complex.

DAVE: But can't it be achieved by just cycling? There are no prerequisite limitations to offering American History one year and World History the next. Student numbers are automatically doubled.

WALT: Right. We'll spend more time with this technique later, but it is just a technique. The school envisioned is more complicated than the idea of installing a jet engine on the rear of the old buggy while leaving the horse in front. We advocate a completely new vehicle.

DAVE: Aren't there quite a few things that impede this accomplishment?

WALT: Yes—primarily the tyranny of tradition. We have developed so much structure that it has become stricture. We have gotten all tangled up with organization. We have tied our own hands and become slaves to our schedules instead of the reverse. One of the basic objectives of the nongraded school is, to borrow the architectural dictum, "Form follows function." The schedule, and the necessary organizational structure, should serve our purposes, not the other way around. The nongraded school attempts to remove impediments to effective learning, to break down some of the artificial barriers to individualized instruction that has been an aim of schoolmen for generations. Our delight in order has made us try to put everything, including courses, teachers, and pupils, into neat little boxes, preferably square. Secondary schools are not that simple, neat, orderly, and easily categorized and administered.

A major difficulty is precisely that it is not only the level of accomplishment that determines the cubbyhole, but also the amount of time a student spends in a given course. For example, not many schools will award credit in French I in March or April, although a student may have reached a point of proficiency that would so warrant.

DAVE: Yet both of our schools have these students.

WALT: The concern for the individual is not exclusively the province of the nongraded school, but we think we've been able to run an orderly, efficient, and exciting school with much less structure than has previously existed. We're not just talking about an organizational system, but also an institutional frame of mind. This attitude is not the exclusive province of the nongraded school, but the nongraded school is not complete without it.

As you recall, we have visited a number of nongraded schools around the country, and I think they have some major characteristics in common. They operate a grouping system such as Frank Brown's phases in the exciting school at Melbourne, Florida. However, the nongraded pattern does not end here. Pupils are grouped on a basis of achievement in individual subjects, regardless of the artificial grade level they happen to be at. Each of the various phases or groups in the nongraded schools are defined, not only in terms of content goals, but behavioral goals as well. In general, the phases or groups tend to demand, or permit, increasing independence on the part of the student from one phase to the next. It's almost like saying that our function is to wean the pupils away from their dependence and reliance upon us, and to prepare them for a lifetime of independent learning that is essentially the way most adults learn. We try, through phasing, to get them out of the academic incubator when they are ready.

DAVE: I like the idea of describing programs for students rather than students for programs.

WALT: Yes, and a nongraded school also actively tries to solve many other particularly nagging questions. For example, the excellent program at Middletown, Rhode Island, is one that seriously questions the desirability or advisibility that a course begin in September and end in June. Traditionally, if a student does not pass a course he must repeat it from the beginning, even though he may not need an entire year to overcome his deficiencies. They try to remedy this situation and, in fact, move pupils along at their own best rates of speed.

The ultimate objective is to create an individual program for each student. This means many things. It means that there is a group of courses he will take, and that he will take these in groups that are most suitable for him. These groups will consider both his achievement and the style of learning expected of him. He will be allowed to achieve the necessary degree of proficiency at his best rate of speed.

It does not accept a preconceived course of study that is deemed appropriate for a mythical, typical student at a given grade level. It says that the only proper course of study, and the only defensible curriculum, is one that takes *each* individual from his present position and attempts to help him develop during the school year. His success or lack of it is more directly related, therefore, to his efforts for this year, and is not influenced as much by his efforts or lack of them last year.

DAVE: Our initial excursions into nongradedness were for structural purposes to serve other ends, but it soon became apparent that it isn't just a framework. We've been called upon to make unprecedented decisions. Questions have arisen that literally shake the basic order of our school's practices and policies.

WALT: The nongrading innovation is one that permeates almost every corner of the institution. It represents a basic and fundamental attitude toward secondary education that ultimately will raise questions in almost every element of the school's operation. In the following issues we will get down to more specifics relative to the way some of those operating programs throughout the country have handled these problems.

DAVE: At that time we should talk about grouping criteria and how they affect the development of programs that serve individual needs.

Criteria for Grouping

DAVE: We've discussed the background that leads to the consideration of a nongraded secondary school. We ought to consider this business of criteria for grouping and how it affects the development of programs that serve individual needs.

WALT: We should make it very clear that when the nongraded school talks about groups or phases, it is talking about a grouping system and not about a disguised form of grade levels.

DAVE: When you speak of grouping we use the term "form," believing it to be apropos in our application. Its usage gives a clearer picture of the shape of grouping practices as they affect our total picture. Each form, described by a number, has a distinctive configuration both in structure and outline.

WALT: If we're talking about a school that uses, for instance, five phases, groups, or forms in a subject such as English, this does not mean that the school has replaced three grade levels with five. It is relatively common that a student may enter his sophomore year in a first form class, remain there for three years, and then graduate. It does *not* mean that a student must begin at first form and proceed through fifth form before he has successfully completed the school program.

DAVE: Some people mistakenly think the term nongraded secondary school refers to a school that gives no indication of a pupil's advancement. The nongraded school suggests the elimination of the artificiality of grade level distinction in terms of a student's progress through his junior and senior high school years.

WALT: In the last issue we talked about the possibilities for flexibility by using five stages or groups within a particular subject. I'll call these groups "forms." We have tried to define each of the forms first, and then, by applying this criteria, we end up with X number of students in each particular form. This is very different from taking an arbitrary percentage of pupils and saying that this is the number that will be in a given form. Our percentages of actual enrollment by forms follows, and is the result of applying the criteria first.

First Form:

Roughly five percent of the student body. Students here work with individualized curricula competing only against their former achievements. These students are generally very weak in basic skills.

IQ—75 to 85

Reading—three or more years below grade level.

Stanines—1 on most standardized achievement tests.

Second Form:

Roughly twenty percent of the student body. This class may contain both genuine slower learners and poor achievers of average ability. These students are also low in basic skills.

IQ—85 to 95.

Reading—one or two years below grade level.

Stanines—2 or 3.

Third Form:

Comprising roughly fifty percent of the enrollment, generally average skills and conceptual understanding.

IQ—95 to 115.

Reading—at or near grade level.

Stanines—4, 5, and 6.

Fourth Form:

Twenty percent of the student body. Better than average in skills and conceptual understanding.

IQ—115 or better.

Reading—beyond grade level.

Stanines—7 or 8.

Fifth Form:

Five percent of the student body. Significantly beyond average in skills and conceptual understanding, advanced in powers of interpretation, willing and able to assume responsibility for own learning.

IQ—over 120.

Reading—considerably beyond high school level.

Stanine—9.

DAVE: You've said this illustration represented a starting point. Are the percentages of the forms and their descriptions as rigid as they seem?

WALT: You'll notice under each form there is a variety of criteria such as IQ, reading scores, and stanine levels on a variety of standardized tests. Actually a student might very well fall in the IQ range for first form, but have achievement scores that fall into the classification of the second form. The range of borderline cases is broad, and the specific classroom performance and the attitudes of the student are the most significant criteria.

DAVE: These criteria measure the student in terms of a particular subject, not his total program.

WALT: When we moved into this program on a schoolwide basis, each of the individual departments independently classified every student. After independently applying criteria developed by each department, 570 out of 600 students had been classified in the same form by both the English and Social Studies Departments. Only thirty pupils were in different forms, and every one of those thirty were only one form away from the designation of the other department.

DAVE: Referring to the illustration again—omitted is the question of student interest. It can be quite a variable in his success or failure. Did you deliberately omit it?

WALT: I referred to this element insofar as borderline cases were concerned. In the beginning we arbitrarily made these rough designations and then handled the borderline cases.

DAVE: We've employed teacher recommendations as well as student achievement. You know, I like your use of the word "we." It might be mistakenly believed that these criteria are administratively superimposed. Student placement or election is a cooperative venture. The illustration above was cooperative, wasn't it?

WALT: The example given here was one developed by our English Department under the leadership of its Chairman, Miss Margaret Spence. The individual department played a major role in the determination of criteria. The Guidance Department provided the teachers with those data they requested, but did not really participate beyond that point.

DAVE: In our efforts thus far to implement a nongraded program, our guidance counselors serve a greater function than that of just providing data in their interrelationship with students while preparing their program for the subsequent year.

WALT: My old grandpappy used to be fond of saying that a good poker player is one who wins. There are significant variables in curriculum development. Existing staff organization, situations, and interests in a particular project will vary considerably and will shape, to a large extent, the way you go about implementing changes. Schools vary significantly in many other respects. While we have approximately five percent of our students in the first form in English and another five percent in the fifth form, other schools might find a different kind of pupil distribution.

DAVE: In our situation we haven't analyzed percentages. We tended to capitalize on your experiences. However, in all honesty, I should mention that in preparing a master schedule we set up sections described by forms. I suppose the number created suggested a percentage. As in your case, our schedule is computerized. We told the computer that we wanted fifteen seats for a fifth form course.

WALT: But this was after the fact, wasn't it? You didn't decide ahead of time that only fifteen students in your senior high school could qualify for a fifth form class.

DAVE: No. A preregistration with Guidance suggested that approximately fifteen students would meet the criteria for this class.

WALT: Actually, the percentages I gave are the result of the application of the criteria. Schools will find that these percentages will vary, depending upon the composition of the student body. This is merely a report of what happened in our situation.

DAVE: This goes back to whether we're talking about a framework or a frame of mind, and here—a frame of reference.

WALT: Having determined various criteria for your forms, this then gives you some guidelines for the development of curriculum appropriate to each particular form.

DAVE: Right. Form is a means of description. Not all forms are used in a given subject. We offer Physics in fourth form, while chemistry is offered in second, third, and fourth.

WALT: We for our purposes offer Chemistry at the fourth form, with the fifth form being Chem Study. There are schools that would consider Chem Study to be the fourth form and advanced placement courses the only ones considered to be fifth form. We use the form designation to serve another purpose. We offer an Art course at the fourth form. This is a demanding course requiring a high degree of competence, but any senior high school student may take it if he has the necessary skill.

DAVE: There's no grade level prerequisite to take this course.

WALT: Exactly. As a general rule, it may be that a student would not be admitted to the course by the department until he has had other courses. However, the department is quick to recognize that some students will enter senior high school with a high degree of skill who can immediately begin at this level.

DAVE: One of the best illustrations of our endeavors to date is a nongraded Math course for slow learners—seventh, eighth and ninth graders. Its content area is less than would normally be given at these grade levels. Some students enter our junior high whose previous success in acquiring mathematical skills goes back as far as the third grade. These youngsters were doomed to fail. Two years ago traditional programs were abandoned. Math was individualized to pick each one up where he had last succeeded. This is no easy task. By the end of the school year we couldn't pass these students into the eighth grade. They lacked necessary skills to pass that course, but they didn't deserve to fail either. Solution: Continue the program; join with them another incoming sixth grade group with similar problems. It's now become a three-year program. Our Math Department determines whether these students have acquired a sufficient mathematical background to receive credit for a year of high school math. If the recommendation isn't forthcoming, a fourth year is required. Students work at their best rate, encouraged to succeed, and are not threatened by failure. There are no set standards of achievement for a given year. These first form classes are small, supervised by a pair of teachers working together. There are several illustrations in your curriculum that bear out this type of arrangement.

WALT: Yes, but I think the example you gave is probably one of the best ones to illustrate the vast potentiality of the nongraded school to solve some of the most persistent, nagging questions in secondary education. What you have described is close to the true ideal of the nongraded school.

I would suggest that our experiences along similar lines have indicated that this approach brings about substantial attitudinal improvement on the part of students who are not currently being punished by, anf for, the sins of omission that they committed in the fifth grade, or even before, when they wouldn't or couldn't master Mathematics at that level. Students have responded well to this approach. They don't feel "stupid" in this kind of situation, and once the real pivotal problem of motivation has been at least partially solved, substantial gains in achievement can and will follow. Interestingly, these particular students will sometimes find themselves in courses such as the fourth form Advanced Art course I referred to earlier.

DAVE: Success is succeeding. A ninth grade student in the math class mentioned might just as well be in a fourth form woodworking course. In these classes he's associating with students both younger and older. Most important—he's not stereotyped! This young man has difficulty in math but has talent in another area.

WALT: This is a very simple, subtle, but nevertheless extremely significant dimension of the nongraded school. Through the scheduling flexibility possible by crossing grade lines, a school is able to do a good deal more in individualizing a student's schedule. I am firmly convinced that as long as a student sees his competence recognized in certain areas he will realistically accept his weaknesses and limitations in other areas. Often at workshops I am asked about the attitude of the student who is in the first or second form. While some students tend to be in these forms in several subjects, rare indeed is the student who is in them in all his subjects. This represents a big difference! A student will accept with good grace his placement in a first form Math or English class if two convictions exist. First, he must find himself in a third or fourth form course in industrial arts, perhaps, or a fourth form secretarial practice course. Secondly, the first form course must be an honest one in which he is not penalized for previous shortcomings, and a real attempt must be made to help him improve in the areas of his weakness. I believe that substantially all students really want to improve.

DAVE: Here's where cooperation of faculty and guidance counselors play the important role. If a guidance counselor will encourage that area of interest, backed by a teacher recommendation, talent can be developed. Students take pride in recommendations to higher forms. In the traditional setting, how often has a particular teacher's evaluation literally damned a youngster against future success?

WALT: True. We attempt to utilize our form designations to serve a number of purposes. I believe that no work is degrading, and that only poor workmanship is degrading. While secondary schools put an emphasis on being comprehensive, there isn't much question in the minds of most students that many so-called comprehensive high schools are really academic high schools with some other subjects thrown in to keep certain students occupied.

DAVE: Don't you think there's a peer aspect to this as well? If students cross grade lines, realizing there are others younger and older who have the same problems or talents—this can tend to be a stimulus to achievement and success.

WALT: Yes, it certainly does tend to work this way. As you'll recall, most of the schools we visited showed evidences of the same thing. I have been consistently impressed with the number of students who have alluded to this and have indicated that if they were in the older end of the age range they tended to work harder so as not to be outdone by a younger member in the same course. On the other hand, I've heard many sophomores tell me they took great delight in excelling in a particular course and beating seniors. This is an example of some of the built-in motivational sources operative in the nongraded setting.

We have deliberately built in elements to assist the teacher in this area of motivation. I am particularly concerned with the nonacademic student and with selling, if you will, the idea that no honest work should be degrading, and that the competence required in a course such as secretarial practice is as demanding as that required in a fourth form academic course.

DAVE: Our acceptance of the nongraded philosophy has opened up "horizons unlimited." Our grade seven to twelve enrollment is 700; yet our master schedule provides twenty-one separate and distinct courses in Math alone, doubling what was formerly offered.

WALT: In a truly nongraded situation there are even more courses than this. For example, in a junior high class of twenty students of lower ability, there are twenty courses of study within that particular framework. This represents very difficult teaching, but I know it can be done. One of the best examples of this, you'll recall, was the math class of twenty-three students we visited last year at the campus laboratory school at Kansas State Teachers College in Emporia. This was a class in which each student was at a different point and was moving at his own rate of speed. That teacher really served as director of the learning activities of the students.

DAVE: The desirability for more courses was teacher-based.

WALT: When did the teachers find the time to develop all these new courses?

DAVE: In our scheduling arrangements all English, Social Studies, and Math teachers have a free preparation period in common. Almost daily these departments meet.

WALT: You've illustrated one method by which administration realistically can, and must, provide built-in time if it is going to expect any substantial curriculum revisions to be made. I don't think that one can expect very much creative revision to take place at four o'clock in the afternoon. A number of schools have employed different practices, but they all have recognized the importance of this planning function.

DAVE: I think it's a credit to your Board of Education and ours that they periodically have afforded our faculties the opportunity to meet for blocks of time. Don't you release your students a half day a month for curriculum development?

WALT: Actually, Newton, Massachusetts has been doing this for many, many years. In our case we dismiss the entire high school at 11:10 one day a month and have the remainder of the day to tackle educational issues. We have been fortunate in receiving some funds for curriculum work during the summer that have been a major help to us in getting some of our programs off the ground. Without this, we could never have brought about some of these changes.

DAVE: Yes, this summer curriculum development time has been our life blood.

WALT: I have tried, though not always successfully, to earmark a minimum of 1 percent of my own operating budget for research and development, including our summer work. This is only one step in the direction needed. A minimum of 2½ to 3 percent of a school district's budget should be spent for research and development.

DAVE: When you consider its importance, this is a pretty minimal figure—considering the implications for the future.

WALT: Speaking about the future, I'm sure that some of the ideas explored here have raised a number of important questions in the area of the nongraded secondary school. The question of content of courses and how you manage the problem created by having some students in the same form for more than one year is a difficult one. We had better plan to get down to cases in the next issue and discuss some of the major ways in which these problems are being solved in nongraded programs.

THREE SOLUTIONS TO THE CONTENT PROBLEM

DAVE: We've discussed some of the criteria necessary for a nongraded secondary school. This, however, suggests several questions in the area of content. What constitutes a school's program of studies? a student's schedule of courses? Nongradedness means more than just pooling students together to create larger groups. We're all familiar with the number of Carnegie units necessary to graduate. Every school has certain required courses.

WALT: A very pivotal and fundamental problem arises in a nongraded school, for example, when you group sophomores, juniors, and seniors together in the same course. At the end of the first year, the seniors have graduated. During the next year you are confronted with a class of which two-thirds were with you last year, and one-third is new. The inevitable question is, what do you present as a course of study? There are currently *three major ways in which this particular problem has been solved*. Basically, they can be referred to as follows:

1. Cycling
2. Open electives
3. Continuous progress

DAVE: Our first attraction to the nongraded secondary concept was in the area of *cycling*—especially with social studies, requiring little prerequisite content. It isn't necessary to offer world history exclusively to sophomores as a prerequisite to juniors taking American history. World history being offered exclusively to both tenth and eleventh graders one year and American history being offered the next quite simply creates a two-year cycle, doubling the number of students taking a given course, as well as doubling the frequency that the course is scheduled during the school day. Many smaller schools have cycled Cicero and Virgil for years.

WALT: You get the maximum amount of scheduling flexibility through the use of the cycle, although there are built-in limitations to the system and problems connected with it. The ultimate decision about the system to use rests with individual schools based upon their own situations. The nature of the cycle may vary somewhat from the one you mentioned. Some schools will create a three-year cycle in English, offering American literature the first year, world literature the second, and British literature the third, and then repeat the cycle. Through this system each student is exposed to each of the areas in a class composed of sophomores, juniors, and seniors. The only difference is that one student may take American literature as a sophomore, whereas another may take it as a senior.

There is another interesting technique for cycling English on a thematic basis. You can establish a system for grouping freshmen and sophomores together, and establish another two-year cycle for grouping juniors and seniors. It is relatively simple to develop a list of themes, Group 1 being offered in odd numbered school years and Group 2 being offered in even numbered years. I'm talking about themes such as The Rebel in Society or Man's Struggle for Individuality.

DAVE: Or concepts like liberty, freedom, or megopolis.

WALT: These concepts could very easily be utilized in English and/or social studies.

DAVE: Note that we've tended to limit this discussion to social studies and English in reference to the nongraded school. The above also applies to a foreign language. Its study is started today in elementary, in junior, and in senior high simultaneously within the same school. Some students inaugurate a second language in the sophomore or junior year, joining colleagues of lower grade levels.

Returning to the point of either thematic or literature cycling in English, it's important to be more specific. What happens to the written or spoken word in the broader interpretations of the language arts?

WALT: All of these traditional elements are still included. Whether you're using the thematic, geographic, or chronological approach for the study of literature, this is a springboard and a focus for your course. It is understood that the students will still do a good deal of writing that can reveal certain weaknesses in rhetoric to be handled on an individual or group basis as the need dictates. The focus of the course and the subject matter of the writing will often spring from the general organization. Furthermore, other traditional items such as vocabulary development and spelling can be easily and effectively worked into such a program.

DAVE: In a theme such as Man's Conflict with Himself, literature would draw from various sources: the novel, the short story, the biography, the essay. Writing would be based on the readings, including subjective interpretations. Vocabulary development and oral work would draw from this same thematic reservoir.

WALT: Exactly. Through the cycling system you get the greatest number of students taking the same thing at the same time, creating the maximum grouping flexibility possible. The problems to consider are those of teacher competence and background. If one used a cycle on a literary basis, someone particularly adept with American literature might find it difficult to handle a sophisticated course in world literature the next year.

DAVE: Right. Cycling suggests the comprehensive content teacher rather than the specialist. Hanging the hat of the English cycle on literature can prove to be a problem. There's much material available in American, less in English, and little in world literature, especially when it becomes necessary to serve the needs of our slower learners and less able readers. The theme or concept approach is more pragmatic. This depends a great deal on the school's staff. Decisions should originate with them as to the best way to solve the problem.

WALT: The dilemma of finding appropriate materials for the less able student is a significant one. It has been handled in a couple of schools by cycling on a literary basis only for average and above-average students. The program for the slower student is essentially reading and writing on a remedial and developmental basis.

DAVE: What's the next means?

WALT: The next method I call *the open-elective system.* It is similar to the system employed in most of our colleges. In this arrangement a body of courses is established on a semester or yearly basis, with subjects such as American literature, rhetoric, speech, drama, and British literature. Students are expected, over a three-year period, to take the equivalent of three full years of English and may take any course at any time without regard to sequence.

DAVE: Students are not limited to just one English course.

WALT: We have established a system of open electives in English and all of them are one-semester courses. This means that a pupil could take two one-semester courses simultaneously in the fall and none in the spring if this would provide him with the best total schedule.

DAVE: I wonder how many times a senior has had to remain for the spring because he lacked the necessary fourth Carnegie English unit to fulfill a graduation requirement.

WALT: This is quite true. I just spent some time this afternoon meeting with a former dropout who told me that he had had ten jobs in the last ten months and is very anxious to come back to school and try to complete his last year. This boy only needs two units to graduate, one in English and one in American history.

DAVE: He could complete requirements by taking four semester courses in the fall.

WALT: Right. In some cases it might be desirable to have a student take additional courses beyond the minimum, but for this particular individual our judgment was that we would serve his best interests by permitting him to complete high school and graduate as soon as possible. He had taken American history and failed it. He will now be enrolled in an American history course. His teacher will work with him on an individual basis, and he will proceed at his own rate of speed outside the framework of the remainder of the class and will be given his final examination as soon as he and the teacher feel he is ready. At this point he will be given credit for American history. In the case of English, he will take two one-semester courses simultaneously, and on his successful completion of these he will complete the graduation requirements by midyear.

DAVE: Isn't it possible to suggest that certain concepts of American history, for example, could be taught simultaneously rather than chronologically?

WALT: Yes. In fact, Meadowbrook Junior High School in Newton, Massachusetts, has developed a fascinating program in social studies based on what could be called "quarter courses." These are, in effect, units that run for one quarter of the school year. A student selects twelve units over a three-year period and may take them in any order. He might take one, two, or even three units simultaneously.

Units like these could be developed using topics such as the following: The Industrial Revolution, The Civil War and Reconstruction, The Two World Wars, an area study course in Sub-Sahara Africa, or a unit from sociology such as Social Stratification.

DAVE: A program of studies would not necessarily be limited to twelve quarter units; as many as sixteen or twenty could be offered from which a student would select his twelve requirements, supplemented by additional electives motivated by interest.

WALT: Right, and certain one-semester courses or certain units could be offered each year; this could be combined with a cycling system that offered other units on alternating quarters, semesters, or years.

DAVE: There is appeal as well as challenge to teacher imagination. One is able to build upon distinct staff talents and strengths: interest, ability, background, and experience. Students will be the beneficiaries of this exploitation.

WALT: Right, and I think this is a significant dimension that shouldn't be overlooked.

DAVE: How was your open-elective system constructed?

WALT: The system of open electives in English was developed by the department. A number of courses that the teachers felt they would be interested in teaching and that would have appeal to the students were drawn up. This list was then presented by the English department to all of the students in a series of meetings, and a survey of interest was taken. The final program was, then, a combination of interests of the department and the students themselves.

DAVE: More recently a third content solution has been applied in an elementary setting that has potentiality in the nongraded secondary school as well—that's the *continuous progress* approach.

WALT: Keep in mind that the notion of continuous progress is more prevalent at the elementary level and is more difficult to implement in the secondary school. In the last issue you gave an example of a continuous progress program in action when you described a junior high school math program for slower learners—each individual student was moving at his own rate of speed and was competing only against his own former achievement. There was no predetermined course of study, but a mathematics sequence had been developed. An evaluation of each student was made individually in an attempt to determine at which point he should begin the year's work. He then proceeded from there, along this continuum, in developmental fashion. This type of teaching is the most difficult kind; such groups shouldn't be assigned to inexperienced teachers.

DAVE: Last year a large group of eighth and ninth graders completed a course in modern elementary algebra. The continuous progress technique was employed. Several students completed course requirements and moved into intermediate and advanced materials before the end of the year. This year this group is taking what would be intermediate and advanced modern algebra rather than interrupt their program with geometry.

WALT: What you've just given is an example of *a developmental approach* to a pure continuous progress concept. Such modified programs are the most practical ones to look at initially. Taking a class in a sequential subject and moving along as far as the group can go is still group teaching. By having the same teacher the following year, you can begin to get away from the idea that a course must begin in September and end in June.

DAVE: This plagiarizes something that has been going on in elementary education for some time. It's not uncommon for a teacher to stay with a self-contained or semidepartmentalized group through first, second, and third grades. Would the use of this principle for secondary schools have to involve the same teacher from year to year?

WALT: Not necessarily. It might be simpler that way, but with reasonably good communication such a program could be operative with a different teacher the following year. However, I think it's important to keep in mind that if you're talking about moving the group along as a group, you're still talking about group teaching or continuous progress for a group, not about continuous progress for each individual member of the group.

DAVE: How frequently could students complete a subject before June, contrasted with classes whose teachers race through the final month to complete a course. In either one of these circumstances all are losers. Either it's a question of time wasted or too rapid class progress.

WALT: A very realistic and practical approach to this problem that I think has great merit, at least as a transitional step, is employed in Middletown, R.I. While purely individualized teaching is extremely difficult and possibly beyond the professional capabilities of many of our current teachers, a teacher *can* work with at least three subgroups within a class. Accordingly, a program has been developed in which close attention has been paid to the sequence of concepts. This approach has great applicability in areas such as foreign language, mathematics, and shorthand, for example.

DAVE: Essentially you're speaking of skill subjects.

WALT: Right. These subjects have a necessary sequence built in. They are also subjects for which a number of fairly good materials have been developed and made commercially available in recent years, facilitating auto-instruction or individualized work by the student. The approach used is essentially simple. A teacher of beginning French very quickly finds that some students are more capable than others, and that it is not too difficult to identify a few students who are ready, willing, and able to progress much faster than the rest of the class, and also to find those who are having difficulty keeping up.

DAVE: This conjures up the timeless elementary classroom whose reading groups are the birds, the bees, and the butterflies. High school classes tend to base all progress on whole group instruction. There's little reason why something as simple as the bluejays', robins', and vultures' principle couldn't be used in this French class.

WALT: I think every secondary school teacher should spend at least one visitation day a year in a good elementary school classroom. The groups, as they tend to establish themselves, permit the differentiation of instruction. An attempt is then made to let a subgroup proceed at its own best rate of speed; your fastest and best students are going to, in effect, complete Level I French some time prior to June. On the other hand, your slower students are not going to complete the program by June. In a traditional setting the whole class is normally kept together. Once the top group successfully completes the work for Level 1, whether it is in March or June, they are given credit for Level I at that point on a basis of competence and performance. On the other hand, *the slow group* that has not successfully completed the course by June *does not fail* the course. However, *the school does not extend credit* for the successful completion of French Level I since the student hasn't finished it. But he is not penalized and forced to take the whole course over. At any point in the year, or at the beginning of the following year, depending upon the size of the school, the classes are regrouped, and a new class is created that reduces the achievement spread. The same thing is done with the faster students, and then these classes quickly begin to jell into their own subgroups. When those in the slower group achieve the degree of proficiency necessary for the successful completion of Level I, whether it is in October, November, or December, credit is then given, even though it might have taken them some time longer to receive it.

DAVE: How much better this might be in handling the problem of unlearning that so frequently occurs over the summer months. This regrouping arrangement beginning the new school year lends itself beautifully to readjustment. Some students are able to carry over a certain amount of learning from June to September, while for others the summer sun seems to evaporate most knowledge. What's suggested here is a refresher-type approach.

WALT: Middletown has developed an interesting reporting system. Students are given two grades based on quantity and quality of work completed. The quantity measure is expressed by a horizontal bar graph showing progress through a particular course, and indicates at a glance the approximate percentage of the normal work for the year that has been finished. How well he has done this work is expressed by a letter grade.

DAVE: Many available testing materials lend themselves to this bar graph proposal, measuring accomplishment or achievement of blocks of material and/or the acquisition of certain skills.

We've previously discussed altering the school day. Why not alter time dimensions of the school year?

WALT: There's nothing sacred about the length of the school year. Sixty years ago in New York State the school year was only 120 days long. At that time I suppose 120 days were considered as sacred as 180 are now.

DAVE: The length of the school year varies from state to state. I'm sure there are many teachers in the Midwest who are capable of accomplishing just as much in thirty-six weeks as some of us in New York State do in forty.

Three approaches have been offered. There are more yet unborn or unpublicized. In terms of the individual school, it depends upon its philosophy, its personnel, and many other variables as to what specific approach or combination of them are used. No school in this country is without a few teachers willing, eager, and able to light one little candle.

WALT: In many nongraded schools I have visited, the teachers who have tended to respond most enthusiastically to opportunities offered when administration has opened the door have been highly experienced veterans who have been wrestling with some of these problems for years.

The three approaches mentioned and their combinations are only beginning steps or implementation devices that I think will ultimately lead to a substantially different secondary school.

DAVE: The nongraded setting provides an atmosphere for creative teachers to flourish. We should focus next on specific school policies designed to establish and maintain this environment.

PART THREE

Team Teaching

Team teaching along with all its variations enjoyed a boom of popularity in the last decade but may still be considered a very recent innovation in the schools. Indeed, despite the wide attention given to team teaching in the literature, many schools have yet to institute this alternative to having one teacher work alone with a class of students. The history of team teaching is difficult to trace. However, it is possible to do so to some degree.

When Andrew Bell arrived in Madras in the late 1700s to become chaplain to the English garrison and also superintendent of the newly established school for the orphans of British soldiers, he faced what became a perennial problem: lack of qualified teachers. He resorted to the expedient of running his school by means of the pupils themselves.

He assigned John Frisken, then eight years old, to be monitor of the ABC class. John's success induced Dr. Bell to extend the experiment. Soon his whole school was operated by monitors. When he returned to London he wrote a report about his superintendency in Madras and published it in pamphlet form. The impact was slight until Joseph Lancaster, spurred on by this report, introduced the monitorial system in London. This monitorial system was a team approach to learning both in its deployment of teaching strength and in its hierarchy of teaching levels.

The Gary Plan, or platoon plan, of the early 1900s in this country provided for two platoons to which pupils were assigned. This may well have been the ancestor of the differentiated grouping schemes presently being used in the large and small group instruction found in some of the team teaching plans. Batavia, with the two-teacher-per-level plan, may well have been the precursor of the collaborative teaching now found throughout the United States. Other team teaching plans have also existed. Ira Singer [1] traces the modern development of team teaching to the work of the National Association of Secondary School Principals, Harvard University (see Anderson's article in this section on SUPRAD, the School and University Program for Research and Development), and Claremont College.

Even though the idea of team teaching has been widely approved, the term *team teaching* does not have a precise definition which is as widely accepted. Nevertheless, there appears to be a common element among the many definitions which renders them in effect slight variations of each other (for example, the definitions offered by Anderson and Olson in their respective articles).

Team teaching is not a method intended for the reduction of the number of teachers in any given school. It is rather a redeployment and a different utilization of teachers. It also results in the regrouping of students, rescheduling of time, redesign of equipment, and rearrangement of teaching space. It is for these reasons that these articles on team teaching are so integrally tied with the others on grouping, flexible scheduling, school architecture, and educational technology.

The full value of team teaching remains to be measured. It is obviously a complex innovation with facets claimed by many to be significant advantages: cooperation among teachers, flexible grouping of pupils, and utilization of each teacher's particular competencies. The reader may find it helpful to note carefully the advantages and disadvantages listed for team teaching in the subsequent articles.

Team teaching is applicable to all levels of the school. Also, there is no one arrangement that fits the needs of every situation. Therefore, the prospective team teacher should read

[1] Ira J. Singer, "What Team Teaching Really Is," *Team Teaching: Bold New Venture*, edited by David W. Beggs, III. Indianapolis, Unified College Press, 1964, pp. 13–28.

the following articles with the intention of establishing a base upon which he can establish a scheme to fit his own particular situation.

Anderson, Hagstrom, and Robinson present a classic account of team teaching in an elementary school. It is this basic design which is still prevalent today. The hierarchy of staff described in their article arose from efforts to provide new avenues for teachers to exert leadership in the schools. In high schools two patterns of team teaching have emerged: the single discipline team and the interdiscipline team. (See the Schlaadt and Georgiades articles in this section for secondary school team teaching.)

The theme of collaboration and planning is fully developed by Goldstein, who contends that cooperative planning is the foundation of effective team teaching. For Goldstein the integration of content and instructional strategies, two elements of effective teaching, are best achieved through team planning.

Rand and English develop the theme of a hierarchial, differentiated staff. For them differentiated staffing emancipates the teacher by offering several avenues for compensation and assignment of responsibility. Are they correct in suggesting that their current heresy may be the accepted practice by the 1980s?

Schlaadt and Georgiades and Bjelke present two research studies on team teaching. Both studies compare team teaching with conventional situations in terms of learning achievement. While the Schlaadt study focuses on one subject—health—taught in a traditional time schedule, the Georgiades and Bjelke study centers on a three-block, flexible scheduling design as well as a team teaching arrangement. Both studies report favorable data. This is not to be interpreted as conclusive evidence about team teaching, for the overall research in this area, as reported by Joyce [2] in his review of the literature, is mixed. Yet these studies, as examples of the research on team teaching, deserve the careful attention of the reader because of the variables treated and the subject matter areas studied.

The closing article by Olson offers reasons for the failure of teaching teams when they do fail. The question of course is whether the factors that lead to failure are inherent in team teaching or whether through careful planning they can be

[2] Bruce R. Joyce, "Staff Utilization," *Review of Educational Research*, 37:323–336, June 1967.

modified in order to reduce the possibility of failure. Prospective team teachers must weigh Olson's points for they stem from his long experience with this organizational plan.

Team teaching has been and still is an exciting idea. It will remain exciting in the coming decade, however, only if team teachers continually reshape it to fit in with the many other changes in the schools. The task is to approach team teaching with an innovative eye—to institute modifications continually just as the originators of the idea did. If not, the result will be a stagnant idea out of tune with both the needs of the times and the hopes embodied in the words *team teaching* themselves.

9 | Team Teaching in an Elementary School

ROBERT ANDERSON
ELLIS A. HAGSTROM
WADE M. ROBINSON

Reprinted from *School Review*, Vol. 68 (Spring 1960), pp. 71–84, by permission of The University of Chicago Press. Copyright © 1960 by The University of Chicago Press.

In 1957–58 the personnel of Franklin School in Lexington, Massachusetts, were reorganized into four teams. Two of the teams were large, composed of five or six teachers. Two were small, composed of three teachers. The titles *team leader* and *senior teacher* were used to designate teachers who had responsibility for leadership in the teams. Classwork in each team was planned jointly by all team members, and through various redeployment procedures the children were taught in groups that ranged in size from six to more than a hundred. Members of the staff of Harvard University shared with the administrators and the teachers in Lexington in the formulation of program plans and in the analysis of the effectiveness of the program.

The Franklin School Project is a major activity within the School and University Program for Research and Development, hereafter identified by its initials SUPRAD. This program involves the school systems of Lexington, Concord, and Newton, Massachusetts, and Harvard University, and is supported in large measure by a ten-year grant from the Ford Foundation. The Administrative Board of SUPRAD approved the broad outlines of the teaching teams proposal in May, 1957, and the planning and recruitment proceeded with considerable speed. The planning provided for the following teams of teachers during 1957–58:

Alpha:	three first-grade teachers (senior teacher in charge)
Beta:	six second- and third-grade teachers (team leader in charge assisted by two senior teachers)
Gamma:	three fourth-grade teachers (senior teacher in charge)
Delta:	five fifth- and sixth-grade teachers (team leader in charge assisted by a senior teacher)

Each team was assigned a part-time clerical aide, and the two larger teams were each assigned a quarter-time teaching assistant. Preparations were completed for the principal and seven teachers to engage in preliminary planning in a six-week summer program under the supervision of Harvard instructors. The program was launched less than two months from the time it was first described on paper.

Among the reasons for establishment of the School and University Program for Research and Development was the belief that public school systems might more easily close the gap between educational ideals and educational realities if they joined with private universities in programs of research and demonstration. Relations analogous to those between medical schools and hospitals were seen as a way toward tough-minded research and unbiased evaluation of new ideas. Among these ideas was the contention that the existing organizational pattern of American schools and classrooms may be inadequate and unsuitable in view of the vast population increase and the severe shortage of professional workers as needs are now defined.

Related to this contention was the belief that too few first-rate people are attracted to teaching, possibly because of the low economic incentives, the low social position of the classroom teacher, and the general inadequacy of supervisory practices and lack of opportunities for professional growth in the typical school. The question was asked: "Would not more first-rate people be attracted to teaching if the economic and social factors were made more attractive and if there were more ready opportunity for professional growth?" Believing the affirmative to be true, SUPRAD set out in the Franklin School to test the feasibility and the effect of a team-teaching organization plan.

Implicit in all efforts to create more attractive conditions (economic, social, and professional) for teachers was the belief that these would lead to better instruction for children, through more effective performance of the teachers. It was hoped that the team organization would permit more flexible and appropriate grouping arrangements to meet individual interests. It was believed that children would be stimulated by association with larger numbers of children and with more than one teacher. It was expected that teachers would find more efficient and interesting ways of presenting lessons through having larger blocks of planning time and through doing more group planning. It was thought that the pooling of teachers' ideas and observations would lead not only to stronger teaching but to better pupil adjustment and more adequate pupil guidance. These and other benefits were seen as attainable if various administrative problems posed by radical changes in personnel organization could be solved.

The first year of the project was seen as an exploratory year, during which the participants hoped to discover whether a hierarchical pattern of team organization was feasible. The traditional pattern of self-contained classrooms, coupled with a system of uniform and undifferentiated salary and prestige for all teachers, was set aside, and a system was initiated wherein prestige roles and responsibilities were assigned to certain teachers and salaries were adjusted accordingly. The teachers in each team were asked to regard all the children in their team as the mutual responsibility of all. They were asked to plan the educational program jointly under the leadership of team leaders and senior teachers. They were invited to experiment with many kinds of class grouping and instructional techniques, using the physical facilities and the instructional resources of the building in whatever ways seemed appropriate and without regard to conventional definitions of the best class size.

One major objective of SUPRAD, and the Franklin School Project in particular, is to discover and to demonstrate new and more promising ways of utilizing teacher competencies. The roles of team leader and senior teacher were set up in an effort to accomplish two purposes: first, to provide rewarding and prestigeful roles to which persons of outstanding competence can aspire, roles which (unlike most supervisory and administrative roles in education) allow teachers to remain in direct association with pupils; and second, to create a collaborative relationship between teachers that offers promise of accelerating and enlarging the development of professional skills and insights. Implied in the latter purpose is that teachers in continuous and intimate association will more readily share their knowledge and express their needs, with the result that each has greater opportunity to learn from and contribute to the others. Hopefully, those persons with the greatest talents and a career dedication to teaching would work toward the prestige roles and through these roles constitute a significant source of strength for teachers of less experience, competence or dedication.

Another objective of the project is to find more effective means of using the services of nonprofessional persons in the community and professionally trained persons who are unable or unwilling to devote full time to service in the schools. In the belief that classroom teachers now devote too much time to clerical and minor administrative duties, it was arranged that each team would have about half-time clerical assistance. Partly to compensate the team members for the extra demands that research activities would make on their time and partly in the hope of demonstrating that good use can be made of the part-time professional worker under team conditions, the two large teams were each assigned a quarter-time assistant teacher.

One hypothesis to be tested in the project is that certain kinds of instructional experiences can be at least as beneficial to children when they are taught in large groups (that is, groups that combine two or more standard size classes) as when they are taught under conventional conditions. It was believed that one prerequisite to testing this hypothesis was the development of instructional techniques appropriate to large groups. It was also believed that various content and skill areas probably lend themselves better than others to presentation in large groups. The teachers were therefore asked to develop such techniques and to identify such content, through various exploratory lessons.

The deployment of children in conventional elementary school situations is usually a static arrangement, each classroom group remaining intact and usually in the same homeroom throughout the day. In departmentalized situations, which are quite unusual below seventh grade, children may move from place to place but the class grouping is usually an unchanging one. Under team-teaching conditions, a number of more dynamic patterns of deployment and redeployment become possible. For example, children can be left in homeroom groups, homeroom groups (or portions thereof) can be combined in large groups, or children can be exchanged between homeroom groups. It is obvious that teachers, too, can exchange locations and instructional assignments. It remained to be tested, in the Franklin School Project, whether these kinds of redeployment under team-teaching conditions would be both manageable and desirable.

That education is an extremely conservative profession is well attested by the slow rate of its progress and by the meager financial and other support for the research on which intelligent change depends. Teachers themselves hold rather doggedly to traditional beliefs and practices, some of which may no longer stand the test of objective examination. The research worker has an almost inexhaustible mine to probe in education, yet his work is frequently blocked or slowed by the diehard forces of tradition and conservatism.

The Franklin School Project is especially notable because of the many beliefs and practices it has chosen to challenge. Among these are such widely held views as the following: individual professional autonomy, as exemplified in the self-contained classroom, is conducive to professional growth and satisfaction; the assignment of differential rewards, status, and responsibility to teachers will lead to poor morale and low productivity; an intimate and continuing one-to-one teacher-pupil relationship is more conducive to pupil security than the more varied relationships necessitated by a three- or five-to-one teacher-pupil relationship; there are advantages in having a single teacher manage all the subject-matter instruction for a given class; the ideal size of classroom groups for all kinds of instructional purposes is somewhere between twenty and thirty; and the lecture technique of teaching and its variants are essentially unsuitable as instructional approaches to young children.

Team organization may be understood best, perhaps, against the background of the more common organizational pattern of self-contained classrooms. In the typical self-contained organization, some twenty to thirty pupils are assigned to each teacher, and each group is placed in a classroom where most of the instruction takes place at the hands of that one teacher. She is expected to have the skills and the knowledge for competent instruction in virtually all the subject-matter areas. She must provide as best she can for the range of individual needs and abilities in her group. In addition, she must ordinarily perform a variety of clerical duties and supervisory tasks of a non-instructional nature. Under typical conditions, she has little contact with other teachers in the building, and she receives little supervision.

In contrast, under the team-teaching pattern, groups of teachers take joint responsibility for the instruction of a segment of the school population. Typically, from three to seven or eight certified teachers take responsibility for the instruction of from seventy-five to 240 pupils of similar age and grade. The clerical and secretarial needs of these teachers are cared for by a clerical aide. The size of the team may be limited by the number of adults with whom a leader can relate effectively and by the number of pupils about whom the leader may reasonably be expected to have fairly specific information.

The teaching team is a formally organized hierarchy whose basic unit is the teacher. Generally, the teacher's experience or training or both have been of a general nature, or he does not wish to assume the responsibilities of a higher position. The position of teacher in the teaching team carries with it the status and prestige commonly accorded the position of teacher in the self-contained pattern today.

Above the position of teacher is that of senior teacher. Depending on the size of the team and the age of the pupils, the team may have one or more senior teachers. A small team may have none. The senior teacher is an experienced teacher who has special competence in a particular subject-matter area or in a particular skill or method. The senior teacher assumes responsibility for instructional leadership—both in his team and, if needed, across teams within the building—in the area of his special competence. Although the positions of senior teacher and team leader are regarded as terminal for many, a possible career line from this position might lead toward the position of team leader or toward such positions as system-wide staff specialist or supervisor or methods instructor at a teacher-training institution.

At the apex of the team hierarchy is the position of team leader. The team leader, as specialist in a content area that complements the areas of his senior teacher assistants, also exercises certain general administrative and coordinating functions. The team leader also has primary responsibility in his team for the identification of pupil needs and readiness and for the assignment of pupils to groups; for directing the continual re-examination and development of the curriculum; and for the training and supervision of junior and less experienced personnel on his team. To discharge his responsibilities effectively, the team leader is released from classroom teaching responsibilities for about a third of the school day. The career line from this position would probably lead to a principalship and perhaps to the superintendency.

In consideration of their additional training and increased responsibilities, senior teachers receive a salary increment beyond the teachers' schedule, and team leaders receive an increment beyond senior teachers'.

The role of the principal under the teaching teams organization will probably become one of enhanced prestige and responsibility, somewhat akin to the present role of director of instruction. Since team leaders and their subordinates are able to attend to many routine administrative and management details, the principal has more time and opportunity for leadership in curriculum development, instructional supervision, and guidance. Although the principal continues to have direct supervisory relations with regular classroom teachers, it is likely that he serves quite often as advisor to the team leaders as they carry out their leadership functions and curriculum building.

A chief advantage of the school organization sketched here lies in the strength of leadership resources that reside in the school whose staff satisfies the specifications for each role. As shown in Figure 1, the principal and the team leaders, for example, may be viewed as an administrative cabinet. These staff members, augmented by the senior teachers, constitute an instructional cabinet. In effect they would together possess the range and depth of competencies of the curriculum-and-methods instructors in a teacher-training institution and hence would be well qualified to appraise and upgrade the school's program.

Thus, a school might expect to operate on the basis of a fairly stable nucleus of upper-echelon career people and a fairly high turnover among teachers with little loss to its total instructional program.

Despite the encouragement of specialization, the project does not advocate departmentalization as it is commonly understood in educational circles. All teachers continue to teach all, or nearly all, subjects. Furthermore, teams may draw on part-time teachers, consultants, and

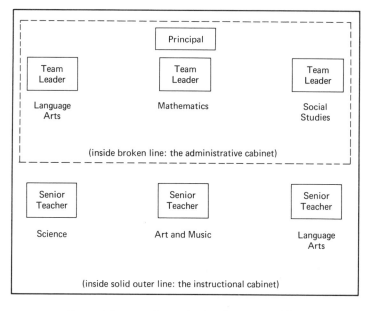

Figure 1. Pattern of organization for team teaching.

resource personnel from the community or nearby institutions of higher education.

The team treats its entire pupil complement as a unit. But both group size and the bases of group composition may vary from class period to class period. The goal is flexible grouping based on specific instructional needs. Thus the team may deal with its pupil complement as a total group, or it may regroup and subdivide the pupils in much the same way that the teacher of the self-contained classroom groups and regroups the pupils who are her responsibility. The entire group of from 75 to 250 pupils may meet as a single large group to hear a lecture or story, to see a demonstration, or to view a movie. Or from the large group the extremes (retarded and accelerated) or a selected individual or group may be withdrawn. The pupils may be redeployed into interest or ability groups of standard size for follow-up activities after a lesson for a large group.

The pupils may be grouped on the basis of one criterion for instruction in arithmetic and on the basis of another criterion for instruction in the language arts or any other subject. Some pupils will have the same teacher for much of their instruction. Other pupils may meet a different teacher for nearly every subject. In the latter arrangement, a presumed advantage to the pupil is that he will come in contact with several adult models and personality types.

Special abilities and disabilities, such as talent in music, proficiency in French, or the need for remedial treatment in reading or speech, can also be accommodated in the schemes for grouping. Furthermore, the number of groups composed on any occasion may be fewer than the number of teachers on the team, thus releasing some teachers from instructional responsibility and enabling them to engage in other professional activities.

Some phases of learning—listening, reading, watching—can be engaged in as well by a large group of pupils as by a small group. Just what the maximum size of these groups may be under different conditions has not yet been determined. However, groups of 75 pupils have met routinely in the Franklin School, and groups of 140 or 215 are not uncommon.

Redeployment of pupils has taken place for instruction in reading and arithmetic at all levels—from first through sixth grade. Pupils in all grades have likewise had instruction in large groups. Data from 1958–59 indicate that about a third of all the instructional sessions involved groups of forty or more pupils and that there was considerable pupil movement and transfer in all grades.

Though groups of twenty to thirty are smaller than they need be for efficient and effective pupil participation in many kinds of learning activities, these same groups are too large for more nearly individual activities. Reciting, discussing, those activities that seem to require a high rate of interaction between pupils or between pupils and teacher can perhaps best take place in small groups ranging in size from ten or twelve down to a few. The flexibility of pupil grouping and redeployment facilitated by the team organization seems to offer a realistic solution to this problem.

Theoretically, then, the team provides the structure within which team leadership personnel engage in some supervisory and curriculum development activities. The team leaders take responsibility for assigning pupils to groups within the team. They coordinate the instructional efforts of junior personnel and also may have more time available for talking with parents. The team structure makes it possible for all teaching personnel to spend more time on planning and on the preparation of materials and less time on clerical and noninstructional supervisory duties. By taking advantage of the opportunities provided through the presence of specialists and clerical aides, and by taking advantage of the released time provided through the scheduling of large group lessons and through the creation of fewer groups than teachers, much more effective use of professional personnel can be realized under team organization than under the self-contained pattern. Furthermore, by holding team meetings before and after school, there is opportunity for discussion of instructional problems. In many respects, the team structure provides

an extension of the training period with its emphasis on planning observation, and evaluation.

The project does not claim that all the components of its program or
model are unique. Many elements have been used in best educational
practice for some time. The project is also aware of the existence of several versions and variants of teaching teams organization that are now
being developed throughout the country. What is unique about the
Teaching Teams Project at Franklin School is the number and the particular combination of elements in its model.

At the beginning of the 1958–59 school year, several changes were
made in the organization of the teams, resulting in the following arrangement:

Alpha: four first-grade teachers (team leader in charge)
Beta: six second- and third-grade teachers (team leader in
charge assisted by a senior teacher)
Omega: eight fourth-, fifth-, and sixth-grade teachers (team leader
in charge assisted by two senior teachers)

Again clerical assistance was provided, and part-time teacher service
was made available to each team for research purposes.

The organizational pattern of Franklin School for 1959–60 is essentially the same as that for the preceding year. The organization may be
presented most vividly, perhaps, by a diagram (see Figure 2).

There are at least two major differences between the organization for
1958–59 and for 1959–60. One is a difference in structure. For 1959–60, a

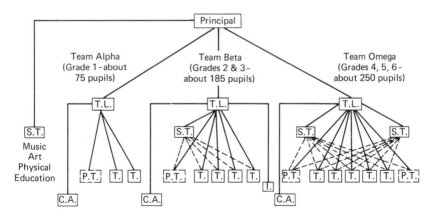

Figure 2. Organization for team teaching in Franklin School for 1959–60.

new senior teacher position was created outside any team organization. This position of senior teacher specialist in art, music, and physical education gives the teaching teams more freedom in program planning and in use of space than they enjoyed under a former arrangement of special visiting teachers who, of necessity, worked on a fixed schedule involving system-wide considerations.

The other change is one of emphasis. Whereas before 1959–60, senior teachers were looked on essentially as grade-level chairmen or as assitant or substitute team leaders, in 1959–60 team leaders and senior teachers alike are becoming specialists in a particular instructional area. The team leader, in addition, assumes administrative responsibility for his team.

In the structure outlined in Figure 2, precise specification of qualifications and functions are still to be written. However, the hierarchy is seen as including a team leader, a senior teacher, a teacher, a part-time teacher, an intern, and a clerical aide.

The team leader (T.L.) is an experienced, mature master teacher of unusual talent who has had considerable experience, who has training well beyond the master's degree, and who has had extensive training in curriculum and instruction, in supervision, human relations, and/or educational sociology. This person would have demonstrated an ability to work with teachers in a leadership role. About a third of his school day might be released for observation and training of subordinates, planning, curriculum development, research and evaluation, and parent conferences.

The senior teacher (S.T.) is an experienced, mature person with above-average talent and considerable advanced training, comparable to the well regarded career teacher today, and with some specialized competence in a particular curriculum area.

The teacher (T.) category is seen as composed of two types of personnel: first, competent, experienced teachers of broad general training, and second, those of relatively little experience. The status of this position is seen as equal to that enjoyed by the typical teacher today.

The part-time teacher (P.T.) is a fully trained teacher, usually experienced, who is unable to teach full time. A combination of two or three part-time teachers might fill a billet which would otherwise require one full-time teacher.

The intern (I.) is a trainee in a program of teacher education doing full-time supervised teaching in a school for one semester. The work of the intern is customarily directed by a senior teacher or team leader working with the training school supervisor.

The clerical aide (C.A.) requires no professional preparation. This person will help with the routine, nontechnical aspects of team operation: typing, rexographing, filing. It is possible that other subprofessional roles can be developed in this category, for example, technicians capable of producing instructional and demonstration materials.

The absence of precise specifications for the qualifications and functions of the several positions has resulted in some frustration and tension as individuals at all levels have tried to work together in ill-defined roles for which adequate criteria for selection were not available at the time personnel were appointed and in which the emphasis, in some cases, has changed markedly during the two years of the project. Personnel have been concerned about the absence of stated expectations for some areas.

The project staff has found that conventionally constructed school buildings with their rows of self-contained cells all the same size, divided by immovable partitions, do not meet the needs of most effective team operation. It is of more than passing interest to note that a new elementary school in Lexington, now on the architect's drafting boards, is being designed with the special requirements of team teaching in high priority.

In grouping, attention has already been directed to the possibilities and flexibility of the situation. But the flexibility and the freedom present problems that can be frustrating. They raise questions about criteria for grouping, about the availability and validity of instruments to evaluate pupils in terms of the criteria, about the transfer of youngsters from one group to another, about the merits of horizontal enrichment and longitudinal progression, and about the justification for large group instruction. These are examples of a host of questions that could be raised about pupil redeployment. It is toward the clarification and understanding of questions such as these that some of the efforts of both the school and university staff are now directed.[1]

In curriculum development, also, the opportunities the team structure offers for reflective and creative work and the challenges provided by the flexibility of the grouping arrangements have dictated a re-examination of the curriculum. Questions are immediately raised as to the objectives of the school, of a particular subject, or of a unit. Issues are raised on the criteria by which content is to be selected and how it is to be organized. Questions of the appropriateness of content, materials, and technique—with perhaps special interest in the use of technological devices—for groups of different composition and different sizes also demand attention. To these and similar questions, the attention of the project is also directed. Efforts are being made to define and clarify the problems involved and to develop and test various sequences of the curriculum.

The opportunity to come to grips with some of these issues in an atmosphere of collaboration and constructive criticism is one source of the attraction and the holding power inherent in the teaching-teams concept.

[1] Further, more definitive analyses of problems and implications are being written and will appear in the literature in the near future.

10 Team Planning: Heart Transplant in Teaching

WILLIAM GOLDSTEIN

Reprinted with permission from *Clearing House*, Vol. 43, No. 5 (January 1969), pp. 272–274.

The best laid schemes o' mice and men
Gang aft a-gley;
An lea'e us nought but grief and pain,
For promis'd joy.

"TO A MOUSE"—*Robert Burns*

Mice do not teach; men do. Burns' philosophical reflection on life should signal a simple *caveat* to the teaching profession —bad instructional planning can yield only bad teaching which ultimately reduces learning no matter how inspiring some unplanned movements may be.

Time was (and lamentably still is all too frequently) when the "development" of lessons sprang Minerva-like from the head of the teacher into full classroom realization, then and there; this unnatural birth, however superficially glittering and sensational, has proven to be consistently inadequate. The absence of sequence and systematic development of material to be mastered results in punctured lessons and wounded curricula.

Thusly, if one accepts the thesis that sound planning is the heart of fine teaching, he may extend the metaphor by recommending a kind of coronary transplant—a shift from academic voodoo to modern medicine.

A KIND OF INTELLECTUAL COLLECTIVISM

Without surrendering independence and imagination in the individual teacher, modern planning for teaching, especially in those schools where a commitment to the idea of the teaming of teachers has already been made, must depend on "team" planning or, as it is called in many circles, "cooperative" planning.

From commerce to academia, the idea of an intellectual "togetherness" has been widely accepted. Terms such as "brainstorming," task forces, commissions, and the like, all give credence to the more-or-less obvious cliché that two heads are better than one, and that such unions may be expected to give rise to better thinking and ideas.

From therapy to think tanks, people work, discuss, and plan in groups, and experience tells us that such liaisons are at least better and more productive than *not* having made them.

What, then, is team planning? It is the *concerted, organized, regularly scheduled* effort on the part of a team or group of teachers to meet and *plan* the program of studies for a group of students. The number of teachers involved really does not matter, and the composition of the group with respect to academic disciplines varies, of course, with purpose of the planning.

In an age of "micro-disciplines," it allows for the development of teaching specialties (e.g., linguistics in the case of a teacher of English) which might otherwise not be possible in a traditional arrangement where the teacher, however excellent his personal preparation for his classes, fails to be provided with appropriate opportunities for specialized development and growth.

Team planning, furthermore, assists in unifying and standardizing desirable instructional practices and programs. It eliminates as far as possible the caprices of instruction and assures some degree of uniformity and exposure for all students to certain necessary basic elements of curricula.

In addition, team planning provides for less expected potentialities as well:

1. Improvement of instruction by inducing colleague observation and self-criticism; i.e., teachers visiting one another's classrooms and constructively learning from and improving one another's performances.

2. Focus of teachers' attention on the need to review instructional goals, reassess teaching techniques, and redeploy teaching personnel.

3. Analysis and adoption of new teaching materials, special groupings for instruction, and better use of space and facilities.

In short, mature and productive team planning eliminates, once and for all, the somewhat childish Panglossian notion that what we have now is the best of all possible worlds.

NATURE OF TEAM PLANNING

The essential nature of anything appears to be dual, both good and bad; team planning is no exception. An idea in its theoretical state generally emphasizes the good, but, if analyzed wisely, guards against inherent risks. Cooperative planning is the heart of cooperative or team teaching, but a cavalier approach to it yields a product which is terminal, primitive, and ephemeral, destroying enormous promise. Let us examine both positive and negative.

Positive Nature of Team Planning

Earlier, team planning was somewhat generally defined. Modern instruction, however, has become sufficiently complicated that general analysis is insufficient; one needs also to look at some detailed by-products. Experience with team planning shows a considerable harvest:

1. Teams of teachers who plan together tend to develop new units of instruction largely oriented to the contemporary world. The present no longer escapes the child because teachers plan for its discussion and analysis, frequently based on thematic and conceptual foundations.

2. "Product" development, so long a bulwark of the thinking of industry may become part of the teacher's vocabulary, in a human sense, of course. With the evolution of evaluation, educators are also thinking of objective assessments of their "products." Increasingly one hears the vocabulary of the statistician, with situations described by their "parameters." While there is a danger in becoming obsessed by a new technical lexicon, there are at least signs of objective and limit-seeking measurements. The Age of the Rampant Guess, so characteristic of educational circles, may be ending.

3. Obviously, a close corollary to product development is the idea of bringing "systems" to work for education. Planning in teams certainly points to the need for relating goals with personnel, materials, hardware, and assessment techniques in a more organized way.

4. Establishing *teaching priorities* should no longer be confined to isolated teachers. What we now know has grown far too complicated, and selecting and ordering ideas are far better achieved through group agreement.

5. Children and how they learn come into far greater focus in

team planning sessions. Sharing ideas on how to get children to learn more and retain longer is hardly better accomplished by planning which is independent of one's colleagues.

6. Research of a fruitful order is seldom carried out in the public schools by public school personnel. The idea of team planning certainly provides some thrust in the direction of changing this situation. One might add that group discussion and analysis cause teachers to review the research of others far more frequently than were they working separately.

7. Stimulating team planning is an in-service education program *sui generis*. It airs ideas; it causes disturbance of status quo thinking; in short, it moves people to come to grips with ideas other than their own.

8. Above all, cooperative planning for better teaching, when successful, develops an atmosphere of mutual respect and assistance among teaching teams; it keeps channels of communication perpetually open, and that, indeed, is something worthwhile.

Negative Nature of Team Planning

On the other hand one is reminded of "the best laid schemes" and all that. Team planning is hardly guaranteed as an elixir of academic salvation. There are problems and they need to be raised:

1. Team planning could become so exotic, especially in its formative stages, that it deals too frequently with the "razzle-dazzle" of instruction and insufficiently with necessary basic substance.

2. Difficulties on the parts of teachers in reaching agreement could cause severe and serious frustrations. It is not enough, for example, to agree on what it is on which the group cannot agree; this serves no really useful instructional purpose.

3. Planning paralysis sets in when team members are snared by the traps of procedure. The idea of team planning presupposes dealing with the substance of material to be taught to children. Continual discussion of the sheer mechanics of teaching surely destroys the elegance of the intent of working in teams.

4. The rigidities of tradition can erode the freshness of mind which develops on a team. Teachers must be willing to "let go" and rethink old ideas. Academic reactionaries, while stabilizing to some extent, also can be ruinous in trying to work out new ideas.

5. Lack of time to plan properly can result only in closure and a perpetuation of the status quo.

6. Contempt for and anger toward the inadequate performances of team members of marginal quality obviously hurt team harmony. Conversely, conspicuous and outstanding successes of other

teachers could create petty jealousies and intrigues which can also damage the team.

7. Cynicism or skepticism on the philosophy of cooperative efforts might also play a role in disintegrating the effectiveness of team planning.

It would not be difficult to apply the controversial domino theory to team teaching—that is, briefly stated, if team planning fails, all else following and connected with cooperative teaching will also fail. On the other hand, were one to write a scenario of the success of team planning, he at least keeps pace with the times and the demands of the times. In the words of T. S. Eliot in "The Love Song of J. Alfred Prufrock":

Let us go then, you and I.

11 | Towards a Differentiated Teaching Staff

M. JOHN RAND
FENWICK ENGLISH

Reprinted with permission from *Phi Delta Kappan*, Vol. 49, No. 5 (January 1968), pp. 264–268.

The acute shortage of teachers and the growing movement toward teacher professionalization are placing unbearable strains upon the present organizational structure in education. The shortage is worst in the nation's largest metropolitan areas, where organizational structures are most rigid and inner-city children in greatest need of good education. In suburban districts there is growing constituent dissatisfaction. Taxpayers are balking at increasing education costs without some proof that the pudding will be better.

Rising militancy and mass "resignations" last fall are signs that teachers are dissatisfied with their roles as mere implementers of administrative decision. Their demands are certainly more inclusive than simply a raise in pay. Teachers are telling us something we should have known or predicted long ago. When a group of people increase their technical competence close to that of the top members of the hierarchy, lines of authority become blurred. The subordinate position begins to rest more upon arbitrary and traditional distinctions than upon competence to perform the job.

Teachers are demanding inclusion in the decision-making process in education. As Corwin says,[1] professionalism is associated positively with militancy. Rather than arouse hostility in administrators and lay boards,

[1] Ronald G. Corwin, "Militant Professionalism, Initiative and Compliance in Public Education," *Sociology of Education*, Vol 38, pp. 310–31, Summer 1965.

it should be welcomed as one sign that the teaching profession is coming of age.

Increasing teacher specialization and competence mean that roles within the present educational structure are in the process of change. Teachers are recognizing that to break out of the ceilings imposed by the single salary schedule they must reexamine the assumptions which support it. The increasing need for high specialization and advanced training means that some teachers should be paid between $20,000 and $25,-000 per year, as are specialists in other fields. So long as we have the single salary schedule, however, no one will get this amount. The money simply cannot be raised without a complete (and in the short run completely impossible) overhaul of tax structures, school financing, and public value systems.

Hence the dissolution of the single salary schedule is a must if the teaching profession is to advance. Teachers will generally admit that not all of them possess the same abilities or strengths. They reject the onus of "merit pay," however, as "unprofessional" or otherwise undesirable. Merit pay plans offer the advantage of dissolving the single salary schedule, but ordinarily make no distinction in job responsibilities of teachers. Added pay is for "merit," not for added responsibility. As long as teaching is considered an art, one man's "superior" teacher is another's "average" teacher. Judgment of teaching "excellence" must be based on careful research just beginning to emerge at some universities. We have a long way to go before we can specify on the basis of empirical evidence what teaching excellence consists of. Hence we do not have the foundation for merit pay.

The Temple City Plan approaches the problem from a different perspecitve. Teachers are not treated the same. They may receive additional remuneration for increased professional responsibilities, which means change in their roles as teachers. These new responsibilities imply increased training and time on the job, and implicit in the concept of advancement is professional competence as a teacher, however it is measured. Teachers are not chosen to be paid more simply for continuing to perform their same functions; they are paid more for assuming increased responsibilities in the instructional program. They are selected on the basis of their experience and qualifications for the job by a professional panel and are retained only as they are able to perform adequately in their capacities. The Temple City Differentiated Staffing Plan, almost wholly designed by teachers, offers a way for teachers to receive remuneration of $20,000 per year by differentiating teaching roles and systematically enlarging their authority and decision-making powers to shape the instructional program.

The Temple City plan is not a brand new idea. Aspects of the plan have been espoused by Myron Lieberman,[2] J. Lloyd Trump,[3] and Robert Bush and Dwight Allen [4] at Stanford University. Allen was instrumental in developing the Temple City project, funded by the Charles F. Kettering Foundation of Denver, Colorado, for an 18-month study. The TEPS program of the NEA has also been active in proposing differentiated roles for professional personnel. The strength of the Temple City concept of differentiated staffing resides in a high degree of staff participation in its development. Indeed, the process of development is every bit as important as the product, i.e., an acceptable organizational design to implement the ideas of the professional staff.

The original model of differentiated staffing was developed by Allen and presented to the California State Board of Education in April of 1966 (see Figure 1). Later it was altered in the work done by Temple City teachers (see Figure 2). At the present, this model is undergoing further revision as a result of financial studies and further staff feedback. A brief sketch of the job descriptions follows.

TEACHING RESEARCH ASSOCIATE

The teaching research associate (TRA) is the "self-renewal" unit of the organization. His primary function is to introduce new concepts and ideas into the schools. He is well versed in research methodology and evaluation of instruction. The TRA may conduct field studies, but his major purpose is to translate research into instructional probes at the school level. The TRA functions in the present structure as a classroom teacher, as do all of the other personnel in the differentiated staffing plan, although in a limited capacity. In this way he does not lose sight of the receivers of his efforts. The TRA represents the apex of professional advancement for the aspiring teacher.

The teaching research associate meets all of Rogers' [5] criteria for initiating planned change in education. These are: (1) base the topics investigated on felt needs of practitioners; (2) create an educational structure to facilitate change; (3) raise the practitioners' ability to utilize the research results. Part of the TRA's responsibilities are implied in the third criterion mentioned by Rogers. Much of his liaison work with staff and cur-

[2] Myron Lieberman, *The Future of Public Education*. Chicago: University of Chicago Press, 1960.

[3] J. Lloyd Trump and Dorsey Baynham, *Guide to Better Schools*. Skokie, Ill.: Rand McNally, 1961.

[4] Dwight Allen and Robert Bush, *A New Design for High School Education*. New York: McGraw-Hill, 1964.

[5] Everett M. Rogers, "Developing a Strategy for Planned Change," paper presented at a Symposium on the Application of System Analysis and Management Techniques to Educational Planning in California, Orange, California, June, 1967.

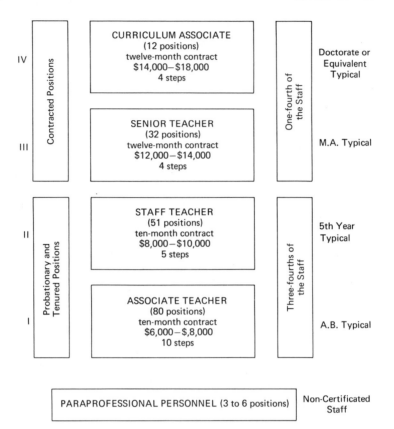

Figure 1. The proposed teacher hierarchy based on differentiated compensation and responsibilities.
This model of a differentiated staffing plan was developed by Dwight Allen and was presented to the California State Board of Education in April 1966.

rent research will be to increase the sophistication level of teachers and help them use it in practice and evaluate its effectiveness.

TEACHING CURRICULUM ASSOCIATE

The teaching curriculum associate (TCA) also must possess knowledge of research methodology, except that his knowledge is more applicable to curriculum theory, construction, and evaluation. In addition, the TCA would be adept at modifying national curriculum studies to meet local needs and local teacher proclivities.

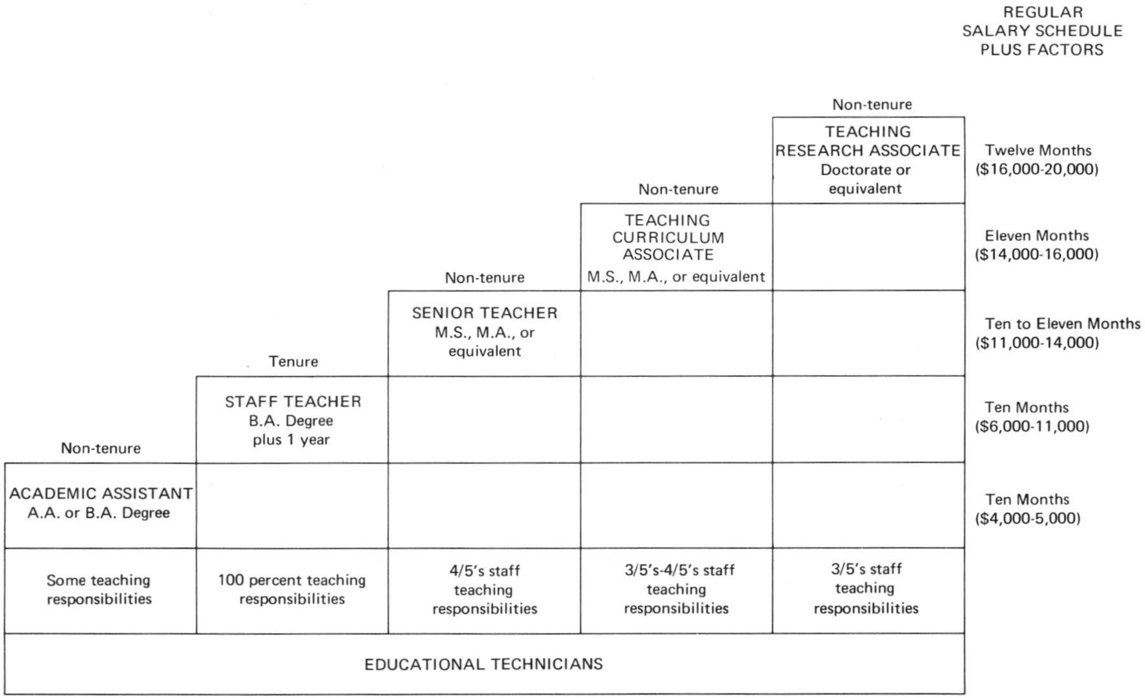

	REGULAR SALARY SCHEDULE PLUS FACTORS
	Twelve Months ($16,000-20,000)
	Eleven Months ($14,000-16,000)
	Ten to Eleven Months ($11,000-14,000)
	Ten Months ($6,000-11,000)
	Ten Months ($4,000-5,000)

ACADEMIC ASSISTANT A.A. or B.A. Degree	STAFF TEACHER B.A. Degree plus 1 year	SENIOR TEACHER M.S., M.A., or equivalent	TEACHING CURRICULUM ASSOCIATE M.S., M.A., or equivalent	TEACHING RESEARCH ASSOCIATE Doctorate or equivalent
Non-tenure	Tenure	Non-tenure	Non-tenure	Non-tenure
Some teaching responsibilities	100 percent teaching responsibilities	4/5's staff teaching responsibilities	3/5's-4/5's staff teaching responsibilities	3/5's staff teaching responsibilities

EDUCATIONAL TECHNICIANS

Figure 2. Temple City Unified School District: a model of differentiated staffing. This model of differentiated staffing was developed by Temple City Teachers. The model is currently being revised to combine the TRA-TCA functions. Salary figures are tentative.

The TCA also works at raising the level of teacher specialization in specific subject areas. He is more of a communications specialist than the TRA. However, due to the overlap in some functions, and because it is difficult to separate research from curriculum and instructional improvement studies, these two functions will probably be combined into one position: the Teaching Research-Curriculum Associate.

THE SENIOR TEACHER

The senior teacher is primarily responsible for the application of curriculum and instructional innovations to the classroom. The senior teacher is an acknowledged master practitioner, a learning engineer, a skilled diagnostician of the learning process. He is the teacher's teacher.

The senior teacher as an instructional advisor heads a subject group and represents this area on the school academic senate. He shares with the school principal the selection, performance, and evaluation of his colleagues in that subject specialty. In a team teaching situation, the senior teacher would function as a team leader. At least one-half of this teacher's day would be with students.

THE STAFF TEACHER

In a sense, all teachers in the differentiated staffing plan are staff teachers. A full-time staff teacher spends his school hours with students. He performs the same professional functions as most teachers in typical school districts. In a differentiated staffing plan the staff teacher is relieved of semiprofessional and clerical duties by employment of the following assistants:

THE ACADEMIC ASSISTANT

The academic assistant is a skilled paraprofessional, or a teacher intern (associate teacher) from a nearby college or university. He works with students and may instruct in special or skilled areas. He may also maintain physical materials, grade papers, and supervise resource center activities or student study.

THE EDUCATIONAL TECHNICIAN

The educational technician assumes many of the clerical and housekeeping tasks that consume so much professional time in the present organization. The technician keeps records, duplicates material, types, supervises student movement on campus, takes attendance, etc. The technician has little, if any, instructional responsibilities.

THE ACADEMIC SENATE

Teachers are formally involved in school decision making through the organization of an academic senate on each campus. One of the responsibilities of senior teachers is to represent the staff in the establishment of school policies relating to the educational program and its improvement.

THE SCHOOL MANAGER

In addition, the principal's role is differentiated by establishing a position called school manager. The school manager assumes responsibility for most of the business functions of school operation and thus relieves the principal for attention to the instructional program. It is hoped that eventually the principal will also refurbish his image as a teacher by assuming some direct teaching responsibilities with students. Most principals would find this impossible now, since they too are overburdened with paperwork and administrivia.

This combination of teacher specialists and administrator generalists would provide the school with the best judgments of all the professionals occupied with shaping a dynamic instructional program. School leadership is clearly enhanced with teachers exercising judgment as to how the instructional program should be improved. The principal's role is strengthened, since he can count on the specialized expertise of his senior teachers in the hiring and evaluation of the instructional staff. Teachers are intimately involved in professionalizing and disciplining their own ranks through the academic senate. This is crucial for full-fledged maturity; effective professional regulation can only occur when teachers assume responsibility for each other's performance. Administrators should welcome this desire for more responsibilities and assist their staffs in learning how to develop and exercise the leadership concomitants to fulfill this important professional role.

A discussion of differentiated staffing would not be complete without mentioning some of the problems the district has encountered in studying this concept. Differentiated staffing challenges a basic assumption inherent in the organizational structure of education. The myth that all teachers are equal exercises a powerful influence upon our thinking. The present organizational structure which assumes that one teacher can be all things to all students is a barrier of the first magnitude, especially at the elementary level.

One way of avoiding change and protecting oneself is for the teacher to shut his door and isolate himself with his 30 children. The position of the teacher in his classroom fortress is easier and more secure without the scrutiny of his colleagues. To differentiate teacher roles is contrary to the standard organizational pattern of elementary education for the last 100 years. When teachers perform different functions and assume new responsibilities they cannot be with children all day long. They must have time during the school day to plan with colleagues and conduct studies or meet with individual students. This implies some type of flexible scheduling, plus dual use of instructional models and resource facilities. This in turn means that teachers must delegate to paraprofessionals many nonprofessional responsibilities that do not demand a high degree of skill and training.

We have found a greater resistance at the elementary level to concepts of differentiated staffing than at the secondary. Some teachers fear that team teaching, use of paraprofessionals, resource centers, and flexible scheduling will permanently "damage" their children. They fail to recall that the present organizational structure established in 1870 at the Quincy Grammar School was organized for administrative convenience and that critics pointed out even then that it rather callously ignored the needs of continuous educational progress for each individual student.

Also we noted that a greater proportion of women than men object to teachers assuming a professional disciplinary role with their colleagues. This is especially true at the primary level, where a traditionally protective environment shields both students and teachers from decision making and colleague interaction.

At the secondary level, the idea of differentiated staffing was received more warmly. Here more teachers are men and the tradition of subject area specialization and leadership through department chairmen has been well established. However, some teachers at the secondary level are just as immobilized in their six-period day, self-contained classrooms as their elementary counterparts.

Some administrators will be uncomfortable in sharing the decision-making process with their staffs. Fear of losing status is an important consideration when proposing new roles for teachers. One must remember that almost all other roles in a school district hinge upon that of the teacher. If the teacher base is expanded upward, a shift is required in functions all the way to the superintendent. This means that in the Temple City plan teachers (teaching research associates) will sit with principals in an academic coordinating council headed by the superintendent. This district-wide group plans and anticipates district movement. Teachers (teaching curriculum associates) will also be a part of the curriculum coordinating council headed by the assistant superintendent. This group articulates curriculum development through the grades. Teacher specialists form an integral part of the decision-making machinery with the administrators of the district.

The Temple City plan of differentiated staffing offers a way to emancipate the teacher. It changes and enlarges the roles of teachers, increases their autonomy and decision-making powers, offers career advancement, and places them in a position to assume a regulatory function of their own profession. From the point of the administrator it enhances the leadership potential of his staff and builds in some guarantee that the instructional program will indeed remain vital and strong in all areas. A board of education and community should be encouraged when their teachers are willing to assume a corporate responsibility for the quality of education in their schools. The fact that teachers are disciplining themselves, are constantly in the self-renewal process, and have the freedom to rise as teachers to the top of their abilities and willingness to work means that the collective human resources which lie fallow in every organization are more fully tapped. In the short time our project has been operative we have been amazed at the talent which has emerged from our staff.

The most difficult barrier of all is not physical or financial but the subtle limitations in our vision, attitudes, and expectations, conditioned by one organizational structure for over 100 years. The validity of this structure may have been eroded, but its form has been firmly implanted in our psyches. The ability to rise above our own conditioning and previous expectancy levels is the most difficult problem, for solutions cannot be devised until problems are accurately perceived. Perception is limited when assumptions cannot be questioned. Our inability to see that some of our frustrations stem from traditional assumptions is a tragic dilemma. Differentiated staffing is a concept which challenges a whole host of notions about how American education should be organized and operated. At the moment it may be heresy; in a decade it may be practice.

12 Evaluation of English Achievement in a Ninth-Grade, Three-Period, Team-Teaching Class [1]

WILLIAM GEORGIADES
JOAN BJELKE

Reprinted with permission from *California Journal of Educational Research*, Vol. 17, No. 3 (May 1966), pp. 110–112.

During the late 1950s and early 1960s several curriculum innovations were proposed. Trump (1960), among others, suggested schemata such as flexible scheduling, team teaching, small- and large-group instruction. While these designs have been discussed in the literature, few of the studies reported have been based on systematic research evaluating the proposals presented (Gibboney, 1963). Since many of these new techniques are now functioning in our school systems, the need for critical evaluation is apparent.

Purpose of the Study

The purpose of this study was to compare English achievement of ninth grade pupils enrolled in a three-period-block, team-teaching (experimental) class with English achievement of ninth-grade pupils enrolled in a conventional (control) class.

[1] The writers acknowledge indebtedness to Drs. Kenneth D. Hopkins of the University of Colorado and William B. Michael of the University of California, Santa Barbara, for suggestions pertaining to statistical treatment of the data.

Hypotheses

The following hypotheses were examined in this study for each of the three measures of achievement: (1) *California Reading Test,* (a) Reading Vocabulary and (b) Reading Comprehension and (2) the teacher-made test:

1. The mean of the experimental group will differ from the mean of the control group.

2. The mean of the high intelligence group (mental age grade placement of 9.7—raw scores of 47 or above—on the Language section of the *California Short-Form Test of Mental Maturity,* 1957 edition) will be greater than the mean of the low intelligence group (mental age grade placement of 9.6—raw score of 46 or below—on the Language section of the *California Short-Form Test of Mental Maturity,* 1957 edition).

3. The mean of the boys will differ from the mean of the girls.

4. There will be a significant interaction between method of instruction and level of intelligence.

5. There will be a significant interaction between method of instruction and sex.

6. There will be a significant interaction between level of intelligence and sex.

7. There will be a significant interaction among method of instruction, level of intelligence, and sex.

METHODOLOGY

The Three-Period-Block Design

This experiment in flexible scheduling and team teaching is in its second year of implementation at Charter Oak High School. During the 1964–1965 school term, 106 ninth-grade students were scheduled to participate in this program, which was comprised of three subjects: algebra, English, and social studies (see Figure 1). In addition, all students in this block participated in a reading laboratory twice a week. Three times per week each teacher, working in one large lecture room equipped with projector, screen, and sound amplifier, conducted a large-group presentation in his respective subject to the entire 106 students. For purposes of small-group discussion and individual instruction, groups of not more than fifteen students met at least twice per week in each of the three subject matter areas. The large group was divided into six of these small groups, designated in Figure 1 as A, B, C, X, Y, and Z, respectively. Time was also provided each week for independent and/or library study

Monday

7:45	8:40	9:20	10:05	10:25
Large Group (100) — Algebra	Large Group (100) — Social Studies	Large Group (100) — English	Nutrition	Medium Groups

Medium Groups (Monday):

(30) Eng.	(30) S.S.	(30) Alg.
C + Z	B + Y	A + X

Tuesday

Small Groups (7:45–9:20) / Independent / Read. Lab.:

(15) Eng.	(15) Alg.	(15) S.S.	Independent	Read. Lab.
A	B	C	Independent	X
B	C	A	Study	Y
C	A	B	Library	Z
X	Y	Z		A

10:05 Nutrition

Wednesday

7:45	8:40	9:20	10:05	10:25
Large Group (100) — English	Large Group (100) — Algebra	Large Group (100) — Social Studies	Nutrition	Medium Groups

Medium Groups (Wednesday):

(30) Eng.	(30) S.S.	(30) Alg.
A + X	C + Z	B + Y

Thursday

Small Groups (7:45–9:20) / Independent / Read. Lab.:

(15) Eng.	(15) Alg.	(15) S.S.	Independent	Read. Lab.
Z	X	Y	Independent	A
Y	Z	X	Study	B
X	Y	Z	Library	C
B	C	A		X

10:05 Nutrition

Small Groups (10:25):

(15) Eng.	(15) Alg.	(15) S.S.	Independent	Read. Lab.
C	A	B	Independent	Y
A	B	C	Study	Z
			Library	

Friday

7:45	8:40	9:20	10:05	10:25
Large Group (100) — Social Studies	Large Group (100) — English	Large Group (100) — Algebra	Nutrition	Medium Groups

Medium Groups (Friday):

(30) Eng.	(30) S.S.	(30) Alg.
B + Y	A + X	C + Z

Figure 1. Basic schedule—three-period flexible scheduling, Charter Oak High School.

for every student. Figure 1 presents the typical weekly schedule of the
three-period-block schema.

It should be noted that the combination of three relatively unrelated
subjects in the three-period-block format just described differs from the
conventional team-teaching design in which two or more teachers cooper-
ate within one class period to teach one subject to a large group of students (Beggs, 1964). In the three-period-block the objective is not necessarily content organization in the core sense, but rather scheduling
organization. Thus, there is little if any breaching of the autonomy of the
individual teachers involved in structuring their own subject matter presentations. Instead, the group planning revolves around the scheduling of
time periods. As a result of this substantial blocking of time, there is po-
tentially a large degree of scheduling flexibility which is not possible in
the conventional one-period, one-subject format.

The Sample

Control Group.—Since the experimental group was taught by an experienced teacher, only ninth-grade English classes being instructed by
other than first-year teachers were used in this study. Eight intact, conventionally taught English classes, involving three teachers and 234 students, comprised the control group. Of these students 64 percent were enrolled in an algebra I class. Excluded from this group were the 35
percent of students on whom no *California Short-Form Test of Mental
Maturity* or *Differential Aptitude Tests* scores were available. There was
no significant difference between the mean on the teacher-made test or
the means of the Reading Vocabulary and Reading Comprehension
scores on the *California Reading Test* of those subjects on whom all
scores were available and the means on the same respective tests of all
control students, both with and without complete intelligence scores.
Consequently the investigators felt reasonably justified that this more
limited sample would not significantly reduce the external validity or
generalizability of this study. Also excluded were an additional 2 percent
who were absent at the time of administration of either the teacher-made
test or the *California Reading Test,* or both. The final control sample
was comprised of 149 subjects, seventy-four boys and seventy-five girls.

Experimental Group.—Consistent with scheduling policy, it was not
possible to assign subjects at random to the experimental group. Because
algebra I was one of the subjects taught in the three-period-block design,
only those students who planned to include that subject in their programs were permitted to enroll. No algebra readiness test was used by
Charter Oak High School, as it is their policy to permit any student to
enroll in algebra if he is interested. In addition, not all students taking
algebra I were enrolled in the three-period-block design. The experimental group was therefore comprised of 106 students assigned to the block

because (1) they had elected to take algebra I and (2) their remaining programs did not conflict with the morning schedule of the three-period-block. Excluded from this group were the 30 percent of students on whom no *California Short-Form Test of Mental Maturity* or *Differential Aptitude Tests* scores were available. There was no significant difference between the mean on the teacher-made test or the means of the Reading Vocabulary and Reading Comprehension scores on the *California Reading Test* of those subjects on whom all scores were available and the means on the same respective tests of all experimental students, both with and without complete intelligence scores. Consequently the investigators felt reasonably justified that this more limited sample would not significantly reduce the external validity or generalizability of this study. Also excluded were an additional 3 percent who were absent at the time of the administration of either the teacher-made test or the *California Reading Test,* or both. The final experimental sample was comprised of seventy-four subjects, thirty-five boys and thirty-nine girls.

The School Environment.—Charter Oak High School is a medium-sized high school (ADA=approximately 1,815) located in a suburb of Los Angeles, California. The community which Charter Oak High School serves consists of persons primarily of middle and upper-middle socioeconomic status. Approximately 69 percent of the graduating seniors enroll in colleges or universities.

The Evaluative Devices

For purposes of measuring the abilities of the individuals in this study, the following standardized intelligence tests were used: (1) *California Short-Form Test of Mental Maturity* (*CTMM*), 1957 edition, Language IQ, and (2) *Differential Aptitude Tests* (*DAT*), Verbal Reasoning (*VR*), and Numerical Ability (*NA*) scores.

For purposes of measuring achievement in English, Form W of the *California Reading Test* (*CRT*), Reading Vocabulary and Reading Comprehension, 1957 edition, a widely used achievement test, was selected.

In addition to the standardized achievement test, a teacher-made test was prepared by the teachers in the English department at Charter Oak High School to reflect specific curriculum objectives and course content common to all ninth grade English classes in the school. This test consisted of 100 multiple-choice and matching items: seventy-two language usage questions and twenty-four vocabulary questions and four library usage questions. The mean and standard deviation of the combined scores of the 337 ninth grade students in the eight control classes and one large-group class were 68.8 and 13.9, respectively. Means in the individual classes ranged from 58.8 to 77.7 and standard deviations ranged from 9.2 to 13.9. The Kuder-Richardson-20 (KR-20) and Kuder-Richardson-21 (KR-21) reliability coefficients (Guilford, 1954) calculated from scores on the teacher-made test of all 337 ninth-grade students in the eight control classes and one large-group class were .92 and .90, respectively. The KR-20's of the individual participating classes ranged from .86 to .93, and the KR-21's ranged from .80 to .91 (Jones, Pullias, and Michael, 1965). On the basis of the above finding, it was determined that this test was sufficiently reliable to be utilized in this study.

Procedures

The standardized intelligence tests (*CTMM* and *DAT*) used in this study had been administered to the subjects in the regular eighth-grade testing program in October 1963 at the three elementary schools (Cedar Grove, Ruddock, and Sunflower) from which Charter Oak High School draws pupils.

The teacher-made test was taken by the subjects as a final examination in January 1965 at the conclusion of the fall semester. This examination was administered by the various classroom teachers involved in this experiment.

The standardized achievement test (*CRT*) was given in April 1965 to the eight control classes and to the experimental class by the various classroom teachers involved. Care was taken by the Coordinator of Guidance and Counseling to acquaint each teacher with the *CRT* and with the specific instructions and procedures required for administration of this test.

Scoring

The number right, not corrected for chance, was used as the score on all achievement tests in this study.

On all tests utilized in this study, raw scores were utilized for analysis of the data.

Research Design

A $2 \times 2 \times 2$ analysis of variance—mode of instruction by level of scholastic aptitude by sex—was employed in this study (Edwards, 1964). Biomedical Computer Programs 3R and 5V (University of California, Los Angeles, 1964) on the IBM 7094 computer were used to analyze the data.[2] Because of the necessity to use intact groups in this study and because of the inequality which resulted between the experimental and control groups, a covariance analysis was also employed. Intelligence or ability, as measured by the *DAT—VR* and *NA* scores combined, constituted the covariate (matching or equating variable) (Edwards, 1964; Walker

[2] Appreciation is expressed to the Western Data Processing Center for making time available to the writers under its cooperative plan of institutional participation in non-profit research activities.

and Lev, 1953). For each of the three dependent variables representing measures of achievement—(1) teacher-made test, (2) $CRT—RV$, and (3) $CRT—RC$—a separate analysis of covariance was computed.

Appropriate significance tests revealed that the variance of the scores in the cells were homogeneous for each of the three criterion variables. Additional statistical procedures revealed that the regression for each subgroup was linear.

Significance Level
The .05 significance level was set as the maximum probability at which the null hypothesis would be rejected.

RESULTS

Inspection of the analyses of variance and analyses of covariance in Table I indicates that although none of the interactions was significant for any one of the three dependent variables, several of the main effects were. Specifically, for the methods variable, the analysis of variance and the analysis of covariance revealed significance of difference in average scores for the teacher-made test as well as for the Reading Comprehension section of the *California Reading Test,* but failed to indicate significant differences with respect to the Reading Vocabulary section. Although the research hypothesis was nondirectional, the statistically significant difference in the unadjusted and adjusted means favored the experimental group. Relative to the second research hypothesis, which was directional in its prediction of greater mean scores for the higher level intelligence group, both the analysis of variance and the analysis of covariance yielded statistical significance beyond the .001 level for each of the three dependent variables. Both the analysis of variance and the analysis of covariance revealed that the third research hypothesis, pertaining to sex differences, was supported for only the teacher-made test.

Table II presents the obtained (unadjusted) and adjusted means on the teacher-made test and the Reading Vocabulary and Reading Comprehension sections of the *California Reading Test* of the three main effects by level as well as the means and standard deviations of the covariates for each level. It is noted that for the method variable, the difference between the mean of the experimental and the mean of the control group was decreased by analysis of covariance both for the teacher-made test and for the Reading Comprehension section of the CRT. In the case of the Reading Vocabulary section of the $CRT,$ the analysis of covariance both decreased the difference and reversed the position of the two means. After analysis of covariance was employed, the mean of the control group

TABLE I

F-Ratios and Error Mean Square Values [a] for Analyses of Variance and Covariance for the Teacher-made Test the *California Reading Test*, Reading Vocabulary and Reading Comprehension Scores

		Analysis of Variance				Analysis of Covariance		
	df	Teacher-made Test F	CRT RV F	CRT RC F	df	Teacher-made Test F	CRT RV F	CRT RC F
Method	1	*** 37.521	.078	*** 24.280	1	** 9.382	3.441	* 5.621
IQ	1	*** 57.733	*** 66.118	*** 79.846	1	*** 11.997	*** 22.020	*** 26.850
Sex	1	* 5.602	1.312	1.153	1	** 10.461	1.008	.979
Method x IQ	1	1.713	.850	.868	1	3.477	1.231	1.010
Method x Sex	1	.099	.102	.902	1	.020	.297	.170
IQ x Sex	1	.113	.714	1.429	1	.526	.008	.131
Method x IQ x Sex	1	.012	.004	.318	1	.017	.000	.369
(Error Mean Square)	215	(107.207)	(58.297)	(75.898)	213	(66.324)	(47.098)	(59.298)

[a] Only *F*-ratios and error mean squares are given since other mean squares are reproducible from these values because the design is a fixed constants model.

* $p<.05$ ** $p<.01$ *** $p<.001$

TABLE II

Test Means and Standard Deviations on the Teacher-made Test and on the Reading Vocabulary and Reading Comprehension Sections of the California Reading Test, Numbers of Subjects, and Means and Standard Deviations of Covariates for Each of the Three Main Effects by Level

		Teacher-Made Test			CRT—RV				CRT—RC				Covariates			
													DAT—VR		DAT—NA	
	N	$\overline{X}$	$\overline{X}_{adj.}$	s	$\overline{X}$	$\overline{X}_{adj.}$	s	Percentile Rank[a]	$\overline{X}$	$\overline{X}_{adj.}$	s	Percentile Rank[a]	$\overline{X}$	s	$\overline{X}$	s
Experimental	74	77.8	71.7	8.6	34.1	31.4	8.7	76	52.9	48.9	10.4	82	22.4	7.8	21.8	6.3
Control	149	65.5	68.5	13.5	31.5	32.8	8.7	66	43.5	45.8	10.1	62	16.8	7.3	15.2	7.5
High IQ	104	77.4	71.8	9.6	37.1	34.2	7.5	82	53.3	49.0	9.3	84	22.8	6.7	21.0	7.3
Low IQ	119	62.7	67.6	12.5	28.2	30.7	7.6	58	40.8	44.5	9.0	54	15.0	7.1	14.2	6.8
Boy	109	67.0	67.4	12.8	32.6	33.1	8.4	70	46.5	46.8	11.0	70	18.3	7.5	17.1	7.4
Girl	114	72.0	71.7	13.6	32.1	31.7	9.1	73	46.7	46.4	11.2	70	19.0	8.3	17.6	8.1

[a] Percentile ranks of obtained means for high ninth grade—1963 norms (California Test Bureau, 1963).

exceeded the mean of the experimental group by 1.4 raw score points. (This difference was not, however, significant.)

Relative to the level of intelligence variable, the mean difference for each of the three dependent variables was decreased by analysis of covariance. There were no position reversals.

For the sex variable, the analysis of covariance decreased the mean difference between boys and girls; however, with analysis of covariance, this difference changed in significance from .05 to .01. For the Reading Comprehension and the Reading Vocabulary sections of the *CRT*, the mean differences were very slightly increased by analysis of covariance. However, these sex differences were not statistically significant.

DISCUSSION

Conclusions

Because of the marked difference in intellectual ability between the experimental and control classes in this study, the analysis of covariance must be considered to be a more realistic evaluation of comparative achievement than the analysis of variance.

Although the experimental group revealed a significantly higher mean achievement level than the control group on the teacher-made test and on the *CRT—RC*, there was no significant difference in the performance of the two groups on the *CRT—RV*. Possibly it was relatively more difficult for individuals in the experimental group to gain in reading vocabulary because they were so far ahead of the control group in this ability at the beginning of the experiment. Or vocabulary building may have been emphasized more by the teachers in the control classes than by the teacher in the experimental class.

The significant difference found between the mean of the girls versus the mean of the boys on the teacher-made test may be a reflection of the nature of the test, which was heavily weighted on language usage. Anastasi (1958) has reported: "Girls maintain their superiority in many aspects of verbal functioning throughout the elementary and high school levels." However, the investigators were unable to determine why this bias in favor of the girls was not reflected in the remaining two measures of achievement as well.

Since no significant interactions were found, it is not surprising that there was a marked degree of significance between the means of the high-intelligence-level group versus the low-intelligence-level group on all measures of achievement used in this study.

While the findings appear to favor the team approach, any conclusions must be tempered with certain limitations:

1. *Teacher Variable.*—Because of the impossibility of selecting at random those teachers who would participate in this experiment and the fact that there was only one English teacher involved in the experimental group and three teachers in the control group, there is a risk that any difference found could be attributed to the teacher variable.

2. *Instrumentation.*—(a) Teacher-made Test—Although this test was prepared collectively by all participating teachers in this study, there is the risk that any one teacher could have been more influential than the others in preparing and selecting test items. (b) *California Reading Test*—Although the *CRT* was selected by the administration of Charter Oak High School as being the most representative of available standardized tests of curriculum objectives and course content, the results of this experiment shall be limited by the relative validity of this test for this particular population and course content.

3. *Selection.*—From the standpoint of the adequacy of experimental design, there were probably selection effects introduced in view of the fact that the students were not randomly enrolled in either the team or one of the control classes.

4. *Interaction Effect of Selection Biases and the Experimental Variable.*—Because of the experimental nature of the three-period-block design, there may be selection specificity, since implementation of this design would possibly be precluded in many high school districts. In addition, although the experimental group was dichotomized into low and high intellectual ability levels, this group was predominately above average on this measure.

5. *Reactive Effects of Experimental Arrangements.*—It is possible that results obtained in this experiment were inflated by the "Hawthorne effect."

In conclusion, since it is felt that this curriculum design itself has certain merits for both student and teacher (Kirkpatrick and Shambeck, 1963), making it a highly effective method of teaching, the investigators were not necessarily looking for greatly improved student performance. However, from the significant results revealed in this study, it appears that the three-period-block is at least initially workable. It must be remembered that a comparison was being made between relative inexperience with one method (team class) and experience with another method (conventional class). Consequently, the evaluation might not have been completely fair to the team method of instruction, since there is a possibility that the teachers have not yet had an opportunity to make maximum use of and to capitalize upon the advantages afforded by this new method. Therefore, the significant findings in favor of the experimental group add further support to the efficacy of the three-period-block design as an instructional method.

Recommendations

The findings of significantly greater achievement in the experimental group tend to support further implementation and evaluation of the three-period-block design.

After further experience with this curriculum structure, it is proposed that this study be replicated with the following changes and/or additions.

1. Use of standardized achievement test other than the *California Reading Test* to determine whether the results of this study were greatly influenced by use of this test.

2. Improvement of the teacher-made test in light of the item analysis obtained in this study.

3. Random assignment of students to the experimental or control groups.

4. Random assignment of teachers involved in the study or at least statistical comparison to insure comparability of experience and training.

5. Evaluation of achievement in both algebra and social studies as well as in English.

6. A follow-up study of the same students in succeeding years to determine whether there may be differential retention.

7. Application of devices designed to measure attitudes of students, teachers, and parents in a systematic fashion.

Summary

In this investigation, English achievement of seventy-four ninth-grade pupils enrolled in a three-period, team-teaching class (including algebra, English, and social studies) was compared with English achievement of 149 ninth-grade pupils enrolled in a conventionally taught class. Since random assignment to the two methods of instruction was not possible, students were equated statistically on the basis of two standardized aptitude tests ($DAT—VR$ and NA). Comparison of achievement was effected on the basis of a 100-item teacher-made test and two sections of a standardized achievement test ($CRT—RV$ and RC). A $2\times2\times2$ analysis of variance (method of instruction by level of intellectual ability by sex) revealed: (1) significant differences in means for the experimental versus the control group on the teacher-made test and on the $CRT—RC$, (2) significant differences in means for the high-level-of-intelligence group versus the low-level-of-intelligence group on each of the three measures of achievement, (3) a significant difference in the means for the girls versus the boys on the teacher-made test, and (4) no significant differential effects; i.e., interactions between the three main effects. It was concluded that the findings were sufficiently positive to warrant further implementation and evaluation of the three-period, team-teaching class.

REFERENCES

Anastasi, Anne. *Differential Psychology*. New York: The Macmillan Company, 1958.

Beggs, David W., III (ed). *Team Teaching—Bold New Venture*. Indianapolis, Indiana: Unified College Press, Inc., 1964.

California Test Bureau. *Manual, California Achievement Tests, Complete Battery*. Monterey, California: California Test Bureau, 1963.

Campbell, Donald T., and Stanley, Julian C. "Experimental and Quasi-Experimental Designs for Research on Teaching," in *Handbook of Research on Teaching* (edited by N. L. Gage). Skokie, Ill.: Rand McNally & Company, 1963, 171–246.

Dixon, W. J. (ed.), *BMD: Biomedical Computer Programs*. Los Angeles: University of California, Los Angeles, 1964.

Edwards, Allen L. *Experimental Design in Psychological Research*. New York: Holt, Rinehart and Winston, 1964.

Gibboney, Richard A., and others. "Curriculum Components and Organization," *Review of Educational Research*, XXXIII (June, 1963), 278–292.

Guilford, J. P. *Psychometric Methods*. New York: McGraw-Hill, Inc., 1954.

Jones, Robert A., Pullias, Calvin, and Michael, William B. "An IBM 1401 Computer Program for Item and Test Analysis," *Educational and Psychological Measurement*. XXV (Spring, 1965), 217–219.

Kirkpatrick, Laurence, and Shambeck, Lillian. *An Evaluation of Staff Utilization Projects in the Centinela Valley Union High School District*. A report prepared by the Centinela Valley Union High School District. Hawthorne, California: Centinela Valley Union High School District, 1963.

Trump, J. Lloyd. *New Directions to Quality Education: The Secondary School Tomorrow*. A report prepared by the National Association of Secondary-School Principals. Washington, D.C.: National Association of Secondary-School Principals, 1960.

Walker, Helen M., and Lev, Joseph. *Statistical Inference*. New York: Holt, Rinehart and Winston, 1953.

13 An Analysis of the Effectiveness of Team Teaching Compared to Traditional Teaching of Health to High School Sophomore Students

RICHARD G. SCHLAADT

Reprinted with permission from *Research Quarterly of the American Association for Health, Physical Education, and Recreation*, Vol. 40, No. 2 (May 1969), pp. 364–367.

This study compared the effectiveness of team teaching and traditional teaching methods in increasing the health knowledge of 114 sophomore high school health students. To determine the difference between the methods, the following groups were analyzed: (a) girls and boys combined, (b) girls separately, (c) boys separately, (d) girls and boys of superior mental abilities, (e) girls and boys of average mental abilities, and (f) girls and boys of below-average mental abilities. All students participating in the study were given the Shaw Health Knowledge Test as a pretest and final test. Although the groups taught by the team-teaching method showed a greater increase in health knowledge than those taught by the traditional method, only the students of superior mental ability taught by the team-teaching method showed a statistically significant gain according to an analysis of variance.

The effectiveness of team teaching compared to traditional teaching has been a major concern in the field of education since 1957. After several years of employing both methods in teaching health education, the author became curious to learn if the team-teaching method is as effective as the traditional method. For the purpose of this study, the terms of this investigation will be defined as follows:

Traditional teaching: Teaching in a self-contained classroom which meets five days a week for 55 minutes each day, with instruction given by the same teacher in the same room.

Team teaching: An arrangement whereby class instruction is offered by two or more teachers cooperatively through the use of large group, medium group or regular class size, small group, and individual study in order to take advantage of teacher specialties.

The following hypotheses were formulated. Team teaching is as effective as traditional teaching in increasing health knowledge of:

1. sophomore high school students taking a semester health course.
2. sophomore high school girls taking a semester health course.
3. sophomore high school boys taking a semester health course.
4. students with superior mental ability.
5. students with average mental ability.
6. students with below-average mental ability.

REVIEW OF LITERATURE

The literature relating to the following aspects of team teaching was reviewed: (a) general secondary school studies; (b) specific secondary school subject studies; (c) elementary and junior high school studies; (d) college and university work in the area; and (e) summaries and conclusions resulting from team-teaching studies.

Relatively few scientific studies have attempted to evaluate the effectiveness of the team-teaching method compared to the traditional method of teaching in increasing student achievement. In the area of health education, the investigator could not find a single scientific study on team teaching. This was extremely disturbing, particularly after reading the article by Pitruzzelo (3) which reported that team-teaching research in physical education and health should be especially important because this is the area with the highest incidence of team teaching. A review of the literature unearthed a variety of general findings in other subject areas, but many of these lacked proper experimental design and statistical treatment. Unfortunately the evidence which has been gathered since 1957 provides little in the way of interpretive analysis.

EXPERIMENTAL DESIGN

In the design of this study the author tried to overcome some of the difficulties which plagued many of the earlier team-teaching studies. This study, conducted during the spring of 1966, used 114 second semester sophomore health students from Centennial High School in Grasham, Oregon. During the 18 weeks of the semester course the classes met five times a week, 55 min./period. The control group consisted of three health education classes which utilized traditional teaching, while the experimental group of three classes used team teaching. The same three teachers instructed the traditional-teaching classes and the team-teaching classes to minimize the teacher variable that has hindered so many team-teaching studies. Control and experimental classes received an equal amount of time, the same content, and used the same state-adopted textbook.[1] Because the school district had purchased this textbook in 1962 it could not be replaced before 1967.

Since physical education and health education were both required during the sophomore year, only half of the sophomore students were enrolled in health education second semester. Starting at the beginning of the alphabet the counselors placed the sophomores alternately in physical education and health education until the classes were equally filled. Sophomores taking health education were then equally divided on an alphabetical basis by alternating students between periods 1 (control) and 3 (experimental). On the basis of this selection, it was felt that classes of similar abilities would be found in the experimental and control groups. There were 57 students in each group, 19 in each class. One of the instructors taught all 57 of the experimental group twice a week in group instruction.

All students participating in this study were given the Shaw Health Knowledge Test (4) as a pretest and as a final test. This standardized test covers the widely accepted areas of health education and has a coefficient of correlation for reliability of .89, which is significantly higher than the reports of reliability of most published health knowledge tests. The Henmon-Nelson Test of Mental Abilities (1, 2) was given to insure that each group was comparable in mental ability. The test also enabled the investigator to group students according to mental abilities as follows: (a) superior mental ability, 111 and above; (b) average mental ability, 90 to 110; and (c) below average, 89 and below. Although the three mental ability levels were arbitrarily chosen, they are comparable to other intelligence test standards. In addition, chronological ages of the students were equated.

PRESENTATION AND ANALYSIS OF DATA

Hypothesis No. 1. Team teaching is as effective as traditional teaching in increasing health knowledge of sophomore high school students

[1] J. Clemensen and others, *Your health and safety* (New York: Harcourt, Brace and Co., 1957).

taking a semester health course.—Although the team-teaching method produced the greatest increase in health knowledge, the analysis of variance results ($F=1.70$) indicated no significant difference at the .05 level.

Hypothesis No. 2. Team teaching is as effective as traditional teaching in increasing health knowledge of sophomore high school girls taking a semester health course.—Although the girls taught by the team-teaching method made the greatest increase in health knowledge, the analysis of variance results ($F=.24$) indicated no significant difference at the .05 level.

Hypothesis No. 3. Team teaching is as effective as traditional teaching in increasing health knowledge of sophomore high school boys taking a semester health course.—Boys in the team-teaching group had a better increase in health knowledge than boys in the traditional teaching group. However, the analysis of variance results ($F=.16$) indicated no significant difference.

Hypothesis No. 4. Team teaching is as effective as traditional teaching in increasing health knowledge of students with superior mental ability.—The team-teaching superior mental ability group had the greatest gain in health knowledge according to the analysis of variance results ($F=6.2$). However, the team-teaching group started lower than the traditional group and this may have affected the outcome.

Hypothesis No. 5. Team teaching is as effective as traditional teaching in increasing health knowledge of students with average mental ability.—Classes taught by the two methods showed about the same increase in health knowledge according to the analysis of variance results ($F=.002$), which indicated no significant difference at the .05 level.

Hypothesis No. 6. Team teaching is as effective as traditional teaching in increasing health knowledge of students with below-average mental ability.—Although the below-average mental ability students made the greatest increase in health knowledge, the analysis of variance results ($F=.21$) indicated no significant difference at the .05 level.

CONCLUSIONS AND RECOMMENDATIONS

The team-teaching method is as effective as the traditional method in increasing the health knowledge of sophomore high school students taking a semester health course. Students of superior mental ability taught health by the team-teaching method showed a statistically significant gain over students of superior mental ability taught by the traditional method. However it should be noted that this group started lower than the traditional group, which might have affected the outcome. It is recommended that:

1. Additional health team-teaching studies utilizing statistical treatment should be conducted on the elementary, junior high school, secondary school, and college levels.

2. Scientific team-teaching studies should be encouraged in other secondary school subject areas to determine the effectiveness of this method in each subject area.

3. Because team teaching is as effective as traditional teaching in health education for girls, boys, average mental ability students, and below-average mental ability students, it is recommended that each school choose the method deemed most effective for the school.

4. Institutions involved in preparing prospective health education teachers should integrate team teaching into their methods courses.

REFERENCES

1. Buros, Oscar K. *The fifth mental measurements yearbook.* Highland Park, N. J.: Gryphon Press, 1959.
2. Lanke, T. A., and Nelson, N. J. *Henmon-Nelson tests of mental ability.* Boston: Houghton Mifflin Company, 1957.
3. Pitruzzelo, P. R. Report on team teaching. *Clearing House* 36:333–36, 1962.
4. Shaw, D. E. *A comparison of the effectiveness of teaching general hygiene by closed-circuit television and by lecture procedures.* Doctoral dissertation, Oregon State University, 1965.

14 | Why Teaching Teams Fail

CARL O. OLSON, JR.

Reprinted with permission from *Peabody Journal of Education*, Vol. 45, No. 1 (July, 1967), pp. 15–20.

Although team teaching is certainly not a new form of school organization, there has been a tremendous emphasis on team teaching in recent years. Virtually every school district has something labeled "team teaching"—a few schools are completely organized on a team teaching basis. Generally teaching teams are organized to: (1) utilize better the talents and interests of teachers, (2) increase grouping and scheduling flexibility and (3) improve the quality of instruction. In theory, team teaching has merit and there are many excellent teaching teams in operation.

As an administrator I have helped organize elementary and secondary teaching teams and have taught on teaching teams. I have observed teaching teams in operation and have discussed team teaching with many educators actively involved in team teaching. *My experience with team teaching has led me to conclude that: quite a few teams are dismal failures, many teaching teams do not make a significant enough contribution to the education of students to warrant the time and effort devoted to them and a few actually retard the educational development of students.* Surely, a sterile, ineffective teaching team is a failure even though it may retain the "teaching team" label.

Teaching teams fail for a variety of reasons. Many teams devote entirely too much time to large group lecturing and others spend too much time in meaningless small group discussion. Very few actually provide significant independent study experiences for students. On many teams the students have much less intimate contact with their teachers than they might normally enjoy in a self-contained classroom. Some teams are dominated by one or more members of the team. For a variety of reasons many teams are rigidly bound to an inflexible schedule. For example, they may be forced to have large group instruction on Monday, Wednesday, and Friday and seminars on Tuesday and Thursday week after week regardless of the needs of the students or the desires of the team members. Although teaching teams may lose vitality and purpose and cease to make a significant contribution to the education of students, all too often they remain in existence.

I recognize that my observations and my main conclusion are purely subjective. (It would be extremely valuable but very difficult to conduct a "scientific" study of the reasons why teaching teams fail. Unfortunately, we educators are usually quite reluctant to admit our failures. Our "experiments" are almost invariably successful; newly established programs rarely fail.) I am not necessarily opposed to team teaching. In fact, I enthusiastically support good team teaching. My primary purpose in exploring the reasons why teaching teams fail is to enable educators considering the formation of teaching teams to examine the "other side of the coin" realistically in the hope that they may be spared some unnecessary disappointment, frustration and work. Secondly, I would hope that the article would be of some value to anyone examining the operation of existing teaching teams.

THE NATURE OF TEAM TEACHING

Many teaching teams fail because those responsible for creating and operating them simply do not understand the nature and demands of team teaching. The theoretical advantages of team teaching will obviously not materialize unless a genuine teaching team is created. Therefore, it is imperative that those planning to organize a teaching team really understand team teaching. In addition, they must agree on their own operational definition of team teaching.

Team teaching is one form of "cooperative" teaching. Although all definitions of team teaching necessarily vary somewhat, essentially team teaching may be thought of as *an instructional situation where two or more teachers possessing complementary teaching skills cooperatively plan and implement the instruction for a single group of students using flexible scheduling and grouping techniques to meet the particular instructional needs of the students.* Cooperative planning of curriculum content and methods of instruction; mutual evaluation of instruction by the entire team; flexible scheduling and grouping and an effort to capitalize on teachers' skills and interests are usually considered the essentials of team teaching.

Many forms of organization labeled "team teaching" are simply not

teaching teams in the sense of the commonly accepted definition presented here. Although they may be excellent examples of "cooperative
teaching" they cannot produce the theoretical advantages of team teaching. For example, if two history teachers each having 25–30 students in a
given period are able to bring their groups together they may be able to
provide some excellent large group instruction but their student-teacher
ratio will not enable them to achieve the flexible scheduling and grouping expected in team teaching.

All too often teachers and administrators expect a teaching team to
produce miracles. Team teaching is no panacea. It will not make slow
learners bright. It will not reduce the range of individual differences in
student achievement and ability. It will not automatically create a spark
of interest in the disaffected student. And, finally, it will not automatically convert mediocre teachers into outstanding teachers.

Many teaching teams have not produced the expected results of team
teaching simply because a genuine teaching team was not created. This
has led to a great deal of unnecessary and unfair frustration for teachers
and students. Everyone involved in team teaching must have a realistic
understanding of what may be expected from team teaching.

THE DEMANDS OF TEAM TEACHING

Additional problems result when those involved in team teaching do
not understand the considerable demands of team teaching. Although a
viable, effective team will make more intelligent use of the teachers' time
and talent and permit more flexible scheduling to better meet the needs
of students, such a team requires a great deal of work and sacrifice on the
part of its members. *Team teaching is not a labor-saving device.* In
many, many ways team teaching requires much more effort and sacrifice
on the part of teachers than teaching in the self-contained classroom.
This point cannot be overemphasized. The difficulties of team teaching
may vary from subject to subject. For example, a "Problems of Democracy" social studies team may have to devote more time to planning than
a geometry team simply because there probably would be less general
agreement on the basic nature of the social studies curriculum and the
methods of teaching.

As indicated above a team must be well planned in order to operate
successfully. The teachers must begin by clearly defining their goals.
They must understand exactly what they expect from team teaching.
Basic instructional materials must be selected. Schedules, techniques, and
criteria for grouping and methods of evaluation have to be discussed
thoroughly and agreed upon *before* the team begins to work with students. This kind of planning requires time. It is unreasonable and unfair

to expect teachers to plan a teaching team while teaching a full load and totally unrealistic to expect it to occur after a team has actually begun to work with students. If a team is to be properly organized the planning should be done on pressure-free "release time." Although release time during the course of a school year may be sufficient, a significant period of summer planning time can contribute a great deal to the success of a team.

After a team has begun to function much day-to-day planning must take place. The planning of truly flexible grouping (with students grouped and regrouped according to their needs, interests, or abilities), the creation of instructional materials and the planning of instruction are very time consuming if done properly. Team activities must be evaluated and future activities planned. When insufficient planning time is provided, the teachers are forced to settle for less than what they would normally believe to be the proper approach to instruction. More often than not this means too much reliance on large-group lecturing. Frequently the scheduling becomes much too rigid. When team teachers do not have enough planning time they simply cannot capitalize on the inherent advantages of team teaching. Team teachers must have a common planning time so they can work together on virtually a daily basis. If planning time cannot be made available during the day, after school time, at the very least, must be kept free for planning.

Periodically, (possibly every summer) teaching teams should be provided with release time to evaluate and, if necessary, change the operation and curriculum of the team and to evaluate and create instructional materials.

Sufficient planning time is vital to the success of a team. If a team does not have adequate planning time or if the members of the team do not devote the necessary time to planning, the team will fail.

A critical factor in the failure of some teams is often the nature of the people selected to be on the team. All teachers are not qualified by virtue of their experience, temperament, or attitude to be members of a teaching team. Team teaching is decidedly different from teaching in the self-contained classroom and, therefore, team teaching requires a special kind of teacher. As mutual evaluation of instruction is an important aspect of team teaching, the members of a team must observe one another teach and, more important, they must be willing to give and accept constructive criticism without ill-feeling. They must respect one another and be able to work together in harmony. This requires much more than the ability merely to "get along" with one another. As constant change is an important aspect of team teaching, the teachers must be flexible. The members of a teaching team must be willing to spend the extra time and effort required of real team teaching. Team teachers find themselves in a variety of instructional situations. As all teachers are not equally capable of performing all the teaching tasks required of a teaching team, the members of a team must possess complementary backgrounds, interests, and teaching skills. To take an obvious example, if all members of a team would prefer to be large group lecturers and none enjoys small group activities, friction and failure may result.

Many teachers prefer the self-contained classroom to team teaching because they feel they can create a more intimate relationship with their students in the self-contained classroom. This kind of relationship can develop in team teaching, although unfortunately it often does not. Teachers who are convinced that an optimum student-teacher relationship can be obtained *only* in the self-contained classroom should not participate in team teaching.

Only teachers sincerely interested in at least giving team teaching a fair trial should be selected for teaching teams. Certainly no teacher should be assigned to a team against his will or, as more commonly occurs, no teacher should be cajoled into team teaching. Team teaching demands too much of teachers. Reluctant or antagonistic team members can and usually do cause teaching teams to fail.

A teaching team must have continuity to insure a smooth operation. If a team has a high rate of turnover, continuity will be lost. Therefore, teachers with a high probability of remaining with a team for a significant period of time should be selected. However, as absolutely no turnover may inhibit the infusion of new ideas and insights, some provision must be made to bring new teachers into existing teams from time-to-time.

The members of a teaching team must be chosen with care if a team is to be successful. The teachers must collectively possess a balance of experience, interest, insight, patience, and ability. They must understand and accept what will be required of them in team teaching or they should not become involved in team teaching.

Poor leadership often contributes to the failure of a teaching team. *A teaching team cannot function successfully without good leadership* any more than a school or an athletic team can be successful without good leadership. Many educators believe leadership will ultimately "evolve" or "emerge" from any social group and, extending this to team teaching, they believe that out of a group of teachers selected to be members of a team, a team leader will ultimately evolve. To a certain extent this is true. However, in team teaching leadership may evolve out of the wreckage of the team. Because the first year of operation is usually difficult and always critical, a team requires good leadership from the very beginning and cannot afford the luxury of waiting for a leader to "emerge." A team leader should be formally designated (either through election by the team or by administrative appointment) and given sufficient authority and time to expedite and coordinate the activities of the team. *All successful teaching teams are built on a foundation of good leadership.*

SOME ADDITIONAL FACTORS

Inadequate physical facilities, instructional materials, or other resources can cause the failure of a team as readily as any of the factors mentioned above. Some of the current literature on team teaching indicates that special facilities are not required for team teaching. In my judgment this is not very realistic. Team teaching *does* require special facilities as well as a different attitude toward the use of available space. Team teachers require flexibility for small group activities and large group instruction. A teaching team must have an adequate place for large group instruction, and, just as important, at least as many small group teaching stations as there are team members. To be truly flexible the team must have control of its instructional facilities. For example, large group instruction should take place when and as often as it is needed and not just when the facilities are available. Instructional facilities must be adequately equipped. A teaching team should have its own planning area. The best physical facilities will not automatically guarantee the success of a teaching team, but inadequate facilities will definitely contribute to its failure.

The building principal has an important role to play in the success of a teaching team simply because a successful team usually cannot be established or maintained without his continual, enthusiastic support—mere acquiescence is insufficient. It is the principal's responsibility to see that the team has the time and the resources to be successful. In particular, if he does not provide his teachers with sufficient planning time, the team will contribute far less than it should and may even fail. The principal must make sure that his entire faculty understands the nature and purpose of the team. If team teachers are valued more highly than others simply because they are team teachers or if the team becomes a public relations device, faculty harmony will be reduced and the entire school program may suffer.

All too frequently adverse parent reaction arising out of ignorance of the nature and the purpose of team teaching has contributed to the failure of the team. Parents should understand the nature of team teaching and particularly that the main purpose of team teaching is to improve instruction for their children. A carefully planned parent orientation program conducted *before* a team goes into operation will prevent problems from arising and will elicit support for the team.

The organization of a teaching team is not a step to be taken lightly.

Teachers and administrators who expect the benefits of team teaching must be willing to pay the price good team teaching demands. Good team teaching is a solution to many, but certainly not all, of the problems we face in our schools today. Team teaching can be rewarding and enjoyable for all involved if the members of the team understand what they are trying to accomplish and are given the time and means to accomplish their objectives. Poor team teaching can harm children, frustrate teachers, alienate parents, and destroy staff morale. There is no justification for establishing a team if it is predestined to fail.

PART FOUR

Various Aspects of Grouping Pupils

Heathers' statement in Part I that grouping may have its epitaph written by the one who does the section on grouping in the next edition of the *Encyclopedia of Educational Research* not withstanding, grouping still remains a very important issue in the whole realm of educational organization.

Ability grouping, or classification of pupils for instructional purposes so that a relatively high degree of homogeneity exists within the group, has had a long and somewhat stormy history. The strong impact made by intelligence tests in the 1920s gave impetus to a popular movement to divide youngsters, at any given grade level, into individual classrooms based on the similarity of IQ score. However, confusion set in rather quickly. The terms homogeneous groups and ability groups took on synonymous meanings. Frequently, these terms are still used interchangeably.

Homogeneous grouping based on IQ scores

alone seems to have passed from the educational scene. Much evidence can be adduced to show that intelligence tests alone are not sufficiently reliable measures on which to base solid unchangeable groups. Additional evidence can also be presented to show that homogeneous grouping does not always make greater provision for individual differences, nor does it reduce the range of actual accomplishment in each grade. It is generally conceded that grouping students on the basis of one ability reduces the class range of that ability alone to some extent, but that complete heterogeneity in many other areas will still exist.

In addition to the problems of arriving at greater precision in establishing ability or homogeneous groups, the whole question of whether or not this type of grouping "squares" with democratic principles is at issue.

Despite the research which, for the most part, indicates that homogeneous grouping based solely on IQ score or reading ability does not in fact yield homogeneity, there still remain vast areas of disagreement among educators. The readings in this section reflect in some measure a paucity of relevant research. Yet, there is now a renewed interest in homogeneous grouping. The question arises as to whether or not, in view of the lack of research, this practice is defensible. However, the summary of arguments, whether empirically established or just hypothetical, are set forth here in the hope that the so-called advantages and disadvantages of ability, partial ability, and homogeneous grouping plans will emerge more clearly in the reader's mind as he approaches this section of readings.

The advantages claimed are that:

- Each child is challenged at his own level and therefore has a real chance to succeed.

- Enrichment fails in heterogeneous grouping because the teachers do not have time for the one or two really bright students, but in homogeneous grouping the teacher is able to care more adequately for all individuals since the total range of the class is somewhat reduced.

- Children have an opportunity to compete successfully, both academically and socially, and the average and slow students have a chance to become leaders in their own groups.

- It is easier for the teacher to teach successfully since there will be fewer groups within the class for skill subjects, and the groups themselves will be made up of students of nearly equal ability.

- Children naturally make friends with others who have similar intellectual ability.

- In real life situations we do not find the barber competing with the chemist but rather with other barbers, and, consequently, it seems more true to life to have children compete with those somewhat nearer their own level.

- Because the teacher has fewer groups to prepare she does a better job.

The disadvantages claimed are that:

- Dividing children into three groups cuts the range of differences by only about one fifth, and most groups are still far more heterogeneous than teachers and administrators realize.

- Regardless of how homogeneous the group is in the beginning, if the instruction is effective the group becomes more and more heterogeneous.

- There is a tendency for the higher ability group to be composed of children from the higher socioeconomic level.

- Children in the lower ability class feel stigmatized and are aware that they are considered slow, dull, or dumb.

- Parents resent their child being assigned to a slow group.

- Many teachers dislike working with the slow group and lack the preparation for dealing with the special learning problems they encounter in that group.

- Children in the "smart" group are aware of their distinction and may become self-satisfied and conceited.

- Often there is a lack of data to allow for successfully grouping pupils.

- Uneven growth patterns and uneven social and academic profiles make homogeneous grouping difficult.

- There has been no conclusive evidence through research that ability grouping leads to improved mastery of subject matter.

- When it is school-wide or intraclass, it limits flexibility.

This list of advantages and disadvantages can only take on meaning as one views the studies from which these points of view are derived.

In the article by Karnes and others, a report is made of a study that investigated the efficacy of placing a small proportion of gifted underachievers in homogeneous classes with high achievers and comparing them with underachieving intellectually gifted children who were placed with children in heterogeneous classrooms. The researchers hypothesized that by placing the underachievers in homogeneous classes with high achievers, it would stimulate them to raise their level of achievement, become more creative, and perceive their peers and parents as being more accepting of them. Their findings suggested that this administrative plan had some merit because it did achieve precisely these results. These findings are in some ways contradistinctive to those that have engendered the great debate over whether we should group homogeneously or not. With the recent research on the concept of the self-fulfilling prophecy (that teachers tend to teach according to their expectations of the class and in fact derive results similar to those expectations), the question of homogeneous grouping both at the low and the high levels becomes a very crucial one to address.

Olsen in his article disagrees with the attempts at homogeneity in grouping. Rather, he looks for a greater approach to individuality in the hope that diagnostic and prescriptive teaching might result in an environment wherein pupils could all reach and realize their own potentialities.

Ogletree, in reflecting on homogeneous ability grouping, British style, offers us some reactions to what for many years has been the streaming process which has been calculated to create a defacto segregation by social class in the British schools. In many ways the reform that is taking place in England, reports Ogletree, is a class power struggle. We should give pause as we think of "tracking" or "streaming" ourselves. These methods of grouping are often too apparent in our schools. What kind of society may this lead to, or indeed, has this already led to in some of the tracking programs found in the city schools of our nation?

Pfeiffer offers a piece of excellent research concerning the verbal interaction and the achievement of cognitive goals on the part of the teacher and the child when placed in ability-grouped classes in English. She found that teachers did not differentiate their patterns of teacher-pupil verbal interactions in classes of different levels of ability. The one great finding she offers is that conflict of results in research may be directly attributable to the fact that teachers who have said they adapt their ability to the group really, in fact, do not. This discrepancy or dissonance between action and perception may contribute to the controversial results in any study on grouping. To Pfeiffer this means researchers must be aware of the problem and that it must be given a closer look.

The short piece relating the pros and cons of various aspects of ability grouping from the *N.E.A. Research Bulletin* and the Shane annotated list sum up this section for the reader who is looking for a careful analysis of what has existed in the whole area of grouping in general in the schools to date.

The Shane list represents an updating of the annotated list of grouping plans taken from his original article, "Grouping in the Elementary School" (*Phi Delta Kappan,* Vol. 41, April 1960, pp. 313–319), which appeared in the first edition of this book. "An Annotated List of 40 Grouping Plans" (March 1970) appears for the first time in print here by kind permission of Dr. Harold Shane. It brings to the reader a resource of definitions and concepts that will aid him in seeing the problems of grouping related to educational planning and growth over the past years. As Shane sums it up, it represents an impressive attestation to educators who, during more than a century, have attempted to come to grips with individuality.

15 | The Efficacy of Two Organizational Plans for Underachieving Intellectually Gifted Children

MERLE B. KARNES

GEORGE McCOY

RICHARD REID ZEHRBACH

JANET P. WOLLERSHEIM

HARVEY F. CLARIZIO

Reprinted from *Exceptional Children*, Vol. 29 (May 1963), pp. 438–446, by permission of the publisher and the authors.

The general area of concern in this study is that of raising the achievement of underachieving gifted children. The specific problem is that of assessing the relative efficacy of two approaches to improving the performance of gifted children whose present performance marks them as underachievers. One approach is that of placing a small number of underachieving gifted children in homogeneous classes with gifted children who are achieving at a level commensurate with their abilities. The other approach to be tested is that of placing underachieving children in heterogeneous classes made up of children with a wide range of intellectual abilities. Since motivation, habits, interests, and attitudes established at an early age tend to affect academic achievement in subsequent years, identification and treatment of young underachievers was deemed to be important. Thus, subjects chosen for the study were intellectually gifted underachievers at the elementary level.

In general, the hypotheses investigated in this study were that underachieving intellectually gifted children enrolled in homogeneous classes with high achieving intellectually gifted children would significantly raise their level of academic achievement, would manifest more creativity, and would perceive themselves as being better accepted by their peers and by their parents. Specifically, the following hypotheses were tested in this study:

1. Underachieving gifted pupils enrolled in homogeneous classes would make greater academic gains relative to expectancy than underachieving gifted pupils enrolled in heterogeneous classes.

2. Underachieving gifted pupils enrolled in homogeneous classes would make greater gains in creativity than underachieving gifted pupils enrolled in heterogeneous classes.

3. Underachieving gifted pupils enrolled in homogeneous classes would manifest greater gains in perceived acceptance by peers than underachieving gifted pupils enrolled in heterogeneous classes.

4. Underachieving gifted pupils enrolled in homogeneous classes would manifest greater gains in perceived parental acceptance and intrinsic valuation than underachieving gifted pupils enrolled in heterogeneous classes.

SUBJECTS

The subjects for this investigation were drawn from a pupil population of approximately 840, consisting of all pupils in attendance at two large elementary schools serving comparable and adjacent upper-middle class socioeconomic areas. A thorough screening procedure was conducted which utilized teacher nominations, group intelligence tests, group achievement tests and individually administered Stanford-Binet (1937, Form L) vocabulary tests. Following the screening, the 1937 Stanford-Binet Intelligence Scale was administered to 465 potential subjects. Appropriate forms of the California Achievement Tests were also given.

Approximately 27 pupils at each of the four grade levels in each of the elementary schools ($N = 223$) were found to have Stanford-Binet IQ's of 120 or higher. Individual grade placement scores in arithmetic and reading for each of these pupils were compared to the Horn formula (1941) corrected values for expected achievement in these areas [Reading $= (2 MA + CA)/3 - 5$; Arithmetic $= (MA + CA)/2 - 5$] to obtain achievement discrepancy scores in reading and arithmetic for each pupil. These two discrepancy scores were averaged for each pupil to obtain the pupil's average achievement discrepancy score. The average achievement discrepancy scores were plotted for each grade level and pupils whose achievement discrepancy was one standard deviation or more below the mean of children at their grade level were classified as underachievers.

Approximately five underachievers were identified in each of grades two, three, four and five at each of the two schools. During the following school year, identification and screening procedures were repeated with all pupils completing the first grade. New subjects ($N = 10$) thus identified at both schools were added to the experimental ($N = 5$) and control ($N = 5$) groups. The subjects for this study, then, consisted of 25 underachieving gifted pupils placed in homogeneous classes with intellectually gifted pupils who were high achievers, and 23 underachieving gifted pupils placed in heterogeneous classes with pupils of varied intellectual ability. (Two subjects moved from the community and thus were dropped from the study.)

At the beginning of the 1959–1960 school year, the gifted pupils in one school were placed in homogeneous classes. Teachers assigned to these gifted homogeneous classes were picked randomly from all teachers regularly assigned to that school. At the other school, the gifted pupils were randomly interspersed among the several heterogeneous classes at their grade level. Regardless of treatment the classes to which the children were assigned were approximately equal in size. All subjects had been in the study a minimum of two years and a maximum of three years.

A summary of the characteristics of the two groups of subjects is presented in Tables 1 and 2.

The two groups, as shown in Table 1, did not differ significantly with respect to boy-girl ratio or chronological age. They did differ, however, with respect to measured intelligence ($p < .05$).

The two groups, as noted in Table 2, did not differ significantly with respect to socioeconomic status as indicated by fathers' occupations ($p = .34$).

PROCEDURE

Instructional materials, curricular offerings and various types of services, such as those of the school consultant for gifted pupils, were made available equally to both schools participating in the study. The treatment of the two groups of subjects differed only in that the subjects were placed either in homogeneous classes whose members had all been identified as intellectually gifted or in heterogeneous classes whose members had intellectual ability ranging from dull-normal to gifted.

Initially, measures of perceived parent attitudes, perceived peer rela-

TABLE 1
Characteristics of Underachieving Subjects

	Homogeneous	Heterogeneous	Statistical Significance of Difference between Groups
N	25	23	
N of Boys	19	14	$\chi^2 = .67; p = .40$
N of Girls	6	9	
Mean CA	11.0	11.0	$t = 0.00; p = .99$
Mean IQ	144.8	135.8	$t = 2.11; p = .04$
SD of CA	1.43	1.36	
SD of IQ	17.23	11.24	

TABLE 2
Father's Occupation as an Index of Socioeconomic Status

Class *	1	2	3	4	5	6 and 7
Homogeneous	12	5	4	2	2	0
Heterogeneous	6	5	2	3	6	0

* Classified according to Warner's Revised Scale for Rating Occupation (1949). Median test yields $\chi^3 = .95$; $p = .34$. The numbers represent categories of decreasing status, with 1 being the category of highest status.

tionships, and academic achievement were obtained from all subjects in grades two, three, four, and five. Thereafter, these measures were obtained from each new group of subjects entering the second grade. Posttests of achievement were administered to all subjects in all grades at the end of each school year. In addition, post measures of perceived parent attitudes and perceived peer relationships were made after the children had been in the project for two or three years. Creativity tests were administered initially to the fourth and fifth grade subjects the first year of the study and again when these subjects were in the sixth grade ($N_{Homo.} = 10$; $N_{Het.} = 9$). Creativity tests were not administered to second and third grade subjects because of their limited ability to respond in writing.

MEASURING INSTRUMENTS

An appropriate level of the California Achievement Tests was used to determine the subjects' level of achievement in reading and arithmetic. Perceived parental attitudes were ascertained by the Perceived Parents Attitude Scale developed by Ausubel, Balthazar, Rosenthal, Blackman,

Schpoont and Welkowitz (1954). The subjects' perceived peer acceptance was measured by the Perceived Peer Relationships Scale as described in a study of overachieving and underachieving gifted pupils carried out by the Champaign Schools. Creative ability was evaluated by tests of creativity used by Wollersheim (1960). The tests of creative ability were entitled the *Unusual Uses* and the *Consequences* tests. A fluency score and a flexibility score are obtained from the *Unusual Uses* test. These two scores measure ideational fluency and spontaneous flexibility respectively. The *Consequences* test yields an obvious score which also measures ideational fluency and a remote score which is an index of originality. Thus, the three abilities of fluency, flexibility, and originality which have been found to be involved in creative ability (Guilford, 1950) were sampled.

RESULTS

The analysis of the differences between the two groups of subjects on the variables investigated was complicated by the unexpected finding that the subjects in the homogeneously grouped classes had a higher mean IQ than did the subjects in the heterogeneously grouped classes. Consequently, the academic achievement manifested by the two groups was compared by using achievement discrepancy scores to correct for differences in IQ. Changes in achievement were compared by subtracting the preachievement discrepancy score from the postachievement discrepancy score. Changes in the two groups in the areas of creative ability, perceived parental attitudes and perceived peer relationships were analyzed in terms of the gain scores.[1] The possibility remains that the subjects in the homogeneous group, because they had greater learning ability, might be expected to make greater gains in the areas of creative ability, perceived parental attitudes and perceived peer relationships. The literature shows, however, that the relationship between creativity and IQ is negligible in groups of children whose IQ's are 120 or above. Furthermore, the relationship of intelligence to perceived parental attitudes and perceived peer relationships also appears to be negligible.

Since it was hypothesized that the subjects in the homogeneous group would manifest greater gains when compared to the subjects in the heterogeneous groups, one-tailed values of significance were used in the interpretation of the statistical tests of the differences between the groups. Only those values which would occur by chance less than once in 20 times ($p = .05$) were considered as representing statistically significant differences. The data comparing the two groups of subjects following treatment are presented in Table 3.

[1] A subsequent analysis of covariance in which differences in IQ were controlled yielded results essentially identical with those herein reported.

TABLE 3
Analysis of Data on Underachievers in Regular and Special Classes [a]

| | Homogeneous | | | Heterogeneous | | | | |
	Mean	SD	N	Mean	SD	N	F [b]	t [c]
Achievement Discp. Score	1.19	.78	25	.67	.89	23	1.30	2.17 *
Per. Par. Attitude Score	4.36	13.34	25	−3.5	20.43	22	2.35 *	1.73 *
Per. Peer Rel. Score	−.76	9.17	25	−1.5	13.49	22	2.16	.21
Creativity Scores								
Fluency	14.0	6.27	10	6.4	8.50	9	1.84	2.23 *
Flexibility	8.2	3.81	10	5.7	4.75	9	1.54	1.27
Obvious	6.1	11.06	10	3.2	6.27	9	3.11	.70
Remote	3.3	5.77	10	3.0	2.87	9	4.03 *	.15

$* = p < .05$
[a] Analysis involved gains obtained by contrasting pretest and posttest measures.
[b] F test contrasting the variances of the two groups.
[c] t test contrasting the means of the two groups.

DISCUSSION

Academic Achievement

It was expected that the academic achievement of the subjects in the homogeneous group would be higher than that of the subjects in the heterogeneous group since the subjects in the homogeneous group would have access to a greater concentration of stimulating ideas and interests and would be under more pressure to aspire to higher goals and standards than would the subjects in the heterogeneous group. Although the expectation that the subjects in the homogeneous classes would have higher academic achievement than would the subjects in the heterogeneous classes was confirmed, the interpretation of this finding was confounded by differences between the two groups that occurred when additional groups of second grade subjects were added in the longitudinal study.

The result of the addition of the second grade subjects was that the mean IQ of the subjects in the homogeneous group became significantly higher than the mean IQ of the heterogeneous group. This was not true the first year of the study. In addition, the subjects in the homogeneous group had a higher mean achievement score (grade 4.4) than did the subjects in the heterogeneous group (grade 4.2). The difference between these mean achievement scores, however, was not statistically significant $(p = .74)$.

The influence of the difference in the learning ability of the subjects in the two groups was expected to be the most pronounced with respect to comparisons of the academic achievement, since IQ and achievement tests scores are highly correlated. A procedure making use of achievement discrepancy score differences was used in an attempt to correct for the influence of learning ability in contributing to the academic achievement of the subjects in the two groups. When the difference in the learning ability of the subjects was so controlled, the mean achievement discrepancy gain score ($\overline{X}=.19$) of the subjects in the homogeneous group was higher than that of the subjects in the heterogeneous group ($\overline{X}=.67$). The difference between the mean achievement discrepancy gain scores of the two groups of subjects was statistically significant ($p<.05$).[2] The finding of higher academic achievement on the part of the subjects in the homogeneous group seems to reflect, with a reasonable degree of certainty, the influence of differences in the treatment afforded the two groups of subjects.

It is possible that the greater gains in achievement made by the subjects in the homogeneous group could have resulted from the higher intellectual ability of this group. The achievement gains of the two groups were compared, however, by gains in achievement discrepancy scores, a procedure which allows for the gain in academic achievement according to achievement expected on the basis of individual learning ability. This procedure would seem to minimize the influence of differences in intellectual ability.

The findings with regard to achievement can be interpreted as being similar to the finding of Dreyer (1953) and Hochbaum (1953) who found that individuals will seek to change their level of performance to agree more with that of the group. This tendency has been found to be more evident in groups made up of persons of homogeneous abilities or opinions, however, than in groups made up of persons of varied ability or opinion (Festinger and Gerard, 1952; and Dreyer, 1953). The possibility also exists that teachers of the homogeneous groups may have changed their teaching behavior in accordance with the advanced interests and cognitive development displayed by the gifted children. There were, however, no measures of changes in teacher behavior included in this study to test such a possibility.

Creative Ability

It was hypothesized that the subjects in the homogeneously grouped classes would manifest a higher degree of creative ability than would the subjects in the heterogeneously grouped classes because the degree of stimulation was assumed to be greater in the homogeneously grouped classes. Creative ability was measured by the subjects' performance in the areas of ideational fluency, ideational flexibility, and originality of thought. The two groups differed significantly on two of the four initial measures of creativity (flexibility and originality). Accordingly, the inves-

---

[2] An analysis of covariance yielded essentially the same findings.

tigation of the differences between the creative ability of the subjects in the two groups was made by evaluating the gains evidenced between pretest and posttest measures of creativity. The differential gains of the two groups in creative ability are considered to be a function of the differences in treatments afforded the subjects in the two groups.

As was hypothesized, the difference in the gain scores of the creativity measures indicated that the subjects in the homogeneously grouped classes had attained a higher degree of ability on certain of the creativity factors than had the subjects in the heterogeneously grouped classes. On the factor of fluency, the subjects in the homogeneous group had a mean difference score of 14.0 and subjects in the heterogeneous group had a mean difference score of 6.4 ($p<.05$). With respect to the factor of flexibility, the subjects in the homogeneous group had a mean difference score of 8.2 while the subjects in the heterogeneous group had a mean difference score of 5.7 ($p=.11$). For the obvious score, which also measures fluency, the subjects in the homogeneous group had a mean difference score of 6.1 while the subjects in the heterogeneous group had a mean difference score of 3.2 ($p=.23$); and for the originality factor, represented by the remote score, the subjects in the homogeneous group had a mean difference score of 3.3 while the subjects in the heterogeneous group had a mean difference score of 3.0 ($p=.42$). The finding that the subjects in the homogeneous group manifested higher gains on the creative ability factors than did the subjects in the heterogeneous group, with a statistically significant difference on the factor of fluency, seems to reflect the more favorable influences accruing from placement in the homogeneously grouped classes. These differences were found despite the fact that measures of creativity were available on only a small number of subjects ($N=19$) and that the subjects had only two years of differential treatment. It seems likely that a greater number of subjects may reveal even greater differences between the two groups.

Perceived Parental Attitudes

It was hypothesized that the subjects in the homogeneous group, when compared to the subjects in the heterogeneous group, would see themselves as more accepted and more intrinsically valued by their parents. The initial measures of perceived parental attitudes showed that the subjects in the heterogeneous group had a higher mean score (139.0) than did the subjects in the homogeneous group (136.4). Although the subjects in the heterogeneous group thus appeared to see themselves as more accepted and intrinsically valued by their parents than did the subjects in the homogeneous group, the difference between the two groups was not statistically significant ($p=.58$). After two years of treatment, however, measures of perceived parental attitudes revealed a mean net increase of +4.36 for the subjects in the homogeneous group while there was a mean net decrease of -3.5 for the subjects in the heterogeneous group. The difference between the mean net gain scores was statistically significant ($p = .05$), indicating that subjects in the homogeneous classes saw themselves as more accepted and intrinsically valued by their parents.

It must be recognized that the change in perceived parental attitudes could have been fostered by the parents of the subjects being made aware of the "intellectually gifted" nature of their children. Since parents of subjects in both the homogeneous and the heterogeneous groups were informed of this attribute of their children in the same way and at the same time, this explanation does not seem adequate for accounting for the observed differences in perceived parental attitudes. There is the possibility that the parents' perception of the pupils as "intellectually gifted" was differentially reinforced with respect to the two groups of subjects, since pupils in the homogeneous groups were placed in "special" classes. It is likely that special class placement proved to be a topic of interest in parent-school-centered activities and groups. The scope of this study did not provide specific measures relevant to this issue which appear to warrant additional investigation.

Perceived Peer Relationships of Subjects in Homogeneous and Heterogeneous Groups

Although perceived peer relationships, like perceived parental relationships, were conceptualized within the framework of this study as being more indirectly related to changes in capacity for making use of intellectual ability, it was hypothesized that the subjects in the homogeneous group would see themselves as more accepted by their classmates after treatment when compared with the subjects in the heterogeneous group. This hypothesis grew out of the expectation that the subjects in the homogeneous group would be more likely to attain a higher degree of academic achievement and the associated successes in meeting goals and standards held by their classmates would propitiously influence these pupils' perceptions of being accepted by their peers.

In the initial measures of perceived peer acceptance, it was found that the subjects in the homogeneous group had a slightly higher degree of perceived peer acceptance (mean = 119.9) than did the subjects in the heterogeneous group (mean = 113.5). This initial difference between the mean perceived peer acceptance scores was not statistically significant ($p = .08$). Contrary to the expected change, the net gains in perceived peer acceptance after two years of treatment were in a negative direction for both groups. The mean gain for the subjects in the homogeneous group was $-.76$ and the mean gain in perceived peer acceptance for the subjects in the heterogeneous group was -1.5. The difference between the mean gain scores of the two groups of subjects was not statistically significant ($p = .40$). Although the loss in perceived peer acceptance was less for those subjects in the homogeneous than for those subjects in the heterogeneous group, the failure of the subjects in the homogeneous group to manifest a higher degree of perceived peer acceptance, especially in the light of their having a higher degree of academic achievement, is puzzling. The finding that the subjects in both groups evidenced a drop in degree of perceived peer acceptance, however, may not be too surprising in view of the low degree of peer acceptance which seems to characterize underachievers as a group.

The data obtained in this study after a minimum of two years of treatment do not support the expectation that underachieving gifted pupils placed in a homogeneous class will have a higher degree of perceived peer acceptance.

Although it was not possible to verify the hypothesis regarding perceived peer acceptance at this stage of the study, it is possible that significant differences in perceived peer relationships may become manifest after a longer treatment period. Although neither group made gains with respect to perceived peer acceptance, it is reassuring to note that gifted underachievers placed in homogeneous classes are able to achieve more academically without appreciably sacrificing their social status.

Representativeness of Findings

This study has compared the influence of placement in homogeneously grouped and heterogeneously grouped classes upon the academic achievement, creative ability, perceived parental attitudes, and perceived peer relationships of two groups of underachieving, academically gifted, elementary school pupils. The subjects were of superior intellectual ability and came from higher white socioeconomic backgrounds. The two groups did not differ significantly as to boy-girl ratio.

The finding that placement in homogeneously grouped classes is conducive to higher academic achievement and higher creative performance is confounded by the fact that the subjects in the homogeneously grouped classes had a higher degree of intellectual ability. The association of special class placement with a higher degree of perceived parental acceptance and intrinsic evaluation may apply only to intellectually gifted underachievers from higher socioeconomic levels where educational achievement is highly valued. The influence of such treatment upon perceived peer acceptance is not clear.

IMPLICATIONS

• Early identification of the underachievers at the elementary levels, as early as the first grade, and placement of these underachievers in homogeneous classes with high achievers seems to be desirable. In addition, although a well developed screening program is needed to identify the intellectually gifted who are achieving, even more precise procedures for identifying the underachievers at a young age are needed.

• The complex problems of the underachieving intellectually gifted suggest the need for a well developed in-service training program for administrators and teachers.

• Since creativity is associated with academic achievement and since the underachievers in homogeneous classes were found to be more fluent after two or more years in homogeneous classes, it is suggested that creativity among underachievers may be fostered by placing these children with others of like intellectual potential and high achievement. Teachers should be aware of the high positive relationship between creativity and achievement, and thus encourage and reward creative expression.

SUMMARY

This study investigated the efficacy of placing a small proportion of gifted underachievers in homogeneous classes with high achievers, as compared with placing underachieving intellectually gifted children in heterogeneous classes. It was hypothesized that placing underachievers in a homogeneous class with high achievers would stimulate the underachievers to raise their level of achievement, become more creative, and perceive their peers and parents as being more accepting of them.

Intellectually gifted subjects in grades two through five were selected from two large elementary schools. A total of 223 pupils were identified who obtained an intelligence quotient of 120 or above on the 1937 Stanford-Binet. Achievement grade expectancies in reading and arithmetic as determined by the Horn formula (1941) were then compared with corresponding achievement test scores. Pupils whose average achievement discrepancies deviated -1 SD or more from the mean of their group were designated as underachievers. Approximately five underachievers at each grade level were placed in homogeneous classes with high achieving gifted children and five underachievers at the same grade levels were placed in heterogeneous classes with children of varying intellectual levels. The following year five additional second grade subjects were added to each group. After a treatment period of from two to three years, data obtained from all subjects were analyzed.

The subject's achievement, perception of parental attitudes, perception of peer acceptance, and creative ability were studied.

Analysis of the data was confounded by differences in IQ between the two groups. Consequently, statistical techniques designed to correct for this confounding were utilized.

Hypothesis 1: Achievement

It was hypothesized that intellectually gifted pupils enrolled in homogeneous classes would make greater gains relative to academic expectancy than underachieving intellectually gifted pupils enrolled in heterogeneous classes. The difference in gains in achievement between the gifted underachievers in homogeneous classes and gifted underachievers in heterogeneous classes, corrected for IQ difference, was statistically significant ($p = .02$). Hence, the hypothesis was accepted.

Hypothesis 2: Creativity

It was hypothesized that intellectually gifted underachievers placed in homogeneous classes would manifest greater gains in creativity than intellectually gifted underachievers enrolled in heterogeneous classes. Although underachieving gifted pupils in homogeneous classes did manifest higher mean scores on all four creativity tests than did underachieving gifted pupils enrolled in heterogeneous classes, the differences reached statistical significance only in the area of the fluency score (fluency, $p = <.05$; obvious, $p = .23$; remote, $p = .42$; flexibility, $p = .11$). Thus, the hypothesis was given only partial confirmation by the data.

Hypothesis 3: Perceived Peer Acceptance

It was hypothesized that intellectually gifted underachievers placed in homogeneous classes would manifest greater gains in perceived peer acceptance than would underachieving intellectually gifted pupils placed in heterogeneous classes. This expectation was not substantiated ($p = .40$). Analysis of the data did not support the hypothesis and, in fact, both groups decreased in perceived peer acceptance.

Hypothesis 4: Perceived Parent Attitudes

It was hypothesized that underachieving intellectually gifted pupils placed in homogeneous classes would manifest greater gains in perceived acceptance and intrinsic valuation by their parents than would underachieving intellectually gifted pupils placed in heterogeneous classes.

The difference between the two groups was statistically significant ($p = .05$). This hypothesis was accepted.

The findings of this study suggest the administrative plan for improving academic achievement among the intellectually gifted underachievers by placing them in homogeneous classes with high achievers has some merit since it appears to foster increased achievement, improved perceptions of parent-child relationships, and improved creativity.

REFERENCES

Ausubel, D. P., Balthazar, B. B., Rosenthal, Irene, Blackman, L. S., Schpoont, S. H., and Welkowitz, Joan. Perceived parent attitudes as determinants of children's ego structure. *Child Developm.,* 1954, 25, 173–183.

Dreyer, A. S. Behavior in a level of aspiration situation as affected by group comparison. Unpublished doctoral thesis. Univ. of Minn., 1953.

Festinger, L. and Gerard, H. B. The influence process in the presence of extreme deviates. *Hum. Relat.,* 1952, 5, 327–346.

French, J. L. *Educating the gifted.* New York: Holt, Rinehart and Winston, Inc., 1959.

Guilford, J. P. Creativity. *Amer. Psychol.,* 1950, 5, 444–454.

Hochbaum, G. M. Certain personality aspects and pressures to uniformity in social groups. Unpublished doctoral thesis. Univ. of Minn., 1953.

Horn, Alice. Uneven distribution of the effects of specific factors. *Educ. Monogr.,* Univ. of Southern California, 12, 1941.

Horney, Karen. *The neurotic personality of our time.* New York: W. W. Norton & Company, Inc., 1936.

Wollersheim, Janet P. The relationship between creative ability and over and underachievement among gifted children. Unpublished masters thesis. St. Louis Univ., 1960.

16 | Should We Group by Ability?

JIM OLSEN

Reprinted with permission from *Journal of Teacher Education*, Vol. 18, No. 2 (Summer 1967), pp. 201–205.

To a very large extent, ability or homogeneous grouping based on intelligence and/or achievement scores is still widely practiced in the public schools of this country (8). This practice rests on the assumption that bright children learn more when they are separated from their slower peers and grouped for instructional purposes with other bright children. We assume that when we place together children who are more nearly alike in achievement and intelligence the instruction they receive will thereby be more individualized. The argument for ability grouping is that if we narrow the range of ability and achievement within an individual class we can increase the quantity and quality of learning in that class.

Today, the validity of this hypothesis is a major issue, not only because it affects the organization of the schools and the kinds of social and intellectual experiences to which students are exposed but also because the practice of ability grouping involves broad social questions. With the busing of children, the locating of many new schools in border areas, and the redefining of neighborhood boundaries, we can be assured that in the immediate future our students will have heterogeneous backgrounds socially, racially, and intellectually. If we look at the issue of ability grouping from a social standpoint, therefore, it takes on a new and important significance.

I think that most teachers and administrators would agree that when a child is confined to a particular ability group he is committed, whether we like to admit it or not, to an education of a very definite caliber. The student who has been placed in a slow class quickly learns that he is in the "stupid" class. In a study investigating the effects of ability grouping on the self-concept of 102 fifth-grade children who had been grouped throughout their school career, Maxine Mann found that, when the children in the lowest group were asked why they were in this particular class, they replied: "I'm too dumb," "I can't think good," "We aren't smart," "We don't think good," etc. Apparently these children felt they were intellectually inferior; any negative feelings they had of themselves as learners when they entered school were simply reinforced by their grouping assignments (17). An analogous study made by Abraham and Edith Luchins of 190 sixth-grade children in a New York City school came up with the same evidence (15).

There is also overwhelming sociological evidence that ability grouping offers a way in which we can create *de facto* segregation in the classroom after we have integration of the schools (20). Low-income children are almost always assigned to the lower-ranking groups, and upper-income children to higher-ranking groups. This is mainly because the lower-income child comes to school with many cultural disadvantages, such as lack of readiness for reading, lack of school know-how, etc., with the result that he gets a low score on the middle-class-biased IQ test (20). Even though we know that these tests do not measure native ability (6), we are still using them to categorize students into low, average, and superior classes. And we do this in spite of the fact that we know that intelligence is not a static entity, genetically predetermined, and that a child's environment and schooling have a profound effect on his mental functioning. As long as educational and social opportunities are unequal, test results will be unequal; yet, through these tests, educators help to strengthen the segregation and class barriers they profess must be overcome.

When students are placed or segregated into ability groups, an intellectual ghetto is created which parallels the social ghetto from which they come, whether that ghetto be Park Avenue or Harlem. In the lower-ability groups, the teacher's expectations of the students' performance are inevitably lowered (7). How many teachers truly believe in the academic potential of students with low IQ's who are often, according to their standardized test scores, "retarded"? This set of expectations must necessarily affect the learning process. The child himself comes to accept his own intellectual inferiority: if the school authorities do not consider him to be very bright, are they not right? Thus students in the lower-ability groups or tracks develop a sense of intellectual inadequacy which they can carry with them for the rest of their lives.

There are other kinds of psychological reverberations for the students in the top classes. In the Luchins' study already cited, the top students admitted they felt snobbish and superior to students in the lower-ability classes. As the superior students put it, "People would think we were dumb if we played with dumbbells." Thus our schools help to perpetuate the social-class stratification that exists in the larger society.

In addition, the better teachers are usually assigned to the better classes, with the result that those children who most need the best teaching do not receive it. Inexperienced teachers are always most heavily concentrated in lower-income schools, and since seniority usually counts when class teaching assignments are made, experienced teachers get the higher-ability classes and the new, inexperienced teachers get the left-over assignments, or the lower-ability classes (20). It would seem that simple justice and common sense would dictate that the lower-ability classes would get the best teachers so that they would have the best teaching available to compensate for their academic deficiencies. But apparently this type of adjustment is not generally preferred.

In the face of the social and psychological price we pay for ability grouping, it is ironic that the research clearly indicates that ability grouping in itself does not improve achievement in children (5, 8, 9). Not only this, but bright children grouped according to ability and taught separately do *not* learn more. Ruth Ekstrom, in her review of the literature on experimental studies of homogeneous grouping, concluded that there is no consistent pattern for the effectiveness of homogeneous grouping by age, course content, or ability level (9). David Abramson's study bears out this point (1). In other words, the research generally shows no significant differences in school achievement because of ability or homogeneous grouping.

Why? IQ and standardized test scores do not provide a valid qualitative index of individual differences in instructional needs, abilities, motivational levels, or learning styles of pupils. We may group students according to intelligence, but any psychologist will tell you that two 110 IQ's on a Wechsler Intelligence Scale is an arithmetical accident because their scores represent different kinds of subtest scatters (5). Or take two students with the same reading score. One child may have excellent comprehension skills in spite of the fact that he is deficient in certain word attack skills. Another child, with the same score, may be competent in his word attack skills but be unable to read for main ideas; in other words, one student's liabilities may be the other's assets. Thus, even though these students have identical standardized test scores, their specific instructional needs are really quite different.

When we multiply these differences by the thirty or forty children in a classroom, we can readily see that our homogeneously grouped class is a statistical myth, not a pedagogic reality. In short, grouping does not solve the problem of meeting individual differences. Rather the practice of ability grouping actually militates against a true differentiation of teaching according to a student's need because we use it to rationalize what we really do in our schools: teach the class as an undifferentiated unit. We may talk about individualized differences, but the real differences in experimental background; academic abilities; verbal, perceptual, and auditory skills; differences in interests and in previous educational background are glossed over and ignored in daily classroom practice.

Soviet schools do not use either IQ tests (11) or ability grouping (12, 20); teachers feel that the use of IQ tests tends to retard the academic progress of students with low scores. Instead, in the Russian school, the child who finishes his work first helps the child who is having trouble with his lesson; and since the Russians feel that teaching is a very good way to learn, the child who teaches is not being penalized. But pupil cooperation and mutual help are not emphasized in American schools. Indeed, we seem to retreat in horror at the suggestion of other ways of meeting the problem of individual differences—of how we can adjust what we do in the classroom to each individual (18). Certainly, ability grouping does not solve this problem. What we must do is *construct a program which makes it possible for teachers to individualize instruction* on the following levels: the content of learning, the level of content, the kind of methodology, and the speed of learning.

Such a program will require the teacher to measure and diagnose continually so that the student can learn according to his needs. But the prime responsibility of the learning process will be on the student, not the teacher. Thus, the program would have self-teaching and self-directing aspects that would decrease the teacher's continual participation (team-learning techniques, for example, would be used); the learner would move at his own pace and in the direction of his interests and needs. In a classroom with this self-instructional emphasis, the teacher's role would be modified: he would initiate activities, work with individual students, diagnose, and supervise the over all direction of the learning process. Above all, he would teach pupils to teach themselves, and he would group and regroup students according to their special needs at a given time in a given content. Thus large-group instruction would be deemphasized and a methodology based on individual, team, and small-group learning would be employed.

Such a structured learning environment would make the practice of initiative and decision making on the part of students a reality rather than a fond dream. The focus of the program would not be, as it is now, upon the extrinsic reward of the mark or grade but upon the intrinsic rewards of the learning process. Students could risk behavior change; the teacher would be working *in conjunction with the student* and not in a judgmental capacity.

To create such an environment for learning is indeed a formidable task. But if we truly believe in our students' ability to grow and realize their potentialities, then I believe we must begin to break through the lockstep methods of grouping and the rigidities of the class lesson and make our programs adjustable to individual pupils rather than adjusting the pupils to the programs. In this way, perhaps we can begin to resolve some of the inconsistencies between what we say and what we, in fact, do.

REFERENCES

1. Abramson, David A. "The Effect of Ability Grouping in the High School upon Achievement in College." Doctor's thesis. School of Education, New York University, 1958.
2. ———. "The Effectiveness of Grouping for Students of High Ability." *Educational Research Bulletin* 38: 169–82; October 14, 1959.
3. Bettleheim, Bruno. "Segregation: New Style." *School Review* 66: 251–72; Autumn 1958.
4. Clark, Kenneth. "Disadvantaged Students and Discrimination." *The Search for Talent.* College Admissions 7. Princeton, N. J.: Educational Testing Service, 1960, pp. 12–19.
5. Cohen, S. Alan. "Reading: Large Issues, Specific Problems, and Possible Solutions." Paper given at meeting of Mobilization for Youth, 1964.
6. Davis, Allison. "Socio Economic Influence upon Children's Learning." Speech given at the Midcentury White House Conference on Children and Youth, Washington, D. C., December 5, 1950.
7. Deutsch, Martin. "Aspects of Ability Grouping." *Integrated Education* 2: 48–49; February–March 1964.
8. Eash, Maurice J. "Grouping: Some Implications from Research." Paper given at the ASCD Conference, October 1960.
9. Ekstrom, Ruth. *Experimental Studies of Homogeneous Grouping: A Review of the Literature.* Princeton, N. J.: Educational Testing Service, 1959.
10. Getzels, Jacob W., and Jackson, P. W. "The Meaning of Giftedness: An Examination of an Expanding Concept." *Phi Delta Kappan* 40: 75–77; November 1958.
11. Giles, G. G. T. "Why Soviet Teachers Oppose Intelligence Tests." *Anglo-Soviet Journal* 14: 1–13.
12. Grant, Nigel. *Soviet Education.* Baltimore, Md.: Penguin Books, 1964.
13. Henry, Jules. "Attitude Organization in Elementary Classrooms." *American Journal of Orthopsychiatry* 27: 117–33; January 1957.
14. Husen, Tortsen, and Svensson, N. E. "Pedagogic Milieu and Development of Intellectual Skills." *School Review* 68: 36–51; Spring 1960.
15. Luchins, A. S., and Luchins, E. H. "Children's Attitudes Toward Homogeneous Groupings." *Pedagogical Seminary and Journal of Genetic Psychology* 72: 3–9; March 1948.
16. MacKinnow, Donald W. "What Do We Mean by Talent and How Do We Test for It?" *The Search for Talent.* College Admissions 7. Princeton, N. J.: Educational Testing Service, 1960, pp. 20–29.
17. Mann, Maxine. "What Does Ability Grouping Do to the Self Concept?" *Childhood Education* 36: 357–60; April 1960.
18. Rabb, Herb. "Grouping in the Classroom." *Mobilization for Youth Newsletter* 2: 1; April 1964.
19. Rudd, W. G. A. "The Psychological Effect of Streaming by Attainment." *British Journal of Educational Psychology* 28: 47–60; February 1958.
20. Sexton, Patricia Cayo. *Education and Income: Inequalities of Opportunity in Our Public Schools.* New York: The Viking Press, 1961.

17 Homogeneous Ability Grouping— British Style

EARL OGLETREE

Reprinted with permission from *Peabody Journal of Education*, Vol. 47, No. 1 (July 1969), pp. 20–25.

Now what I want is facts. Teach these boys and girls nothing but facts. Facts alone are wanted in life. Plant nothing else and root out everything else. . . . Nothing else will be of service to them.[1]

This statement by Mr. Gradgrind in Charles Dickens' novel *Hard Times* in part reflects one of the necessary means that British education has used to attain and maintain its intellectual standards. These goals have been traditionally and firmly established by the eleven-plus, by the grammar school, and ultimately by the university. Not only have these standards determined the curriculum and methods, but also the beneficiaries.

In order to serve the highly selective university system, a sorting-out process has evolved over the past half century. This has resulted in a system of rigidly streamed primary schools, which, in turn, has tightened the links between the primary school organization, secondary achievement, and university entrance. The system is so firmly entrenched that only 50 percent of all English children are admitted to or request the eleven-plus tests. Of these, approximately only half succeed in gaining admittance to the grammar schools. And only 17 percent of all grammar school pupils go on to the university.[2] However, in recent years there has

---

[1] London: J. M. Dent and Fawcett Sons, Ltd., 1931.

[2] Charles L. Bereday, *Comparative Method of Education*. New York: Holt, Rinehart and Winston, Inc., 1964, p. 122.

been a revival of the discussion on the effects of streaming children in the primary school.

Streaming, which evolved as a means of accomplishing more efficient teaching of the varying individuals within a grade level, has spread to the majority of primary schools in England, Wales, and Scotland. Not until the recent Plowden Report has streaming really become a major issue. Although one of the main recommendations of the Report was to welcome unstreaming in the infant schools with the hope of it spreading to the junior schools, it has not had the impact of reducing the practice of streaming as some educationists had hoped. The percentage of junior schools employing streaming had not been reduced substantially. The latest figures show that 56–70 percent of the junior schools practice some form of streaming.[3] Slowly this figure is being reduced, but to what extent is not actually known. Some hopefully place the reduction at 17 percent, leaving 37–50 percent of the schools streamed.[3] The method of classifying the children into various streams is based on the infant school report and internal and external examinations. In a study conducted by Brian Jackson, it was found that most of the schools used the class teacher's recommendation nearly 80 percent of the time.[4] Fewer than half of the schools employed IQ tests. The headmaster with the consensus of the teaching staff determines whether a particular school will be streamed or unstreamed.

PRO AND CON

The arguments for streaming include the following: "It is the only arrangement which 'stretches' the most able pupils and encourages the weakest. Ability grouping is advantageous to both staff and pupils; pupils and their parents know what is expected of them. To put poor pupils with more able ones results in the former developing feelings of inferiority. The demands of the eleven-plus examination makes it necessary for the most able to be pressed. Streaming arrangements follow naturally individual differences in levels of educability. Pupils are kept on their toes and work hard to hold their positions or to gain promotion." As Sir Cyril Burt philosophically stated:

> After all every one of us, however successful, has sooner or later to acknowledge that there are others better than we are. It should be an essential part of the child's education to teach him how to face a possible beat-

[3] *Children and Their Primary Schools: Report of the Central Advisory Council for Education,* (England), Vol. II. London: H.M.S.O., 1967, p. 550, p. 553.

[4] Brian Jackson; "Teachers' Views on Primary School Streaming," *Educational Research,* LV (June 1961), 66–71. (The Plowden Report substantiated the continuous use of unscientific criteria to allocate children to streams).

ing in the eleven-plus or any other examination, just as he should learn to take a beating in a half-mile race, or in a bout with boxing gloves, or a football match with a rival school.[5]

They also argue that the system of transfer is an integral part of the streaming organization, pupils can easily be placed in the correct group, free to move at their proper pace.

The opponents of streaming hold contrary views. They argue: "It is used primarily as a convenience for the teaching staff. It is unnatural and undemocratic and deprives many less able pupils of the stimulus and leadership to be gained from learning alongside the more able. Streaming is based on quite small and often unreliable differences in performance which suggests that there should be frequent transfers, but these are rarely made. Given a wider spread of ability within a group, teachers are compelled to devise more effective teaching methods." They feel that the concept of streaming is based on the false premise of innate ability. They rationalize that most pupils are a mixture of strengths and weaknesses, with good motivation of special interests; a pupil could actually be found working in a number of different groups. Even if streaming on the basis of ability were sound and gave true homogeneous groups, it ignores the more subtle aspects of the personality and the education of the social aspect of man.

RESEARCH

Most of the investigations into streaming have been at the junior school level. For example, J. C. Daniel found that the policy of non-streaming significantly increased the average IQ of children by about three points and reduced the standard deviation or significant differences between the children's IQ scores.[6] Slow learners were helped by the policy of nonstreaming to a greater degree than were the brighter children in which arithmetic scores were given a decided boost by the policy of nonstreaming. This result, however, might have been caused by decreases in the dispersion of arithmetic scores. The UNESCO Report on the attainment of primary school children in 12 countries reported that England by far had the largest dispersion of test scores.[7] Scottish schools, which also employ streaming, were second. Jackson's study of one

[5] Cyril Burt, "The Examination at Eleven-Plus," *British Journal of Educational Studies*, VII (May 1956), p. 110.

[6] J. C. Daniel, "Effects of Streaming in the Primary Schools." *British Journal of Educational Psychology*, XXXI (June 1961), p. 69.

[7] *Educational Achievement of Thirteen-Year-Olds in Twelve Countries*. Hamburg: UNESCO, 1962, p. 62.

hundred sixty-two junior school children in a comparative unstreamed and streamed situation indicated that unstreamed classes not only increased the achievement of all children but it especially helped the slow learners who would ordinarily be placed in the low stream.[8] Other studies indicate that streamed groups achieve no more than unstreamed. Although the recent Plowden Report found that streamed pupils surpassed their nonstreamed peers in academic attainment, it indicated however that the difference reported may have been erased had the two types of schools been controlled for social class differences.[9]

From the research on streaming, it seems to this writer that two valid conclusions can be drawn: All children improve somewhat in the unstreamed school, and the least academically able children gain the most. Perhaps the reason for this is the notion of teacher expectancy or the standard of work expected by the teacher of his pupils as well as the degree of concern for the development and nurturing of abilities and capacities.

TEACHER EXPECTANCY

The rationale for streaming being based on the belief that academic achievement is limited by innate ability, has resulted in the opinion that achievement and IQ *cannot* be altered by the climate of the school. According to the UNESCO Report, this ". . . indeed has led to the general acceptance of the practice of streaming (in England)." Streaming viewed as an administrative device resulting from the acceptance of this belief does in fact enhance its effects, the self-fulfilling prophecy is manifested. That is, administrators and teachers expect wide differences in performance between the levels of streaming, and this is what is achieved. This accounts not only for the positive effects of nonstreaming on the academically weak child but also for the great dispersion of achievement scores as reported by UNESCO.

Contrary to the argument by the protagonists of streaming that a system of transfers is an integral part of the organization, fluidity between the streams is almost nonexistent. After several years of streaming the only avenue open for transferring is downward, from A to B to C streams. The opposite direction is a practical impossibility. The number of pupils actually transferring across streams is approximately 5 percent a year.[9]

---

[8] Brian Jackson, *An Educational System in Miniature.* London: Routledge and Kegan Paul, 1964, pp. 110–111.

[9] Plowden, p. 589, p. 551, p. 576.

TEACHING METHODOLOGY

There is a theory of teacher practice that is worthwhile mentioning which may explain what differences of homogeneity signify for achievement. The theory is based on the proposition that a teacher instructs the heterogeneous class on an individual basis and that the instruction is shared among the class members; whereas the instruction of a homogeneous group is more of a collective nature, adapted in content and design to the class average. Hence, the more the child deviates from the average, the poorer the instruction he receives.

Streaming also influences the way teachers view the organizational system as well as their teaching style. In general, it was found that teachers in streamed schools are more traditional and rigid in their approach than teachers in nonstreamed schools. Because of their lack of experience with any other form of grouping, streamed teachers are committed to the system, if not philosophically, at least practically. Discussions with teachers, who had been teaching streamed classes for a number of years, revealed a "Die Hard" commitment to a streamed teaching style. They confessed a certain lack of confidence in their ability to teach heterogeneous classes. Most of the teachers preferred top streams over lower streams. Hence teachers and students alike were streamed.

The Plowden Report stated that organizational factors may well mask more important and persuasive influences of the attitudes of teachers. Teachers' attitudes not only manifest themselves in the achievement of their students, but in their attitude toward self, school, and society. The effects of streaming upon the attitudes of pupils is presently being studied by the National Foundation of Educational Research. The findings will be released in the coming year or so.

ATTITUDES

Although the protagonists of streaming insist that streaming reduces the feelings of inferiority by grouping children of similar intellectual capacities, there is little evidence to support their position. Most of the research conducted in England indicated that pupils in lower streams possess a sense of failure, resulting in a decline in morale, effort, and attainment. As a group of interviewed pupils put it: "I think it is better without streaming because with it there is jealousy: usually those in the lower grades are not encouraged much." "People who are not clever, yet try hard are discouraged if they are put in the lower class, and the people in the top class become snobs." [10]

[10] Wm. Patterson, "Streaming in Schools," *Educational Review* (Oct., 1963), 229–35.

Since streaming in England is initiated in the infant school, children may naturally and without awareness assimilate the streams role. The nonacceptance of an inferior role might be an incompatible situation in terms of the level of academic expectancy. If transferred, a child would more than likely be at the bottom of his new class, whereas previously he had been at the top of his former class. However, Rudd found that in general no long term effects were attributable to streaming.[11] Transfer did not increase the homogeneity of the streams, nor did it improve academic achievement. Transfer however was accompanied by temporary traumatic difficulties, resulting in aggressive, resentful, less cooperative behavior.

Since there is a definite relationship between social class and academic achievement, many have labelled streaming as a system of "de facto" segregation by social class. A number of studies, including the National Foundation for Educational Research, have shown that nonstreamed pupils had great opportunity for the formation of inter-social class relationships. The NFER study revealed that only 9 percent of the friendships recorded in streamed classes were between children in higher or lower streams, whereas in the nonstreamed classes the figure was 20 percent.[12]

A number of English sociologists and educators believe that streaming reflects social background, privilege, accident, and handicap. There have been several studies which show that middle-class children move into stream A and working class children into B and C. The Plowden Report also evidenced age as a factor in stream placement in which younger children are generally placed in lower streams and older children in upper streams.[9] Therefore, a steady decline in average age is noted as one proceeds from the A streams to the lower streams.

The contaminations of the findings of the Plowden Report by the variables of age, social class of pupils, and the attitudes and the methodology of teachers, left some doubt in the minds of the researchers as to the valididty of their findings. Even they ask themselves, "Is streaming really worth it?"[9]

Nevertheless there seems to be an educational reformation on the horizon. The eleven-plus examination is gradually falling into disuse in many areas as an exclusive means of selection. The Labor Government instructed the LEA's in 1965 to submit plans for the reorganization of secondary education along comprehensive lines. Although it has not substantially reduced streaming *inside* schools and year-groups, there was some hope that it would severely reduce selection for separate secondary

[11] W. G. A. Rudd, "Psychological Effects of Streaming by Attainment." *British Journal of Educational Psychology*, XXVII.

[12] Peter Healey, Janet Bouri, "Some Sociometric Characteristics of Children in Streamed and Nonstreamed Junior Schools," N.F.E.R. Study (London, England, March, 1965).

schools, the grammar school, and the secondary modern. According to a number of headmasters, the increased number of comprehensive schools, in many cases, have become nothing more than a common facility for the secondary modern and the grammar school, academic segregation being maintained.

The crux of the problem, as most educationists view it, is the limited number of available university places. The percentage of students in the university is seven to eight percent of the student population. Admission policy changes are being considered and implemented, new universities constructed and old institutions expanded. But the recent economic problem in England will severely cut into these plans.

Some view the problem of reform as a social class power struggle. As Bereday asserted: "Until the controlling elite group adopts and supports such recommendations (expansion of higher education by Crowther and Robbins Committees) England will have a highly selective system of education." [2] Streaming will remain.

18 Teaching in Ability Grouped English Classes: A Study of Verbal Interaction and Cognitive Goals[1]

ISOBEL L. PFEIFFER

Reprinted with permission from *Journal of Experimental Education,* Vol. 36, No. 1 (Fall 1967), pp. 33–38.

A persistent problem inherent in mass education is effective teaching of individual pupils. To confront this problem teachers have used a combination of group activities and adjustments for individual pupils, e.g., differentiated assignments, individual assistance, and selection of appropriate materials. Individualization of instruction has often been a focus of attention in the schools. Various administrative procedures have been used to facilitate such teaching. One device, long popular with teachers and administrators, is ability grouping, called homogeneous grouping by some. Theoretically, this procedure of assigning pupils to class sections on the basis of some measures of achievement or academic ability narrows the range of student ability and achievement within the class and enables the teacher to work more effectively. Its proponents argue that with pupil variability thus constricted, goals may be set more specifically and teaching activities may be planned to fit the group and the individuals comprising it.

Although the logic of homogeneous grouping is convincing to most

---

[1] This study was undertaken at Kent State University as a part of a doctoral dissertation under the supervision of Dr. O. L. Davis, Jr. The major portion of this paper was presented at the annual AERA meeting in Chicago, February 1966.

teachers, research has failed to substantiate the educational advantages claimed. Since unequivocal conclusions have been unavailable, moves to install ability grouping in schools have been accompanied by differences in opinion. This controversial issue in the public school, ability grouping, has been periodically questioned in terms of its effectiveness and its democratic basis. In general, evidence collected in research on ability grouping has related to pupil achievement under different systems of grouping, psychological effects of different patterns of grouping on pupils, teacher attitudes, and parents' views of different grouping practices. A fundamental assumption in most studies and in most schools where ability grouping is practiced, apparently, has been that when a teacher is assigned a class of a certain ability level his teaching style, goals, materials, and evaluation are accordingly adapted to the general ability level of the class. This basic assumption, however, seems not to have been tested empirically and, therefore, must be questioned. The absence of information about teaching behavior in classes of different ability levels has been called to the attention of educators by Wrightstone (9), Franseth (6), and others. Drews (4: 28), for instance, suggested that probably little goes on in the homogeneous class that would not have happened in an ungrouped, or heterogeneous, situation. Yet no one has done research to verify or refute such a supposition and to provide relevant evidence. If teachers assigned to classes of different ability levels do not differentiate their behavior, the case for ability grouping has been undermined on at least two points:

1. Teachers are deceiving themselves, and administrators are wasting a great deal of time in assigning pupils to appropriate ability groups.
2. The teacher, by his action, denies his importance as a factor in individualization of instruction.

The possible failure of teachers to differentiate their teaching may explain some of the contradictory results of studies of ability grouping. If the teaching is not different in classes grouped by ability, pupils' subsequent learning can not be expected to be different. As Davis (3: 215) has pointed out, "Attention to the process of grouping itself is less important than the type of instruction which is given to the group."

This study investigated certain aspects of teacher behavior when teaching at two different ability levels. Teacher-pupil verbal interaction in the classroom and cognitive goals were analyzed.

PROCEDURE

Eleventh-grade English teachers teaching classes of two different levels of ability in a large suburban high school were the subjects. The investigator visited six successive class sessions of the ten classes involved, that is two different ability levels for each of the five teachers in the study, and completed the Flanders' Interaction Analysis (5). Interaction Analysis was selected as an appropriate observational technique. Some factors involved were the following (5): Teacher-pupil verbal interaction has been established as an effective index of classroom climate and teacher influence; this system is unique in considering the sequence of verbalization; the relation of indirect teacher influence to greater student achievement and favorable attitudes has been established. The teachers were interviewed to obtain estimates of time emphasis on cognitive goals, teacher talk, and student talk in each class. They were asked about differentiation in their own teaching and their preference of classes: enriched classes (for pupils having IQ's of 130 and above), adjusted classes (for pupils who were two grades below grade level on English achievement tests and who received below average English marks), or average classes (for the remaining pupils in the 11th grade). Two tests for each class were analyzed according to the cognitive goals inferred from the test items, using the six major categories of Bloom's *Taxonomy of Educational Objectives: Cognitive Domain* (1956): knowledge, comprehension, application, analysis, synthesis, and evaluation.

The *Taxonomy*, a carefully prepared classification plan, is inclusive and yet the arrangement as a hierarchy of increasingly complex activities affords an instrument for analysis of test items. The authors of the *Taxonomy* (1: 20–4) indicated that to be a useful and effective tool it must be communicable, comprehensive, stimulating to thought regarding educational problems, and acceptable and useful to workers in the field. According to Cox (2), who reviewed over thirty studies relevant to these four standards, the *Taxonomy* has met the criteria. He considers increasing interest in and utilization of the *Taxonomy* as further evidence of its validity.

FINDINGS

Teachers did not differentiate their patterns of teacher-pupil verbal interaction in classes of different levels of ability. Verbal interaction was significantly similar in classes of different ability levels taught by the same teacher. See Table 1 and Figure 1.

Four of the five teachers utilized more than half of the class time for their own talk; they used direct influence (lecture, criticism, directions) more than indirect influence (use of student ideas, praise, acceptance of student feelings, questions). Teachers' emphasis on content was greater in their classes of higher ability.

Student initiated talk in a class generally was greater when the teacher followed such talk with indirect verbal influence. The lower ability class

TABLE 1
Spearman Rank Correlation Coefficients for the Classes of Two Ability Levels
for Each Teacher

Teacher	r_s Based on Ten Categories	Level of Significance	r_s Based on Teacher Talk Categories	Level of Significance
Teacher A	.83	.01	.96	.01
Teacher B	.95	.01	1.00	.01
Teacher C	.95	.01	.96	.01
Teacher D	.92	.01	.88	.05
Teacher E	.82	.01	.96	.01

usually did not initiate as great a percentage of ideas as the other group.

Most of these teachers had a preference for teaching classes of certain ability level or combinations of classes of different ability levels. Three of the four teachers indicating a preference used more indirect influence with the class preferred. This finding has potential value in assignment of classes since research by Flanders and his associates (5) and Furst (7) has indicated a positive relationship between superior student achievement and indirect teacher influence.

Teachers' estimates of time spent on cognitive goals indicated a differentiation of goals between average and adjusted classes. The emphasis for adjusted classes was on less complex skills: knowledge, comprehension, and application. Goals of average classes included the higher cognitive processes: analysis, synthesis, and evaluation.

Teachers' test items revealed a differentiation of operational cognitive goals for their classes of different ability levels. There was more concern with the less complex mental skills; the more complex skills received little attention.

Teachers' estimates of time spent on cognitive goals were not significantly related to goals inferred from tests given to that class. Teachers indicated one pattern of cognitive goals was important and tested for another. See Table 2.

Teachers in this study did not realistically classify classroom talk. They especially misjudged how much they had talked. They underestimated student initiated talk of adjusted classes.

Three of the four teachers teaching adjusted classes believed little progress could be expected from this lower group. The teachers indicated that these expectations were reflected in limited assignments and restricted goals.

DISCUSSION

Mitzel's (8) multidimensional approach to teacher effectiveness enumerated presage, process, and product as important dimensions of teach-

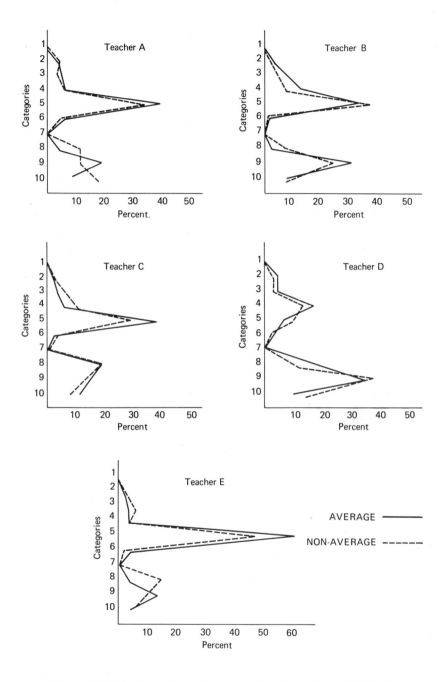

Figure 1. Profiles for each teacher comparing interaction data for two classes observed.

TABLE 2

Spearman Rank Correlation Coefficients for Each Class Comparing Teachers' Estimates of Emphasis on Cognitive Goals [2] and Cognitive Goals Inferred from Tests [3]

Teacher	Average	Nonaverage
Teacher A	.43	.44
Teacher B	−.16	.55
Teacher C	.62	.52
Teacher D	.21	−.46
Teacher E	−.49	.29

ing. Presage referring to teacher personality, training, characteristics, and similar variables has been unproductive in providing insights to teacher effectiveness. This study focused essentially on the second aspect or process, teachers' behavior while instructing classes of two different ability levels in eleventh-grade English. Previous studies of ability grouping have concentrated on the product dimensions of teaching, i.e., student achievement, attitudes, study habits, and adjustment.

Examination of the classroom verbal interaction, using Flanders' Interaction Analysis, revealed that teachers in this study did not differentiate their verbal behavior in classes of different levels of ability. The evidence from previous studies of ability grouping has been conflicting but has indicated that no consistent and significant advantages characterized ability grouping. These results might be explained by the lack of differentiation of the behavior of the teacher in the classes of different levels of ability. Similar teaching might be expected to effect similar products. Consequently, the findings suggest that the product dimension in ability grouped classes has not been different from results under heterogeneous grouping because the behavior of the teacher has not changed; the teaching style of the teacher has not been modified to facilitate teaching students at designated ability levels. The fallacy of assuming that teachers adapt their behavior to classes of different abilities is indicated by the interaction data in this study. The claim of teachers that homogeneous grouping provides a better teaching situation was not verified by their adjusting verbal interaction to groups of different levels of ability.

Teachers in this study seemed to differentiate the cognitive goals between classes of different levels of ability in both their estimates of class emphasis on goals and in the goals inferred from test items. However, these teachers did not test the same cognitive goals on which they said they

[2] Teachers' estimates were indicated on separate scales for each category for each class.

[3] Test items were classified by three judges and evaluated using the hierarchic arrangement of the *Taxonomy*. The most complex category was given half the value of the item; the preceding categories shared the other equally.

spent time. Such findings indicate that these teachers failed to rethink and adjust their procedures and did not actually know what cognitive skills they required in test situations. These teachers possibly deceived themselves and actually believed that they were consistent in their stated and operational goals

Results of the study indicate that teachers seem to practice self-deception. If this estimate is accurate, the situation is a critical one, yet it goes unnoticed because the pressures of numbers of students and increased curriculum content are more obvious and urgent than systematic analysis of teacher behavior. The teachers in this study believed that they differentiated their teaching behavior according to the ability level of the classes they taught. However, no significant differences in verbal interaction patterns were found for these teachers between their classes of different ability levels. These teachers misjudged how much they talked and what kind of classroom verbalization they used. The contributions of students, particularly in adjusted classes, were underestimated. The cognitive goals which these teachers felt they emphasized were not the goals which they tested in the different classes. Such misconceptions make self-understanding and improvement virtually impossible. Knowledge about where he is, in what direction he is headed, and where he is going is essential for the teacher who would seek to improve his teaching. Clearly these teachers had little, if any, precise knowledge of how they were handling different ability groups in their classrooms. Their predicament may well be shared by other teachers.

This situation of teachers may be compared to that of the pilot in one of the early planes. A pilot knew whether or not he was flying upside down only when he could see the horizon. In bad weather such a discrimination about his position proved more difficult. Today, using the precise instruments available to him, he can determine his position regardless of the visibility. Likewise, teachers in the past may have been unable to determine their positions because of the lack of suitable instruments, but times have changed. Tools now are available to help the teacher to determine where he is. Flanders' Interaction Analysis is such a device in regard to teacher verbal influence in the classroom, and Bloom's *Taxonomy* is an instrument to assess position in regard to cognitive goals. Neither tool is an evaluation device, for the teacher like the pilot decides where he is going and in what attitude he wants to proceed. But such decisions are significant only after the teacher has determined his present position. These tools, Interaction Analysis and the *Taxonomy,* offer potential power to preservice and in-service educational programs.

A number of studies by Storlie, Amidon and Simon, Zahn, Kirk, Hough, and Amidon and Furst seem to be in agreement that training in Interaction Analysis results in changes in attitudes and behavior. This evidence from in-service work with teachers and preservice programs in teacher education should stimulate efforts toward professional growth. Since student achievement and favorable attitudes have been related to indirect teacher influence, the improvement of instruction can be a specific and objective program. A teacher could use Flanders' system to analyze his own teaching by taping classroom discussions, listening to these tapes, recording the interaction, constructing and interpreting his own matrices. A supervisor using Interaction Analysis, moreover, could help a teacher gain insights into the verbal interaction in his class, encourage the setting of realistic and desirable goals for changing interaction, and appraise teacher progress; and all this could be without rating or evaluation.

The *Taxonomy* can be used effectively as a basis for improving teacher-made tests as well as evaluating curricula and teacher instruments (2). The teacher, individually or with others, could use this instrument in planning his teaching activities, preparing tests, and revising curriculum. Interaction Analysis and the *Taxonomy* are tools which can be used by teachers and student teachers to study their own teaching behavior and work toward achieving the verbal interaction and cognitive goals which they select.

This study, then, suggests that one factor which may account for conflicting results in research which compared ability-grouped and heterogeneous classes is the teaching behavior in the classes. Although teachers have indicated that their teaching behavior was adapted to the ability of the group, evidence in this study revealed no such differentiation. A discrepancy also existed between cognitive goals which the teacher indicated as emphasized in a class and the cognitive goals which were included on the tests for the class. Such a similarity of teacher behavior, confusion about cognitive goals, and emphasis on simpler mental processes undoubtedly contribute to the controversial results of studies on ability grouping.

REFERENCES

1. Bloom, Benjamin S., (Ed.) *Taxonomy of Educational Objectives, The Classification of Educational Goals, Handbook I: Cognitive Domain* (New York: David McKay, 1956).
2. Cox, Richard C., "An Overview of Studies Involving the Taxonomy of Educational Objectives: Cognitive Domain During Its First Decade," Paper presented to the American Educational Research Association in Chicago, February 1966. (Mimeographed)
3. Davis, O. L., Jr., "Grouping for Instruction: Some Perspectives," *Educational Forum*, XXIV (January 1960), pp. 209–16.
4. Drews, Elizabeth Monroe, *Student Ability Grouping Patterns and Classroom Interaction* (U. S. Department of Health, Education, and Welfare, Office of Education, Cooperative Research Project No. 608, East Lansing,

Michigan: Office of Research and Publications, College of Education, Michigan State University, 1963).

5. Flanders, Ned A., *Teacher Influence, Pupil Attitudes, and Achievement* (U. S. Department of Health, Education, and Welfare, Office of Education, Cooperative Research Monograph No. 12. Washington, D. C., 1965).

6. Franseth, Jane, "Research in Grouping: A Review," *School Life* XLV (June 1963), pp. 5–6.

7. Furst, Norma, "The Multiple Languages of the Classroom: A Further Analysis and a Synthesis of Meanings Communicated in High School Teaching," Dissertation Abstract, Temple University, Philadelphia, Pennsylvania, 1967. (Mimeographed)

8. Mitzel, Harold E., "Teacher Effectiveness," *Encyclopedia of Educational Research,* Third Edition, edited by Chester W. Harris (New York: The Macmillan Company, 1960).

9. Wrightstone, J. Wayne. *Class Organization for Instruction.* What Research Says to the Teacher, No. 13. Prepared by the American Educational Research Association in Cooperation with the Department of Classroom Teachers. Washington, D. C.: National Education Association, May 1957. 33 pp.

19 | Ability Grouping

RESEARCH DIVISION OF THE NATIONAL EDUCATION ASSOCIATION

Reprinted with permission from *NEA Research Bulletin*, Vol. 47, No. 3 (October 1968), pp. 74–76.

Studies of ability grouping have been conducted for more than four decades. Considering the amount and duration of interest in ability grouping, it might be thought the issue would be settled by now, either adopted as a successful measure or discarded as ineffective. School programs, however, have had variable success—ability grouping has been considered a beneficial practice by some and a detrimental and undemocratic procedure by others.

PROS AND CONS

Much controversy exists as to the best methods for grouping pupils. Some arguments advanced in favor of homogeneous ability grouping are:

- It allows pupils to advance at their own rate with pupils of comparable ability and achievement.
- It challenges the pupil to do his best in the group to which he is assigned, or to qualify for assignment to a higher group.
- Pupils associate with others of different abilities in athletic programs, assemblies, clubs, and other joint activities, so that democratic living is present.
- Methods and materials used with homogeneous ability groups are directly applicable to all pupils because of the pupils' similarity. Instruc-

tional material of varying levels of difficulty which must be provided for each heterogeneous classroom is expensive and inefficient.

• Pupils with less than average ability are able to receive more individual attention from the teacher when they are placed together in a class. Children of greater than average ability also receive greater attention in homogeneous ability groups.

• Providing for individual differences within the heterogeneous classroom becomes complex and time-consuming with the great variation of individual differences.

• When heterogeneous grouping is used, the teacher tends to slant his teaching toward the average or below average pupil. As a result, the classroom becomes less of a challenge, and educational standards are necessarily lowered for above-average learners.

Some of the reasons for which educators claim that homogeneous ability grouping is less desirable are:

• True homogeneous ability grouping is impossible, since any particular factor used for such grouping may be the only point of similarity in the class.

• Test data may vary from one situation to another, and homogeneous ability grouping may depend too much on the validity of these data.

• In homogeneous ability grouping, teachers may have the tendency to assume that pupils are similar and neglect their differences. Since individuals have different patterns of ability, heterogeneous grouping allows those abilities to come forth with pupils of the same age.

• A stigma may be attached to the pupil if he is placed in a slow group; the pupil placed in a fast group may develop snobbishness and an inflated view of his worth. Members of either a slow or fast group have a loss of social contact with their peers.

• Heterogeneous classes provide personal contacts similar to the kind the pupil will encounter as an adult.

• Pupils need the experience of working with others of different abilities.

• Pupils of less ability may profit from learning experiences in association with those of more ability.

RECENT RESEARCH

A brief summary of the findings and conclusions from 50 research studies published since 1960 follows:

• Research on the relative merits of different organizational procedures for ability grouping as they affect pupils' achievement was extensive. However, the results were inconclusive and indefinite.

• Available evidence indicates that factors other than ability grouping
per se may account for the many differences that occur in achievement
test results when children grouped according to ability are compared
with their counterparts in a heterogeneous situation.

• Some studies showed gains in achievement in favor of ability grouping and some in favor of heterogeneous grouping. Others showed little or
no statistical difference among grouping methods in pupil achievement
as measured by standardized tests.

• Ability grouping tends to succeed when there is modification of materials, objectives, curriculum, and teaching methods.

• Most of the studies on ability grouping deal with the effects on academic achievements as measured by standardized tests, but only a few
have attempted to examine the effects of grouping procedures on pupils'
attitudes, self-concepts, and other factors in their development. It may
well be that for some children at least, ability grouping does produce undesirable effects in specific areas of development.

• Little research has been conducted to determine the possible effects of different ways of grouping on pupils' growth in such areas as ability to think, on the development of creativity, on the development of
values, and the like.

• Research studies indicate the difficulty of attempting to group
children according to ability. Especially in the early years, it is likely that
grouping by ability cannot be accomplished with assurance and accuracy.

• Empirical data supporting either a positive or a negative judgment
with regard to the merits of ability grouping are almost nonexistent.

Ability grouping seems to mean various things in various places. Considerable diversity exists in both methods of organization and aims of instruction. It would not be an exaggeration to state that there are probably as many different types of ability grouping as there are different
school systems which utilize such arrangements. What is important is that
the particular structure under consideration be clearly and carefully described, and that extrapolation of research findings be applied only to
groups operating in the same manner.

MORE RESEARCH NEEDED

Despite all the diversity in evaluation, opinion, and practice with regard to ability grouping, there appear to be three major areas of agreement:

1. Ability grouping *per se* has yet to prove itself as an administrative device to meet both effectively and efficiently the individual needs of all pupils in most areas of educational concern. Teachers, however, tend to prefer ability grouping.

2. More and better research studies which account for or control a larger number of the variables involved are needed.

3. Objectives, materials, curriculum, and teaching methods should also change to fit each of the homogeneous groups at different ability levels.

Experimentation with flexible homogeneous grouping procedures, which vary according to instructional purpose and pupil need, and the results of recent large-scale experiments may yield some helpful information. Several conditions appear to hold promise for further study of the many unanswered questions related to ability grouping: (a) the individual school system's approach to flexible ability grouping, (b) the use of improved measures of the instructional inputs, processes, and outcomes, and (c) the use of multivariate analysis.

20 | An Annotated List of 40 Grouping Plans

HAROLD G. SHANE

Printed with the permission of the author.

For over a century of U.S. education diverse grouping plans have been initiated, discarded, modified, or gradually accepted on a widespread scale. Here is an overview, with annotations, of some plans and programs that have been introduced in U.S. schools or discussed by educational writers.

1. *Ungraded groups.* Originally found in the seventeenth century Dame school and eighteenth century "district" school, ungraded groups were taught by one teacher who handled all subjects in the first eight grades. One room ungraded schools are still commonplace in many areas, but have decreased sharply since the 1940s.

2. *Primary-intermediate grouping.* When the one room school grew too large for a single teacher to handle, it often was split into a two room establishment with children in grades 1–4 and grades 5–8, respectively, assigned to two instructors.

3. *Grade-level grouping.* Introduced around 1848 in Boston's Quincy Grammar School, the graded type organization permitted one teacher to work with a given grade group. In practice, this is the same as chronological age grouping or heterogeneous grouping. (See 4 below)

4. *Heterogeneous grouping.* Essentially, this is the *absence* of an especially structured plan. Children, when entering grade one, are assigned to a given teacher irrespective of such factors as intelligence, social maturity, or achievement that might have been scrutinized at the kindergarten

level. Individual differences may be dealt with through such means as program enrichment, accelerated promotion, or interclassroom grouping as in primary reading.

5. *Homogeneous grouping.* A misnomer for *ability* grouping, this approach frequently uses intelligence test data, reading ability, or generalized achievement scores as a basis for placement in a given classroom.

6. *XYZ grouping.* A form of ability grouping in which "X", "Y", and "Z" refer to levels of intelligence, or to three levels of assumed potential performance in such a subject as arithmetic. Teaching procedures are modified to allow for differences among the three groups.

7. *Intra-subject-field grouping.* This plan is generally used in departmentalized junior and senior high schools. (See "departmental grouping" below.) For example, in the New Trier Township (9–12) High School (Winnetka, Illinois), a student may be in an "advanced" ability group in English and in a "middle" ability group in mathematics. As many as five levels have been used in such groupings.

8. *Departmental grouping.* The practice of having pupils move from one classroom to another for instruction by teachers in each subject field. A departmental program is the antithesis of the unit classroom program in which one teacher handles all, or nearly all, instruction in subject fields. Rarely used below the intermediate grade, departmentalization becomes most commonplace in grade seven and above.

9. *"Vestibule" groups.* The label here suggests the idea of an anteroom or small entrance room or hall into which one comes before entering the main rooms of a house. To illustrate, in some school systems such as Chicago, there are "1-c" groups in which less mature children are enrolled prior to entering "1-b" and "1-a" classes in first grade. Thus without "failing" or repeating, certain pupils spend one and one-half semesters in grade one. "Vestibule" groups also have been used at the threshold of high school to help slow learners and children with cultural flaws to increase their prospects of success in secondary education. That is, students may spend four and a half or five years in progressing from eighth grade to the high school diploma.

10. *Hosic's Cooperative Group Plan.* Originally conceived by James F. Hosic in the 1920s, this plan calls for *teachers* to work in small cooperative groups under a group chairman. It is a novel twist, since nearly all other plans involve grouping *children*. Under it, staff members were in charge of special rooms (e.g., a literature, composition, story-telling, reading, and spelling center) but were not so much "subject specialists" as specialists in teaching children. Work for a given group of children was planned at frequent intervals by the "cooperating group" of teachers, who sought to extract from their special area rooms the contributions that each center might make to a unified learning experience.

11. *Winnetka Plan grouping.* Pupil progress in Winnetka has been

influenced for many years by self-instructional materials and what might be called an "individual-within-the-group" approach to instruction. The basic classroom unit in grades 1–6 in Winnetka is heterogeneous, but individual progress continues to be personalized by the use of record forms or "goal cards," which encourage optimum academic growth by each child. Thus, in a sense, individual progress within the group constitutes a grouping device which has many of the merits of ability grouping without some of the problems of so-called homogeneous grouping.

12. *Dalton Plan grouping.* The classic Dalton Plan was based upon individual progress, group interaction, and a time-budgeting "contract plan" to facilitate individual achievement. Subject matter was grouped in two component parts, the academic and the physical-social. The former was presented predominantly by individualized instruction, the latter by the wholeclass method. The work for each grade was laid out in the form of "contracts," which described work to be done over a period of weeks.

13. *Multiple-track grouping.* This is a type of ability grouping in which children of varied ability complete a given number of units or topics at different rates of speed, their progress being contingent upon individual ability. An historically important multiple-track plan was developed late in the nineteenth century by Preston W. Search in Pueblo, Colorado. In brief, the multiple-track plan permitted some children to finish eight years of elementary school in seven years, while others (on a slower track) might take up to nine years to complete the same tasks. Thus three ability levels were involved, and the *amount,* not the *nature,* of requirements were "scaled down" for slower learning children in a given year, although all children presumably completed the basic requirements before leaving the elementary school.

14. *Platoon grouping.* Platoon grouping goes back to 1900, when it was devised by William A. Wirt for use in Bluffton, Indiana. In broad terms, this plan sectioned children into two groups (platoons) so scheduled as to have one group studying fundamental subjects in classrooms while the second group used special rooms for activities. As originally conceived, the plan was designed to encourage efficient use of the school plant and to achieve balance between academic and social activity or creative work. The platoon plan also was known as the Gary Plan (since it was best known for its application in Gary), and as the "Work-Study-Play" plan.

15. *Social maturity grouping.* A rather loosely defined concept, this one suggests that grouping be heterogeneous but that children can be grouped when they leave kindergarten, for example, into three first-grade rooms on the basis of social development and friendship patterns rather than on the basis of ability or of sheer chance. This plan implies the exercise of professional judgment and the use of available test data in assigning boys and girls to "well balanced" groups, with the most mature and the least mature assigned to separate classrooms.

16. *Developmental grouping.* Another term used loosely, this one apparently connotes an approach to grouping roughly comparable to "social maturity" grouping.

17. *Organismic age grouping.* Also a loosely used term, organismic age grouping was apparently coined by persons attempting to apply Willard Olson's concept of organismic age to the grouping of children at varied levels of maturity. In practice, the term probably implies policies similar to those associated with "social maturity" grouping, plus study of various indices of organismic age as determinants of group structure.

18. *Social maturity-teacher personality grouping.* This refers to "social maturity" grouping coupled or linked to a consideration of teacher personality in the assignment of children to a given classroom. It recognizes that teachers as well as children vary as individuals and implies recognition of the assumption that some teachers are more effective with less mature children and that some are most effective with the more mature children in an ungraded primary or "social maturity" grouping situation.

19. *Ungraded primary groups.* This term may be used to describe a situation in which grade levels as such are abandoned at the primary level and where children work together in an environment conducive both to individual and to group progress without reference to precise grade level standards or norms. The teacher in the ungraded primary may work with the same group for two and occasionally three years. It is her purpose to help children progress as far and as fast as they can with less regard for conventional minimum essentials than for total human development.

20. *Ungraded intermediate plan.* Not widely used, the ungraded intermediate approach to grouping involves assigning a group of children in, say, grades 3–5 or 4–5 to one teacher. The program or curricular design is appreciably influenced by teacher-pupil planning. As distinct from the split or "hyphenated" group (see 21), the ungraded intermediate grouping is intended to enrich and to improve learning rather than merely to compensate for uneven distribution of pupil enrollment.

21. *Split grade or "hyphenated" groups.* The "hyphenated" or split group is one enrolling children from two and occasionally three grade levels. As a rule, groups are split in smaller schools when, for instance, there are too many children in the fourth and fifth grades for efficient instruction, yet too few to justify dividing both grades. When this situation occurs, a division may be made as follows:

1960–61	*1961–62*
3rd grade—40 pupils	4th grade—30 pupils
4th grade—40 pupils	4–5 grade—20 pupils
	5th grade—30 pupils
Total 80 pupils	
	Total 80 pupils

The "hyphenated" grouping plan is obviously an administrative-organizational device for securing smaller classes while adding one rather than two new teachers.

22. *Intraclassroom grouping.* A number of teachers make use of various schemes for grouping within the classroom. This is especially true of primary teachers, who create two or more groups when teaching reading. As a rule, intraclassroom grouping is "part-time ability grouping," designed to permit the teacher to work with youngsters of roughly comparable ability. (See also 25, "grouping through teacher-pupil planning".)

23. *Interclassroom grouping.* Some schools have developed the idea of grouping children not within the classroom but within a given grade or grade range for instruction in a particular subject field (commonly reading), presumably to allow for individual differences. This type of grouping requires that all three teachers in grade five, for instance, schedule reading at the same hour. Then each of the three fifth-grade teachers works with the children who remain in or come to her room (on the basis of reading ability) for instruction in reading. Frequently several grade levels are involved in this temporary interclassroom grouping. For example, all children may, at a given time, exchange rooms for reading activities, the children going to the classrooms which presumably correspond to the level of their reading ability; e.g., the fourth-grade child reading at the third-grade level would report to the third-grade room.

24. *Intergrade ability grouping.* This is very similar to interclassroom grouping (described above) and to departmentalized grouping, but is limited exclusively to shifts made within a single grade. For example, three fifth-grade teachers may schedule their mathematics period for a given hour daily, then shuffle their enrollment according to ability so that one teacher works with the children in the top-achieving group, one with the middle-, and one with the slow-achieving section.

25. *Grouping within the classroom through teacher-pupil planning.* Such grouping involves the creative or emergent planning of experiences with children in such ways as will eventuate in the selection of various pupil activities to be developed and pupil responsibilities to be carried out. Once a topic, project, or unit has been selected, the teacher and children discuss: (a) What do we already know about this topic? (b) What do we want to find out? (c) How shall we go about it? At point (c) various class committees or groups are formed, each of which assumes certain responsibilities for assembling information, for construction work, etc. Teacher guidance is essential to insure that the children volunteering for or assigned to these temporary groupings are challenged by the committee work on the one hand, yet are not frustrated by a too difficult task on the other.

26. *Self-selection grouping.* This term is rather closely related to 25. It implies the creation of a rich environment which is also diversified so as

to provide a variety of activities or projects from among which children can "self-select" work in which they will engage (individually and/or in groups) in conjunction with a topic or subject which promises to be a sound "center of interest" or "group interest" compatible with the developmental levels in the group.

27. *Extracurricular activity grouping.* Especially in the upper grades, many children may be involved in such activities as band, orchestra, or sports. This type of grouping is designed to group children (especially in semidepartmental or departmental programs) so that those in, say, the orchestra can be free to rehearse or practice at the same hours during the week. To serve this purpose, children in the school orchestra, for instance, have their programs so designed as to free them for rehearsal at the same hour of the day.

28. *Special grouping for the gifted.* In schools with large enough enrollments to permit it, there may be special groupings for high IQ children which go beyond the provisions of mere ability grouping and which segregate these high IQ pupils in special programs or even in special schools or centers. Such groups usually are derivatives of one of the plans already mentioned.

29. *"Opportunity Room" grouping for the slow learning or mentally handicapped.* For many years, the educable mentally handicapped or trainable mentally handicapped child has, in some schools, been placed in special ungraded groups with small teacher-pupil ratios. Special instruction and training are provided, usually for children with IQ's of 70 or below.

30. *"Self-Realization Room" grouping for the gifted.* The S-R room is the reverse or antithesis of the so-called opportunity room for the slow learner and, indeed, is a "grouping" plan only in a very broad sense. In brief, the S-R room is one presided over by a highly capable teacher, well-equipped with study and research aids, and open during the day for gifted children in grades 1–6 or 1–8 to use as they see fit. This plan is based on the assumption that the gifted will be placed in the regular classroom but will also be free to supplement their personal-intellectual development under expert guidance when they have completed basic work with their peers or age-mates. In a school of 500 or 600 pupils, perhaps twenty to thirty would have S-R room privileges and responsibilities. That is, only from one to three youngsters would be likely to come from each grade level.

31. *Ungraded four- and five-year-old kindergarten grouping.* A few places have introduced "ungraded" kindergarten programs for four- and five-year-olds. Depending on his social and intellectual maturity, the child may spend from one to three years at the kindergarten level. This approach to grouping is designed to reduce the range of individual difference.

32. *The Woodring Proposal.* A plan for reorganizing the American school system advocated by Paul Woodring in 1957 has certain features which involve grouping. In brief, Woodring envisioned grouping aimed at helping both the slower and faster pupils in a manner somewhat reminiscent of the multiple-track and other historically interesting proposals. Woodring suggested that the K-8 organization be divided between an ungraded primary school and a middle elementary school. The more able children would spend as little as two years in the primary, moving to the middle school as early as age seven. The less able might remain in the ungraded primary through age nine. He envisioned the bright children leaving elementary school at age 11, the dull leaving at, perhaps, age 13. Woodring suggested that the K–8 organization be divided between an un-ungraded, multiple-track, homogeneous, and individualized concepts (6).

33. *The Trump Proposal.* Described in a report of the National Association of Secondary School Principals (5), the Trump Proposal advances the idea of a limited amount of large group instruction coordinated with small classes and individually guided independent study at the high school level.

34. *The Newton Plan.* A proposal from the Newton (Mass.) Public Schools suggesting some class groups of from 50 to 200 students. It is somewhat similar to the Trump Proposal, and involves classes of varied size, restructuring of teachers' time schedules, changes in space and equipment utilization, and curriculum modification to meet individual differences (1).

35. *The Rutgers Plan.* Formulated by teachers of English meeting on the Rutgers campus. Designed so that ". . . no English teacher need ever meet more than twenty-five students at a time except by choice (2)." Other components of the plan include one day per week for each (English) teacher without scheduled classes, biweekly class periods, testing and self-correcting homework periods, outside reading and increased independent study, and the use of college educated but noncertified personnel as readers.

36. *Grouping through team teaching.* In recent years there has been a good deal of interest in the kind of grouping made possible through team teaching. In general, this type of grouping can best be described through an example. In a conventional school, say, at the third-grade level, each of three teachers may teach classes of 30 children or a total of 90 in all. The team teaching approach is one in which one of the teachers commonly is designated as a team leader and, with his two associates, coordinates the experiences of all 90 children. Essentially, each of the teachers brings his particular skills and abilities to all 90 boys and girls rather than working with 30 of them all day long. For example, if one person is particularly good in science or in mathematics, he may work with all 90 of the children in these fields, while another member of the team with strength in the language arts or social sciences may assume re-

sponsibilities to an enhanced degree in these fields. To sum up, team teachers working with youngsters at approximately the same age level in such ways as will maximize the teachers' personal and academic contributions. The grouping that results is flexible, often changes from day to day, and grows out of cooperative planning among the teachers involved.

37. *The Dual Progress Plan.* First received wide attention when a book with this title by George D. Stoddard appeared in 1961 (5). The plan divides content between "cultural imperatives" (language arts, social studies) and "cultural electives" (science, arts, music, etc.). A core (the "imperatives") are taught by a classroom teacher and specialists work in the other fields, on a vertical basis, with the children.

38. *"Self-contained" classroom grouping.* The "self-contained" classroom approach assigns a group of children to the same teacher for all or most of the day. This plan is the same as 4 above (heterogeneous grouping) and can be done on an ability or so-called "homogeneous" basis. See 5.

39. *Nongraded grouping.* Reference has been made to *un*graded groups (See 1 and 19–20), hence a distinction should be made between *un-* and *non*graded grouping. As noted, *un*graded groups (as in a one-room rural school of yesteryear) are composed of children of a wide-ranging age spectrum (e.g., from grade 1–4 or 1–8) working together or in rotation with the same teacher. The *non*graded school abandons the structures of graded organization and is linked (by Goodlad and Anderson) to the "continuous progress" concept listed below (3).

40. *Continuous Progress plan.* This is difficult to separate from the nongraded school and often there *is* no distinction other than a semantic one. Essentially, there are no grade level lines through which one is promoted in the continuous progress school. Rather, one moves through a K-12 continuum at his own rate. Breakneck progress is reduced by lateral enrichment, and slow learners receive special attention, to keep them with age-mates insofar as possible.

The list of 40 plans and proposals sketched above, while by no means comprehensive, serves, by its impressive length, to emphasize the many ideas that have been voiced for purposes of personalizing teaching and recognizing individual differences during more than a century of U.S. educational history. Patently, the challenge of human individuality has engaged the attention and stimulated the imagination of scores of educational leaders.

REFERENCES

1. Bissex, H. S., "Newton Plan Challenges Traditions of Class Size," *The Nation's Schools,* 65:60–64, March 1960.

2. Diederich, P. B., "Rutgers Plan for Cutting Class Size in Two," *English Journal*, 49:229–236, April 1960.

3. Goodlad, John I., and Robert H. Anderson, *The Nongraded Elementary School*, New York: Harcourt, Brace and Company, 1959, 248 pp.

4. Stoddard, George D., *The Dual Progress Plan*. New York: Harper & Row, 1961, 225 pp.

5. Trump, Lloyd J., *Images of the Future*. Washington, D. C.: The National Association of Secondary School Principals, NEA, 1959, 48 pp.

6. Woodring, Paul, *A Fourth of a Nation*. New York: McGraw-Hill, Inc., 1957, pp. 143–158.

PART FIVE

Individualized Instruction

The 1964 Yearbook Committee of the Association for Supervision and Curriculum Development introduced its book, *Individualizing Instruction,* with the belief that "achieving individualization which effects release of human potential has long been an important function of classroom teachers." [1] Indeed, they are correct. Individualization has been one of the educational tenets of our democracy. That is to say, the strength of our democracy depends on the development of each individual's potential in order to bring about his independence as a citizen. The individualization of instruction is but one procedure for developing each citizen's potential for independence.

Nevertheless, as is evident from the articles in this section, individualization of instruction—along with its partner, independent study—is not as widespread as it might be. We talk about individualization of instruction, but we too often fail to implement it. A great need exists and it grows greater as we enter the decade of the 1970s—a decade of mass communication, mass

[1] *Individualizing Instruction,* 1964 Yearbook of the Association for Supervision and Curriculum Development, Washington, D.C., The Association, 1964, p. 7.

transportation, mass participation, and mass everything else.

The implementation of individualized instruction rests on what the concept means to us in the first place. We alert the reader to two sets of distinctions to aid him in his reading. First, individualization of instruction can mean that the teacher works on a personal, one-to-one basis with each student. This essentially means a tutorial program. Individualization can also mean the tailoring of instruction to the particular needs and abilities of the student. This may mean the establishment of an individual curricular program within a group framework and/or on an individual basis. The key lies in the context of the usage, for *instruction* can refer either to the act or the content of instructing.

Secondly, individualization of instruction can refer to the level of the learnings—the lesser learnings and the larger learnings. These two levels are explored astutely by Frazier in his article. Frazier suggests that most often individualization refers to the mastery of the lesser learnings. He, however, contends that today we must devote most of our attention to the larger learnings, for they are the ones so necessary to a person of the twentieth century. These learnings, for Frazier, are "the powers of physical being, of responding, of loving, creating, and enduring." If we grant Frazier his point—and surely we must agree that these powers, or processes, are significant today—we then must consider how we are to instruct students in these powers. Most likely our response to this question will lead us to rethink our entire concept of schooling.

Hedges devotes his article to the lesser learnings. He bases his approach to individualized instruction on the concept of mastery. In practice this means that a student moves on to new work only after he has mastered his current work. It is interesting to note that individualized instruction begets other changes in the school (for example, rearrangement of classroom and school space). Hedges also specifically points out how the student becomes a teacher in individualized instruction.

Hillson presents another case for individualization of instruction which rests on admission of individual differences and the need to go beyond consensus and conformism. For him, the individualization of instruction entails a continuous progress program as the facilitating overall school organization plan. To what degree, however, can and must a teacher individualize instruction (whatever the definition accepted) within a graded school plan?

Bolvin, the director of the Individually Prescribed Instruction Project which is a cooperative venture between the University of Pittsburgh and the Baldwin-Whitehall suburb of Pittsburgh, presents his program of individualized instruction as it occurs in the Oakleaf Elementary School. The Individually Prescribed Instruction project is an application of the principles of programmed instruction. In this program each student works on his own level at his own pace as he masters the material to be learned. Obviously an important element is the shifting role of the teacher from direct transmitter of knowledge to programmer, diagnostician, and prescriber. What skills, then, must the teacher learn in order to program, diagnose, and prescribe? What tools does he need for these tasks?

The Richardson article presents a case study of one program which implemented the individualization of instruction through independent study on the secondary school level. Richardson shows that students can act responsibly when they are offered the opportunity. Furthermore, he shows in the research part of his article that significant gains in learning are achieved by the students involved in independent study. He also shows that independent study entails flexible scheduling and more physical mobility for the student. This independent study program at Valhalla, New York, is testimony that the idea of individualization can be implemented when teachers care to do so. Prospective implementers are invited to study the three vital ingredients and organization of Richardson's Valhalla group.

The reader is encouraged to compare the Individually Prescribed Instruction program with the independent study program at Valhalla High School in regard to basic premises about teaching, learning, and students. Would it be possible, for example, to institute IPI in Valhalla High School? Would independent study (Valhalla style) work on a middle school or elementary school level?

The research article by Zahorik does not focus on a comparison of achievement in a group situation versus achievement in an individual situation as might be expected—not at all. This short and unique study focuses on the quantity and quality of verbal interaction in group versus individual situations. The focus on the teacher's verbal behavior is in keeping with the point made in the five preceding articles: individualization of instruction necessitates a shift in teacher role. If teachers are to have another role, then we must prepare them for it. To do this it is necessary to know what kind of verbal interaction now occurs. The implications of Zahorik's study are many, and he himself suggests several. In doing so he too refers to ASCD's 1964 Yearbook, *Individualizing Instruction,* for ways of developing each student's potential.

The reader is asked to consider how, through individualized instruction, we can prepare both whistlers and poets, to use Frazier's terms. The question focuses on "How?", for at this point we all must admit that the answer to "When?" is "Right now!"

21 | Individualized Instruction*

ALEXANDER FRAZIER

Reprinted with permission from the *California Journal for Instructional Improvement,* a quarterly publication of the California Association for Supervision and Curriculum Development, Vol. 11, No. 1 (March 1968), pp. 31–44.

> *You must know what you want to hear.*
>
> —Edwin Zilz [1]

> *When poets repair to the enchanted forest of language it is with the express purpose of getting lost; far gone in bewilderment, they seek crossroads of meaning, unexpected echoes, strange encounters; they fear neither detours, surprises, nor darkness. . . .*
>
> —Paul Valery [2]

For half a century we have been committed to individualized instruction as the answer to the problem of how to teach everybody what everybody needs to know. Yet only now have we been able to put together in proper relationship the necessary elements to enable us to act on our conviction with the prospect of true success.

And as we approach success, we begin to wonder whether we are going to succeed at the expense of much that we have valued and still do. To put it another way, we have the prospect of success partly because we have reduced our conception of education to what would lend itself to individualization as we presently understand that process. Now we are concerned about what we may have left out or lost.

---

* This article is based on a speech delivered at the Los Angeles CASCD (California Association for Supervision and Curriculum Development) Conference, November 15, 1967.

[1] *How To Whistle Songs: An Easy, Enjoyable Guide to Beautiful Whistling.* Los Angeles: The Stanton Press, 1961; p. 19.

[2] *Aesthetics.* Translated by Ralph Manheim. New York: Pantheon Books, 1964; pp. 48–49.

THE ELEMENTS OF SUCCESS

Let us examine the elements that we have defined and combined that promise us success in teaching everybody what everybody needs to know. We need to understand the nature of individualized instruction as we now think of it in order both to celebrate our triumph and to lay a foundation of agreements as to what else we may need to think about and work on as we move ahead.

Here are some of the elements:

Goals

We have revived mastery as a goal in our new approach to the problem of succeeding through individualized instruction. Continuous progress is a term familiar to all of us. While that term may sometimes be used as a euphemism for merely moving ahead, however imperceptibly, it is a sign of where we are hoping to go. Failure-free learning is another such term that indicates direction.

But beyond these terms is the very tough-minded assertion by an increasing number of persons that we can if we will really teach everybody what everybody needs to know—and do it for most of them the first time around.

Nature of the Learner

Learners start out with much less difference in capacity to learn than we have thought. If at any given point in time, they seem unequal, it means that native capacities have not been properly developed or that we did not get to some of them early enough or that we do not know how to reach them. At any rate, the idea that capacity is fixed is much in question. Some people are saying, "Don't tell us about their IQ or their home background or anything else. Just tell us what you want them to learn, and leave the rest to us." Others, more disturbingly, are going a bit further: "Tell us what you want them to learn, put them in our charge— and leave the rest to us."

What essentially is being contended is that learners can and will learn if those who are teaching know enough about how to teach.

Content Analysis

Part of our problem has been that we have sometimes tried to teach what is not true or adequate and therefore has been very hard to teach. The more scientific analysis of the nature of knowledge that has come out of the emphasis on its structure is promising to help us identify what is learnable. The teaching of modern language has been revolutionized by the reexamination of content as well as by the redefinition of the goal as mastery. The teaching of mathematics and of science is being similarly affected. As we learn how to put the pieces together again in our competing analyses of beginning reading, we may anticipate that we will be increasingly successful in teaching the first steps of that most complex and mysterious set of learnings.

We have learned more ourselves about what is learnable, that is the point, and it is making a great difference in our prospects for successful teaching.

Materials

We have discovered how to prepare materials that are much more studyable than any we have developed before, much more precise and detailed and geared much more directly to eliciting the responses needed for learning than anything we would have been able to imagine in the past as either possible, necessary, or perhaps desirable. A recent brochure [3] on 20 programs designed to teach pieces or segments of knowledge describes the reusable booklets as containing "ten short sets of 25–50 frames, each designed to be worked in 15 to 30 minutes." The booklets have been developed in terms of two conditions: "(1) satisfactory terminal behavior (mastery of the subject) and (2) an error rate of less than 10 percent." Topics for which programs are available include "Cells: Their Structure and Function," "Latitude and Longitude," and "Figures of Speech."

In short, we now have for the first time the kind of study materials we have needed in order to make it possible to individualize instruction toward mastery—and will soon have them in quantities greater than we have thought.

Methodology

We have broken through another barrier, one of the most unlikely breakthroughs in educational history. For a long time, we have used as a kind of symbol of individualized instruction the apocryphal image of a student on one end of a log and Mark Hopkins on the other. Now we are faced with the prospect of having a student on one end of the line and by computer who knows whom on the other. That part of the problem of individualizing instruction represented by the need for providing a one-to-one correspondence of teacher and learner, however eerie or unearthly or unheavenly their relationship may seem to us likely to be, is already resolved.

We will know a great deal more about what this is going to mean for us in the very near future as the education industry begins to get itself into full production.

---

[3] "20 Learning Programs from Coronet," Coronet Learning Programs, Coronet Building, Chicago, Illinois 60601; 4 pages.

Evaluation

One of the chief worries we have had under our efforts to individualize instruction has been to find out when help was needed and in general to check on progress among 25 to 30 learners working independently. The new care in spelling out specific objectives; the elaboration of study materials, with built-in feedback of some kind to the learner; and now the computer—all have helped or will help to make the flow of evaluative information not only continuous but, in terms of quantity and precision, more than we can handle. In fact, in some situations, clerks are being employed to manage and control the flow so that it will become most useful.

We certainly now have the information we need for evaluation in individualizing instruction although we may still need to consider how best to handle it.

Organization

The matter of grouping learners for individualized instruction has been the one element of the problem above all others to which we have been historically most attentive. We have tried everything and anything. Now, however, we have suddenly found ourselves with a choice of alternatives, partly perhaps because of our inventiveness but also because other elements in the problem have been clarified. We can organize our pupils in relationship to successive levels of progress through a well-defined sequence of study materials. Or we can organize them in larger units of 100 or so, with an augmented staff and plenty of open space, and leave the internal grouping and scheduling to the teacher corps. Or we can run students through study or learning centers more or less at random, leaving their assignments and supervision to whoever is in charge of their stations. In the latter case, where for this portion of the day the learner is to work independently, with programmed materials entirely on his own or under the tutelage of a remote computer, grouping is merely a question of housing.

We really face no difficulties any more as far as organization goes, that is, supposing that we accept individualization of instruction as the overriding or even the sole concern.

THE SOURCE OF OUR DISCOMFORT

How surprised we are, when we look the situation right in the face, to find that we really have triumphed over the problem of how to teach everybody whatever everybody needs to know. By reviving mastery as our goal, letting go of the notion of limitations in capacity to learn, analyzing more scientifically what needs to be and can be learned, preparing dramatically different and more studyable materials, inviting in the computer assistant, letting loose in consequence a flood of information about how well learning is progressing, and organizing learners in new and inventive ways—yes, by redefining and relating all these elements of individualized instruction, we have licked the problem.

We can truthfully say that when it comes to the education of the whistler, we know what we want to hear. And we can teach just about anybody to whistle *Yankee Doodle* or *Dixie*.

Still, to return to our discomfort in the face of such triumph, we may wonder at what we have paid or seem willing to pay for the prospect of such success. We know, when we think of the realm in which success is to be expected, that in order to succeed we have altered our conception of what education is all about, reduced it, limited it, fundamentalized it.

Thus, we are at this moment uneasy. In fact, some of us may be more than uneasy, we may be horrified at what success would seem to mean. To some zealots of the new era, it would seem right and proper that the realm of what everybody needs to know should be extended into everything that anybody might want to learn. If we can, they seem to be saying, through the use of this process of instruction, succeed with a piece of the program, why not move ahead to all of it. Let us analyze, atomize, technologize, prescribe, and so truly individualize the entire curriculum.

But for most of us, while we may be surprised that anybody would conceive of the total curriculum as lending itself to such treatment and may be disappointed perhaps at the waste of effort going into wholesale attempts to misapply the process of individualized instruction as we have described it, we are puzzled now and more than a little apprehensive at something much more likely to be hard to accept. We can trust to the general good sense to take care of excesses of zeal in the routinization of teaching. But are we now ready to assume responsibility for redesigning our program to provide more adequately for the larger aspects of learning that successful routinization of the facts and skills segment is going to give us?

We have had to spend so much time on the facts and skills segment in the past that we have not done what we would have liked with the rest of the curriculum. Now the prospect of success in teaching the facts and skills means that we will have the time and space to do more with the rest.

What we are faced with, at the prospect of success in individualizing instruction is the necessity of redeveloping the curriculum to subordinate and transcend the segment for which routinization is appropriate. We have the time and space to do more with the larger learnings.

What is involved in this task? The first thing is to clarify the differences between the lesser and the larger learnings in terms of the elements already defined. Let us run through these quickly so that we are clear about there really being genuine differences.

Goals

For the larger learnings, the goal is not mastery. There is no reachable end-point on the way to which highly specific steps or objectives can be spelled out. Continuous growth is the goal.

Nature of the Learner

The question of equality of capacity is not central since mastery is not the goal. What is of concern is "an ability, a power . . . the possibility of growth." [4]

Content Analysis

With the emphasis on the development of powers or their growth, analysis of what needs to be learned is very different here. It is concerned with the nature of the process through which powers develop.

Materials

The total environment is of greater concern than any piece of material. The concern is for richness and diversity rather than precision.

Methodology

Powers are personal. Their growth comes necessarily from individual use. The concern is to provide many opportunities for their responsible exercise.

Evaluation

Since growth or "carrying power forward" [5] is the goal, evaluation is concerned with the individual rather than the group and is likely to be seen in global rather than concrete terms.

Organization

While room needs to be made to insure independent functioning, many personal powers require the presence of others in the picture for their proper development. The isolation booth is an inappropriate site for the larger learnings.

Now such a contrast serves to make plain that we are still dealing with individualization of instruction. We talk of the person here, however, and of his powers and of their growth. It might be useful at this point if we were to propose two definitions for the individualization of instruction: (a) the individualization of instruction that leads to the achievement of mastery in the lesser learnings and (b) the individualization of instruction that leads to the development or growth of power in

---

[4] John Dewey, *Democracy and Education.* New York: The Macmillan Company, 1916; p. 49.

[5] *Ibid.;* p. 61.

the larger learnings. The former aims at success despite individual differences; the latter aims at success in terms of individual differences, perhaps actually seeking to make the most of them toward a greater range of human variability, at least in all the generally desired directions or arenas of growth.

But the distinction attempted in these definitions may still strike us as abstract and poorly expressed. What we may need in addition is the exemplification of the larger learnings. If we are going to have to redevelop the curriculum to make good use of the newly vacated time and space, what are we going to be trying to do? The growth of which personal powers are we to try to forward? What is the nature of the realm of the larger learnings?

THE REALM OF THE LARGER LEARNINGS

Perhaps what we are moving into now is the education of the poet as compared to the education of the whistler.

"I believe in individuals." [6] This is the way Anton Chekhov responded to a correspondent inquiring about his politics. "I see salvation in a few people living their own private lives," he continued, "scattered throughout Russia—whether they be intellectuals or muzhiks, the power is in them, though they are few." Elsewhere Chekhov, whom we may take to stand for the poet, defined the realm of personal powers: "My holy of holies is the human body, health, intelligence, talent, inspiration, love, and the most absolute freedom—freedom from violence and lying, whatever forms they may take. This is the program I would follow if I were a great artist." [7]

Let us try to say what such larger learnings are, and, with more attention from us, might be.

Physical Being

We may begin with the powers of physical being. If we had more time and space in the curriculum to attend to physical growth and development, what might that mean?

For one thing, it would encompass but go far beyond mastery of skills although skills would certainly be there—skills of walking and running, of throwing and catching, of surfing and sailing, of skiing and hiking and dancing. Information would have its place also, of course—about diet and safety, drugs, and diseases.

[6] Anton Chekhov, *The Personal Papers of Anton Chekhov*. Introduction by Matthew Josephson. New York: Lear Publishers, Inc., 1948; "Letter to I. I. Orlov, 1899," pp. 194–195.

[7] *Ibid.*, "Letter to A. N. Pleshcheyev, October, 1889," p. 154.

But in our enlarged program, much more time and space would be provided for free play, for self-chosen games, dancing, swimming, and gymnastics; and for loafing—for refreshment and relaxation. The environment would be designed for physical functioning and physical freedom all day long—and the school would extend its responsibility to outdoor sites for hiking, pack trips, camping, visits to the beach.

The expanded program would focus on more opportunities for physical development, for using the physical powers enjoyably and for experiencing the world through the body, including not only the natural world (air breathed in deep, the feel of sun and wind and rain) but the world of other persons—through racing, tagging, wrestling, helping up, striking out, gaming, forming circles, dancing, pairing off.

We have never had time really to celebrate the physical powers and their growth and development. Now we well may have.

Sensibility

"Experience is never limited, and it is never complete," begins Henry James, in his famous definition of what it means to be fully conscious of one's own existence; "it is an immense sensibility, a kind of huge spider-web of the finest silken threads suspended in the chamber of consciousness, and catching every airborne particle in its tissue." This mechanism of sensibility "takes to itself the faintest hints of life, it converts the very pulses of the air into revelations." Such sensibility is "the power to guess the unseen from the seen, to trace the implication of things, to judge the whole piece by the pattern, the condition of feeling life in general so completely that you are well on your way to knowing any particular corner of it. . . ." [8]

Education of the power or powers of sensibility—of responding fully to experience, of being thoroughly conscious of the world about one in all its manifold meanings—incorporates mastery of certain skills and information, it is true. Being able to identify the structure of the cell or the figures of speech may help. But the development of the powers of responsiveness and consciousness necessarily comes through many encounters with rich, raw experience and the chances one has to respond to these encounters, the demands made upon awareness.

The message of Marshall McLuhan is highly relevant here. We live in an image-bearing environment so rank and dense with multilayered meanings that we must learn to respond to it all at once. Today the school is often less stimulating than the out-of-school environment, more restricted, blander, relatively impoverished.

[8] Morton Dauwen Zabel, editor, *The Portable Henry James*. New York: The Viking Press, 1951; "The Art of Fiction," pp. 401–401.

What would the school look like to the learner if it were designed to be experienced as were the exhibits of Brussels and Expo '67?

What kinds of new and specific learnings would be needed if we were to value responsiveness to the broader environment in terms of the visual arts—graphic arts but also sculpture, architecture, landscape, and town planning? If we were to take films and television seriously? If we wanted to increase awareness and enjoyment of the world of music old and new, eastern as well as western?

If we were to venture deeply into the realms of human awareness outside the arts—the world of feelings and values personally expressed, the spoken and nonverbal cues to feelings and values?

What changes in environment, what additions to specific learnings, the inclusion of what kinds of in- and out-of-school experiences for the exercise and development of sensibility might we have if we were to redesign the curriculum to make use of new time and space in this field of larger learning?

Love

How does one learn to love? It is something that can hardly be spelled out, detailed, programmed. Yet the power to empathize, reach out, relate, identify with, to seek with others community of some kind in increasingly wider circles is surely among the larger learnings with which we will want to do more as we make good use of our new time and space.

Perhaps love as we are thinking of it begins with simple wonder at and respect for the force of life. Marian Catlin in Wallace Stegner's beautiful new novel, *All the Little Live Things,* represents such an aspect of love. Cancer-ridden and pregnant, hoping to live to bear another child, she expresses through her care that nothing living be uprooted or destroyed a neurotic obsession with life, an obsessive love. Her husband, an ethologist, tells of how the baby California gray whale gains a ton a month, and the narrator wonders: "What in *hell* is in whale's milk?" Looking back after Marian's death and recalling that metaphor for her agonizing effort to survive with her baby's birth, the narrator supposes her to be saying to him: "You wondered what was in whale's milk. Now you know. Think of the force down there, just telling things to get born, just to be!" [9] The narrator, an old man aroused from what he comes to call a "twilight sleep" of detached retirement, would amend her feeling —but it remains as a symbol of love.

And love extends to and encompasses death as well as birth. In grieving over and reflecting on his mother's death at 80, Sean O'Casey com-

---

[9] Wallace Stegner, *All the Little Live Things.* New York: The Viking Press, 1967; pp. 66 and 344.

forts himself by seeing her as having passed into the endless stream of humanity. "It wouldn't do to say that each differed from each in some trivial, imperceptible way, blade of grass from blade of grass; leaf of tree from leaf of tree; human face from human face. Who is he who having examined each blade of grass, every leaf of every tree, would say no one of them was like its like? And though human faces might differ, and did, the darkness of hatred, the light of love, the glint of fear, the lightning flash of courage shone the same from every human eye, and the thoughts surrounding them were, in essence, the same in every human heart." [10]

Between the emergence of life and its extinction or translation lies the great range of occasions for valuing and supporting others and expressing love in its many guises. Is this a field in which our powers need to be extended and strengthened? With time enough and space, what more can be done with love in the redeveloped curriculum?

Invention

For the poet, the power to shape and reshape his experience is that which he needs most of all to test and extend. What Sartre says of the meaning of history, the poet would say of the meaning of life: ". . . the problem is not to *know* its objective, but to *give* it one." [11]

While there are specific and lesser learnings that need to be there to be called upon, the development of the power to deal creatively with fresh experience, to search it out (to "seek crossroads of meaning, unexpected echoes, strange encounters") and to work with it (fearing "neither detours, surprises, nor darkness") until it yields both form and substance —this kind of development depends on openness to new experience and a great freedom of experiencing. When what is to be known is all laid out for the learner, the power of invention gets little enough exercise.

Providing in the new curriculum more time and space for richer experiencing that will stimulate the learner to alter or amend, compose, design, discover, recast, reorder, shape and reshape his world would seem obviously to be of the greatest importance.

Endurance

Grace Norton, a friend of Henry James', who in his words seemed to "make all the misery of all the world" her own (she "suffered," as they said then), received a letter of consolation from James under the date July 28, 1883. "Sorrow comes in great waves . . . but it rolls over us, and though it may almost smother us it leaves us on the spot, and we know

[10] Sean O'Casey, *Inishfallen: Fare Thee Well*. New York: The Macmillan Company, 1949; p. 38.

[11] Jean-Paul Sartre, *Situations*. Translated by Benita Eisler. New York: George Braziller, 1965; "Reply to Albert Camus," p. 103.

that if it is strong we are stronger, inasmuch as it passes and we remain. It wears us, uses us, but we wear it and use it in return; and it is blind, whereas we after a manner see." [12]

Years later, James wrote to Henry Adams, who had sent him a "melancholy outpouring" of "unmitigated blackness" about their being "lone survivors": "I still find my consciousness interesting—under *cultivation* of the interest." And he suggests that perhaps this survival of interest comes "because I am that queer monster, the artist, an obstinate finality, an inexhaustible sensibility." [13]

Of his reaction to the first-night failure of *The Sea Gull*, Chekhov wrote to a friend: "When I got home I took a dose of castor oil, and had a cold bath, and now I am ready to write another play." [14]

In his account of the San Francisco earthquake, William James, who went into the city from Stanford where he was spending a few months, remarked on the resilience of the victims, of their "healthy animal insensibility and heartiness." [15]

One of the powers, then, that we know we need to include among the larger learnings is the power to endure. In a television interview with Ernest Jones some years ago, Lionel Trilling asked the aging biographer of Freud how he would summarize the lesson of the master. Jones' reply was this: "To look life straight in the face—and endure it." We might find this message a little bleak ourselves and wish to amend it, but we would have to concede that physical being, sensibility or consciousness, love, and shaping and reshaping our experience rest as powers on this rock-bottom hardiness, this power simply to be and to endure.

An environment arranged or prepared for learning, an environment ordered for simplicity and certainty toward prescribed ends, a failure-free environment—whatever its uses, such an environment may be inadequate for developing fully the power to endure. Much of life "out there" beyond the school or around the school, before and after school, is disarranged and unprepared, disordered and complex and uncertain, formless or littered with discarded forms, ambiguous, full of incongruity, possibly meaningless. To learn to live in this world one needs to be in it, with it, so to speak.

Can we set the school scene for adventures into this world that has to *be accepted first* to be experienced, has to be endured to be shaped, to be loved, to be responded to, to be physically enjoyed? The education of the poet really begins as he risks his life, so to speak, in venturing into the enchanted forest. Perhaps we can help him develop the power not merely

[12] Zabel, *op. cit.*, p. 650.

[13] *Ibid.*, p. 675.

[14] Chekhov, *op. cit.*, "Letter to A. S. Souvorin, October 22, 1896," p. 173.

[15] William James, *Memories and Studies*. New York: Longmans, Green, and Company, 1912; "On the Mental Effects of the Earthquake," p. 226.

to endure the darkness, the detours, the surprises but possibly to seek life out, even to welcome the bewildering and wonderful world.

Certainly as educators, we are convinced that in the long run the great human tragedy is the person who drops out, not to tune in and turn on but merely to be safe somewhere in the dusty ruts and routines of the half-alive, the twilight valleys of the living dead.

What we have tried to do here is first to celebrate the prospect of success in individualizing instruction under what we have chosen to call definition (a): the individualization of instruction that leads to the achievement of mastery in the lesser learnings.

Then we have noted that this prospect should mean that our curriculum will be open to redevelopment. The teaching of facts and skills will occupy less time and space than in the past.

We have proposed that we use this time and space to individualize instruction under definition (b): the individualization of instruction that leads to the development or growth of power in the larger learnings.

We have tried to identify some of these powers—the powers of physical being, or responding, of loving, creating, and enduring.

We have tried to imbue our analysis with a sense of urgency. If we do not see and accept the challenge of curriculum redevelopment on some such terms as these, there may be those less broadly based than ourselves who will move into the freed time and space with something or other, probably more and more of less and less.

Samuel Beckett, after conducting one of his heroes through a series of misadventures, deposits him finally alongside a highway where the hero narrator tries to attract the attention of occasional passersby. "I tried to groan, Help! Help!" the hero complains. "But the tone that came out was that of polite conversation." [16]

So it may be with this present effort.

In closing, we may return to an attempt William James made to call attention to the great waste that exists in the undeveloped powers or energies of men. The questions of the extent of our powers and "the various keys for unlocking them in diverse individuals" were to him those that "dominate the whole problem of individual and national education." [17]

"Compared with what we ought to be," James challenged, "we are only half awake. Our fires are damped, our drafts are checked." [18]

Perhaps that is still the challenge to us both as educators and as members of a democratic society. We need whistlers, certainly, but we need poets even more.

[16] Samuel Beckett, *Stories and Texts for Nothing.* New York: Grove Press, Inc., 1967; "The End," p. 62.

[17] W. James, *op. cit.;* "The Energies of Men," p. 263.

[18] *Ibid.,* p. 237.

22 | What Is Individualized Instruction?[1]

WILLIAM HEDGES

Serious attempts to individualize instruction are sweeping the country. These efforts appear in many forms. There are the reading experts who are recommending a more flexible curriculum in which children progress continuously according to achievement, including using the heretofore "sacred and untouchable" basal readers of the next or higher grades. There are the mathematics experts who are recommending children be allowed to proceed at widely varying rates through precisely defined but variably sequenced mathematical skills and concepts. There are the school organization experts who speak of nongrading or continuous progress plans or of ungradedness. And there are the philosophers who speak of providing each child with those environmental challenges (experiences) which are clearly designed to contribute toward his achieving the goals which (in the teacher's judgment) are what that child should encounter regardless of any preconceived grade level expectations.

Whatever their name and no matter whether they are primarily concerned with reading, arithmetic, science, physical education, or any other area, all attempts at individualized instruction have a common goal, i.e., to provide for the tremendous differences in student aptitude, student achievement, student interest, et al., of which every elementary teacher is

[1] References to the "Oakleaf Project" are based on the material found in *Programmed Instruction in the Schools: An Application of Programming Principles in "Individually Prescribed Instruction,"* by C. M. Lindvall and John O. Bolvin; Chap. VIII (pp. 217–254) of the Sixty-sixth Yearbook, Part II, of the National Society for the Study of Education. All rights reserved. Used by permission.

keenly aware, and to provide for these differences in a society committed to the goal of mass education.

If your school is seriously contemplating moving toward more individualized instruction, there are certain characteristics of such instruction of which you should be aware. I just do not see how you can individualize or nongrade or develop continuous progress on more than a superficial level unless you are prepared to confront, to come to understand, *and to cope with and accept* these factors:

CHARACTERISTICS OF INDIVIDUALIZED INSTRUCTIONAL PROGRAMS

FACTOR 1: Students do not leave one unit and begin a new one until they have attained a predetermined level of proficiency in the former unit.

The above assumes the child has been carefully and properly placed. Under this condition the practice of allowing children to "move on" to new material, new skills, new concepts, having earned a percentage grade of say 75%, is no longer followed. Rather, *assuming the child has been properly placed,* it becomes necessary to introduce a variety of teaching strategies (and materials) until the teacher is prepared to say: "I think John really understands this concept or has mastered this skill." For example, suppose the skill was as follows:

> John can perform column addition using two addends and with three or more digit numbers which do not require carrying. He can check these addition problems by adding in the reverse direction.[2]

You *can* ascertain whether John can do the above because it is highly specific and is expressed in behavioral (observable) terms. When John leaves this "unit" he must have achieved close to 100 percent mastery—not 75 percent—hence letter grades become meaningless. All students achieve mastery—but the time and methods required to achieve this mastery must vary and this leads us to our second factor:

FACTOR 2: Students must be allowed varying amounts of time (and practice) to achieve mastery of specific instructional goals.

Traditionally we have taught using fixed lengths or periods of time for groups of students, and have allowed mastery to vary from high to low as

---

[2] Richard C. Cox, *The Project for Individually Prescribed Instruction,* (Oakleaf Project), Learning Research and Development Center, University of Pittsburgh, Sample Test Packet Level D. Addition, p. 2.

represented by the letter grades of A through F. For example, we have assumed at the secondary school level that all students need 180 clock hours of teacher instruction in order to learn enough to receive one Carnegie unit of credit; we have assumed in the junior high school that all students should study the metric system in science classes for about ten days each year; we have assumed in the elementary school that all children should have the same amount of time in school each day to reach a certain level of mastery in spelling. In short, we have kept the time factor constant, and have allowed a large percentage of our children to fail or to perform very poorly. The result has been that as these children have progressed through school they have become increasingly handicapped because the new tasks confronting them have rested upon the presumption that they have mastered the previous work.

The situation is very different with the more individualized program. Having defined the goals with precision and having demanded each student achieve mastery, we must then allow the heretofore fixed factor of time to become elastic. Time becomes the major variable. What we are really saying is that we will (for the first time outside of a tutorial context) recognize variations in aptitude for learning. We are saying we are prepared to give more than lip service to the fact of individual differences. We are saying there is an almost inverse ratio between aptitude for learning something and the time that will be required to master it, i.e., the greater the aptitude the less the time required.

We are *not*, however, saying that a child must learn something just because he is such and such an age or in such and such a grade as was the case years ago in America when some eighteen-year-olds were still in the first grade. Contingent upon requiring mastery is the clear knowledge by the teacher that the student has been properly placed, i.e., has been confronted with tasks which he can master. This leads us to our third factor:

FACTOR 3: Permitting students to proceed at varying rates necessitates provision for frequent and diagnostically oriented evaluations of each student's progress.

No longer will all students take their unit tests at the same point in time —ready or not. Multiple forms of tests for each specific skill and concept will have been made out and filed. When a student is deemed ready, he is administered the mastery test. This test, while covering only a very small, discrete area, is comprehensive and diagnostic *of that area*. The scoring of this will reveal not only whether the student has achieved mastery, but if not, wherein the student seems in need of help. This information in turn provides the basis for new materials and new teaching strategies pointing toward those same skills or concepts.

The above type of detailed and frequent but irregular evaluation of each student necessitates very comprehensive record keeping, test scoring, and the like. This means that the teacher who would individualize must have clerks to aid her. This leads us to our fourth factor.

FACTOR 4: The teacher's role changes from being primarily one of disseminating information to one of (1) diagnosing pupil needs, (2) planning and preparing each child's instructional program, (3) working with pupils in small groups or individually and (4) supervising teacher clerks, teacher aides, and junior or less experienced teachers.

With an array of information at her fingertips derived from a variety of sources, the teacher moves into the role of figuring out the needs of her pupils. This role requires a more sophisticated teacher than formerly, because it requires the teacher to know and to be able to apply a great deal in the area of child growth and development and learning theory. Also, and because the teacher is not busy "talking all the time," she now has some time to locate or prepare materials. Preparation might include the making of a listening tape in arithmetic, while locating might include the assignment of John to an SRA tape already on file in the learning resources center.

Whereas the superb elementary teacher of former years found it possible *albeit very demanding* to have as many as three reading groups, three math groups, etc., this new type teacher will find it possible to have many groups of two, three, four, or even only one student. You ask, of course, "Just *where* is the teacher to find all this extra time?" This question leads us to our fifth factor.

FACTOR 5: Students become more actively involved in the learning process than before by assuming more responsibility for their own development.

Rather than listening to the teacher for such a high percentage of the school day (50–75 percent), the student is engaged in much more independent study. With good classroom organization, students can carry out assignments (and not infrequently complete them) with only limited assistance from the teacher. We have assumed far too long that the most effective medium for learning is through the human ear. We have assumed far too long that everything a child was going to do that was "new" had to be explained or predigested for the child. Today we are discovering that frequently it is only when the child is "stuck" that he should come to you in some subject areas or on some assignments. We have conditioned far too many of our students to sit and wait until the teacher has carefully explained everything, or to wait until they arrive home at night so that mother can do their thinking for them. Under more individualized instructional systems, the child is more directly involved in trying to understand the directions, or in trying to decide whether he should go back and view that five minute film clip a second time, or in electing to hear the teacher's explanation of an arithmetic concept on tape a third time. The teacher who cannot move into this new role comfortably—the teacher who is bothered by seeing herself at what she considers to be the periphery of the teaching process—the teacher who would rather be "up front" and "talking at" the children— this teacher is probably going to be uncomfortable in a school which is moving into a more individualized instructional program.

But a note of caution is in order here. If we are to respect the individuality of students, we must not ignore the individuality of teachers. There are some teachers who work more effectively in certain contexts and using certain methods. It is very probable, also, that there are some students who will profit more from association with certain teachers than in working with other teachers. Can we bring these together? Recognition of the above approach can often help to resolve otherwise impossibly difficult conflicts in regard to nongrading. If we can identify those children who should be with one teacher and with that teacher's methods for a major part of the day, we can aid both teacher and students by bringing them together.

FACTOR 6: With individualized instruction almost every child becomes a teacher part of the time.

With increased responsibility for their own learning, students can go to their peers for help much more frequently than before. No longer need they contact just the teacher while "hiding" or shielding their work from their peers. Nor need the teacher or teachers worry very much about the cheating factor because the student who copies much of his work will soon enough be found out on the diagnostic mastery tests and will soon enough come to understand that he has been wasting his time. This student will discover this fact because he has to stay with a unit until mastery, and he eventually comes to understand he is not achieving mastery by copying. Students vary in the rapidity with which they acquire this insight; for some have been very indoctrinated with the belief that what is important is *how fast* one "covers" material and turns in completed work, rather than with the belief that what is important is understanding. The new type teacher is not interested just in whether or not the homework or seatwork has been completed, but is most interested in student mastery—in fact as well as in statement.

And it will amaze some of us to note that it is not just the bright students who become the teachers. Some of our so-called "slow learners" can and do become teachers in certain areas or in certain specific respects. Not always is the glib, verbal child who understands an arithmetic process the one to whom another child goes when he wants help. The child needing help may go to a youngster who had great difficulty when *he* was working on that unit. Remember we are speaking here of a situation characterized by multiage grouping and variable sequencing of learning tasks. In addition, one of the findings from some of the Federal education programs has been that one way for a slow learner to learn is to make him a teacher.

It is a source of amazement that we have not thought of this before, because most of us as teachers have said at one time or another: "I learned more my first year of teaching than I did in all my student teaching. . . . ." What we were really saying was that because we were *involved,* i.e., because we were talking, explaining, writing, waving our arms, drawing diagrams (trying to communicate with and get someone to understand), we had a great deal of learning theory going for us and we did learn. If we apply this theory of involvement in allowing our students to help one another, we will see that the helper is helped as well as helping. The helping becomes a double-edged process. In particular we discover that the student as teacher (1) learns better how to express himself so as to be understood (and this is one of our major goals for each student), and (2) becomes more aware of the study habits which should or should not be employed—which are or are not efficient. Also, the "slow" student perceives he actually does know a great deal and this knowledge serves to enhance his self-image. We also discover that much more can be accomplished when a student does not have to wait to contact the teacher to obtain help. The above is in sharp contrast to the traditional procedure of allowing only the more able child to be a teacher.

FACTOR 7: Our classrooms must be arranged differently in a physical sense.

If we are to have classrooms in which students are working through different materials or varying rates and using different methods and within a variety of groups, then we must drastically rearrange the physical setting so as to facilitate learning. Rather than classrooms, we must have learning resource centers. We must have individual study booths in which a single student can watch a film clip and hear and see a dialogue; we must have a small library center with reference books and work spaces; we must have small three- and four-pupil conference booths where students can confer without their conversation interrupting the others in the class; we must have a listening center for tapes; we must have a construction center for the use of simple tools; we must have . . .

In short, our classrooms must increasingly come to resemble spaces that are designed for a variety of strategies for learning rather than spaces wherein information can be efficiently disseminated by means of the teacher's voice. A classroom designed for *teaching* has rows of chairs facing toward the front of the room; a classroom designed for *learning* looks much like a modern kindergarten—with provisions for a virtual plethora of activities in a large flexible space that can be rearranged as often as necessary. The acoustics are good; the lighting is adequate; there is carpeting on the floor; and walls are movable.

FACTOR 8: We must begin to apply a "systems analysis" approach to schools as learning centers.

On a modest scale, the crucial test of the efficacy of the technology in a school is whether teacher time is saved and teacher production rises. The day—still prevailing in some schools—when the teacher had to "go get the film projector, thread the film, operate the projector, dismantle and return it to storage, etc." must go. Instead, the teacher should be able to dial for the film. The teacher must have an increasing array of machines at her fingertips and be able to feel secure in the knowledge they will work for her most of the time. The technology of information retrieval has shown tremendous advances in the past decade and it is past time for schools to put it to use.

By beginning to bring scientific analysis to the school as a system much as is being done in business, we can begin to identify and eradicate some of the obstacles to learning for students and the obstacles to working for teachers. Most schools today are organized in ways that make it possible for them to be efficiently administered rather than organized on a basis which reflects what we know about how children learn. This cannot continue in a school which is serious about individualizing instruction.

Examples of technology that are showing signs of helping us to individualize to a greater extent include: (1) the computer which enables us to build heretofore impossibly complex schedules; (2) computer-based teaching which is now in an embryonic stage but which is able to employ the concept of feedback with individual students; (3) easily accessible libraries of film clips; (4) closed circuit TV; (5) modern language laboratories, etc. These are just the beginning.

SUMMARY

This newsletter has described the essence of individualized instruction, i.e., *what is implied* for a school faculty seriously interested in providing differentiated instruction for its students. Obviously, it is *not going to be easy* and it is *not going to be accomplished quickly*. But, virtually every school can begin in some small degree to modify its program so as to introduce some individualized instruction.

23 | Individualizing Instruction: Educational Fad or Educational Fulfillment?

MAURIE HILLSON

Reprinted with permission from *Hillson Letter Number Four, The Nongraded Elementary School*, pp. 1–4, © 1966, Science Research Associates, Inc. Reprinted by permission of the publisher.

SOCIETY AND THE INDIVIDUAL

Not long ago, a major educational association saw fit to publish a yearbook devoted entirely to individualization (*Concern for the Individual in Student Teaching,* Forty-Second Yearbook, Cedar Falls, Iowa: The Association for Student Teaching, 1963). There is no question that the individualization of instruction is one of the issues of our times.

This presents an interesting phenomenon. For many years the profession of education has given verbal testament to the concept of individual differences. Colleges taught the preservice teachers the techniques for assessing individual differences in their child growth and development classes. In the classes on methodology they were taught ways to differentiate instruction to meet the needs which they found resident in the groups of learners they faced. Endless hours of discussion have been spent concerning ideas, techniques, and ways of coping with the variations found in a classroom.

Even if the concept of individuality is generally embraced by the oft-quoted educational shibboleth, "we recognize individual differences in children," rare are the instances where classrooms exhibit those experiences which carry beyond the recognition stage. Recognition does not necessarily mean that viable programs are set in motion to capitalize on these recognized differences. In fact, the opposite is often the case.

Most administrators are accustomed to the necessity for dividing pupils up into groups which display some homogeneity along some dimension. They use for this purpose the intelligence dimension or age dimension, or possibly, an ability dimension. They want to classify and cluster pupils in a way so that they know where the pupils are. These clusters frequently become fixed groups. They become crystallized. They do indeed become homogenized—if not homogeneous. They replicate other aspects of our culture in their unvarying uniformity and in the uniformity that they seek.

One may add to this kind of grouping activity the manner in which teachers project their own problems into a classroom. Because of their own reference groups they carefully shape the behavior that they want displayed by their children (Jules Henry, *Culture Against Man,* New York: Random House, 1963). David Riesman points out that teachers are measured *not* by the way they teach, but rather in terms of their competence in the use of techniques for gaining consensus or cooperation from their charges (David Riesman, *et al., The Lonely Crowd,* Garden City, N.Y.: Doubleday & Company, Inc., Chap. 2, 1956). It would be a mistake not to recognize the fact that, in general, teachers accept the statements concerning individual differences. But they do it uncritically. Their practices concerning these differences are usually superficial.

When teachers are faced by an ever increasing number of students, the explosion of knowledge that they are expected to transmit, and the limited hours that they have to work with children, the tendency is to reach out for an easy device to classify the pupils into handy groups for instruction.

We are presently in what the sociologists call a "togetherness-oriented" society. It is also referred to as a "corporate" society. Everybody seeks to get along with one another. Consensus is a byword in the culture. What eventually happens in this kind of culture is yet to be seen. But one thing is certain: when the major aim of a society is consensus which is reflected in the schools through teacher behavior and pupil activity, a docility sets in which undermines scholarship and creates a conformism which leads to mediocrity. Fathers reinforce corporate behavior in their homes. Mothers, in turn, play their roles in making the behavior work. When teachers and schools stress grades and other external awards for advancement; when they reinforce these symbols by their classroom behavior; and when mothers and fathers in turn reward their children with "dollars for A's," we move to the real calamitous aspect of conformism. We clutch the tangibles. We submerge the imagination. Through this kind of activity we get an intense externality. We achieve a big-show kind of existence which is bereft of sincerity. How unfortunate! With a very great number of alternatives available, and with more being made available through study and research, to seek a uniformity of practice by dealing only with external appearances limits the potential and growth of the culture as a whole.

The question of whether the individualization of instruction is a fad or really something that leads to educational fulfillment is a crucial one. It is crucial in an historic sense. In Europe, the peasant was bound to his family. From his birth he was labeled for life. His personal talents were submerged and the incentive to develop an individual personality was frowned upon, or if attempted—shattered. He was very likely to be born, grow, live out his life, and die in the same village. If these physical circumstances are hard to imagine as you read this letter hundreds or maybe thousands of miles from your own birthplace, contemplate for a moment the intellectual constrictions that enchained the mind of the peasant in the European societies. There was no room for even the slightest alteration of fixed sets of customs. Novel ideas or creative endeavors were taboo. Traditions were crystallized, established, and passed on in an intellectual world as immutable as the physical one that encapsulated many people in historic societies.

Modern America, on the other hand, represents the growth and triumph of individualism. The American family nurtured this. The school, first the agent of the church and then the agent of the state, fostered and became the social institution that ratified and guaranteed it.

This short analysis leads directly to the problem that concerns educators: the individualization of instruction and teaching the individual learner.

Individualization of instruction and the bolstering of responsible individualism is crucial. If one compares our present physical and intellectual situation with those of the European peasant, it becomes readily apparent that individualism with its attendant concomitants underpin freedom and liberty.

In a free society where the traditions of individual freedom have been nurtured and practiced, man never again need be only a piece of chattel buffeted by historical forces. Some of the present-day totalitarian states offer us much insight as it concerns conformism. Individualism endows and encourages one to be autonomous, exercise choice, and vouchsafe democracy.

THE SCHOOLS AND THE INDIVIDUAL

Any critical analysis of the schools yields the finding that individualization as a theme for learning is not widespread. There are schools where very real attempts are being made to individualize instruction. But more often school systems write in their philosophies of education or curriculum guides about their commitment to the individual child without a commensurate adoption of methods and strategies, or teacher-training programs to insure the actual practice of individualization. If a person learns to be responsible by being responsible, then surely it must follow that one truly becomes an adequate individual by being treated as an individual. Life degenerates into mere routine if the boundaries of individuality are not readily and steadily extended. It is the job of the school to readily and steadily extend the boundaries.

This cannot be done successfully in a graded school. This cannot be done by sloganizing. This cannot be done by inflexible grouping procedures. This cannot be done by endlessly expending efforts to create a kind of homogeneity among learners—a homogeneity, by the way, that really is unattainable because is is quite nonexistent. And, most importantly, this cannot be done without some intensive reschooling of teachers and administrators.

In order to make a change toward giving increasing attention to the needs of the individual learner, we must come to see the organization for learning in a different light. The themes that presently run through our schools and which support the present activities of pupil assessment, programs, and school progress are insufficient if individual differences are really to be recognized, evaluated, probed, and capitalized on in the schools. If real commitment to individualization were to become the "law of the land," it would naturally activate new themes. For example, the term *below grade level* would have no place in a school organized to develop the competencies of self-instruction. The term *promotion* would be archaic or vestigial in a school where the activities are aimed at developing competencies to deal with any kind of intellectual problem.

An excellent example of this kind of individualized approach is seen in the Meadowbrook School, Newton, Massachusetts. At Meadowbrook they have taken five hundred youngsters and ungraded them. These youngsters are in what would be the customary grades 7, 8 and 9. Individualization is not only embraced philosophically, but it becomes a practical reality in that each pupil makes an individual contract with each subject-matter teacher. Each teacher sits down with each pupil and designs a contract for that pupil. Because the school is broken up into houses (a collection of youngsters and teachers) each pupil has a house advisor. The house advisor has two groups of fifteen youngsters. He sits down with the youngster as often as he thinks necessary. With the added feature of blocks of unscheduled time available, the pupils can be trained to be more independent. They schedule themselves. They involve themselves. They become responsible in creating their individual programs. Many teachers are not readily able to move to this kind of a program.

Teachers who are competent in individualized instruction are very difficult to find. Too many rarely know how to define the goals that they are seeking. Too many do not know how to evaluate a learner's status. They do not know how to test or when to use ratings. And unhappily, too many do not have the techniques for teaching pupils *how to learn*.

Individualization *is not* a fad. Indeed, it may be the very quintessence of our educational system. We will not be able to achieve it unless we greatly improve the competency of the student to learn alone or in a group situation. Students will have to learn to conduct their own learning semiautonomously if we are to create true individualization. To accept this as a professional charge means to accept a whole host of new approaches: nongrading (a major concept attendant to any attempt to individualize), programmed learning, computerized instruction, team learning, team or collaborative teaching, flexible scheduling, and other yet undiscovered methodologies and schema for teaching and learning.

Most importantly, however, when we accept the very viable position that individualization is the prerequisite educational theme needed to assure learning in a democracy, we also accept the orientation of what education is all about. Then it remains to think and create the imaginative activities in schools which are fresh, alive, exciting, and powerful for the individual learner. Gradeless schools are plausible organizational possibilities. The short history of the nongraded school in America is impressive. An analysis of this is prerequisite to creating the fresh departures that will insure individualization.

24 | Individually Prescribed Instruction

JOHN O. BOLVIN

Reprinted with permission from *Educational Screen and Audiovisual Guide*, Vol. 47, No. 4 (April 1968), pp. 14–15, 43.

Educators have long professed the need for an educational system attuned to the background and abilities of individual students. This concern has, in fact, been the basis for most of the recent changes and innovations in school organizations.

Due to the importance of this problem and the potential contribution to educational practice that could result from any significant progress in the development of procedures for providing for the many individual differences among students, the Learning Research and Development Center at the University of Pittsburgh is devoting major attention to this problem. Another reason for centering attention on this problem is that problems of this nature demand rather long-term commitments to develop and are the types of problems research and development centers, now being funded by the U. S. Office of Education, have the unique opportunity to investigate.

The Project on Individually Prescribed Instruction represents an investigation of the problems encountered in the individualization of instruction and involves the development of one type of program for achieving this goal. The essential aspects of individualization that are presently being provided for in this program as operating are: (1) individualization of rate at which students proceed through a carefully sequenced set of objectives for a given subject; (2) mastery of subject matter content by individuals to enhance discovery or creativeness as they proceed through a set of objectives; (3) some self-direction, self-evaluation, and to a limited degree, self-initiation on the part of the learners; and (4) individualized techniques and materials of instruction. These aspects are predicated upon the definition of individualized instruction as an instructional system which provides for the planning and implementation of an individualized program of studies. This system can be tailored to each student's learning needs and his characteristics as a learner that can facilitate his acquisition of new skills.

SIX MAJOR COMPONENTS

The model for individualization is conceived of as consisting of the following components: (1) sequentially established curricular objectives in each area stated in behavioral terms; (2) a procedure and process for diagnosis of student achievement in terms of objectives of the curriculum and the proficiency level desired for each student and each objective; (3) the necessary materials for individualizing learning to provide a variety of paths for attainment of mastery of any given objective; (4) a system for individually prescribing the learning tasks the student is ready to undertake; (5) the organization and management practices of the total school environment to facilitate individualization; and (6) strategies for continuous evaluation and feedback of information for teacher decision making as well as information for continuous evaluation of the curricular for the curriculum developers.

As presently operating, the project involves students for that portion of each school day set aside for study in the three basic content areas: (1) reading, (2) mathematics, and (3) primary science. For the remainder of the day, students are engaged in study under procedures followed in most elementary schools.

IMPLEMENTATION

The curricula presently being implemented in the Individually Prescribed Instruction Project represents a consensus of recent thinking in each of these areas. Members of the project staff, including teachers, psychologists, and subject specialists, examined a variety of curricula currently being offered in each of the subjects to define a sequence of learning experience which could provide the necessary flexibility involved in individualizing instruction. Since it is important that students be able to work through the sequence with a minimum amount of teacher direction, it is necessary to express the curricula in carefully defined objectives with each succeeding objective built upon what preceded. These objectives tend to insure that lessons be directed toward specific student competencies so that more precise evaluative devices could be developed to determine pupil achievement. Each of the curricula is divided into levels, units and objectives, or skills. A level consists of a set of operational tasks grouped into categories and represents a level of achievement at the end of a large sequence of work. Each category within a level is called a unit. Within each unit the subtasks needed to master the unit are called objectives or skills.

Once the sequenced objectives in each area had been stated, diagnostic instruments were developed to measure the specific tasks to be learned. As presently operating, there are four general types of instruments being utilized: placement tests, pre-unit tests, curriculum-embedded tests, and post-unit tests.

Placement tests are administered at the beginning of each academic year to determine general placement in each of the units of each curriculum. From the results of the placement tests, the teacher assigns each child to a pre-unit test for a particular unit. These pretests measure each skill within a unit. Mastery of any of the skills within a given unit means that the child can skip these particular skills and concentrate on the skills within the unit for which there is lack of mastery. Once the child has been assigned work in a given skill and indicates from his manipulation of the tasks that he has mastered that skill, the student is given a curriculum-embedded test—a test which measures the particular skill which he has been assigned. Mastery on this instrument indicates that he is ready to move to the next skill within the unit. When a child has completed all of the work assigned within a unit and successfully indicates mastery on the curriculum-embedded tests, he is assigned a post-unit test covering all of the skills. The posttests are, in essence, an alternate form of the pre-unit tests which the student took prior to working on a unit.

NECESSARY FLEXIBILITY

Materials for individually prescribed instruction have been selected and developed to teach each of the objectives. These materials, for the most part, must be developed for self-study, leading the child from what he knows to what he must know next to progress through the curriculum. Presently there is considerable reliance upon worksheets, tape and disc recordings, programmed materials, individual readers, and manipulative devices. In some instances, it is necessary and desirable for the teacher to present new ideas and processes in each of the subject areas and this is done individually, in small groups, or in large group discussions.

The basic materials for each of the subjects have been organized according to the objectives of the curriculum. For example, for each objective within the mathematics curriculum there is a master file of materials that can be utilized in teaching a single objective. A major task of the Learning Research and Development Center is to develop alternative sets of materials to provide a variety of approaches to the same objectives.

Once the placement testing has been completed, the teacher can determine where each pupil is ready to begin instruction. On the basis of the diagnosis of the student's weakness, a prescription is developed for each child. This prescription, one for each student for each subject, lists the materials for the objectives in which the child should begin studying. For this initial prescription the teacher will generally consider the following factors: (1) the ability level of the child in each subject being prescribed, (2) the general maturity of the child, (3) certain learner characteristics as they relate to the particular learning, and (4) the student's general reaction to IPI. These prescriptions are prepared prior to the scheduled time for the subject and arranged for ease of dissemination as the class begins.

The student then begins work independently on the prescribed materials. This is done in a large room which provides space for all the students from a particular group, e.g., primary, first, second, and third graders. In this area there are, generally, three or four teachers and two or three teacher aides assigned to these students. Most of the students can proceed through the prescribed materials with a minimum of teacher direction and instruction. When assistance requiring extended explanations or instruction is required the team of teachers will decide cooperatively who should give this instruction and to how many. The team responsible for the instruction of a particular group also decides on the sharing of other responsibilities such as administration of pre- and posttests, large group instruction, and prescription writing that may be necessary during class period.

EVALUATION PROGRAM

In order to free the teacher for instructional decision making, tutoring and evaluation of student progress, the scoring of worksheets, tests, etc., is either done by the teacher aides or by the children themselves. The teacher aides also assist the children in locating materials and performing other noninstructional tasks.

An essential aspect of individualized instruction is the provision for charting progress of each student as he moves through the curriculum and the availability of these reports for teacher use. A program for computer-assisted management for the project is presently being developed and will be in operation within the next few months. With the implementation of this management system, teachers will be able to obtain more quickly relevant information on a particular student, reports as to how many and which students are working in the same units or objectives, and daily summaries of the progress of each student. Additional functions of this system will be added as we are able to move the system into operation and train teachers to utilize the system more efficiently.

As indicated earlier, work on this type of a problem demands a rather long-term commitment for development on the part of all parties concerned. Thus far, evaluation on the program has been limited to information feedback that assists in improving the program itself. Assisting in this evaluation, Research for Better Schools, Inc., the U. S. Office of Education sponsored Regional Laboratory in Philadelphia, is field testing the project in 23 elementary schools to obtain data on the model in various settings to determine its reproducibility, cost factors involved, types of teacher training needed in the various settings, and variables related to the implementation and monitoring of an individualized program. In general, what has been accomplished to date in the development of the program has convinced the staff that some degree of individualization of instruction is possible with this type of program.

25 | Independent Study: What Difference Does It Make?

DON H. RICHARDSON

Reprinted with permission from *The Bulletin of the National Association of Secondary School Principals*, Vol. 51, No. 320 (September 1967), pp. 53–62.

Five periods a week, 40 weeks a year equals one unit of credit. That is the time prescription of many years' standing for the typical high school subject. Its yield is one Carnegie Unit, the arbitrary coin of academic earnings. It has a basis in custom as solid as King Henry's nose-to-fingertip measure of a yard. It is educational dogma that regular attendance on each of the five days of the school week is necessary for the success of the student. Indeed, the more class time, the better.

But a revolution is going on in secondary schools that challenges this traditional time arrangement of classes. The well-known work of the NASSP and J. Lloyd Trump has done much to stimulate varying period lengths and instructional groupings. One of the elements of the "Trump Plan" is time for independent study, and many schools now are freeing students from the traditional required time in class to carry independent work.

PROOF NEEDED

It is one thing to release a student from class; it is quite another to be sure that this is effective. There are many questions concerning the selection of students, guidance of independent study, relationship to the classroom teacher, what latitude to allow the student, and finally evaluation of what he has learned.

Many schools give students varying degrees of independence; few, if any, have systematic research evidence of learning results. It is this critical problem of proof that is the substance of this report.

At Valhalla High School in Valhalla, New York, the independent study program enters its fifth year with its values well recognized. The Valhalla program has had the special benefit of research evaluation.

GUIDANCE IN THE VALHALLA PROGRAM

Setting a student loose without guidance is a mistake. "They offer students too much independence and too little program," according to Don Marquette, district principal in Valhalla, speaking of some independent study programs. "In most of these so-called programs," says Mr. Marquette, "students spin off on fantastic flights through a scholastic never-never land. They get a dab of extra reading, some laboratory work, a little field work, and an occasional cigarette in the parking lot. What they should be experiencing—a challenge, stimulation, a taste of true scholarship, a sense of achievement—just never materialize."

Three vital ingredients are needed: student *projects,* student *planning,* and close staff *guidance.* The program at Valhalla emphasizes these key elements. Thus the title, "Directed Independent Study Program," with emphasis on "directed."

WHAT THEY DO

One senior taking dramatics wrote a history of the drama, another in physics undertook an electronic circuitry project that culminated in the construction of a television receiver. A mathematics student studied advanced mathematics through the use of teaching machines and sophisticated programs. A history student used his time to deepen his knowledge of economics; he prepared essays on the writings of Owen and Fourier.

Some pursue intellectual interests not offered in the usual high school curriculum. One such student developed a project dealing with science and philosophy. He completed extensive reading of the works of Immanuel Kant and Thomas Huxley. Another gifted student related his independent study program to outside course work at a nearby university.

Failure confronts some. One science student attempted to construct a mass spectrograph from an old TV tube. As a result of the many problems he encountered, he read widely on the electronics of the instrument. He was not successful in attaining his goal, but he learned much in the process.

HOW IT WORKS

Any interested student may apply. The independent study program is open to all ages in the junior-senior high school at Valhalla. The student applies in a particular subject. In practice, the more mature, academically able student is most likely to apply and be accepted.

Before a student is freed from regular class attendance his plan must survive the critical review of the selection committee. Each student's selection committee includes his subject teacher or teachers, his guidance counselor, the directed independent study program director, and often the principal.

The committee verifies the student's seriousness of purpose and the feasibility of his plan. Constructive suggestions often help the student improve his plan.

Once accepted for independent study in one or more subjects, the student is given the freedom to make up his own daily schedule. His is the responsibility for deciding when he goes to class and when he works independently.

Close coordination between student and teacher is vital since the freed student is still responsible for the major tests and assignments of the class, though he is excused from daily assignments.

When free of the regular classroom, the student with the help of his adviser may use varied resources. His work may take him to the school library, the science laboratory, to a conference with his adviser, or outside the school as in some of the examples already mentioned. Resource people are brought into the school for group or individual interests. For example, one group of independent students gained much from a seminar meeting with the school psychiatrist.

THE TEACHER'S ROLE

A guidance counselor and a subject adviser are assigned to each student in the program. The adviser is usually the classroom teacher of the subject the student is studying. Teacher direction is vital for the student. At the early stage, the student is bursting with energy and enthusiasm. He's raring to go—anywhere. Staff members have to direct this energy into practical channels without killing enthusiasm and independence.

A supporting attitude on the part of the classroom teacher is essential in order to help the student plan when to attend class and when to work independently. A truly professional teacher is required, in order not to be petty about the time the student "misses" class periods.

One extreme example of student success out of class involved a senior girl who was on independent study in American history. She earned 95 percent on the three-year American History and World Backgrounds III Regents examination, and she attended class only twice!

It is not always easy for a teacher to accept the fact that a bright student can sometimes learn as much without the teacher as with him. Staff members need to develop perspective to see that the independent student actually does need the teacher but in a more sophisticated, project-adviser role.

WHAT IS THE PROOF?

From this description it may seem that independent study at Valhalla High School is similar in one way or another to programs in many other schools. The distinguishing feature at Valhalla is the research evaluation.

Subjective opinions might conclude that independent study is an unalloyed blessing. But is it? What evidence is there to substantiate the conclusion? If directed independent study is to be more than the latest educational fad, there has to be documented evidence of its values and limitations.

The New York State Education Department has funded a research project on independent study to find out if students who were out of class a substantial amount of time would learn as much as those who attended regularly. The factors investigated were achievement, school grades, critical thinking, study skills, research and library techniques, originality, and enthusiasm for school.

Francis Lodato of Manhattan College headed the research team. In 1964–65 an original group of 24 high schools agreed to participate. A total of 623 students were involved in the first formal testing. The continuation of the research in 1965–66 included seven more high schools. Valhalla, which had started its own independent study program in 1962–63, joined the project and contributed its experiences.

The following research description is based on a report by Mr. Lodato and his staff which covers statistical studies of 1964–65 and 1965–66. The findings reported here are based on 1965–66 unless otherwise indicated.

CONTROL GROUPS ESTABLISHED

The study which began in the fall of 1964 was designed to compare the learning of two groups of students. One group engaged in a program of independent reading and attended class two or three class periods a week in a given subject, while the matched or control group attended classes on a regular basis. The two groups were matched in age and intelligence and were enrolled in the same subject.

The results of the study compared students, both boys and girls, participating in independent reading programs in eleventh- and twelfth-grade English and eleventh- and twelfth-grade history with control groups in the respective areas.

While the experiment included students in other areas such as mathematics and science, the sample in those areas was too limited to be analyzed statistically.

PREDICTION

An additional purpose of the research was to discover what measures were best for predicting which students would derive the greatest benefits from the program of independent study. Therefore, the following tests were administered to students before independent study began: Henmon-Nelson Tests of Mental Ability, High School Personality Questionnaire, The School Inventory, Test of Critical Thinking, Survey of Study Habits and Attitudes, A Library Orientation Test for College Freshmen, Uses for Things Test, and Metropolitan Achievement Tests. Most of these were also given in the posttest battery.

WHAT HAPPENED
Grades

In school grades, experimental students did as well as or better than control students, even though they spent up to three-fifths of the class periods in independent study outside of the classroom. Their absence from the classroom did not have a detrimental effect on the grades assigned to them by their teachers in those subjects. One difference, in twelfth-year history, favored the second-year experimental boys at the .01 level of significance. Although only this one difference was significant, seven of the eight obtained differences favored the experimental groups. See Table 1.

Regents (statewide tests given in New York State) grades were also compared. Once again students in independent study did as well as or better than students in the control groups. The Regents grades for girls in eleventh-grade English favored experimental students at the .05 level of significance. The scores obtained by the other three experimental sections were higher than the control groups, although the differences between the two sets were not statistically significant. See Table 2.

Gains in Achievement

An analysis of achievement gains of eleventh- and twelfth-grade girls and boys showed that the experimental groups did as well as or better

TABLE I
Final Grades of Both Groups in Subjects in the
Independent Study Program

Section	Sex	Year in Program	Independent Study Group		Control Group			
			N	Mean Grade	N	Mean Grade	t	p
English 11	B	1	23	80.43	21	79.84	.23	N.S.
English 11	G	1	22	81.71	27	79.69	.93	N.S.
History 11	B	1	27	84.73	17	85.42	.41	N.S.
History 11	G	1	24	85.87	21	84.76	.59	N.S.
English 12	B	2	17	86.13	14	83.56	1.08	N.S.
English 12	G	2	14	87.64	13	85.18	1.31	N.S.
History 12	B	2	53	87.02	40	81.86	2.67	.01
History 12	G	2	54	84.21	29	81.81	1.43	N.S.

than control groups though experimental groups were out of class up to 60 percent of the time.

As measured by the Metropolitan Achievement Tests, the gains for eleventh-grade girls on independent study in English showed no gains significantly superior to those of girls in the control group. The same was true for boys. However, achievement gains for girls who participated in the eleventh-grade independent reading program in history showed a significant advantage in the social studies vocabulary test at the .05 level.

Boys who participated in the eleventh-grade independent reading program in history showed superior gains over the control group in the two social studies tests. The gains were not statistically significant, however. Boys in the twelfth-grade independent reading program in social studies showed gains superior at the .05 level of significance to those of the control group.

The achievement gains of experimental and control groups were also compared in computation, problem solving, science concepts, and science information. There were no significantly superior gains for the experi-

TABLE II
Regents Grades of Both Groups in Subjects in the
Independent Study Program

Section	Sex	Year in Program	Independent Study Group		Control Group			
			N	Mean Regents Grade	N	Mean Regents Grade	t	p
English 11	B	1	21	83.1	21	80.5	1.34	N.S.
English 11	G	1	20	84.3	25	80.2	2.05	.05
History 11	B	1	26	85.3	16	83.7	.87	N.S.
History 11	G	1	23	84.6	20	83.0	.72	N.S.

mental group in any of these areas. However, they performed as well as the control students.

SECOND-YEAR IMPROVEMENTS

The 1965–66 achievement gains in language for experimental groups showed a gain over 1964–65, when experimental groups showed no advantage over control groups. It is apparent that independent reading in English becomes more effective as teachers and students become more familiar with independent study or else that independent study has a cumulative effect.

In general it was found that students who were in the program for a second year showed impressive gains over first-year participants. First-year participants (eleventh-grade groups) showed superiority over control groups in only one area, social studies vocabulary. Second-year students showed significant advantage over control students in four out of six achievement areas. The remaining two areas favored experimental students but not at a statistically significant level. These latter two achievement areas were computation and science information, both of them unrelated to areas of independent study experimentation.

Creativity

Experimental and control groups were compared in creativity gains. None of the independent reading groups made progress significantly superior or inferior to the control groups in creativity scores. At least as measured by *Uses for Things Test,* absence from class does not have an adverse or beneficial effect on growth in creativity.

School Satisfaction Better

Satisfaction with school as measured by *The School Inventory* was analyzed according to subject of study, sex, and group. The findings favored the independent reading groups in four of the eight mean differences. Three of the four differences were statistically significant. In the first-year independent study groups, only one of the differences was significant. School satisfaction was better for History 11 boys, English 12 boys, History 12 girls, and History 12 boys. It is interesting to note that three of the four groups were boys.

Study Habits and Attitudes

Among the second-year groups, three of the four mean differences in study-habits gains as measured by the *Brown-Holtzman Survey of Study Habits and Attitudes* significantly favored the experimental group. Only one of the mean differences in study-habits gain significantly favored the first-year experimental group. Although the four other mean differences in gains were not significant, they all favored the experimental groups.

It is clear that independent study markedly affects study habits and attitudes, and the results improve as schools and students gain more experience with the program. In view of the goal of educating youth for greater responsibility for their own learning in college, these results have particular importance.

Library Skills Improved

Significant gains in library skills were shown in favor of the independent reading groups. The data were analyzed according to subject of study, sex, and group. Six of the mean differences in library orientation favored the experimental groups at a significant level. The second-year results showed higher gains for independent study pupils than the first year, when only three of the differences favored the experimental groups instead of six.

It would appear that independent reading programs are quite effective in producing gains in library skills as measured by the *Library Orientation Test for College Freshmen*.

PREDICTION

Study-habits scores and certain personality traits were the best predictors of achievement gains and gains in library skills. Students who measured as conscientious rather than undependable and as individually resourceful rather than group dependent and who also scored high on study skills were able to handle the challenge of independent study better.

The correlations between the Conscientious Dependable section of Cattell's *High School Personality Questionnaire* and gains in achievement test scores in the area in which independent study was undertaken were significant at the .05 level of confidence among the girls in the eleventh- and twelfth-grade history groups. Study habits and individual resourcefulness versus group dependence correlated with achievement, as did conscientiousness versus undependability; the lowest correlation, obtained with the later test, was .23.

Four predictor variables correlated with gains on the *Library Orientation Test*. The four significant correlations were between pretest scores on study habits and gains in library skills among both boys and girls in independent twelfth-grade social studies reading and between pretest scores on individual resourcefulness versus group dependence and gains in library skills among both boys and girls in twelfth-grade social studies. All four correlations were significant at the .05 level of confidence.

Independent Study and College Grades

A follow-up was made of the students who participated in the independent reading programs at the twelfth grade and then went to college. The small-size sample made use of a test of significance unsound. However, the average second-semester mean quality point indices of the four groups suggest the existence of a systematic difference.

Experimental Girls — 3.2 $(N=12)$
Control Girls   — 2.9 $(N=9)$
Experimental Boys — 3.1 $(N=12)$
Control Boys   — 2.8 $(N=7)$

Progress Report

As previously indicated, the findings summarized here represent the results of the two years of the New York State research project. While these findings show advantages in only some areas for students in independent study, they establish clearly that such students did just as well as control students even though they attended classes about half of the time. The second-year results show gains over the first year as students and teachers became better oriented to the program.

BRIGHT POSSIBILITIES

Many implications for secondary school improvement are seen in the independent study program at Valhalla and from the New York State research results. Following are a few promising interpretations:

1. It is now certain that more responsibility for their own learning can effectively be placed on the more able and mature high school students.

2. Much greater flexibility of scheduling and what is studied is practical. It is quite possible, for example, to schedule a whole class made up of students on independent study on a two-or-three-times-weekly basis such as the typical college class.

3. Use of teacher time and the nature of the teacher role can be greatly changed. The teacher with a class that meets three times a week instead of five will have more time for planning and for conferences with individual students. The role of the teacher as a guide to individual learning will be enhanced by such arrangements.

4. Perhaps most important, procedures for independent study give the school new ways of awakening interests and talents of students whose zest for learning might otherwise be stultified by the regime of the traditional schedule of class study.

5. Finally, independent study shows promise of helping young men and women to develop qualities of resourcefulness and self-guided learning that will improve their future education and indeed help prepare them for independent lifelong learning. This broader spirit of individual inquiry is well expressed by John Gardner: "The ultimate goal of the educational system is to shift to the individual the burden of pursuing his own education." [1]

[1] John Gardner. *Self-Renewal: The Individual and the Innovative Society.* New York: Harper & Row, 1964.

26 Individual Instruction and Group Instruction: A Case Study

JOHN A. ZAHORIK

Reprinted with permission from *Journal of Educational Research*, Vol. 62, No. 10 (July–August 1969), pp. 453–455.

The purpose of this investigation was to explore differences in teaching during individual instruction as compared to group instruction. Several qualitative and quantitative aspects of teacher verbal behavior were examined. Data were obtained by analyzing transcripts of five individual and four group mathematics lessons taught by the same teacher. Significant differences were found in relation to amount of teacher verbal behavior displayed, types of thought required by teacher solicitations, and types of logical operations required by teacher solicitations. During individual instruction there was more teacher talk, less use of higher thought level solicitations, and less use of a variety of logical operation solicitations than during group instruction.

Descriptive research of the past several years has made it inappropriate and inaccurate to make the statement that almost nothing is known about the teaching act. Although a great deal of knowledge about this complex and mysterious phenomenon does not exist, some valuable inroads have been started by Flanders (3), Hughes (5), Gallagher (4), Bellack (2), Smith (7), and others.* These researchers have investigated many different facets and aspects of the teaching act. They have examined such things as teacher influence, productive thought, pedagogical moves, and logical aspects of teaching. Pervading this variety and differ-

---

* For an anthology of these studies on teaching see *Teaching: Vantage Points for Study,* edited by Ronald T. Hyman. Philadelphia, J. B. Lippincott Co., 1968. M. H. and R. T. H., editors.

entness, however, is one common element. All of these studies were concerned with teaching in its usual context. They dealt with what typically occurs in almost all classrooms: teacher controlled group instruction.

Focusing on group instruction is a viable action and has yielded significant data, but it is somewhat retrogressive. That is, it provides information about teaching as it is or has been rather than how it might be. It describes the norm rather than the new.

One aspect of teaching or context in which teaching occurs that has received little attention by researchers of teaching is individual instruction. Individual instruction in reading, mathematics, and other areas as a planned form of curriculum organization rather than a periodic remedialization technique is being increasingly employed. Unfortunately, however, there is a paucity, if not a complete absence, of knowledge concerning teaching in a one-to-one situation. It seems reasonable to assume, as Jackson states, that "the teacher's activity during these tête-à-tête sessions differs in several ways from his behavior in front of the entire group . . ." (6:11). Is this a valid assumption, and if so, how does teaching differ in these two situations?

STUDYING INDIVIDUALIZED INSTRUCTION

In an effort to begin the description of teaching during individual instruction as compared to teaching during group instruction a case study of one teacher's teaching in these two situations was carried out. The study centered on four comparisons of verbal behavior between the two situations: (a) total verbal behavior and pauses, (b) teacher verbal behavior and pupil verbal behavior, (c) thought levels required by the teacher solicitations, and (d) logical operations required by the teacher solicitations.

The subject of this study was a fourth-grade teacher. She was observed during her teaching of nine mathematics lessons; five of the lessons were individual lessons and four were group lessons. The size of the groups varied from the total class of twenty-three to a group of four pupils.

The mathematics lessons that were taught were part of an individualized mathematics program developed by the teacher. The program consisted of fourth- and fifth-grade mathematics textbooks divided into topical segments, and assignment sheets giving directions concerning assignments, when to consult with the teacher relative to the introduction of a new skill, and enrichment activities. Each pupil could progress through the program as rapidly as his ability permitted. Whenever he needed to consult with the teacher he signed up for a conference. Generally, pupils were seen individually, however, if several pupils were ready for the same new skill or had a common difficulty the teacher met with them as a group. The individual lessons and the group lessons did not differ in purpose or intent.

All of the nine mathematics lessons were tape recorded, and notes concerning various nonaudible behaviors were taken. The lessons were then transcribed verbatim and analyzed. Analysis consisted of timing total verbal behavior and pauses, counting teacher words and pupil words, and categorizing teacher solicitations with a modified Gallagher system (4) to determine thought levels and with Smith's criteria (7) to determine logical operations. The thought levels into which the solicitations were sorted were cognitive-memory, convergent, evaluative, divergent, and routine, while the logical operations were defining, describing, designating, stating, reporting, substituting, evaluating, opining, classifying, comparing and contrasting, conditional inferring, explaining, and managing. Total frequencies and percentages of these verbal behaviors were determined for the individual lessons and for the group lessons. To ascertain significance of differences the null hypothesis was assumed in each case and the chi-square test employed.

The major results of the study were the following:

1. There was no significant difference in the total verbal behavior and pause time between the individual lessons and the group lessons. In both situations approximately 85 percent of the time talking was occurring, while silence occurred 15 percent of the time.

2. There was a significant difference (.05) in the quantity of teacher verbal behavior and pupil verbal behavior between the individual lessons and the group lessons. In the individual lessons the teacher talk amounted to 89 percent of the total talk and the pupil talk amounted to 11 percent. In the group lessons the teacher talk was 78 percent and the pupil talk 22 percent.

3. In the use of cognitive-memory solicitations and divergent thinking solicitations there were significant differences (.05) between the individual lessons and the group lessons. During individual instruction the teacher employed cognitive-memory solicitations 45 percent of the time while in group lessons she used them 36 percent of the time. Divergent-thinking solicitations were not used with individuals, but were used 7 percent of the time with groups. All other differences in relation to the thinking level required by the teacher solicitation were not significant. No evaluative thinking was required in either situation.

4. Between the two types of instruction there were significant differences (.05) in the use of five kinds of logical-operation solicitations: substituting, describing, reporting, classifying, and managing. During the individual lessons substituting was used 17 percent of the time while during group lessons it was used 6 percent. All the

remaining four logical operations were employed more frequently in group instruction: describing—5 percent with groups, but not used at all with individuals; reporting—5 percent with groups and 2 percent with individuals; classifying—8 percent with groups and 2 percent with individuals; and managing—25 percent with groups and 16 percent with individuals. Differences in relation to the other logical operations were not significant. Opining was not called for in either type of instruction.

It can be concluded from these results that this teacher's teaching did differ in several respects in these two instructional situations. Her individual lessons may be characterized by comparatively more teacher talk and less pupil talk, comparatively more lower thought level solicitations (cognitive-memory), and comparatively less use of a variety of logical operation solicitations. Her group lessons can be described as consisting of comparatively less teacher talk and more pupil talk, comparatively more higher thought level solicitations (divergent thinking) and comparatively greater use of a variety of logical operation solicitations.

INDIVIDUALIZATION AND INDIVIDUALITY

The outcomes of this brief case study take on meaning when one focuses on the purpose of individualization and how it can be developed by the teacher.

Individualization deals with individuality. Its purpose is to recognize, enhance, and develop individuality. It is to help individual children to grow in individual ways, to become what they might become, to extend their vision and promise. The goal of individualization is to make unique persons more unique.

The Association for Supervision and Curriculum Development 1964 Yearbook Committee (1) voices this purpose when it states that the chief object of individualization is the release of potential in individual learners. Further, it suggests some possible ways for releasing potential through teaching. Several of these suggestions are:

1. Observing and listening to learners with increased care and concern
2. Achieving openness in pupil-teacher relationships, to permit improved response and interaction
3. Recognizing and accepting different ways of responding, according to learners' individualized styles and needs
4. Questioning, probing, and responding in ways that lead learners to assume responsibility

5. Standing aside judiciously to let the learner discover and exercise his own resources

6. Placing learners in varying roles

7. Achieving free and constructive communication with learners

8. Clearing the way, by whatever means, for stretching learners' minds and abilities in creative, self-fulfilling endeavor (1:160–1)

A comparison of this teacher's individualized instruction with these suggestions indicates that individuality may not have been emphasized as much as it could have been.

It seems reasonable to expect more pause time in individual instruction than in group instruction if individuality is being developed. Pause time would permit the pupil to discover and exercise his own resources. It would also permit the pupil to reflect and digest and thereby stretch his mind and ability. This teacher, however, did not provide more pause time during her individual instruction.

If observing and listening to learners, being open in pupil-teacher relationships, and achieving free communication with learners are important in fostering individuality one might expect the ratio of pupil talk to teacher talk to be greater in individual instruction than in group instruction. In this particular teacher's teaching, however, the teacher talk was greater and the total pupil talk was less during the individual lessons. Of course, although the pupil talk was less, it was the talk of only one pupil; therefore, his verbal behavior probably was greater during the individual lesson than during a group lesson. Nevertheless, if the teacher monopolizes 89 percent of the talk, it is difficult to understand how individuality is being developed.

In addition to pauses and general verbal behavior, examining the teacher solicitations in light of these suggestions brings further doubt that individuality was really being developed during the individual lessons. If the teacher had been recognizing different ways of responding; questioning, probing, and responding to encourage responsibility; putting learners in different roles; and, in general, stretching learners' minds in individualized instruction, it would seem that divergent and evaluative thinking solicitations and much greater variety of logical operation solicitations including comparing, inferring, and explaining would have been employed. Again, the fact that more divergent thinking solicitations and a greater variety of logical operation solicitations occurred during group instruction is surprising.

In this one instance, then, individual instruction was indeed different from group instruction and the difference does not appear to be one that enhances and facilitates the goals of individual instruction. It is obvious, but yet striking, that the establishment of this individualized mathematics program did not necessarily insure the growth of individuality.

More obvious still, is the need for continued analysis and description of individualized teaching and other types of teaching if teacher classroom behavior is to become conscious and controllable. Certainly this teacher's individual instruction in other subject areas should be investigated. Also, the individualized teaching of many other teachers at a variety of grade levels and in all of the subject areas needs to be researched. In addition, the effect of various sized groups on teacher behavior should be studied.

REFERENCES

1. Association for Supervision and Curriculum Development 1964 Yearbook Committee. *Individualizing Instruction* (Washington, D.C.: National Education Association, 1964).
2. Bellack, Arno, and others. *The Language of the Classroom,* Part Two, Cooperative Research Project No. 2023 of the U.S. Office of Education (New York: Institute of Psychological Research, Teachers College, Columbia University, 1965).
3. Flanders, Ned A. *Teacher Influence, Pupil Attitudes and Achievement,* Cooperative Research Project No. 397 of the U.S. Office of Education (Minneapolis, Minnesota: University of Minnesota, 1960).
4. Gallagher, James L. *Productive Thinking of Gifted Children,* Cooperative Research Project No. 965 of the U.S. Office of Education (Urbana, Illinois: University of Illinois, 1965).
5. Hughes, Marie M., and associates. *The Assessment of the Quality of Teaching: A Research Report,* Cooperative Research Project No. 353 of the U.S. Office of Education (Salt Lake City: University of Utah, 1959).
6. Jackson, Philip W. "The Way Teaching Is," *The Way Teaching Is,* pp. 7–27, Report of the Seminar on Teaching, Association for Supervision and Curriculum Development and the Center for the Study of Instruction (Washington, D.C.: National Education Association, 1966).
7. Smith, B. Othanel, Milton O. Meux, and others. *A Study of the Logic of Teaching,* Cooperative Research Project No. 258 (7257) of the U.S. Office of Education (Urbana, Illinois: University of Illinois, 1960).

PART SIX

Flexible Scheduling

For many years educators have simply accepted the fact that the school day runs from about 8:30 A.M. to 3:00 P.M. and these six and one-half hours are divided into daily regular units of about fifty minutes each. For long this was felt to be an immutable concept. This is especially true in the secondary schools, where student programs are often prepared according to Carnegie Units acceptable for college admission. But the problem of rigid time is not restricted to the secondary school. With the advent of such innovations as team teaching, individualized instruction, and continuous progress, the "old schedule" suffered irreparable damage. The articles in this section all make this point: changes in school demand a fresh look at how the school schedules its time.

Since the key concept underlying the other innovations is flexibility, the educators who began to look anew at time also accepted flexibility as their guideline. They began to think in terms of flexible time and realized that this concept allowed them to plan for "using our time" rather than "spending our time." Some schools dropped the fifty-minute period as their basic unit and instituted the module. (The length of a module differs from school to school but usually it is fifteen, twenty, or thirty minutes long. In any case, a module is a short length of time which can be used alone or in combination with other modules so as to fit the particular needs of the various activities going on simultaneously in the school.) Some schools maintained the old daily schedule but changed the weekly schedule so that it became flexible.

Whatever the approach is, as the very titles of the articles in this section show, the attempt now is to be flexible. This flexibility in arrangement and use of time has several concomitants. It is not only demanded by other innovations, but it also serves to permit still more innovation. This point is made quite strongly by Polos and it deserves to be underscored here. Flexibility in time also encourages student responsibility in that the student himself now schedules at least part of his school time and now has significant freedom of movement during the school day. These connections with team teaching, individualization of instruction, continuous progress, and congenial space are emphasized in the articles that follow.

Johnson opens this section with a description of his flexible schedule at Interlake High School in Bellevue, Washington. This flexible schedule, contrary to many, is built around the conventional six-period school day. Note that it is a deliberate choice to remain with the conventional six periods rather than choose modules or floating periods. The unique blending of the students' schedules and the teachers' schedules deserves careful study in the light of the three goals that Interlake's staff established.

In contrast to the Interlake schedule is the Archbishop Ryan High School schedule based on seventeen modules a day of twenty minutes each. Here, however, "once the schedule for each pupil is established it becomes as rigid as the traditional schedule." Yet the initial flexibility is sufficient to bring about self-motivated students operating with reduced tension where no bells ring. Moore lists over twenty promising outcomes of Ryan's modular schedule.

The schedule at Thurston Intermediate School in Laguna Beach, California, as reported by Gehret, demonstrates that flexible schedules are suitable on the middle school level. Here the student has even more responsibility for his own time schedule than the students in the high schools discussed above. The Thurston schedule points up the ability of young students to be responsible in making decisions affecting their school life. What is more, the apparent effect is a gain in overall vitality in the school on the part of teachers and students. The interconnections among time flexibility, ability grouping, team teaching, individualized instruction, a differentiated staff, use of the computer, and a continuous progress program are evident.

In the final selection, Polos treats the advantages and disadvantages of flexible scheduling based on the program at Claremont High School in Claremont, California. The reader is asked to weigh the listed advantages against the disadvantages to determine the net result of Claremont's flexible schedule. Do these advantages and disadvantages apply to other schools' schedules as well?

Flexible scheduling appears primarily at the high school level at this point. It appears in the middle schools and elementary schools where there is some form of continuous progress or team teaching. Most schools, at all levels, still maintain a rigid scheduling of time. Perhaps, during the coming decade, we will give more and more students—high school, middle school, and elementary school students—the opportunity not only to be flexible in their use of time but also to demonstrate their responsibility by scheduling their own use of time.

Polos asserts that flexible scheduling of time is not a panacea for all the problems which arise in a school. He also specifically notes that it is not time which is flexible, but rather man who is flexible in his arrangement and use of it. These two points need to be remembered by anyone expecting to implement schedules similar to those reported here. Like other innovations a flexible schedule needs constant adjusting in order to keep it flexible and useful. Although it is a facilitating innovation, those who change to it from a traditional, rigid schedule must not let their fascination with it consume them. They need to keep in mind that flexible scheduling is but one important means to their pedagogical ends and not an end in itself. Yet they must, as Schopenhauer says, try to be men of intellect and use their time wisely. Serious attention to the dimension of time can serve to increase pedagogical opportunities (see Polos' article for these points by Schopenhauer and Wood), and flexible time is a significant factor facilitating that end.

27 | Flexibility in the Secondary School

HOWARD M. JOHNSON

Reprinted with permission from *The Bulletin of the National Association of Secondary School Principals,* Vol. 53, No. 339, (October 1969), pp. 62–72.

The word "flexibility" has received much attention in recent years, particularly in our secondary schools, where fixed special arrangements and somewhat rigid scheduling have long been the standard practice. To cite just a few examples, flexibility has been used to describe newer facility designs which incorporate either demountable or operable walls, patterns of staffing which utilize varying levels of professional training and competence, and a wide variety of deviations from traditional time-scheduling practice. Because this increased use of the term "flexibility" indicates a greater willingness to look at learning as an individual rather than group endeavor, our increased use of the term has sometimes been accompanied by a looseness in interpretation and, in some cases, an almost complete misuse of the word.

It seems inappropriate, for example, to say that any variance in the size of classes or the mere adoption of a so-called modular schedule will automatically result in a more flexible learning situation. If, as Webster suggests, flexibility involves a capacity for being adapted or modified, we don't get it by simply replacing a traditional facility or schedule by some other rigid pattern of instructional organization. The experience at Interlake High School in Bellevue, Washington, over the past two years shows how one school faculty has attempted within certain obvious limits to create a program which does have flexibility and one which encourages student responsibility and staff communication.

SCHEDULE DEVELOPS FROM EDUCATIONAL GOALS

Interlake High School opened in September, 1967, with an enrollment of 900 students. The facility emphasizes the use of both operable

266

and demountable partitioning of interior space and is designed to house approximately 1300 students in grades 10–12. The school serves a typically suburban, middle class, residential area and is used extensively for community and adult education activities. The limited tax base of the community and the extremely rapid growth within the school district forced designers of the building to eliminate certain desirable educational features. The completed structure did, however, incorporate a sizable learning center, provision for the latest in audiovisual instruction, and project or work areas associated with the various disciplines. These features provided a unique opportunity and challenge for the professional staff, and particularly for the administrators who were charged with the responsibility of selecting and organizing a new faculty for a new kind of school.

Recognizing that the schedule is really a means of bringing together in an orderly fashion the various components of the learning process, we began with certain assumptions about the way in which these components could best be joined to assure a flexible learning environment. We had to recognize at the outset that many of these educational components, such as rooms and teachers, would be limited in number. This meant that certain compromises had to be made in the scheduling process. A most important concern for any faculty in designing a schedule format is to see that these compromises are made consistent with certain prior assumptions or educational goals.

Such goals were established early in the planning stage at Inerlake. Long before the school opened, the principal, assistant principal, activity coordinator, and other key staff members decided on three major goals for the Interlake program and schedule:

1. *The schedule must permit each student the opportunity to structure some portion of his own school time.*

Most research in education indicates that real learning requires an active rather than passive role on the part of the student. The student becomes an active participant in the learning process only when he has an opportunity to initiate inquiry in his own way and on his own time. Far too many independent study programs in our high schools today are limited to those few students who already show maturity and an ability to work without immediate supervision and direction from a teacher. It is little wonder that many students find it difficult to structure their own time when they reach college or go to work on a job. All too few of our high school graduates have really had an opportunity to develop the skills of independent study; and unless we can find ways to permit the development of these skills within our regular secondary school program, we have little chance of preparing students for a world in which a proper balance between leisure and work is required of all.

2. *The schedule must provide some considerable time during the regular school week for teachers working in teams and/or related disciplines to meet and plan together.*

The traditional secondary school schedule generally affords only limited opportunity for team planning. Certainly, teachers on a particular team can be given a common planning period. However, anyone who has worked closely in building a master schedule knows that the number of teams that can be accommodated in this manner is limited. Even with a modular schedule, where the possibility of setting aside common planning time for teams of teachers is somewhat greater, it is extremely difficult to bring together large segments of the faculty during the regular school day. With this in mind, the Interlake staff has developed a rather unusual schedule which encourages staff members in related disciplines to work out common problems together. The staff is divided into three parts with each having common planning time built into the weekly schedule. Hopefully, this division and team planning time can do a great deal in breaking down the traditional discipline and subject-matter lines found in today's secondary schools. It also tends to reduce the amount of time required in general faculty meetings held on an after-school basis.

3. *The schedule must provide some flexibility and variety in the structure and size of classes.*

One of the major drawbacks to traditional schedules is the requirement that all classes meet a set number of periods each week; rarely is the opportunity provided for any variance in the standard length of period or the number of class periods per week. At Interlake, we give at least some attention to the fact that a daily course meeting is much more important in a subject like mathematics or foreign language than it is in science or history. Furthermore, we hope to give each teacher some flexibility in designing the structure of his own classes.

A SCHEDULING MODEL FOR INTERLAKE

After examining the above assumptions, it became obvious to us that none of the commonly used scheduling patterns [1]—including traditional,

---

[1] Of all the present scheduling models, the modular schedule would best approach the three goals already stated; however, it is doubtful that the modular schedule could provide an opportunity for as much as one-third of the staff working in related disciplines to meet during the regular school day. It was also felt that the modular schedule, once established, is actually quite rigid and provides very little opportunity for teacher variance. The Interlake facility, with its extensive use of operable walls, does not require a modular-type schedule as a means of creating variable class sizes.

PERIOD ╲ DAY	MONDAY	TUESDAY	WEDNESDAY	THURSDAY	FRIDAY
1					
2					
3					
4					
5					
6					

LANGUAGE ARTS DIVISION PLANNING TIME
(Includes teachers of English, speech, drama, bookkeeping, typing, and shorthand)

MATH-SCIENCE DIVISION PLANNING TIME
(Includes teachers of biology, chemistry, electronics, physics, mathematics, physical education, industrial education, and driver training)

SOCIAL STUDIES DIVISION PLANNING TIME
(Includes teachers of history, art, music, home economics, social sciences, and foreign language)

Figure 1. Basic scheduling structure.

floating period, rotation, and modular—would answer the Interlake requirements. It was at this point that we attempted to create a schedule which could develop from the basic structure of Figure 1. Special features of this format include the opportunity for each student to individually structure several class periods each week and a considerable amount of common planning time for each of the three faculty divisions. The way in which the student structured time (SST) program operates within this schedule format is perhaps best illustrated by applying it to a few student schedules. Notice that students A, B, and C of Figure 2 each have five or more SST periods per week. The SST periods fall on a certain day for each horizontal period, depending upon the division or area of the teacher involved. For example, Student A has SST on Tuesday, period 1, because the teacher of his period 1 class is a member of the social studies division.[2] Similarly, students B and C have SST on Thursday and Friday during period 1 because the teachers of the first period classes are assigned to the math-science and language arts divisions, respectively. In

---

[2] According to Figure 1, the social studies teachers are free for planning on Tuesday, period 1, and therefore this is the day upon which students assigned in any social studies class receive their SST. A regular class meeting is held the other four days of the week.

STUDENT A

PERIOD \ DAY	MONDAY	TUESDAY	WEDNESDAY	THURSDAY	FRIDAY
1	HISTORY 11		HISTORY 11	HISTORY 11	HISTORY 11
2	ART		ART	ART	ART
3	BIOLOGY	BIOLOGY		BIOLOGY	BIOLOGY
4		SPEECH	SPEECH	SPEECH	SPEECH
5	TYPING	TYPING	TYPING		TYPING
6	ENGLISH 11	ENGLISH 11	ENGLISH 11		ENGLISH 11

STUDENT B

PERIOD \ DAY	MONDAY	TUESDAY	WEDNESDAY	THURSDAY	FRIDAY
1	GEOMETRY	GEOMETRY	GEOMETRY		GEOMETRY
2	ENGLISH 10	ENGLISH 10		ENGLISH 10	ENGLISH 10
3	SPEECH		SPEECH	SPEECH	SPEECH
4	FRENCH 2	FRENCH 2	FRENCH 2	FRENCH 2	FRENCH 2
5		PHYSICAL EDUCATION	PHYSICAL EDUCATION	PHYSICAL EDUCATION	PHYSICAL EDUCATION
6		HOME ECONOMICS	HOME ECONOMICS	HOME ECONOMICS	HOME ECONOMICS

STUDENT C

PERIOD \ DAY	MONDAY	TUESDAY	WEDNESDAY	THURSDAY	FRIDAY
1	SHORTHAND	SHORTHAND	SHORTHAND	SHORTHAND	
2	CHOIR		CHOIR	CHOIR	CHOIR
3	DRIVER TRAINING			DRIVER TRAINING	
4	OFFICE ASSISTANT	OFFICE ASSISTANT	OFFICE ASSISTANT	OFFICE ASSISTANT	OFFICE ASSISTANT
5	ENGLISH 11	ENGLISH 11	ENGLISH 11		ENGLISH 11
6		HISTORY 11	HISTORY 11	HISTORY 11	HISTORY 11

   Student Structured Time (SST as used throughout the text)

Figure 2. Sample schedules.

general, the students pick up their SST periods according to the division planning assignments of their teachers.

During a typical SST period at Interlake, the student is given his choice of several educational and social activities. He can study in the large learning center, socialize in the student commons, shoot baskets in the gymnasium, practice his typing, or work on an art project. While a student may change from one approved activity to another at any time (except the last five minutes of any period, which is designated as a "freeze" time), aimless wandering from one area to another is not permitted. Students who wander without purpose or who fail to maintain standards of behavior appropriate to the various approved areas are assigned to supervised study during the SST periods. Provision is made for petitioning back into the regular SST program after a designated time in supervised study.

THE TEACHER'S SCHEDULE

A sample teacher schedule built around the format of Figure 1 is shown in Figure 3. Notice that each class meets four periods per week

DAY / PERIOD	MONDAY	TUESDAY	WEDNESDAY	THURSDAY	FRIDAY
1	GEOMETRY	GEOMETRY	GEOMETRY		GEOMETRY
2					
3	GEOMETRY	GEOMETRY		GEOMETRY	GEOMETRY
4	FUNDAMENTAL MATH	FUNDAMENTAL MATH		FUNDAMENTAL MATH	FUNDAMENTAL MATH
5		GEOMETRY	GEOMETRY	GEOMETRY	GEOMETRY
6	MATH ANALYSIS		MATH ANALYSIS	MATH ANALYSIS	MATH ANALYSIS

DIVISION OR TEAM PLANNING
(This time may also be used for individual planning when cooperative efforts are not required.)

SUPERVISING DUTY ASSIGNMENT
(This assignment may include membership on a general supervising team, responsibility for a supervised study group, or availability as a resource person in an open laboratory area.)

INDIVIDUAL PLANNING

Figure 3. Sample teacher schedule (Math-Science division).

and the teacher receives supervising duty assignments in addition to the regular classroom load. These supervisory assignments generally relate to the SST periods. Some general supervision and assistance is required during these periods when approximately one-third of the student body is not assigned to regular classes. While the particular teacher's schedule in Figure 3 shows only two individual planning periods per week, the number generally exceeds that amount. Whenever team or division planning periods are not utilized for the designated purpose, they can simply be added to the teacher's individual planning time. In practice, most teachers at Interlake end up with four to six individual planning periods per week.

As further clarification of this utilization of nonclassroom time for teachers, let us look again at the teacher schedule shown in Figure 3. This particular teacher is assigned to five mathemtaics classes and his 10 periods of nonclassroom time per week. In a typical week, the teacher may, in addition to regular classroom teaching, attend one general division meeting on Wednesday (periods 3 and 4) to discuss general problems such as improper placement of students in mathematics classes, the need for more faculty assistance in student science projects, or the failure of some students to make productive use of their unscheduled time. The teacher may be scheduled into the student commons during period 2 on Tuesday and into the math resource center during period 2 on Wednesday. The teacher may work individually with certain Math Analysis students during period 6 on Tuesday or, even more likely, work together with several of the students on a certain kind of problem missed on a previous examination. Period 5 on Monday might be used to develop, with two other mathematics teachers, specific objectives for the basic geometry course.[3] The remaining four nonclassroom periods (period 2 on Monday, periods 1 and 2 on Thursday, and period 2 on Friday) can then be utilized for individual planning or for working with students on an individual basis.

Because both students and faculty have considerable unscheduled time, there is usually no limit to the student demand for individualized help. Most teachers find that their planning time is difficult to preserve, but they also realize the educational advantage for the student in having an opportunity to confer with his teacher on an individual basis. Having examined the basic scheduling structure and sample student and teacher schedules, we can now go on to raise several questions about the actual flexibility of the schedule and the practical problems experienced in its implementation.

[3] Such objectives are required as part of the school's accreditation with the Northwest Association of Secondary and Higher Schools. Interlake is scheduled to complete the accreditation procedures during the 1969–70 school year and has found division planning time to be extremely useful for discussing accreditation matters.

FLEXIBILITY, A FUNCTION OF SCHEDULE AND FACILITY

The schedule structure already described does not by itself assure flexibility in the instructional program. It is only as this particular structure shows itself to have capacity for teacher modification and change that it can truly be labeled flexible. It is at this point that Interlake's capacity for spacial modification becomes extremely important.

All the general classrooms at Interlake are clustered in groups of four. This means that careful placement of team classes permits immediate change in group size and instructional methods.[4] Interlake's potential for spacial modification, coupled with the basic scheduling structure already described, offers a degree of flexibility unequaled in any other school known to this author. Let us examine certain specific ways in which this flexibility can be realized.

• Rather than freezing a team teaching class into a certain prearranged pattern of large, regular, and medium sized groups, the Interlake plan permits teachers to make this decision on a daily basis. The operable walls permit the teaching staff maximum control over modification of classroom activity and group size.

• Teachers often find it impossible to work with small groups of students on specific problems, particularly when faced period after period with classes of 25 or more students. The Interlake schedule provides considerable flexibility in this regard. During SST time, teachers can meet with groups of varying sizes. The foreign language teachers quite often call selected students in during all or part of the SST period associated with the particular class (See Figure 2, Student B). This permits an opportunity to work closely with students experiencing specific learning problems. Mathematics teachers also utilize this fifth day option in certain classes and are encouraged to do so. The only limitation is that during those times a division or team planning meeting might be called. Since team meeting demands in the foreign language and mathematics disciplines are somewhat limited, this has presented no real problem to the overall program and certainly increases the teacher satisfaction with the schedule.

• Quite often in a conventional program, teachers are unable to permit advanced students to work apart from the class on individual assignments or projects. There is generally either no place to send them or no one available to assume responsibility for them. At Interlake, this provi-

---

[4] It is well to note here that the modular schedule with its more definite assignment to large, small, or regular sized areas does not permit this same kind of instant modification of spacial arrangements.

sion is built right into the schedule format. Since SST is operating three days per week for each of the six class periods, it is quite simple to send a limited number of students to the Learning Resource Center or some other part of the building during these three class periods. For example, Student C in Figure 2 attends driver training only two days each week instead of the usual four. He becomes part of the regular SST program the other three days. This permits a better balance of class and driving time for the teachers in the driver training course and can be used to a limited extent by teachers in other areas who feel that less class time and more independent study best suits the particular area or unit of study. Several Interlake teachers are experimenting this year with optional attendance on certain days of the week. This option to reduce time in formal class instruction does a great deal to individualize the approach to instruction.

SOME LIMITATIONS

Like any other operating schedule, the one just described has certain practical limitations. Even with extensive back scheduling [5] into classrooms vacated for SST, it is doubtful that space utilization will be quite as efficient as that achieved using a large study hall and a more conventional schedule. It can be argued that the traditional study hall has, for a long time, been little more than a convenient mechanism to accommodate more students in an already crowded facility. With this in mind, the Interlake schedule will hardly be applicable in a school system whose secondary facilities cannot accommodate at one time all its students in real learning situations.

Perhaps the most important practical consideration associated with the Interlake schedule is the staff attitude toward working with students individually and in small groups. Unless teachers and administrators are willing, as they are at Interlake, to extend themselves to help students during their SST periods and are tolerant of a rather free (and sometimes confused) atmosphere about the school, very little purpose is to be served by adoption of this schedule. The Interlake schedule is no different from any other successful innovation in its requirement of faculty acceptance and its demand for a new staff attitude toward the process of education.

This faculty acceptance and support of the Interlake schedule is a direct result of the fact that it gives each teacher a maximum of control over his own classroom schedule. Teachers and division chairmen have also appreciated the opportunity to provide significant direction to the

[5] Back scheduling as used here refers to the scheduling of selected classes into areas vacated by SST. Since for each horizontal period there exists three SST periods, several classes meeting on a three-day per week schedule can be accommodated within the schedule format.

selection of courses to be handled by teaching teams and the selection of teachers for the various teams. The teacher enthusiasm carries over to the students, 90 percent of whom voted at the end of the first year to continue with the present schedule format. Their comments, for the most part, indicated that the independent study time given to all students and the opportunity to meet individually with teachers are the major strengths of the Interlake plan.

At a time when teachers are increasingly concerned about a greater role in developing the structure for learning in the school, it seems appropriate that all schools look at current scheduling practice. All too often, we place students in an unnecessarily rigid schedule which allows very little opportunity for teacher or student modification. This particular discussion has shown how one suburban high school is trying to increase the teacher control over instructional patterns and activities. The extent to which Interlake or any other school has encouraged schedule flexibility goes beyond the fancy tables and charts and looks directly to the matter of teacher control over modification of the instructional schedule. Obviously, the development of such teacher control over the schedule pattern along with a preservation of order and integrity in the total school operation must be the major goals of those searching for a more flexible schedule for today's secondary school.

28 | An Approach to Flexibility

ARNOLD J. MOORE

Reprinted with permission from *Educational Leadership*, Vol. 24, No. 8 (May 1967), pp. 691–695. Reprinted with permission of the Association for Supervision and Curriculum Development and Arnold J. Moore. Copyright © 1967 by the Association for Supervision and Curriculum Development.

There is little question but that those associated with the American secondary school must initiate change dynamisms if the qualitative aspects of education are to receive their proper emphasis. If we are really serious about excellence in our high schools, then schools must break away from traditional practices and experiment with new and promising ideas. Perhaps then some of Trump's predictions in *Images of the Future* [1] will become realities. At least this has been the case in one school in Omaha, Nebraska.

A sincere concern for the qualitative aspects of its educational program caused Archbishop Ryan High School, a private coeducational school, enrolling approximately 1,050 students, to initiate a full-scale modular schedule [2] for the 1966–67 school year. Thus Ryan High, under the direction of Sister M. Pacis, O.S.F., principal, in the ninth year of the school and after two years' preparation with the staff, students, parents, and local community, became the first school in Nebraska to implement such a schedule.

[1] J. Lloyd Trump. *Images of the Future.* Commission on the Experimental Study of the Utilization of the Staff in the Secondary School. Washington, D.C.: National Association of Secondary-School Principals, 1959.

[2] Basically modular scheduling divides the school day into equal units of time which are considerably shorter than the traditional class period. These shorter units, called modules are combined in a variety of ways to meet the individual needs of both the student and the teacher. Consequently, the size of student groups, media for learning and time requirements evolve from the arrangement of modules.

Modular scheduling was adopted because of the incongruity of student ability and achievement. Careful studies of student performances on national tests over the eight years of the school's existence consistently showed excellence in ability whereas actual achievement within the school and for four years with alumni at colleges and universities consistently was below valid expectations.

THE PROBLEM OF UNDERACHIEVEMENT

A study of the parental background of the students and community revealed that a large portion of the school's enrollment came from highly nationalistic ethnic groups in which, in some cases, English was the second language in the homes. Summer remedial reading programs for selected incoming freshmen were used as an attempt to reduce the difficulties language barriers present. Additional studies of the curriculum and subsequent revisions were instigated in attempts to accommodate contemporary society and the 75 percent college-bound student enrollment.

None of the modifications or plans seemed to have the inherent motivational aspects so essential to student achievement. Consequently, the next effort was to investigate teaching methods, program structure, and personal involvement in learning by the student. This led to the decision to consider a modular schedule.

INITIATING THE MODULAR SCHEDULE

Sister Pacis undertook a cooperative staff study of modular scheduling which included its purposes, operation, and feasibility. This exploratory phase evolved into an orientation program which included faculty-wide in-service programs, visitations by faculty to other schools, and the utilization of resource people. Once the decision was made to proceed with the development of a modular schedule an inventory of facilities and resources—both physical and human—was undertaken.

This inventory included departmental requests as to time allocations —scheduled and unscheduled—for each of the courses and modes of instruction proposed. Reports from the departments indicated space needs and suggested modification of facilities, present usable material resources, and requests for additional materials. The personnel inventory contained the strength and weakness of staff members as they related to the various modes of instruction and any additional personnel requirements. Then the principal and staff, using the inventory as the basic document, arrived at mutually compatible decisions about curriculum content, time allocations, modes of instruction, staff needs, and space requirements.

At Ryan, originally built as a traditional school with self-contained classrooms and laboratories for classes of 30 to 35, the necessity for physical changes was minimal. One wall was removed between two traditional typing rooms to make one large business lab with a flexible wall being installed to provide for subdivisions. Room utilizations became more efficient when the large music rooms and the cafeteria were used for large group instruction areas and a supervised study room. In the future, other classrooms, the library and the gym may need to be modified to provide additional flexibility.

Ryan High used a program designed by Charles Elliott and the facilities of the McDonnell Automation Center, St. Louis, Missouri, as an aid in preparing the master schedule, but did not have the computer generate the final schedule. The school prepares its own master schedule manually because this control facilitates better personnel interpretation for both student and teacher needs.

Procedures used in developing the schedule at Ryan were:

1. Register the students for their course selections.

2. Code on a course-request form the name of each student with his courses specified by course number, track and semester. Submit to the computer which prepares a conflict matrix.

3. The conflict matrix is used to schedule large group lectures, avoiding conflicts in student requests, rooms, and teachers. Then schedule the small groups tied to the large groups. Code and resubmit to the computer which will schedule and return individual student conflicts.

4. Resolve individual student conflicts manually and send back. Individual class lists and student programs are generated by the computer.

RYAN'S MODULAR SCHEDULE

At Ryan, the school day is reshaped from the traditional lockstep method of programming to a seventeen module day of twenty minutes per module with three minute passing periods. While the basic module is twenty minutes, school subjects are scheduled for a varying number of modules depending on the nature of the course and the request of the teachers of given departments. A class does not meet formally each day, but may be scheduled once, twice, three, or four times a week, depending, again, on departmental requests, nature of the learning activities, and the amount of individual student study or research needed. However, once the schedule for each pupil is established, it becomes as rigid as the traditional schedule.

Basically, learning takes place within three kinds of situations. First, a team of teachers in a subject area is responsible for presentations to a large group of students ranging in number from 90 to 250. Such presentations occur once or, at most, twice a week. The student, in such a large group, obviously cannot ask questions, but follows an outline which the team prepares and distributes in advance.

The second approach involves sessions in which students are placed in small groups according to their talent. Each small group consists of from 8 to 20 students, with an ideal of about 11, and meets two or three times a week with a teacher as a resource person. Here the students question, discuss, investigate, validate, and evaluate their understanding of concepts.

A third type of activity is independent study. Each student has about one-third of his program unscheduled. During this time he can channel his activity as he needs to. He might do research on his own (either teacher or self-directed) in the library, prepare experiments in a science laboratory, pursue some project in one of the fine or practical arts laboratories, study independently or with a fellow student, confer with a resource teacher, or work in a supervised study hall.

Since classes do not meet for uniform lengths of time, and because modular scheduling tends to place the responsibility on the student for being present for a given class activity at a designated time, there are no intruding sounds of bells. A natural outgrowth of periods of variable length and the concomitant staggered arrangement is that only a small percentage of the student body moves at any time.

There is no congregating in corridors, no waiting for the bell. Instead, students go directly to their next class. Shorter passing periods are needed and the quiet atmosphere which is so much in evidence is enhanced. Without bells the students are made to feel that they have "appointments to keep" rather than meeting for classes, with a resultant increase in self-reliance and sense of responsibility.

The emphasis has shifted sharply in the school from a place in which teachers present information to a largely passive audience to a milieu in which students learn through an active involvement in instructional media. Professionalism is enhanced on the part of the teacher as he assumes the role of a resource person who occasionally lectures, but with many opportunities for overt interaction with the students.

This does not minimize the role of the teacher who has additional opportunities to work with individuals rather than groups. In fact, teachers are more important as their efforts become more meaningful and professional in nature. The dominant people in the system are self-directed and motivated students, who are actively engaged in the process of learning.

PLANS FOR EVALUATION

A longitudinal study is in progress in which several evaluation instruments and techniques are being used to collect data to determine the impact of the new approach of programming on the students, staff and patrons of the school. This study involves the cooperative efforts of the Ryan staff, Creighton University, and the Mid-Continent Regional Educational Laboratory.

Since it is agreed that the fundamental purposes of an education are to effect changes in the way the student thinks, feels, and acts, these factors will be evaluated. In addition to measures of subject matter achievement, the changes in student self-concept of academic ability, patterns of study habits and attitudes, and problem-solving skills and critical thinking modes will be assessed.

Such instruments as the Brown-Holtzman Survey of Study Habits and Attitudes, the Michigan State General Self-Concept of Ability Scale, the Iowa Tests of Educational Development, and the Scholastic High School Placement Tests will be used. Student interviews and questionnaires are also included in the study. The staff is also keeping accurate records of usage of the independent study facilities, i.e., science, fine arts, and other laboratories, incidence of discipline problems, and school attendance. The librarian is recording the kinds of library materials being used and the number of student visitations.

Teacher questionnaires, supervisor reports, course syllabi, teacher projects, faculty departmental and interdepartmental meetings will reflect changes in faculty interaction, morale, and effectiveness. Student questionnaires should indicate the changes in teacher-student relationships and the amount of faculty-student interaction. The patron perception of the modular scheduling program will be elicited through a questionnaire and solicited and unsolicited comments.

Conferences with parents should yield information about their viewpoints on the effectiveness of the changes in the Ryan program. Perhaps, at a latter date, interviews with individuals selected at random in the community will be incorporated in the study. Data from another follow-up study of alumni will be contrasted with the results of the first studies.

PROMISING OUTCOMES

Those associated with the Ryan program and its evaluation are cognizant of a possible Hawthorne effect and of the subjectivity of some of the data. Based on one semester of experience and with the preceding limitations, the following statements by categories are presented.

1. Students

a. Label it a program to eliminate boredom.

b. Scores on departmental tests are significantly higher.

c. Semester course failures reduced from 63 to 21.

d. Preparation for classes is somewhat increased.

e. Discipline problems reduced 65 percent, with no incidents in classrooms.

f. Behavior is self-motivated, with concomitant reduction of tension.

g. No truancy or unexcused absences.

h. Greatest benefits accrue to high- and low-ability students.

2. Faculty

a. Self-concept of professionalism enhanced considerably.

b. Respect for colleagues greatly increased.

c. Developed a new respect for the school's instructional materials.

d. Increased utilization of a multi-text approach, especially in the social studies.

e. Preparation for classes significantly increased.

f. Agreement on increased student responsibility for learning.

g. Greater progress in course syllabi, both in breadth and depth.

3. Parental Reaction

a. Encourages student maturity and responsibility.

b. Student's study habits are improved with an increased interest in school.

c. Places the accent on the student.

d. Students benefit from the continuous availability of an appropriate resource teacher.

e. Concerned about the effect on the low-ability student.

f. Wondering if students will neglect subjects they dislike.

g. Eighty-nine percent of the respondents approved the program.

4. General

a. Changes in attitudes and performance of both faculty and students exceeded expectations of principal.

b. No accurate tally of inquiries about the program, but 339 administrators and teachers from six states visited the school during the first semester. Some individuals have returned four times, with one school basing its decision to adopt modular scheduling on the visits.

Sister Pacis has stated that the modular scheduling is the first phase of Ryan's implementation of a nongraded school. It is anticipated that Ryan will be using such a plan in about two or three years.

29 | Nancy Draws Up Her Own Daily Schedule at Thurston

KENNETH G. GEHRET

Reprinted with permission from *The Christian Science Monitor,* © 1970 The Christian Science Publishing Society. April 4, 1970, p. B16. All rights reserved.

Nancy Porter scanned the master-schedule sheets on her desk. "Student government at 9 o'clock and Spanish at 1:30. I'm 'officed in' on these—no choice, you see," she explained to a visitor, while quickly entering both subjects on her personal schedule for the day.

The attractive, poised 14-year-old continued: "Now, I can take English either at 10:30 or at 11:15. If I list it for 10:30, I'll have trouble fitting in phys ed." She pondered a moment.

"There, that does it," Nancy soon announced, handing the completed schedule of classes to the visitor to puzzle over.

On the duplicated schedule form, she had entered opposite each time period the class she expected to attend at that hour. Within minutes, she had managed to plan her entire school day in such a way as to include all the required subjects plus several electives without leaving any time slots open.

Nancy is one of 450 students enrolled in the Marie Thurston Intermediate School here at Laguna Beach, California, who order their day on the basis of "daily demand flexible scheduling."

Thurston school officials devised the system, which is now in its second year after a pilot program. They consider it a virtually unqualified success. So does the United States Office of Education, which continues to bring in educators from points at home and abroad to view the system in operation.

Nancy Porter also gives the system high marks. "It's great because you don't have to go to the same room at the same time every day. That's deadly," she says with a grimace.

There's more to Thurston's scheduling plan than options for students on when to attend classes—more, too, than developing the sense of responsibility which Nancy and her classmates evidence in making decisions about their schedules.

"Our program offers a continuum of degree of difficulty," explains Wick Lobo, scheduling counselor. "It challenges the student to do his best. It takes account of individual differences, providing him the fullest opportunity to master areas that seem difficult without penalizing him in areas in which he excels."

Thurston students move ahead at their own pace. They are grouped into four "ranges," corresponding roughly to grade levels, subject by subject. In a conventional school, these students would be classified as 7th and 8th graders. Class work at these levels is identified as Ranges 1 and 2, respectively. Range 3 represents advanced studies beyond 8th grade; Range 4 indicates that the student does not need to take a specified unit of work but may elect another subject or take a study period instead.

Thus in the same semester a student could conceivably place in Range 1 in English, Range 2 in math, Range 3 in history, and Range 4 in science. He need not remain in any of these categories throughout the entire semester. He is free to challenge any range placement at any time, and of course he can be dropped back if his work is unsatisfactory. Movement, both up and down, is frequent within the school term. (Thurston operates on the trisemester plan, with breaks at Christmas and Easter.)

Students have a wide selection of subjects. But required studies come first in the daily scheduling. Each pupil must take at least two modules (30 minutes) of history, English, math, and physical education daily and of science three times a week. He can decide which of several periods of repeated classes he will attend. Then, as his over all schedule permits, he may choose from a lengthy list of selective subjects and activities to round out his day, which extends from 8 a.m. to 2:30 or 3:30 p.m.

Homeroom teachers check each student's schedule carefully before approving it.

The arrangement of classes is a formidable challenge to the Thurston staff. Teachers turn in their departmental schedules by the week. These are reconciled five days in advance of going into effect with the aid of the school's IBM 1620 computer, under Mr. Lobo's supervision. Further adjustments can be made on two days' notice. Final changes—necessitated by a teacher's absence or other last-minute developments—are made by announcements over the loudspeaker system at the start of the school day.

Flexible scheduling is only one innovative feature in the Thurston program. Nongraded classes (range groupings) are also important, as are team teaching and individualized instruction.

It all adds up to "a vibrant school, in which people—students and staff—really get involved," according to David Lloyd, principal at Thurston. "There's an intimate relationship that brings student and teacher together. The staff likes it because here they become professionals; they're not babysitting any more."

The Thurston plan helps the student, Mr. Lloyd points out, by providing teachers with a pupil "performance profile" every two weeks. This aids teachers in spotting weak points, counseling students, and offering extra help when needed.

The system is more efficient, too, the principal maintains, despite higher-than-average costs. "You get so much more for the money," he claims.

"We have cut the student-teacher ratio by having just one teacher to a class when needed [for tests, lectures, or films], and at other times often by using a paraprofessional [aide] in place of a second teacher.

"Further," Mr. Lloyd adds, "we see our system as a vehicle that allows us to solve our problems as they arise."

One problem that the school has well in hand is discipline.

Although there are occasional incidents, few students take unfair advantage of the high degree of freedom which Thurston allows. Students appear to respond to the confidence placed in them. They also know that a system of reminders, backed up by punishment, is rigorously enforced.

But probably the biggest factor in maintaining order is that—in the words of Mr. Lloyd—"students are having a good time learning."

30 | Flexible Scheduling— Advantages and Disadvantages

NICHOLAS C. POLOS

Reprinted with permission from the April–May 1969 issue of *Education*. Copyright, 1969, by the Bobbs-Merrill Company, Inc., Indianapolis, Indiana.

A short time ago F. F. Brown wrote: "The bravery with which schools introduce new heresies can be compared to the quavering whistle of a man taking a short cut through a cemetery at midnight in the dark of the moon. We must take care that promising new heresies do not become dull new orthodoxies." The accent today is on change. We are not suffering today from the malady of "chronic and excessive caution."

This is a time when we urgently need research and experimentation in education; however, resistance to change is built into our educational practices. Many educators fear change because of the difficulties, foreseen or unforeseen, which they might encounter, and seem to prefer what P. M. Blau calls "ritualistic conformity." Perhaps they lack Reisman's "nerve of failure," and consequently refuse to face up to the shortcomings of any program in their school but prefer to quietly bury it under some isolated educational rug.

Another favorite game today which has become very popular since the explosion in experimentation began is called the "genie game." This game, played under the mystical rays of Aladdin's educational magic lamp, attempts to find one magical cure-all, a panacea if you will, for all of the educational ills. If, for example, the adoption of flexible scheduling exchanges a new set of problems, then some educators immediately take their daily exercise by jumping to the conclusion that flexible scheduling does not have the charismatic powers of complete flexibility, and after all our motto today should be "In flexibility we trust!" Systems and structures of time and staff utilization are never flexible—these are mere instruments which are to be manipulated by people who are flexible.

There are as many attitudes as there are educators, ranging all the way from the "time is not ripe" educator to the "hollow imitator for publicity purposes" educator suffering from that common school ailment known as "bandwagonism." Somewhere in the middle of this range is the judicious educator who has carefully weighed all of the possibilities, examined many programs that are in the field, and then proceeded with intelligent action. He is aware of E. Dale's statement that wisely counsels: "But it is the weak man, not the strong man who wants absolute certainty. It is the essence of leadership not only to live successfully with uncertainty, but also to be challenged by it. . . ."

CLAREMONT ADOPTS FLEXIBLE SCHEDULE PLAN

Willing to risk uncertainty and operating on the premise that "time is the fourth dimension in learning," Claremont High School, located in Claremont, California, the home of the Associated Colleges (Pomona College, Scripps College, Claremont Men's College, Harvey-Mudd College, the new Pitzer College, and the Claremont Graduate School and University Center) after careful and serious planning adopted a "Flexible Schedule Plan." It does seem rather odd that in the construction of an educational equation educators have paid far too little attention to the important factor of time—the stuff of which life is made. In her excellent assay of education and time, Helen C. Wood wisely points out that "time is one of the dimensions of opportunity . . . To find and recover more time is to increase opportunity."

Technological change and the new educational media undoubtedly call for a better use of school time—perhaps solid blocks which are uninterrupted by the traditional school intrusions. This is the point Trump makes when he says: "One basic problem concerns the necessary departure from a conventional school schedule . . . A first step in solving this problem is to view time in larger blocks." We see now that the heavy hand of custom and tradition and the ease of scheduling, aided and abetted by the constant tyranny of the Carnegie Unit, forced many schools into the Procrustean mold of fixed scheduling.

After examining the important factors which influence scheduling priorities, i.e., time, facilities, pupils, courses, and the role of the teachers, Claremont High School, the Claremont Unified School District carefully planned methods to avoid "timetable" troubles. Many times schools that have plunged into flexible scheduling have done so without carefully examining the internal program of their school.

Flexible scheduling is not "a punch card toy," or a "modular game," at Claremont High School because at its inception stage the school carefully and critically reviewed its entire school program, its educational philosophy, and made several important decisions. Realizing that flexible scheduling is only a means of using time wisely, and that flexibility is not the by-product of some organizational plan or method; on the contrary it must purposefully be built into the school curriculum. Time of itself has no magic. If changes are to be made in the scheduling of the students then educators should ask themselves, time changes for what?

PURPOSE OF FLEXIBILITY

One of the important decisions made at Claremont High School was that the purpose of flexibility was to provide a large curriculum in diverse areas of knowledge. The Claremont Curriculum Guide offers the student 149 courses in subjects ranging from algebra to science. Large group and small group instruction, directed or tutorial programs, better use of teacher's time, independent study programs for each student were all incorporated into the flexible schedule.

Libraries, resource centers, independent study areas, open laboratory programs now took precedence over the gymnasium. This is not to say that physical education is not an important part of a student's education, for we hold to the maxim that the Romans once extolled: "Mens sana in corpore sano." It is to say that several firm decisions must be made before any school attempts to embark upon a "time-smashing" program. Non-academic matters (administrative or clerical), any cancerous growth of runaway extracurricular programs should be controlled in any educational program; therefore, flexible scheduling in and of itself would not erase these evils without overt planning. The program possesses enough adventure without adding the variable factor of bad planning.

CLAREMONT ATTITUDES FAVORABLE

There is no doubt that the adventures of the other high schools into this "terra incognita" which we call flexible scheduling may have been different from the Claremont experience. Claremont High School, Claremont, California, had a "built-in" advantage that many other schools did not have. (The other schools are Homestead High School, Fremont Union High School District, Sunnyvale, California; Lincoln High School, Lincoln Unified School District, Stockton, California; Marshall High School, Portland Public Schools, Portland, Oregon; and Virgin Valley High School, Clark County, Nevada.) It is a college community already oriented to diverse time factors in educational procedure, and there was a willingness to experiment and to listen cooperatively to the public relations program which the Clarmont schools share with the community. This was of vital importance, for the success of the program depended a great deal on community understanding and citizen participation.

ACCOMPLISHMENTS OF FLEXIBLE PROGRAM

After two years of flexible scheduling the ledger of education at Claremont showed the following credits:

1. We were able to "individualize" each student as a person. The Claremont Plan did not endow students with maturity but simply provided the opportunity to mature.

2. We have opened up time for teacher preparation and planning.

3. We were able to provide a varied curriculum that had both variety and depth in subject areas.

4. Our guidance and counseling program was purposely improved; and our "walk-in" trade in which students were now able to drop in for counseling assistance or even to chat with some understanding adult became an intrinsic part of our daily program.

5. We learned to be flexible and did not buy permanence at the expense of performance. When one arrangement did not work well we were willing to change it. Flexible scheduling is only the "skeleton of time," which must be covered with the flesh of educational substance.

6. We found that time tailored to a particular curriculum (i.e., physics and the laboratory) provided improved instruction.

7. Students could now take advantage of the expanded facilities, such as the new library, social science resource center, the laboratories, and the reading, listening, experimental, and exploratory areas in modern languages.

8. We found that we could offer new programs in independent study such "directed readings," or what we call the tutorial; expand our seminar reading programs and elective programs.

9. By increasing the school day it was possible for students to do more of their school work at school where instructional assistance was readily available.

10. Each student could structure his own course of study, and some of our students took as many as eight or nine courses in a week.

11. We were able to make better utilization of the community re-

sources of a city which has seven colleges and a graduate school; and also to take part in the rich and varied program of speakers, musical, and dramatic activities offered by these educational institutions. Indeed, many of our upper division students often took courses at these colleges due to our flexible program.

12. We found that it was possible to entertain team teaching projects which had been stifled in the past under the Procrustean, traditional, fixed "seven period" day.

13. We found that we could expand our programs not only for the gifted student, but also to provide special attention for the below-average student and the very slow learner. Thus we were able to expand our remedial reading curriculum, and to devise multidisciplinary courses to achieve these objectives.

These were only some of the advantages derived from our experience in flexible scheduling. One "caveat" should be entered here. The attempt to find solace by fleeing into a refuge within the shadow of "King Computer," as though the electronic machines will mysteriously develop sound educational concepts as underpinning for the sagging educational structure, is indeed naive. The SCHED Computer Program is a valuable assistance for modern education, but the Program cannot guarantee that simply because the school time is rearranged in blocks better learning will result.

DISADVANTAGES OF THE PROGRAM

On the debit side of the educational ledger we found that:

1. Over the years some of the students seemed to lack initiative, and were not able to use their independent study time wisely. This, too, is a part of the education of the student.

2. Resource and independent study facilities needed to be expanded. This is not a formidable obstacle and can be overcome with intelligent planning.

3. We had some difficulty in planning the physical education program, but this has been corrected.

4. We found that it was necessary to "slay the dragon" of reprehensibility, i.e., reassuring the community that all educational shortcomings were not due to flexible scheduling, but were genuine problems that belonged to modern education in general.

5. We found that we had to change our system of attendance since accountability became more complex under a system of flexible scheduling. In time this problem was solved.

6. We found that flexible scheduling brought about some traffic pattern problems as the students got on the "modular merry-go-round," and that the independent study program placed a heavy burden on the school's facilities. However, wise administrative assistance and planning soon corrected these problems.

7. We found in the first year that the length of the modular school day (from 8 o'clock to 4:15) posed a problem to both parents and students. This has been rectified (in the second year) by revising the school day.

8. We found that many times the student's program showed a lack of dispersion of time or a "spreading out" which caused him to be scheduled with too little "in class" time on other days. We have wisely attempted to balance out each student's program by careful counseling and preprogramming.

In general these were some of the debits on the maroon side of the educational ledger (maroon is the school color). We did not suffer from the "disarming influence." We knew beforehand that time manipulation would not decrease student enrollment, provide more needed space, or correct deficiencies in our curriculum. We attacked these problems separately.

We were also aware of the pattern of possible rigidity, and tried to avoid this educational pitfall. Like a suit of clothes, education often has to be tailored to the student, and we made an overt effort to do just this. We quickly isolated some of the minor problems (overlapping in programming, the matter of proper grouping, readjustment of time blocks commensurate to the needs of certain subject disciplines such as languages and mathematics, proper supervision for slow learners, and the rapid adaptation of school facilities to the present program), and made an honest and realistic attempt to find humanistic solutions.

CONCLUSION

There is no doubt that the new school of the twenty-first century which is emerging from a traditional agricultural past will be "time-oriented." This is not due to the fact that teachers and students greet the new approach with acclaim and welcome this new horizon but because the burgeoning of knowledge of our nuclear age demands that educational time be used differently. Here there is uncertainty and risk, but also a great challenge. Schopenhauer once remarked, "Ordinary people think merely how they spend their time; a man of intellect tries to use it."

Here we have a commitment to learning shared by all. Alistair Cooke must have had Claremont in mind when he said, "America may end in spontaneous combustion, but never in apathy, inertia or uninventiveness." We are not averse to change, and we are pursuing with great energy a new way to develop creativeness and excellence in learning.

PART SEVEN

Educational Technology

This is the age of sophisticated technology. It is the age of the computer, the television, the telephone, the photocopy, and the film. It is the age of giant communications corporations. It is the age when technology has begun to invade—not just enter—the field of education in general and the schools in particular.

For years technologists worked their wonders in the fields of aerospace, the military, consumer manufacturing, and public communications. Only within the last decade have these same frontier technologists begun to apply their ideas and skills en masse to education. This is not to imply that technology's products were absent from the schools previously. Surely the schools used textbooks, wall maps, 16 mm. films, filmstrips, and phonograph records. Yet such use was peripheral to the dominant teacher–student talk and promoted generally by small corporations. It was as if education got the crumbs of technology's menu.

Today the situation appears to be changing both in the quantity of technological innovations and the diversity of products. What is more, many people seem to be putting greater faith in technology's potential for creating a panacea for

for solving education's problems. For some, an educational
revolution is galloping in pursuit of the schools.

It is to this educational technology that the articles in this
section devote themselves. Robert Heinich begins with the
case for using technology in instruction. His term *mediated instruction* is well chosen, for it applies to the many textbooks,
disk and tape recordings, films, filmstrips, and printed or computerized programs. His case rests primarily not on greater
achievement by the student but rather on the awareness about
teaching created by using technology. His points about the visibility of instruction, teaching style, sequencing, feedback, revision, and the development of a theory of instruction are significant.

The reader will note that following Heinich are
treatments of only two basic technological innovations: computers in education and filmmaking. To treat each of the
many technological innovations would be impossible because
of space limitations and because of high-speed obsolescence.
That is, by the time this book is one year old there will be
several new technological advances that are obviously not included here. We have chosen computers and student filmmaking because they are on the furthest frontier at this point in
time. This in no way denigrates innovations focusing on:

closed circuit television
8mm film loops
programmed textbooks
video tape recorders
electronic study carrels
the language laboratory
talking typewriters
filmstrips and slides
airborne television transmission
educational television (ETV) for school and home
16mm film
audio tape recordings
3-D wall maps and charts
radio
scale models

Anyone wishing to read about these innovations can find a
host of articles in the many journals devoted to audiovisual

and electronic technology as cataloged in any library today. We believe that Heinich's article on mediated instruction includes the most important feature of these omitted areas.

Saettler traces the rise of programmed instruction (PI), which is the immediate predecessor to computer-assisted instruction (CAI). He treats some historical antecedents, terminology, basic early research in Denver and Manhasset, and also the learning theory which underpins most of mediated instruction today. This treatment is necessary lest we think that programmed instruction and computer-assisted instruction burst forth full grown in the last decade. Saettler notes that the introduction of programmed instruction in the schools led to other innovations, too. We have pointed this out in the other overviews as well. The reader must consider whether he himself accepts the Skinnerian base of most programmed instruction for it may run counter to other ideas he holds about education.

Suppes, who is without doubt the leader in the use of computer-assisted instruction, and his colleague Jerman discuss the several uses of computers in education. They do not even question the rationale for using computers. They do not even cite the research on learning achievement and other aspects of CAI. (Feldhusen and Szabo in their review of the research on computer-assisted instruction show that "the evidence clearly indicates that CAI will teach at least as well as live teachers or other media, that there will be a saving in time to learn, that students will respond favorably to CAI, that the computer can be used to accomplish heretofore impossible versatility in branching and individualizing instruction, that true natural instructional dialogue is possible, and that the computer will virtually perform miracles in processing performance data.[1]) Suppes and Jerman, rather, launch directly into a discussion of the types of computer-based programs. The reader should note that they also treat computer-based simulation games, and computer-based management systems. (See the Geddes and Kooi article for a development of this latter idea.) It is also important to note that in discussing terminal hardware these two strong advocates of CAI wisely say, "The curriculum produces whatever learning takes place, not the hardware."

Geddes and Kooi develop the use of a system for giving prompt feedback to the teachers concerning the achievement

---

[1] John Feldhusen and Michael Szabo, "The Advent of the Educational Heart Transplant, Computer-Assisted Instruction: A Brief Review of the Research." *Contemporary Education*, Vol. 40, No. 5 (April 1969) p. 271.

of the students. Their computer-based instructional management system rapidly presents data ordinarily lacking to the teacher, diagnoses areas of weakness, and prescribes new material. The requirement for this system as with programmed instruction (see Saettler) and computer-assisted instruction (see Suppes and Jerman) is the defining of specific objectives to be achieved. They have developed this system with mathematics and reading. (Note that these areas also are the ones most often used in PI and CAI.) Is it possible to do the same with such fields as social studies, science, and the humanities?

Holden's research deals with another aspect of computer-based instruction. He studies the effect of computer-based resource units on instructional behavior. His data are important in that they show that teachers using such units both increased the number and improved the quality of many individualized instruction tasks. Such tasks include the significant items of "encouraging pupils to engage in independent thinking" and "creating an accepting atmosphere in the classroom." This is contrary to the expectations of some critics who believe the computer dehumanizes classroom instruction.

The article by Carrico is most important for it treats an innovation which makes the student a creator (producer) rather than a consumer. In virtually all of the innovations based on educational technology the student is a consumer using the products created by adults in order to learn prescribed knowledge and skills. Carrico discusses filmmaking based on technology which permits the student to be a creator. (Compare this with the article by Gehret in another section which describes Nancy as her own schedule maker.) The rationale in student filmmaking is simple yet profound: it is an invaluable way to give the student a new way of seeing.

We urge the reader to give this article close attention for it deals with both the why and the how of filmmaking in practical terms. What are the implications for three of Carrico's points: (1) In filmmaking the students are clearly superior to the print-oriented teachers; (2) Creativity cannot be taught but only given a chance to grow and to be channeled; and (3) "Hands-off pedagogy" is difficult and the student-as-creator requires more of the teacher than student-as-consumer?

The closing article by Oettinger serves to caution us about our faith in educational technology. He makes an important point, distinguishing between ultimate promises and immediate possibility. He questions—and rightly so—whether we can successfully apply technology to education as we have applied it to aerospace. He questions computer scheduling as practiced today. He questions individualized instruction as it is often practiced today. He touches on the "lack of an empirically validated theory of teaching" and thereby calls to mind Heinrich's earlier article in this section.

Yet, Oettinger accepts the system's viewpoint and offers many possibilities arising from an educational technology. His call for broad learnings (see Frazier's article on individualized instruction in another section) is most appropriate. So is his call for pluralism, diversity, and flexibility. And so we ask, will technology aid us or deter us in our efforts to achieve these goals?

31 | Technology Makes Instruction Visible

ROBERT HEINICH

Reprinted with permission from the EPIE Institute from the March 1968 *Educational Product Report*, pp. 9–12, Vol. 1, No. 7.

In one of the most charming statements I have had occasion to read, a media teacher revealed an essential difference between mediated instruction and classroom instruction. He said:

> After a year and a half as a television teacher, I still have a tiger by the tail. It pulls me from the typewriter to the studio to the classroom and back again. I dare not stop, lest the camera find me without message, mood, or music. There are days when I would trade it all for my own little empire—a classroom behind closed doors where no one watches to criticize or writes daily evaluations.

This comment illustrates a unique peculiarity of classroom teaching: the privacy of instruction. While the product is usually observable, the practices are normally so hidden that attempts to associate cause and effect meet with difficulty. The profession zealously guards privacy of instruction to the point where most efforts at assessment are either deprecated from the start or clothed in individual anonymity. Achievement tests are never used as a basis of comparison, for example. The guild structure of the profession militates against any salary arrangement that suggests differences in teachers based on ability to teach. If five high school teachers begin in a district in a given year and maintain equal levels of course work, their salaries will be identical, and the teachers are, as far as the public and profession are concerned, equal. This is reflected in the literature by frequent reference to the "good" teacher and what he "can" do. But can we assume that the "good" teacher is the average teacher, and that what "can" happen does happen?

Some years ago, I had occasion to preview the introductory film in the John Baxter Chemistry series (EBEC) in the company of a science supervisor. In the film Baxter introduces the branches of chemistry with some elaborate experiments, including one using blood. After the film, the science supervisor was asked what he thought of it. He indicated that the material was important but that any "good" chemistry teacher "could" do the same thing. Asked if he knew of any "good" chemistry teachers doing it, he admitted he didn't, but failed to see the point of the question. After all, they "could" do it, couldn't they?

There has been quite a bit of activity directed toward identifying effective classroom teaching by analyses of teaching situations. The studies may eventually be very helpful in providing colleges of education with guides to help preservice teachers improve their teaching techniques, but several problems attend the mode of operation and the results.

N. L. Gage (1966) criticizes the functionalistic basis of the research by pointing out that the upper limit of the results will be the best teachers *now teaching,* rather than the best performance possible. Stephen M. Corey (1966) makes the same point when he states that lack of information on cause and effect in the studies is similar to observing "that healing and a general health improvement often occur during the exorcising rituals of witch doctors" and that to improve health we "single out the witch doctors with the best client records, and develop a program to make all witch doctors behave like those who appear to be most successful." Another question that is begged by the research pertains to repeatability of the performances and whether or not the qualities detected are transferable. There can be no assurance that the good teacher will be the average teacher.

The magnitude of this problem may be better appreciated by considering the results of a survey by the National Council of Teachers of English on the preparation of English teachers:

Only half of the high school English teachers earned college majors in English. One third of the rest did not even have majors in a related field, such as speech or journalism.

The average English teacher has taught for nine years, but during the past decade 30 percent have taken no course work in English; 25 percent, no course work in education.

Although almost 90 percent said they wanted to study intermediate or advanced composition, the average secondary teacher has completed less than one semester hour in composition or linguistics since starting to teach.

Evaluating themselves, 86 percent of the secondary school teachers did not feel well prepared to teach reading; more than 69 percent felt ill-prepared to teach composition or speech; and more than 40 percent felt inadequate to teach literature and language.

Fewer than 20 percent of the elementary teachers have majors in English. Although English comprises 24 percent of the elementary program, courses in English and the teaching of English total less than 8 percent of their course work.

But we still write about what the "good" teacher can do.

Television has been responsible for revealing just how poor much instruction often is. A report from the Ford Foundation on learning by television states that "the most conspicuous result of television teaching has been an incidental by-product: the medium has displayed in public what had heretofore gone on behind too many closed classroom doors—uninspired teaching." Team teaching has the same effect, but, unless media are used, it is not as widely visible.

Nevertheless, television and other media, offer the best hope for improvement *because* instruction is made visible. As Fred Hechinger once described it:

> Bad teaching is magnified many times over on TV. By the same token, good teaching is not only magnified by TV, but becomes contagious. In spite of the difficulties and problems faced in the Washington County, Maryland, TV system, there is a beneficial effect of TV, not only on the carefully trained TV teachers, but through the effect of these teachers on the other teachers. This doesn't merely mean that the TV teachers are the superior teachers, but it means that we have broken the confinement that has forced teachers to become locked up in their classrooms (after they finish their practice teaching) with no criticism of their work. This criticism is something TV is offering us now by opening an avenue of comparison.

Because mediated instruction is generally observed apart from the presence of the person who had conducted the lesson, teachers tend to be more critical than they would if they had witnessed the same vent in the presence of the instructor, even though they may subsequently adopt some, or all, of the displayed techniques. In a graduate class one day, I was showing a pilot TV program in elementary science. The television teacher, selected on the basis of resourcefulness and appeal, had full use of supervisory, scholarly, and technical help. After the program, the class, all experienced teachers, were critical of a number of procedures used. I then asked them, "If this was the best teacher available and had the advantages of personnel and services for this program, what do you think is happening in all those invisible classrooms out there?" It was evident from the discussion that followed that none had ever thought about it that way—because any "good" teacher "could" do as well.

TECHNOLOGY CONCENTRATES INSTRUCTION

Technology makes teachers aware of instructional styles, characteristics, and shortcomings of which they may not have been conscious before.

Language teachers, faced with the necessity of preparing language laboratory lessons, suddenly become acutely aware of their accents. The same situation will make teachers very aware of the inadequacy of a preparation which would have served for classroom use. Jerome Bruner (1963) indicates that teachers become very conscious of the sequencing of content and the objectives of instruction when called on to devise programmed instruction. Teachers also become aware that television teaching is "tighter" than classroom teaching because much of what the teacher needs to do during the presentation, or is in the habit of doing, is handled by someone else, e.g. slide changing, writing on the chalkboard. Teachers are not aware how much instructional time is taken up with noninstructional activities.

This leads to a problem which needs more study. Because technology concentrates instruction, students tire more quickly. Classroom teachers, observing student restlessness after a period of time, often believe the students are bored with mediated instruction. Sometimes this is true, but experience indicates that the student may need a break. In a language class, for example, there are many opportunities for the student to relax by "tuning out." In the laboratory, he is engaged with the mediated teacher all the time. Much more study is needed on optimum lengths of time for various kinds of mediated lessons.

BUILDING INSTRUCTIONAL THEORY

But the main thing that technology makes us aware of, and what improves as a result, is instruction itself. Mediated instruction as a product of technology may be tried out and revised many times before being "frozen"—and even then, depending on the medium, adjustment may be made. The opportunity to pretest the instructional sequence, until student response assures validity, is a potent way to build instructional theory. N. L. Gage seems convinced that programmed instruction, for example, is a superior method of studying development of *complex cognitive behavior* than classroom teaching, particularly if individual learning styles are important. He quotes Hilda Taba at length on the results of her studies in teaching concept formation and raises this question:

> This is only an example of the kind of complexity that teaching for certain kinds of cognitive objectives must face. If Taba's analysis is valid, and it certainly sounds valid, then we ought to face the question of whether teachers can ever be trained to cope with such complexities on anything approaching a scientific basis.

Philip W. Jackson (1966), in a summary of research on teacher behavior, regretfully concludes that very little has been discovered. The major problem in this type of research is that there is virtually no way to alter the stimulus situation, with any degree of reliability and repeatability, in accordance with student response. The result is usually a study of teacher characteristics. The intersubject confirmability is extremely low. On the other hand, mediated instruction permits repeatable adjustments to student response with, when revised to criterion, very high intersubject confirmability.

A number of experiments in television, programmed instruction and film research have established this, but two are worth mentioning because they illustrate the improvement of a technological product by application of further technology. Philip G. Schrag and James G. Holland (1965) applied programming techniques to a PSSC * film. The printed program, fed through a machine, instructed the student at appropriate places in the program to turn on the projector which would automatically stop at the end of the desired segment. The latter portion of the film, a lecture, was cut out and recast into a programmed sequence. Student gains from the new format were significant.

Another approach was used in the study conducted by A. W. Vander-Meer et al. (1965). Two selected films were augmented and devices, designed to improve learning, inserted directly into the films. A number of the techniques "paid off" and others didn't. The important point though is that once improved, the new instructional sequences would produce the same results with other comparable groups.

Gage's singling out complex behavior as particularly appropriate to research using programmed instruction is an answer to critics who insist that programming is limited to relatively simple skills. Lauren D. Resnick (1963) in a very thorough article concurs with Gage on this way of investigating learning of complex behavior. Both David Ausubel (1963) and Robert M. Gagné (1965) have authored books which deal with learning higher cognitive skills. Gagné's is more directly instructional, particularly in connection with programming, but certainly Ausubel, whose emphasis is more on learning theory, would not disagree with most of Gagné's approaches. The technology of instruction is probably the best approach to converting learning theory into theories of instruction.

MEASURING PERFORMANCE

Jerome Bruner has made a great deal of the necessity for the specific sequencing of certain crucial phases of child development. Mediated instruction offers him the best hope of having those sequences presented in the proper order. If classroom instruction is relied on, there is no way of monitoring the presentation. Only mediated instruction can make the

---

* Physical Science Study Committee. MH and RTH, editors.

claim that the "good" teacher is the average teacher, or, to borrow some terms from psychological testing, that maximum performance is typical performance, that is, the performance is repeatable at the same level. One of the reasons why "no statistically significant differences" conclusions result from so many television versus classroom teaching experiments may be that classroom teachers are spurred to "maximum" performance.

Evidence of this was indicated in the Anaheim, California, television experiment, by Dr. Kenneth D. Hopkins, one of the principal investigators, in a public statement at the University of Southern California. Each successive year of the five year experiment witnessed a drop in classroom teacher performance while the mediated instruction remained the same. However, all indications are that classroom teaching is considerably improved as a result of television teaching and remains above prior levels. Looking at this another way, if televised teaching had been measured against classroom teaching of the year *before* the experiment began, the results might have been quite different. Or if at all possible, an experiment should be conducted where the classroom teachers in a district are unaware that a comparison is being made so that typical performance is measured; again the results might be quite different.

Video taping of teachers in training is another example of attempting to improve instructional skills by making their efforts visible. This practice is no doubt valuable in sharpening teaching style but suffers from the same limitation mentioned before. Unfortunately, it tends to place the main emphasis on teacher performance rather than on student behavior. It is using video tape as a way to improve only one means (the classroom teacher) of achieving instructional ends. The advantage of mediated instruction is that the ends of instruction, i.e., student behaviors, are kept uppermost, and its visibility is a better assurance of revision and eventual success.

REFERENCES

Ausubel, David P. *The Psychology of Meaningful Verbal Learning.* New York: Grune and Stratton, 1963.

Bruner, Jerome S. *Toward a Theory of Instruction.* Cambridge, Mass.: Belknap Press, 1966.

Corey, Stephen M. "The Long Run," *The Way Teaching Is.* Association for Supervision and Curriculum Development and the Center for the Study of Instruction, NEA, 1966.

Davis, Gladys D. "The Challenge of TV Teaching," *NEA Journal.* Vol. 55, No. 4, April, 1966.

Educational Television: The Next Ten Years. Stanford: The Institute for Communication Research, 1962.

Gage, N. L. "Research on Cognitive Aspects of Teaching," *The Way Teaching Is.*

Gagné, Robert M. *The Conditions of Learning.* New York: Holt, Rinehart and Winston, 1965.

Jackson, Philip W. "The Way Teaching Is," *The Way Teaching Is.* Washington, D.C., National Education Association, 1966, pp. 7–27.

National Council of Teachers of English. *The National Interest and the Continuing Education of Teachers of English.* Champaign, Ill.: NCTE, 1964.

Resnick, Lauren B. "Programmed Instruction and the Teaching of Complex Intellectual Skills: Problems and Prospects," *Harvard Educational Review.* Vol. 33, No. 4, fall, 1963.

Schrag, Philip G. and Holland, James G. "Programming Motion Pictures: The Conversion of a PSSC Film Into a Program," *Audio Visual Communications Review.* Vol. 13, No. 4, winter, 1965.

VanderMeer, A. W., et al. "An Investigation of the Improvement of Educational Motion Pictures and a Derivation of Principles Relating to the Effectiveness of These Media," *Audio Visual Communications Review.* Vol. 13, No. 4, winter, 1965.

32 | The Rise of Programmed Instruction

PAUL SAETTLER

Reprinted with permission from *A History of Instructional Technology* by P. Saettler. Copyright © 1968 by McGraw-Hill, Inc. Used with permission of McGraw-Hill Book Company, pp. 250–267.

We have seen that much of the historical development of instructional technology has been focused on the use of media for presenting stimulus materials rather than on psychological learning theory as a basis for a technology of instruction. The recent rise of programmed instruction offers a distinct contrast to this historical motif. In the case of programmed instruction, psychological theory actually spawned media for the purpose of incorporating principles of learning, instead of merely introducing a post hoc theoretical rationale for instructional media.

BEGINNINGS OF PROGRAMMED INSTRUCTION

The concept of programmed instruction can probably be traced to the Elder Sophists of ancient Greece (see Chapter 2). We know that Comenius anticipated programmed instruction five hundred years ago. Also, we know that early devices for automating particular teaching functions were invented in the first decade of the nineteenth century.

Montessori: Pioneer of Modern Programmed Instruction
Probably the first systematic attempt to implement a psychological theory of learning with a mechanism was made by Maria Montessori soon after she initiated her first Casa dei Bambini in Rome in 1907 (see Chapter 4). The Montessori didactic apparatus anticipated modern con-

cepts of programmed instruction. One of her devices, for example, consisted of a block of wood with ten holes of different diameters and ten wooden cylinders to fit the holes. This device was dependent on the activity of the young learner for its use. It was necessarily self-corrective with immediate feedback since (1) a learner could not put a cylinder into too small a hole, and (2) if he put one into too large a hole, he would have, at the end of the sequence, a cylinder left over that would not go into the only remaining hole.

In another type of device, the child was presented with a series of wooden forms and insets. After learning to place the pieces in position quickly and accurately, he was given a set of cards bearing blue silhouettes of the same forms, followed by another card series in which only the contours were shown in heavy blue lines, and finally a set showing the contours in a fine blue line. The learner's task was to place the wooden insets first over the corresponding silhouettes, then over the heavily drawn outlines, and finally over the line drawings. Since each wooden inset covered the corresponding silhouette or outline exactly, if any portion of blue showed, the learner knew he had made a mistake.[1]

Early Contributions of Pressey

Sidney L. Pressey, a psychologist at Ohio State University, exhibited a device anticipating the contemporary teaching machine at the 1925 meetings of the American Psychological Association. This device had four multiple-choice questions and answers in a window, and four keys. If the student thought the second answer was correct, he pressed the second key; if he was right, the next question was turned up. If the second was not the right answer, the initial question remained in the window, and the learner persisted until he found the right one. Meanwhile, a record of all tries was kept automatically.

There were two unique features of this early device that are still unrealized. First, a simple mechanical arrangement made it possible to lift a lever which reversed the action and transformed the machine into a self-scoring, record-keeping, testing device. Secondly, a simple attachment made possible the placing of a reward dial set for any desired goal-score which, if attained, automatically gave the learner a candy lozenge.[2] Thus Pressey's device both taught and tested by providing immediate feedback to the learner as to whether or not he was learning what he was supposed to learn.

Meanwhile, Pressey's former student, J. C. Peterson, devised "chemo-

[1] Maria Montessori, *The Montessori Method*, tr. by A. E. George. Philadelphia, J. B. Lippincott Company, 1912, p. 190.

[2] Sidney L. Pressey, "Autoinstruction: Perspectives, Problems, Potentials," in E. R. Hilgard (ed.), *Theories of Learning and Instruction*, Sixty-third Yearbook of the National Society for the Study of Education, part I. Chicago, The University of Chicago Press, 1964, pp. 355–356.

sheets" in which the learner checked his choice of answers to multiple-choice questions with a swab, finding that wrong answers instantaneously turned red and correct ones blue.[3] Later Pressey devised a punchboard device and a selective-review apparatus using cards.[4] In more recent years, he has urged what he calls adjunct autoinstruction, which calls for a whole array of instructional media—textbooks, films, television, etc.—to be used in conjunction with programmed instruction.

Pressey developed a number of other devices and conducted many experiments with autoinstruction during the 1920s and the early 1930s, but their impact on instructional technology was almost inconsequential. Although he discontinued this first phase of his work in 1932 because of lack of funds (Pressey financed most of his device construction out of his own pocket), he remained confident that automated instruction would eventually generate an "industrial revolution" in education.[5] Except for sporadic developments (mainly during World War II), Pressey's work was virtually forgotten until B. F. Skinner of Harvard University stimulated a new surge of interest in programmed instruction in the middle 1950s.

Programmed Instruction during World War II

Several military training devices constructed in the 1940s and 1950s were developed to teach skills by individualized self-instructional methods. These devices, called phase checks, both taught and tested. Each step of a skill, such as the disassembly-assembly of a piece of equipment, was organized on the assumption that constructed responses with immediate automatic feedback had a special value in learning. This was a linear program in which the learner's problem was to complete the steps involved in learning a manual skill or to accomplish certain terminal behaviors.[6] Thus the basic concepts of contemporary programmed instruction were anticipated.

Crowder's Intrinsic Programming

Norman A. Crowder developed a programmed instruction approach somewhat similar to Pressey's in the 1950s when he was associated with

[3] *Ibid.*, p. 356.

[4] When using Pressey's punchboard device, the student punched with his pencil through a cover paper. His pencil went deepest when he found the right answer.

[5] Sidney L. Pressey, "A Third and Fourth Contribution toward the Coming 'Industrial Revolution' in Education," *School and Society*, vol. 36 (1932), pp. 1–5.

[6] H. B. English invented a device used in 1918 to help train soldiers to squeeze a rifle trigger. It provided visual feedback through the use of a manometer which revealed to the soldier a change in the height of a liquid column. If he squeezed the trigger smoothly or spasmodically, the mercury column would rise correspondingly and provide visual feedback. See H. B. English, "How Psychology Can Facilitate Military Training: A Concrete Example," *Journal of Applied Psychology*, vol. 26 (February 1942) pp. 3–7.

the United States Air Force and engaged in training troubleshooters to find malfunctions in electronic equipment. Crowder's intrinsic or branching style of programming, as represented in Tutortexts or "scrambled textbooks," consists of steps which contain a limited amount of information, usually less than a page, and a multiple-choice question presented at the same time. After reading the text, the learner chooses whichever answer he thinks is correct and then proceeds to the step indicated by his choice. If an incorrect answer is given, the learner is directed to information designed to overcome the cause of his error and is then returned to the step where the error occurred. Thus the Crowder program simulates a tutor by performing the functions of presenting material, examining the learner, and providing corrective instruction or advancement to new information, based on the learner's performance.[7]

Skinner: Father of the Contemporary Programmed Instruction Movement

In a 1954 paper entitled "The Science of Learning and the Art of Teaching," [8] B. F. Skinner of Harvard University supplied the first significant impetus to the contemporary programmed instruction movement. Although Skinner's techniques of programmed instruction were not wholly new, he was the first to call the attention of the academic community to the educational possibilities inherent in programmed instruction and the first to demonstrate a simple, practical learning device based on the principles of operant conditioning.

Skinner, like Pressey before him, focused attention on the device and christened it a "teaching machine." Since the machine rather than the instructional program within drew primary attention, more machines than programs were produced during the first years of the movement, and many commercial companies competed in their development.

The programming approach designed by Skinner was based almost exclusively on work which he and his colleagues had done in animal laboratory research. As to the applicability of this research, he pointed out that "the advances which have recently been made in our control of the learning process suggest a thorough revision of classroom practices, and fortunately, they tell us how revision can be brought about. This is not, of course, the first time that the results of an experimental science have been brought to bear upon the practical problems of education. The

---

[7] N. A. Crowder, "Automatic Tutoring by Intrinsic Programming," in Arthur A. Lumsdaine and Robert Glaser (eds.), *Teaching Machines and Programmed Learning: A Source Book*, Washington, D.C., Department of Audio-visual Instruction, NEA, 1960, pp. 286–298.

[8] This paper was presented at a conference on current trends in psychology at the University of Pittsburgh in March, 1954, and it also appeared in *Current Trends in Psychology and the Behavioral Sciences*, published by The University of Pittsburgh Press, 1955.

modern classroom does not, however, offer much evidence that research in the field of learning has been respected or used." [9]

The basic Skinner approach to programmed instruction is based on the notion of operant conditioning in which the learner's responses are "shaped" to pronounce and to write responses correctly and whereby his behavior is brought under various types of stimulus control. Thus a relatively small unit of information, called a *frame,* is presented to the learner as a *stimulus.* The learner is then required to make a *response* to this information by completing a statement or answering a statement about it. By a *feedback* system, he is informed as to the correctness of his response. If he has been wrong, he may even be told why; if he is correct, his response is *reinforced.* The learner is next presented with a second frame and the stimulus-response-reinforcement cycle is repeated until a series of hundreds or thousands of frames present a complete *program* in a logical sequence of information.

Effective Skinnerian programming requires instructional sequences simplified to such a degree that the learner hardly ever makes an error. If the learner makes too many errors—more than 5 to 10 percent—the program is considered to be in need of revision.

During the decade following the introduction of Skinnerian programs, a majority of those produced were Skinnerian or variations. Yet research had already raised doubts concerning the theoretical validity of Skinnerian programs, despite extravagant claims for the method (see last section in this chapter on Programmed Instruction and Theories of Learning). It is possible that within another decade Skinnerian programs may become obsolete, to be replaced by new methods of programmed instruction with a sounder theoretical underpinning. Whether or not this is so, Skinner must be credited with reviving the concept of programmed instruction and with setting the stage for a closer relationship between the behavioral sciences and instructional technology.

EARLY SCHOOL USE OF PROGRAMMED INSTRUCTION

American schools have been generally slow to adopt programmed instruction. As yet, there has been no widespread movement of school systems to train their teachers in the use of programs nor any general movement, even in colleges and universities, to introduce programmed instruction. In 1962 and again in 1963, the Center for Programmed Instruction, at the request of the U.S. Office of Education, conducted a survey to determine patterns of use of programmed instruction in schools

[9] B. F. Skinner, "The Science of Learning and the Art of Teaching," in *Teaching Machines and Programmed Learning,* op. cit., p. 107.

throughout the country.[10] In each year, the largest single category of responses was obtained from school administrators who considered themselves nonusers of programmed materials. It was reported, however, that nonusers were usually familiar with some of the terminology of programmed instruction and indicated that they had seen programmed instructional materials of some kind or had read some of the basic literature.[11] Within those schools using programs in 1962, teachers and curriculum coordinators played the dominant role in initiating programmed instruction: by the 1960s, the principal had replaced the curriculum coordinator as an innovator.

Although the most common use of programmed materials indicated by the 1962 and 1963 surveys was within large school systems, the programs were tried in most cases with individuals or small groups of students, rather than with entire classes. There also appeared to be more frequent use of programmed materials in junior high schools than in either senior high or elementary schools. Most programs used were in the areas of mathematics (60 percent), followed by English (21 percent), foreign language (4 percent), spelling (4 percent), science (3 percent), and social science (3 percent). Teacher evaluations of programs (four out of five came from commercial sources) were generally favorable with only about 5 percent opposed.[12]

First School Use of Programmed Instruction

We have seen that the first sustained use of programmed instruction occurred in Montessori's Casa dei Bambini and in later Montessori schools which implemented her methods. Aside from the early experiments of Pressey and others [13] in the 1920s and 1930s, programmed instruction was first employed in higher education, on a regular basis, as part of courses in behavioral psychology taught by B. F. Skinner and James G. Holland [14] at Harvard University in 1957. The second pioneer-

[10] Center for Programmed Instruction, *The Use of Programmed Instruction in U.S. Schools.* Washington, D.C. 1965.

[11] Two journals devoted exclusively to programmed instruction are the *Journal of Programmed Instruction* and *Programmed Instruction,* published by the Center for Programmed Instruction of the Institute of Educational Technology, Teachers College, Columbia University, New York City. The Center for Programmed Instruction, under contract from the U.S. Office of Education, publishes an annual catalog of programs available.

[12] *The Use of Programmed Instruction in U.S. Schools, op. cit.*

[13] James K. Little used Pressey's devices as part of the regular class procedure throughout a course in educational psychology in 1934. See James K. Little, "Results of Use of Machines for Testing and for Drill upon Learning in Educational Psychology," *Journal of Experimental Education,* vol. 3 (September, 1934) pp. 59–65.

[14] James G. Holland, "A Teaching Machine Program in Psychology," in E. Galanter (ed.), *Automatic Teaching: The State of the Art.* New York, John Wiley & Sons, Inc., 1959, pp. 69–84.

ing use of programmed instruction in higher education occurred in 1958 when Evans, Glaser, and Homme [15] of the University of Pittsburgh printed programs in a unique book format designed to simulate certain characteristics of a teaching machine.

The first sustained use of programmed instruction in a public elementary school began in 1957 at the Mystic School in Winchester, Massachusetts, when Douglas Porter [16] conducted, under the sponsorship of the U.S. Office of Education, a year-long experiment in teaching spelling to second and third graders. The first use of programmed instruction in a secondary school was started in 1959 when Eigen and Komoski [17] conducted an experiment in teaching modern mathematics.

A Case Study: Denver, Colorado

The public school system of Denver, Colorado, was among the first large city systems to investigate the possibilities of programmed instruction. It was through superintendent Kenneth Oberholtzer's personal interest that, in 1960, Denver became the first school system to free teachers from classroom duties to be trained as programmers.

The pioneer in the Denver development was Jerry E. Reed,[18] a supervising teacher of English who, in the spring of 1960, was sent to Collegiate School in New York City to learn about programmed instruction. Reed spent three weeks at the Collegiate School and then returned to Denver to begin preparing programmed materials on English correctness. Meanwhile, six other English teachers were relieved of classroom duties and assigned to work with Reed. Together they produced 2,800 frames, covering sixteen units of work, during the summer of 1960. When the teachers went back to their classes in the fall, their programs still needed testing and editing. However, just about this time a decision was made to try English 2600, a new commercial program which covered almost the same ground and was aimed at the same tenth-grade level as the Denver teacher-made units.

In trying out English 2600, Denver was assisted by a research team from the Stanford University Institute for Communication Research that

[15] J. L. Evans, R. Glaser, and L. E. Homme, "An Investigation of 'Teaching Machine' Variables Using Learning Programs in Symbolic Logic," *Journal of Educational Research*, vol. 55 (June–July 1962), pp. 433–450.

[16] Douglas Porter, *An Application of Reinforcement Principles to Classroom Teaching*. Cambridge, Mass., Graduate School of Education, Harvard University, May, 1961.

[17] L. D. Eigen and P. K. Komoski, *Research Summary No. 1 of the Collegiate School Automated Teaching Project*. New York, Center for Programmed Instruction, 1960.

[18] The decision to send Reed to New York City was made on the basis that he was *not* attracted to programmed instruction. The rationale of this decision was that if Reed became enthusiastic about the method, then other English teachers also might be expected to accept it.

was engaged jointly with the Denver schools on an educational television project. A research design was made and the English 2600 program was tested during the school year of 1960–61.

The results of this experiment showed that there was substantial learning in all ability groups. It was also discovered that the program proved to be more effective with accelerated classes but that the accelerated students were also the ones who complained most because they were bored with the repetition. The regular classes did about as well with the program as with class practice. On the other hand, the low achievers who did not use the program scored higher in achievement than those who did.

It was obvious from this experiment that the English 2600 program did not meet Denver's needs for low-ability students. As a result, attention was shifted again to the 2,800 frames prepared by the Denver teachers, and in the summer of 1961 Reed recruited the best writers from the previous year for additional work on the English programs. They revised portions and developed short booklets to implement the "lay reader system" of teaching English composition. Under this system, developed by Paul Diederich of the Educational Testing Service and pioneered in the Denver schools, the student's written work was first checked by a lay reader for the purpose of identifying specific key errors. Each type of error was recorded on an error grid (an ingenious device which provides the English instructor with a profile of his students and the kinds of errors they make). With the error grid serving as a basis for diagnosis, the student was assigned to a series of programmed units to remedy the types of errors revealed by his written work.

In another major experiment with programmed instruction—its second—Denver assigned Del Barcus, a young teacher of Spanish, to a full-time task of constructing a sixth-grade Spanish program. This was to be part of the Denver-Stanford research project designed to test the use of programmed materials in combination with instructional television in the teaching of Spanish. One aspect of this experiment was to use television to facilitate the transition from the wholly audiolingual method of language teaching, which the students had experienced up to the sixth grade, to a combination of speaking-listening and reading-writing. Since there was no program in existence to meet these needs, Barcus began developing a program, designed to teach word recognition, reading, and writing. Barcus worked through 1960–1961 and much of 1961–1962 before he had developed and thoroughly tested his program.

When it came time to implement the program, Denver had already learned from its experience with the English programs something about the effective introduction of programmed instruction. Thus, teachers who were to use the Spanish program were paid to come to a series of Saturday morning workshops where they had an opportunity to try parts of the program and discuss its use. The value of these workshops cannot be underestimated because they contributed in large part to the ultimate success of the Spanish program.

The results of the Spanish program experiment, which involved more than six thousand students, provided the general finding that when the new program was used for part of the classroom time, the amount of learning was substantially increased. In other words, the program plus classroom teaching was more effective than either alone. Another significant finding of the experiment was that the more enthusiastic the teacher was about programmed instruction, the better work the students did on the program, even though they worked privately or on an independent basis. Another significant finding was that there appears to be an optimum time to introduce certain types of programs to particular learners. For example, many of the sixth-grade students who used the Spanish program in the first semester could not take full advantage of the program because they had not acquired sufficiently the necessary skills of listening and speaking. When the program was first introduced in the second semester, it proved to be more effective.

The success of the Spanish program created a new climate for programmed instruction in the Denver schools and generated great enthusiasm among the teachers as well as the administration. As a consequence, teachers began to ask for programs, and some of them took steps toward preparing their own. Another development occurred in 1963, when Barcus was appointed as a supervising teacher with primary responsibility for programmed instruction in Denver.

In reviewing the early programmed instruction experiences of Denver, it is clear that no dramatic instructional innovations were produced. Perhaps the one exception to this generalization might be found in the instance of the creation of a teaching team, consisting of a master television teacher, a classroom teacher, and cooperative parents, whereby Spanish was taught to elementary children. Teachers usually thought of programs as part of teaching teams, headed by the classroom teacher. For example, a mathematics teacher used a program to teach his students to use the slide rule, or a third-grade teacher used a programmed tape to drill his students on the multiplication tables.

As we look back on the Denver experience, it is apparent that the most significant lesson learned is that it is a difficult, time-consuming task to introduce programmed instruction as an instructional innovation. This appears to be true whether the school system prepares its own programs or whether it selects commercial programs. Despite its early difficulties, however, Denver has made a growing commitment to programmed instruction.[19]

[19] See Wilbur Schramm (ed.), *Four Cases of Programmed Instruction.* New York, Fund for the Advancement of Education, 1964, pp. 30–40.

A Case Study: Manhasset, Long Island, New York

Early in 1960, the Manhasset Junior High School administration enthusiastically supported the use of programmed instruction and began to make plans for an experimental study. After three months of preliminary study, the experiment began in January, 1961, with the same English 2600 program used in Denver. The experimental design was such that one seventh-grade class and two eighth-grade classes would be taught solely by the English 2600 program, while all other classes in these grades would continue to be taught by the usual methods. Grammar was taught to the experimental group in three half-hour class periods per week and the students were given minimum assistance by monitoring teachers. Teachers in the other classes taught grammar, as before, as part of a ninety-minute English-social studies block period.

The results of this experiment revealed that the experimental groups in grades seven and eight made significantly higher grades. However, Herbart and Foshay found it difficult to interpret the findings and observed that "the test used was the one designed to test the material of the English 2600 program, and no clear evidence exists that the content taught in the other classes was comparable." [20] Although the experimental design was far from adequate, the conclusions drawn from observations convinced the administration and the eighth-grade teachers that it would be worthwhile to continue the program. The seventh-grade teachers, on the other hand, decided against using the program during the subsequent year because they felt the English 2600 program was far beyond the scope and depth of what was customarily taught in grade seven.

The eighth-grade teachers used the English 2600 program the following year to teach all eighth-grade classes, with some changes to meet those needs of students which had become apparent during the previous year's observation. It had been noted, for example, that students worked better when they were encouraged to call on a teacher for help with a difficult frame. What was needed was a less formal classroom climate in which there could be more teacher-learner interaction. Thus the plan for the use of the English 2600 program during the second year called for a large room equipped with enough desks to seat over one hundred students, where different class goups could simultaneously complete their programs. As each student finished his program, he joined a teacher in another room where he could write compositions and receive individual assistance in conferences with the teacher.

The second-year results led teachers to examine a number of assumptions [21] they had held about teaching and to organize new instruc-

---

[20] *Ibid.*, p. 20.

[21] It had been anticipated that the brighter students would be the first to finish the program, but in practice, it was the students of low ability who were first to leave the large program group since they found the program beyond their capacity and desired individual help.

tional patterns. For example, the teachers began to develop an informal, team teaching structure which enabled them to become involved in joint planning, teaching, and evaluation of the program. In addition, they began to hold individual conferences once or twice a week for each student, they established a class in remedial grammar, and they developed a system of grouping homogeneously in relation to speed and accuracy in English grammar.[22]

The Manhasset experience with programmed instruction did not provide the model that Denver did for introducing programmed instruction. In this respect, it was somewhat disappointing. Also, the use of only one regular program and the lack of precise experimental data deprived the project of the scope and depth one might have otherwise expected from an administration which had so strongly supported the concept of programmed instruction. Although some worthwhile instructional innovations were introduced, they were by no means foreseen by the Manhasset administration when programmed instruction was first initiated in 1960.

Comparative Analysis of the Denver and Manhasset Case Histories

The case histories of Denver and Manhasset are only two illustrations of the early American school use of programmed instruction. Other early experiments in the school use of programmed instruction were conducted in such diverse places as Roanoke, Virginia (1960),[23] Provo, Utah (1961),[24] and Pittsburgh, Pennsylvania (1962); [25] but it is apparent from a study of the case histories of these early uses that certain themes run through the Denver and Manhasset cases which tend to be representative of many of the early school histories of programmed instruction.

The Denver and Manhasset cases indicate that while programmed instruction may introduce a more flexible instructional pattern, it can also generate new problems. Since programs are more difficult to adapt to curriculum changes than textbooks, a change in the curriculum could easily make a program obsolete, or a program could hamper or obstruct a desirable curriculum change. In the case of the Manhasset district, for example, when it discontinued the Encyclopedia Britannica Films elementary algebra program TEMAC to change to new mathematics, the TEMAC teaching became obsolete since the machines could not be adapted to the new subject matter.

Both the Denver and Manhasset cases illustrate different attitudes toward individualized instruction. In Denver, the teacher-made programs

---

[22] Schramm, *op. cit.,* pp. 18–27.

[23] E. Rushton, *The Roanoke Story.* Chicago, Encyclopedia Britannica, Inc., 1963.

[24] Schramm, *op. cit.,* pp. 66–94.

[25] R. Glaser, J. H. Reynolds, and Margaret C. Fullick, *Programmed Instruction in the Intact Classroom.* Pittsburgh, Learning Research and Development Center, University of Pittsburgh, 1963.

were designed, from the first, to be teacher aids; the goal was to keep the
students together rather than to encourage divergent rates of progress. In
Manhasset, some efforts were made to individualize the study of English
grammar in the eighth grade. On the other hand, Denver chose to dis-
card the English 2600 program in favor of individualizing instruction,
while Manhasset considered the same program an ideal way to free the
teacher for individualized instruction.

In both the Denver and Manhasset cases, it is clear that teacher attitudes toward programmed instruction proved to be a critical factor in
the success of programmed instruction. For example, in Denver it was
found that students did better with a program when the teacher's attitude was favorable toward programmed instruction. This was quite obvious in the cases of the Denver teachers of Spanish and the eighth-grade
teachers in Manhasset. It even held true when all the teacher did was
keep order!

Finally, the Denver and Manhasset cases support the need for structuring the learning environment to bring about optimal learning conditions. The Manhasset teachers, for example, who initially attempted to
use the grammar program for individual instruction soon found that they
would have to make extensive modifications in existing classroom structure and organization and that they would need to adopt new teacher
roles before individualized instruction could be accomplished. Thus it
seems clear that the use of programmed instruction may eventually serve
as a vital agent of educational change.

PROGRAMMED INSTRUCTION
AND COMPUTER-BASED SYSTEMS

In recent years a number of computer-based systems have been developed and used experimentally in programmed instruction, but the tendency has been to use computers to simulate a Skinner-type program or a
Crowder-type programmed text rather than to achieve instructional goals
which would be impossible or impractical to accomplish by other means.
What is more, the instructional potential of computer-based systems has
thus far been largely unrealized because the concepts of cybernetics have
been generally unknown in the field of instructional technology.[26]

Pask: Pioneer of Adaptive Teaching Systems
Gordon Pask of the Systems Research Laboratory in London, England, developed the first so-called instructional adaptive machines in

---

[26] See Karl U. Smith and Margaret F. Smith, *Cybernetic Principles of Learning and
Educational Design*. New York, Holt, Rinehart and Winston, Inc., 1966.

1953. These devices are not well-known to educators because they have thus far been concerned primarily with the teaching of skills needed by the industrial and military sectors. Perhaps the best known adaptive teaching machine is one devised by Pask for the training of card punch operators. This device, known as SAKI (Self-organizing Automatic Keyboard Instructor), consists of (a) a near-vertical display panel which exhibits exercise materials; (b) a real-size keyboard which the trainee must learn to operate without actually looking at the keys; (c) a "cue information" display of lights which helps the trainee to locate particular keys without his having to look for them directly; and (d) an adaptive computer which senses characteristics of the trainee and adjusts the training routine to suit his requirements.[27]

Lewis and Pask [28] constructed and experimented with an adaptive teaching system whereby a centralized computer induced students to teach each other or placed them in tutorial relationship to one another. To implement the general principles involved in this system a group of three students was used. Whereas typical programmed materials are designed to handle the task of instructing and testing students, this particular system "provides an adaptively controlled environment in which the students are invited and encouraged to develop interaction patterns that enable them to become their own best instructors." [29] In order to implement this system, the computer system "computes objective measures of the progress made by any particular students (and combinations of students), and, on the basis of these computations, it adjusts their working conditions in ways that seem most likely to insure that progress will continue." [30] Pask's work, provocative as it now appears, is but the first of many steps toward a computer-based programmed instructional system which will adapt itself to the responses and needs of individual students.

Autotelic Responsive Environments
A direct influence of Pask can be seen in the example of handling individual differences offered by the work of O. K. Moore at Hamden Hall Country Day School near New Haven, Connecticut. Moore's instructional approach, first begun in 1960, is designed to develop an instructional situation which he calls an autotelic responsive environment. To date,

[27] Brian N. Lewis and Gordon Pask, "The Theory and Practice of Adaptive Teaching Systems," in Robert Glaser (ed.), *Teaching Machines and Programmed Learning, II, Data and Directions.* Washington, D.C., Department of Audiovisual Instruction, NEA, 1965, p. 242.

[28] Pask, "Interaction Between a Group of Subjects and an Adaptive Automaton to Produce a Self-organizing System for Decision-making," in M. C. Yovits, G. T. Jacobi, and G. D. Goldstein (eds.), *Self-organizing Systems—1962.* Washington, D.C., Spartan Books, 1962.

[29] Lewis and Pask, *op. cit.*, p. 259.

[30] *Loc. cit.*

Moore's work has focused on the teaching of nursery-school children (starting as young as two years old) to read and type.

In teaching children to read, Moore has them strike the keys of a computer-based electric typewriter so engineered that the typewriter becomes actively responsive to the keys pressed by the child. Thus, as the child sees the letter struck, he simultaneously hears the name of the letter from an auditory response within the system. After a period of free exploration on the keyboard, further programmed instructions tell the child what letter to strike. By keeping all keys except the named one fixed, the electronic teacher gradually teaches the child the entire keyboard. By means of additional programming, the child is able to take dictation from the computer, pressing keys and forming words and sentences with little error.

The results of this experiment provided the impressive evidence that children who had experienced this approach during its first two years in use had entered the first grade with a fourth-grade, or higher, level of reading ability. Moreover, the motor dexterity and control of these children, as reflected in their writing, was like that typical of seven- and eight-year-olds.[31]

Moore's programmed instruction approach holds challenging implications for the future directions of computer-based programmed instruction. It seems likely that all students will get individualized programs which they may determine themselves and complete at their own pace. The most apparent implication of computer-based programmed instruction is that we must develop our knowledge about the more complex instructional strategies which cannot be implemented in any way yet known other than by the use of the computer-based system.

THE MACHINE-PROGRAM CONCEPTUAL DICHOTOMY

Two opposed schools of thought arose in the programmed instruction movement, which might be characterized as the machine-program conceptual dichotomy. The early machine viewpoint emphaizsed the use of machines and the problems of developing highly sophisticated instrumentation for automating the instructional process. The concern of this view focused on discovering decisive machine functions and specifying the manner in which each is to be accomplished, rather than on methods of programming or implementation of learning theory.

The program (and current) school of thought places emphasis instead on the development of programs based on an analysis of learning and the

---

[31] O. K. Moore, "Autotelic Response Environments and Exceptional Children," *Special Children in Century 21*. Seattle, Wash., Special Child Publications, 1964.

goals of instruction. The predominant concept inherent in this orientation is that programmed instruction should be based on learning theory. What is more, this view holds that programmed instruction should provide a means for studying more complex experimental designs to determine teacher-learner interactions so that more effective instructional strategies may be developed.

This conceptual dichotomy has cut deeper than might be assumed and has been further exacerbated by competing commercial interests in the development of machines and programs. For example, the Finn-Perrin survey [32] revealed that an almost equal number of companies were occupied either with producing machines or developing programmed instruction and were prone to make exaggerated advertising claims without adequate program testing. In most cases, commercial producers have supported almost no research on programming nor have they made any serious attempt to stray from familiar formats or introduce programming innovations. As a result, programs have tended to congeal into stereotyped forms just at a time when more flexible approaches to programmed instruction might have been expected.

Another facet of the machine-program dichotomy is the prevailing conception that programs (software) are more important than machines (hardware). Also, machines and programs are now perceived as having separate, distinct functions. It is obvious that the simple nature of most current teaching machines makes it appear as if the program is the essential item and the device in which it is placed is merely a dispensing mechanism. This arbitrary division of functions appears questionable in the light of the recent development of more sophisticated computer-based instructional systems. Thus, with specially constructed man-machine computer-based teaching systems operating in accordance with cybernetic principles of learning, it will be difficult to separate machine from program functions. They both will be accomplished by a complex combination of display, switching, and computer operations. Therefore, in considering the relationship of a machine and a program, it is important to understand that the prevailing concept of a teaching machine is indeed quite primitive and in need of reformulation.

PROGRAMMED INSTRUCTION
AND THEORIES OF LEARNING

Although a whole range of learning theory positions have been reflected in programmed instruction to date, there is little question that the

[32] James D. Finn and Donald G. Perrin, *Teaching Machines and Programmed Learning, 1962: A Survey of the Industry.* Washington, D.C., NEA Technological Development Project, 1962.

movement has thus far been dominated by the Skinnerian operant conditioning theory of learning, as previously stated. It is still too early to assess the final effects of this theoretical envelopment on the future evolvement of programmed instruction, but it is apparent that there is increasing opposition to the Skinnerian view and that a countermovement has already begun. It is hardly surprising to find that the traditionally antagonistic theoretical positions of S-R (stimulus-response) associationists and gestalt-field psychologists have each become a rallying point in programmed instruction.

Programmed Instruction and Learning Theory Crisis

According to a recent view of Pressey, "there is disturbing evidence that current autoinstruction is not up to the claims made for it, that the current 'boom' might be followed by a 'bust.' " [33] Further, he declared:

> The archvillain leading so many people astray is declared to be learning theory! No less a charge is made than that the whole trend of American research and theory as regards learning has been based on a false premise —that the important features of human learning are to be found in animals. Instead, the all-important fact is that human has transcended animal learning. Language, number, such skills as silent reading, make possible facilitations of learning, and kinds of learning, impossible even for the apes. Autoinstruction should enhance such potentials. Instead, current animal-derived procedures in autoinstruction destroy meaningful structure to present fragments serially in programs, and replace processes of cognitive clarification with largely rote reinforcings of bit learnings.[34]

Thelen's provocative critique of Skinnerian concepts of teaching machines and programmed instruction voices the following doubts and criticisms:

> First, the notion that the learner must be rewarded at each step is by no means proved. Experiments similar to Skinner's studies on rats have shown that latent learning unguided and unrewarded does take place.

> Second, if we assume that reward is necessary at each step, the question becomes one of deciding how to give the reward. The present answer is to have steps so easy that the student makes very few errors. . . . The doubt is that continuous success is in fact rewarding. . . . Reports that boredom sets in after the first few hours of programmed instruction seem to be practical evidence.

> Third, the criterion of a good linear program so far used is that it be error free; but the relationship between this criterion and any educational criterion remains completely unestablished.

[33] Sidney L. Pressey, "Teaching Machine (and Learning Theory) Crisis," *Journal of Applied Psychology*, vol. 47 (February, 1963), pp. 1–6.
[34] *Loc. cit.*

Fourth, while the art of programming is very much concerned with developing an effective sequence of items, two experiments have already revealed that the students learned just as much when the items were presented in random order as when they were presented in the sequence designed by the programmers. This finding suggests that if the purpose of the program is to give information, then sequence does not matter. If the purpose is to teach principles that must be developed over a set of items, then it appears unlikely that principles will be learned through present types of sequences.

Fifth, the role of the teacher is unspecified.

Sixth, the talk of individual differences is misleading. The same program is used with all the students, the mental skills required of all the students are the same, and the content is covered in the same way.

Seventh, the notion that learning is better when it is active and that the machine requires activity is uncertain in its application to present programs. A number of experiments show no differences in learning when the student actually makes the responses as compared with when he merely reads the items.

Eighth, there is no control over student purposes or motives. His posture is to be extraordinarily docile, and he is not expected to participate in goal-setting.

Finally present programs are designed to be teacher-proof and self-contained . . . they cannot deal with unanticipated or emergent purposes, feelings, or ideas.[35]

The above objections to the Skinnerian assumptions underlying programmed instruction are reflected in many of the controversial issues which have arisen in recent years. An S-R-theory-centered programmer considers learning a change of behavior which occurs as the result of practice or doing. To a gestalt-field programmer, learning is a cognitive process of developing new insights or modifying old ones. In preparing programmed materials, the gestalt-field programmer is concerned with helping the learner to pursue his purposes, see new ways of utilizing elements of his environment, and get a sense of, or feeling for, pattern or relationships. Learning, according to this view, is essentially a purposive, explorative, imaginative, creative enterprise. This conception breaks completely with the Skinnerian concept that programmed instruction is mainly a process of shaping complex forms of behavior in passive learners by bringing it under many sorts of external stimulus control.

The theoretical issues which have arisen in programmed instruction are not only pertinent to programming approaches but are likely to be basic in any theory of instructional technology.

[35] Herbert A. Thelen, "Programmed Materials Today: Critique and Proposal," *The Elementary School Journal*, vol. 64 (1963), pp. 189–196. Copyright 1963 by the University of Chicago.

Toward a Field-centered Approach
to Programmed Instruction

Since it is obvious that a countertendency away from Skinnerian programmed instruction neo-orthodoxy has already begun, it is of historical
importance that we examine the less familiar field-centered approach to
programmed instruction. Thelen has summarized the following specifications as a starting set for programmed materials:

1. The student would be able to define his purpose in using the materials in terms of a question to be answered, a relationship to be sought, a
skill to be learned, and he would have solid reasons which, for him, justify his learning of these things.

2. The materials would present reasonably large or molar "situations"
containing many elements, and the student would devise his own path
through these elements, taking them in any order he chooses, going back
and forth among them. . . .

3. Each of these molar situations would involve at least two phases:
discovery of the pattern followed by immediate application, summarizing,
prediction, or raising of further questions. . . .

4. During the "search" phase, the student would get immediate feedback when he had classified each element appropriately.

5. During the application or assimilation phase, feedback could not be
built into the program because any of a large number of speculations or
answers might be right—at least from the point of view of the student.
The feedback for this phase would have to be reserved for a nonmaterial
third phase: class discussion which begins with the testimony of several
students.

6. The programmed materials thus would lead into class discussion;
the reported speculations and difficulties of the students during the second phase would be testimony from which the agenda for discussion is
generated.

7. The discussion would be concerned both with the students' speculations and conclusions and with the way in which the students arrived at
these answers.

8. Diagnosis of the discussion would lead into the formulation of what
the students need to study next, and a variety of activities as appropriate,
including further work with programmed materials, would then be initiated.[36]

It is of interest to note that current work in adaptive teaching systems
and computer simulation of learner-machine interactions has already
begun to incorporate some of the foregoing specifications. There are also
many indications that programmed instruction is shifting toward explo-
rations of the significant interactions in integrated instructional systems

---

[36] Herbert A. Thelen, "Programmed Instruction: Insight vs. Conditioning," *Education*, vol. 83 (March 1963), pp. 416–420. Copyright, 1963, by the Bobbs-Merrill Company, Inc.,
Indianapolis, Ind.

composed of teachers, learners, media, and subject matter. Instructional systems research and development are not likely therefore to be confined to specific machines or techniques but will extend to a cybernetic analysis of the learner as a feedback system in the context of his interactions with his total environment.

33 | Computer-Assisted Instruction

PATRICK SUPPES
MAX JERMAN

Reprinted with permission from *The Bulletin of the National Association of Secondary School Principals*, Vol. 54, No. 343 (February 1970), pp. 27–40. Reprinted by permission of the National Association of Secondary School Principals. Copyright 1970 by the National Association of Secondary School Principals.

The number of applications of modern computer technology has increased steadily since the first commercial computer began operation in the Census Bureau in 1951 (2), and none is more exciting than the application of computer technology to education and, in particular, to instruction.

Leaders in education and industry cite several educational requirements that make computer-assisted instruction (CAI) inevitable. Among the most prominent are: (a) the current emphasis on individualizing instruction, (b) the increasing amount of new information to be learned, (c) the shortage of qualified teachers, and (d) the growing need for periodic upgrading of one's education throughout life.

The question of whether CAI will play an increasing role in education is no longer debated. Rather, the question is "When will CAI begin to play a more prominent role?" The state of the art or CAI is the subject of this paper in terms of both available programs and available hardware. We begin our discussion by considering some of the types of curriculum programs now in use.

TYPES OF CURRICULUM PROGRAMS

Drill and Practice

Instruction provided by a drill-and-practice program is supplementary to the regular curriculum taught by the classroom teacher. A drill-and-practice program may be under partial control of the classroom teacher; that is, the sequence of topics studied by students may be specified in advance by the teacher. Concepts are first introduced in class, and students later review and practice fundamental skills on an individualized basis at instructional terminals.

The drill-and-practice approach lends itself readily to many subject areas in both elementary and secondary schools, and provides an opportunity for teachers to be creative in introducing and developing new concepts in class. Teachers, however, are not able to provide immediate feedback to 30 or more students as they work through a set of exercises. The computer *is* capable of presenting individualized lesson material of appropriate complexity to a number of students almost simultaneously, in addition to providing immediate feedback and correction. Further, a report on each student's performance is furnished the teacher as an aid in evaluating student progress.

The structure of a drill-and-practice program that includes branching, evaluation, and review is quite complex. For example, in the Stanford drill-and-practice program in elementary mathematics, the content of the year's work at each grade level is divided into 30 concept blocks. Each block contains lessons for seven days' work. The lessons are arranged sequentially in blocks coordinated with the development of mathematical concepts introduced by popular text series. Adapting this program to any given text usually requires no more than reordering the blocks in the required sequence. Blocks from other grade levels may be inserted in the sequence for either rapid or slow learners. It is not unusual for each class to work on a different sequence of blocks.

The first day's lesson of each block is a pretest which serves to identify the achievement level for each student on each concept. On the following day, based on his pretest performance, the student is automatically assigned one of five lessons each at a different level of difficulty. The student's performance is computed automatically after each lesson in terms of percent correct, and the student is given a lesson of greater difficulty, the same difficulty, or of lesser difficulty the following day. The level of lesson difficulty assigned each student is a function of his own performance on the previous lesson. A posttest is given on the seventh and last day of each drill block. In Figure 1, each darkened circle represents a lesson. Level 1 is the most remedial in nature, and level 3 the most difficult. The average student is expected to work at level.

Essentially, what happens is that students are given a pretest on each concept, such as addition and subtraction, and, based on individual scores, are then assigned to one of three mathematics groups, each working at a different level of difficulty. The students are reassigned automatically to appropriate difficulty-level groups at the end of each lesson. In addition, students are given individual review lessons (noted "r" in Figure 1) selected from the block in which they had the lowest posttest score. Each

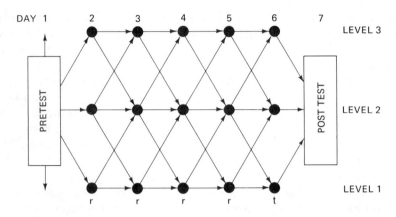

Figure 1. Branching structure followed in constructing sets of exercises for concept blocks.

student may be reviewing a different concept, again at one of three levels of difficulty as determined by his posttest score. Following four days of review, the student is given a review test (noted "t" in Figure 1). The review test score that replaces the previous posttest score determines whether review lessons will be selected from this concept block in the future. The daily lesson in the regular concept block constitutes approximately 70 percent of each day's work; the remaining 30 percent is individual review. Thus, each student periodically reviews his weakest area throughout the year.

Individualized instruction is provided by arranging the sequence of concept blocks, adjusting the sequence as needed, selecting blocks from different grade levels for use by a given class, and providing lessons automatically at five levels of difficulty for each student. Students may work through material as rapidly as they desire simply by taking more than one lesson each day. They may catch up following an absence in the same way. Poor students, as well as students of high ability, can have successful experiences because the difficulty level can be adjusted to their individual needs. In addition, students are reinforced immediately following each response.

Drill-and-practice programs in the areas of elementary mathematics, elementary reading, spelling, and language arts are available from commercial organizations or from university centers.

Tutorial

The tutorial instructional program assumes the burden of instruction. All, or nearly all, necessary information is programmed into the instructional sequence. Provisions for remedial help or skipping ahead are often built into programs of this kind. Most CAI programs developed to date are tutorial and were designed either as special supplementary units or as fullcourse sequences. Teachers incorporate tutorial units at appropriate points in the curriculum sequence in much the same way as they would programmed texts. Tutorial sequences, however, are usually prepared for schools that have the highest pupil-teacher ratio or for special content areas where expertise is not readily available.

Hickey (1) cites 310 available CAI programs from various centers in the United States. Upon examination of the ENTELEK file, which describes the programs, one is struck by the fact that most programs listed are less than an hour in length. Many are available only to a select audience near the computer center.

Some of the programs available for use in schools are Stanford's 3-year logic-algebra program, a college-level Russian language program, and a beginning reading program for grades 1 to 3. Florida State University has produced a college-level physics course which is offered for credit. A science program for seventh-, eighth-, and ninth-grade students is also being field tested. Students in the program at Florida State combine laboratory work with work on instructional terminals. The University of Illinois, University of Texas, State University of New York, and other places have similar projects in several subject matters underway.

A somewhat different approach to tutorial instruction is the program in which the student is a player in a game-type situation designed to develop an ability to deal realistically with problematic situations that face him in the game. In this approach, the student learns from experience the consequences of his decisions rather than from direct instruction. In perhaps the best known of these game programs, the student assumes the role of priest-king of a Sumerian city-state of 3,500 BC (5). The program is available on a limited basis only.

Problem-solving programs also are included under the tutorial heading, since it is possible for students to learn course content at the instructional terminals. In this instance, the classroom teacher directs student interactions and aids in planning and program preparation. Many of these programs are designed to teach students to solve mathematical problems using the computer as a tool. Students learn and use languages such as ALGOL, FORTRAN, BASIC or APL. The course of instruction consists of a sequence of graded exercises drawn from such fields as physics, engineering, and economics.

A description of all the various tutorial programs is beyond the scope of this paper. The reader is referred to the ENTELEK publications for descriptions of other available programs.

Now we turn to a brief consideration of some instructional terminals.

TERMINAL CONFIGURATIONS

Before discussing the terminal hardware itself, one ought to list criteria for evaluating a given system. In order of importance these criteria are: (a) content of curriculum, (b) level of student population, (c) ease of operation, (d) efficiency of operation, (e) reliability, and (f) capacity for data retrieval.

Decisions concerning the subject content and the student population should be made before considering hardware. What is it that needs to be taught to whom? Administrators, often pressured to be innovative, take whatever is available instead of making a selection on the basis of need. Good programs can produce excellent results when they are used as they were intended with a needy population.

Terminals should be easy for students to operate, efficient in terms of response time, and reliable; that is, not subject to frequent breakdowns. The student should not have to follow an elaborate procedure to operate the terminal; rather, he should be faced only with the instructional problem. Response time should be low. Our experience indicates that the system should respond in a mean time of $\frac{1}{2}$ second after the student presses a key or touches a screen. Response times longer than 2 seconds result in loss of motivation and lower learning rates.

The system also should provide feedback to the teacher or administrator on student performance. Daily or weekly reports on each student's performance aid in the over all evaluation of progress and permit teachers to help students in specialized areas.

Simple Configurations

Currently, the simplest configuration for an instructional terminal is a teletype machine or electric typewriter connected by telephone line to a computer. Many drill-and-practice and tutorial programs run on systems with student terminals of this type. Instructions and lesson material are typed to the student under computer control.

Another simple terminal device is a telephone with touch pad. Under computer control, lesson materials are given to the student over the telephone, and the student responds by using the keys on the touch pad. An arithmetic program for elementary school children has been successfully tested in New York City. The computer required to produce the digitized audio used in this program is not a simple device, but the student terminal is. Student responses for each of these configurations are handled by the system's central computer. Branching decisions and adjustments are handled automatically as the student responds. Detailed information can be available to teachers at the end of each day's run.

Intermediate Configurations

In addition to a teletype or typewriter, student stations may include a slide projector, a tape recorder, or both. Many systems which have these devices operating simultaneously under computer control have been less than satisfactory for at least two reasons. First, slide projectors and tape recorders are subject to frequent breakdown. Second, in spite of the anticipated advantages of visual and auditory capabilities, many programs run on these systems failed to show better results. This is not to say that we are not in favor of visual or auditory displays—we are. It should be kept in mind, however, that the curriculum produces whatever learning takes place, not the hardware.

Complex Configurations

Student terminals in this category consist of a cathode-ray tube (CRT), with audio or film display, or light pen, or any combination of these features. Under computer control, a wide variety of stimuli may be presented. Students respond by using the keyboard or by pressing the light pen to the face of the CRT at the appropriate location.

A wide variety of curriculum materials may be presented on a configuration of this type. Its versatility lends itself to the presentation of curriculum content appropriate to students of all ages. The complex configuration, however, is subject to the same sort of reliability problems as the previous configurations, and it is the most expensive of the terminal configurations.

CAI VERSUS PROGRAMMED INSTRUCTION

Programmed instruction is an attempt to individualize instruction in a limited way. There are programs that emphasize the benefits and advantages inherent in greater remedial branching through adaptation of programs to accommodate individual difficulties and differences. Examination of the structure of many programmed texts reveals that for students who make few or no errors, the program is essentially linear in nature. It is not surprising that about all that can be claimed for programmed instruction is that students learn approximately as much as students learn from regular classroom instruction in somewhat less time. The entire content of the course is contained in the linear main line. This is not to say that this is bad; however, it does not make sufficient allowance for individual differences either in terms of student background or achievement level. The instructional sequence is not truly individualized, since stimulus items are not dependent upon student responses. Many small frames in programs often are redundant to the point of boredom and fail to require the thought and knowledge of results at the level required for effective learning. Reinforcement is not truly immediate in programmed materials, since students must check answers by moving masks or turning pages. Neither are hints easily available for students having difficulty. Evaluation is difficult since a teacher must check each response to see where errors were made if a student's performance was less than expected on some criterion test.

Computer-assisted instruction, on the other hand, does provide for immediate reinforcement and correction as the student works through a lesson. In the Stanford arithmetic program, for example, students who type an incorrect character are stopped within 1/10 second and told "No, try again." The idea is to correct the error as it occurs, often before the student has even completed the whole answer. Once the student corrects his answer, he completes the exercise from that point on. A large number of hints may be stored in computer memory; an appropriate set is available at certain points in the program. Students who type "H" for "help" or "hint" receive a clue on how to proceed.

Branching is handled automatically in a variety of ways by the computer without the student's being aware that he is being channeled into a different sequence. Students simply respond to the item presented and, according to their performance, the computer automatically selects and presents the next stimulus item or set of items.

There is considerable discussion in the current literature about the development of CAI programs which take into account a variety of personality, aptitude, and achievement variables when selecting appropriate curriculum items. None of these programs is in operation to our knowledge. The existing programs select material on the basis of achievement only. Perhaps this is as it should be, since our experience indicates that the best predictor for a student's future success is his immediate past performance. Keeping records is, of course, one of the things a computer does well. Students are programmed into new curriculum material on the basis of immediate past performance, and reports of student performance are given periodically to teachers.

One of the greater advantages of CAI is the approximation to dialogue possible in such a highly responsive environment. The student is more involved in solving even a simple arithmetic problem step-by-step, for which he receives reinforcement on each character, than in solving a problem using pencil and paper and checking the answer. A description of two such programs follows.

NEW CURRICULUM PROGRAMS

The Strands Program

The objectives of this program are: (a) to provide supplementary, individualized instruction in elementary and secondary mathematics on a daily basis at a level of difficulty appropriate to each student's level of achievement; (b) to allow each student to accelerate in every concept area in which he demonstrates proficiency; (c) to provide remedial help for each student in each concept area as needed while continuing to provide a degree of success which remedial students often need; and (d) to provide each teacher with a weekly detailed profile report of each student's position in each concept area.

A strand is a series of problems of the same operational type (e.g., counting and place value, addition, subtraction, fractions) arranged sequentially in equivalence classes according to their relative difficulty and running across the entire six years of elementary school mathematics and beyond. Table 1 shows the 15 strands in the program. The strands ap-

TABLE I
Strands in the Arithmetic Program

Strand	Description
1	Counting and place value
2	Vertical addition
3	Horizontal addition
4	Vertical subtraction
5	Horizontal subtraction
6	Equations
7	Horizontal multiplication
8	Vertical multiplication
9	Fractions
10	Division
11	Large numbers and units of measure, time, money, linear measure, dozen, liquid measure, weight, Roman numerals, metric measure
12	Decimals
13	CAD laws
14	Negative numbers
15	Problem solving

proach provides perhaps the highest degree of individualization to date because each student's lesson is prepared for him daily by the computer, the lessons are presented as mixed drills at a level of difficulty in each concept determined by the student's prior performance in each concept, and the student moves up each strand at his own pace.

Advancement
Although a student may be working in several strands simultaneously, he begins each new strand with the class of lowest difficulty or at a grade level determined in advance by standardized achievement test scores. Each day's lesson consists of a distribution of problems from three different classes in each strand. One third of each lesson contains problems

from the student's grade-level class, the second third is selected from the next higher class, and the last third from the next lower class for review. Thus, the lesson contains problems from the class just below the student's grade level, problems at grade level and problems from the next higher grade level. Branching decisions are made on the basis of student performance on each set of six to twelve problems in each strand. The exact criterion varies across strands and grade level.

A student can work through the material at his own pace by taking more than one lesson each day. He can catch up in the same way following an absence. Working at a level suited to his ability, the poorer student, as well as the student of high ability, has successful experiences. Further, the immediate reinforcement the student receives after each response is one of the more positive features of the entire CAI program.

Assignment of New Strands

The choice of strands to which a student is assigned rests with the computer-assisted instruction program. After the initial grade placement at the beginning of the school year, a new strand is added for each student when his average grade-placement score reaches the grade-placement level of the lowest difficulty class of the next strand.

When several strands are being worked on simultaneously, the computer selects problems from each strand for each lesson as described above. The remainder of the problems for any given lesson is selected from the strands in which the individual student is weakest. For example, if Figure 2 represents a student's grade placement in each strand, the program is so constructed that the student will receive problems from strands 1 to 5, followed by a review of the strands for which he had the lowest grade placement; in this example, strands 1 and 3. Thus, the student is assured of an opportunity to advance in each strand and also is given more practice in individual areas of weakness.

Other strands include the commutative, associative, and distributive laws of arithmetic and integers. Problem solving and algebra strands are also in preparation.

Dialogue

At Stanford we are just beginning to develop dialogue programs. These programs aim at a much richer interaction between the student and the computer program. In principle, the objective of a dialogue program is to achieve an interaction similar to that between a talkative student and a talkative tutor. However, it does not take much reflection to realize that we do not understand in any clear scientific fashion the nature of dialogues. When each of us engages in a conversation, we are not aware of the principles we use in responding to previous statements in

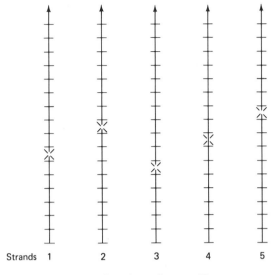

Strands   1   2   3   4   5

Figure 2. Sample student profile.

the conversation, how we process these statements, how we select from them the content on which to concentrate for additional remarks, etc.

In some areas of curriculum, nevertheless, it is possible to develop explicit dialogue programs. As might be expected, mathematics is the easiest and most obvious area in which to begin. Our first dialogue programs try to scan the student's work and to offer comment on the deficiencies in what he has done thus far when he asks for it. The programs also ask him leading questions about what he is trying to do, and how he plans to accomplish both final and intermediate ends. We should like to emphasize that we believe it will be some time before operational dialogue programs will be in widespread use in schools. The investigation of such CAI programs is an important area of research and should be pursued intensively at the research level before implementing them in schools.

THE ROLE OF GOVERNMENT AND INDUSTRY

Most of the work in computer-assisted instruction thus far has been funded by various projects sponsored by the federal government. This probably will continue to be the pattern over the next two or three years. Yet the success of CAI in a broad operational sense will depend upon these efforts' becoming a part of local and state school budgets. Hardware and software costs are just beginning to reach the level at which individual school systems can hope to pay for limited facilities out of their own budgets. CAI efforts in secondary school computer programming and related data-processing topics will perhaps be one of the earliest areas of concentration, especially in terms of the use of local and state funds.

It is also apparent that at the community college and four-year college level considerable funds probably will be expended by state and local funding agencies in order to implement programs that are large in number, but that require a technically well-qualified teaching staff. It seems a reasonable prediction that CAI will be an especially useful tool for basic and remedial courses in mathematics and English in two-year and four-year colleges over the next decade.

As it has in most other instances of educational innovation, much of the initiative will necessarily come from educational institutions. The role of industry, however, is particularly important in the field of computer-assisted instruction because the sophisticated equipment is manufactured and marketed by industry, and educational institutions will be dependent upon industry to provide, at the very least, technical know-how in operating and maintaining computer systems.

As might be expected, a number of firms are interested in CAI and will continue to contribute toward its development. On the one hand, we have large computer manufacturers like IBM, RCA, and Honeywell. On the other hand, we have small software firms interested in the programming and curriculum aspects of CAI. These firms run from traditional publishers like Harcourt, Brace & World to special software firms such as Bolt, Beranek and Newman in Massachusetts, and Computer Curriculum Corporation in Palo Alto, California. A large number of additional firms have some peripheral interest in computer-assisted instruction. As the market develops, it can be anticipated that industry will devote more attention to CAI. Undoubtedly, publishers will expend greater effort than they now do in the development of CAI courses and curriculum, as they sense the growth of a sizable market that will make commercially feasible a substantial investment in curriculum development.

In a very general way, the role of industry in CAI should be similar to the role of publishers in the production and marketing of textbooks. Yet, because of the sophistication of the technology and the requirements for operating and maintaining computer systems, as opposed to the simpler matter of placing books in a school, the relations and areas of responsibility between industry and educational institutions will have to be closer and more carefully thought out than they have been in the case of publishing.

CONCLUDING REMARKS

In this article we have attempted to give a sense of current activities in computer-assisted instruction and to project at least in a modest way some of the future directions. We have not delved into many important details nor even into some central topics. For example, we have not attempted to survey the work undertaken in evaluating CAI programs or what is an appropriate methodology of evaluation. For a report of some fairly extensive evaluation results, the reader is referred to Suppes and Morningstar (4). For a detailed discussion of the first stages of developing a CAI program, and the sorts of attitudes encountered by teachers, students and parents, the reader is referred to Suppes, Jerman, and Brian (3).

On the vexing subject of CAI economics, we do not think the appropriate analyses have yet been published. One of the difficulies is that projections too often are based on the technology of last year or the year before, and in a field that is changing as rapidly as that of computers, it is difficult to prepare sound economic cost forecasts that can be depended upon to be reliable and accurate over the next few years. For those who are interested in installing and operating CAI systems, we caution that they should believe neither those who argue that the cost is very slight nor those who counsel that the cost is inordinately high. The installation and operation of CAI courses does entail substantial cost, but many aspects of standard instruction also are expensive. In areas like that of computer programming it is simply the case that many secondary schools are not able to find qualified teaching personnel. The offering of computer programming courses in a CAI context may be the only feasible alternative. For example, as the national need for languages such as Russian, Chinese, and Japanese increases over the next decade, the only hope for offering them on a widespread basis at a sufficiently high quality will be through the use of CAI courses. Finally, we believe that much of the remedial work in mathematics and English in the present high-school curriculum can be made more attractive and more efficient by placing it in a CAI context. Again, the cost of these programs will not be negligible, but the increased gains in student performance and achievement will, we would predict, offset the costs.

REFERENCES

1. Hickey, A. *Computer-Assisted Instruction: A Survey of the Literature.* (3rd ed.) Newburyport, Massachusetts: ENTELEK, Inc., 1968.
2. Macy, J. "Automated Government." *Saturday Review,* 1966, *49*, 24.
3. Suppes, P., Jerman, M., & Brian, D. *Computer-Assisted Instruction: The 1965–66 Stanford Arithmetic Program.* New York: Academic Press, 1968.
4. Suppes, P., & Morningstar, M. *Evaluation of Three Computer-Assisted Instruction Programs.* In press.
5. Wing, R. "The Production and Evaluation of Three Computer-Based Economics Games for the Sixth Grade and Game Simulation for the Sixth Grade." Final Report. Cooperative Research Project No. 2841, June, 1967, Board of Cooperating Educational Services, Westchester County, New York.

34 | An Instructional Management System for Classroom Teachers

CLEONE L. GEDDES
BEVERLY Y. KOOI

Reprinted with permission from *The Elementary School Journal*, Vol. 69, No. 7 (April 1969), pp. 337–345, by permission of the University of Chicago Press. Copyright © 1969 by the University of Chicago Press.

During the 1967–68 school year, a computer-aided management system was used to help first-grade teachers in two schools in Los Angeles manage the daily affairs of their classrooms. The teachers operated under the Instructional Management System, which is being developed jointly by the System Development Corporation and the Southwest Regional Laboratory for Educational Research and Development.

The Instructional Management System is designed to help the teacher monitor the progress of her pupils and make decisions on the pace of instruction, the grouping of children, the sequence of lessons, and the individualization of instruction. The system helps the teacher answer such questions as: "How fast should these children progress from one lesson to the next?" "Do I have my pupils grouped to allow the most efficient learning?" "Do my pupils know their reading vocabulary well enough for me to spend today on the more difficult skill of sentence comprehension?" "Exactly what kind of help should I be giving this particular child?" The Instructional Management System helps the teacher by providing information almost daily about each child's achievement and by suggesting specific activities to help the pupil when he does not learn what is presented in any particular lesson.

The Instructional Management System provides a framework for making decisions on classroom management at any grade level, but some one level had to be selected for initial development and demonstration. The project staff wanted to encounter and solve the most difficult problems during early design and development of the system. For this reason, we decided to work with first-graders. They cannot read instructions, are not accustomed to classroom instructional routines, and have almost no previous experience with tests.

Usually each class we worked with was divided into three reading groups so that the teacher could work more closely with a few children at a time. A ninety-minute period was generally reserved for reading; during this ninety minutes the teacher worked directly with each group of approximately ten children for twenty to thirty minutes. While the teacher worked with one group, the other groups pursued independent activities or did workbook sheets that followed up their reading.

The teachers were satisfied with the practice of moving the children from one small-group situation to another in the classroom, but realized that there were problems that needed attention. The children were grouped according to the teacher's best judgment of how well they kept up with the group, not according to their mastery of skills; lesson assignments were made to the group as a whole and were based largely on the teacher's intuitive judgments about what the children needed. There was little opportunity for individual instruction. Any regular information the teacher gathered about her pupils' progress depended on her. She could observe the children in class or grade lessons or give tests that she herself planned and assigned, but she had no help in planning her observations and assignments or in analyzing the results. Consequently, she could not use the data effectively to pace or sequence instruction, or to discover what help she should give any one child, if she found time to give it.

In developing a management system, the System Development Corporation has tried to provide the information teachers know they lack. No attempt is made to force immediate changes in classroom routines that seem satisfactory to teachers. By trying the Instructional Management System in classrooms, we are discovering what information and what assistance actually help the teacher help each child. When we provide that information and assistance, more flexible, individualized routines will follow.

The classroom that uses the Instructional Management System has carrels wired for sound. Otherwise it looks like a typical classroom. Many classrooms have listening centers with tape recorders or phonographs and headsets. Classrooms that use the Instructional Management System have adapted these teaching aids to present instructions for diagnostic tests that resemble regular workbook exercises. The children in one group work on the tests at individual carrels during their regular follow-up portion of the reading period while the teacher is working with another group.

The tests have a simple format of multiple-choice items. The children mark their responses in pencil directly on the test booklet. The tests are collected each day and taken to the System Development Corporation, where they are first checked for identification and extraneous marks, then processed through an optical scanner. Data from the scanner are put on a tape for insertion into the computer, and the computer evaluates the responses for correctness and achievement of teaching objectives. A report is printed out showing the results of the tests for the group as a whole and for each individual child. A sample of this report is shown in Figure 1.

The report is in the teacher's mailbox when she arrives at school the next morning. The first part of the report shows the group's achievement on the test; the second part shows scores for individuals.

When the performance of a group or a child is not up to standard, an activity, or "prescription," is recommended. The activities are designated by code numbers. In the report shown in Figure 1 the activities recommended include those assigned the code numbers R28–0203 and R28–0204. The teacher selects the lesson designated by the code number from her files and uses it for the day's instruction. The prescription may be given to the whole group or to a single child. When there is no prescription, the class can move to the next unit of work.

| Teacher 53 | Date 05/22/68 | Test 9928, WHITEHOUSE |
| Grade B1 | Subject READING | Review Group 1 |

A. GROUP REPORT

General Objectives	Score	Activities Recommended
2 WORD RECOGNITION	87	R28–0203 R28–0204
9 PARAGRAPH COMPREHENSION	94	
TOTAL SCORE	88	

B. INDIVIDUAL REPORT

| | | General Objectives Score This Test | |
| | Total | | |
Student Name	Score	2	9
RUTH STERLING	97	96	100
CARLA REECE	97	96	100
DONNA PRENTICE	94	92	100
CATHY WILTON	91	89	100
LORI MATTHEWS	89	85	100
203 (70) R28–0203			
DANIEL LARSON	86	85	88
DALE SCHULTZ	81	78	88
204 (62) R28–0204			
MICHAEL ROLLINS	72	71	77
203 (60) R28–0203			
204 (62) R28–0204			
902 (66) R28–0902			

Figure 1. Test report.

COMPONENTS

The first component of the Instructional Management System is the objectives. They define the goals of instruction. The items in each test are keyed to these objectives. The second component consists of the tests, which measure the children's achievement of the objectives. The third component is the system of reports prepared by the computer. The reports provide the most frequently used information on a daily basis and more detailed information as necessary. The fourth component is made up of the activities prescribed to remedy deficiencies.

OBJECTIVES

The instructional objectives were defined early in the development of the system; they were based on actual instruction in various classrooms rather than on what we, as educational psychologists, might believe appropriate. To describe a first-grader's progress (or lack of it) on an almost daily basis, we had to know what is expected of him on a daily basis—what the instructional goals or objectives are. For example, what should a child learn and be able to do after he has "covered" any particular story in his preprimers or primers?

To identify objectives that we could state in operational terms, we examined publishers' guides and city school curriculum guides, we observed first-grade classes, and we consulted teachers. From these sources we derived several general objectives in reading and mathematics. Though we defined objectives and wrote tests for both arithmetic and reading, the greater thrust was in reading. Only the reading system will be described here.

The general objectives for reading are broadly defined skills that can be associated with successive levels of content as they are introduced in first grade. For example, at the end of each reading lesson in first-grade the child should be able to pick out a reading vocabulary word from all others; he should be able to select a written word when he hears it pronounced; he should recognize the sounds or key letters in his reading vocabulary words; and he should understand the meaning of the words, the sentences, and the paragraphs in his reading lesson. Thus, the general reading objectives are visual discrimination, word recognition, phonic analysis, structural analysis, word comprehension, sentence comprehension, and paragraph comprehension.

Though these general objectives seem fairly specific, they are not specific enough to indicate what should be in a test question or what examples the teacher should use in teaching a lesson. Each general objective, therefore, must be translated into a number of specific objectives from which specific instruction and test items can be drawn. Some specific objectives tell exactly what content should be included; other specific objectives show what skills should be taught and tested. Take the general objective in phonic analysis: The child is to show that he recognizes the sounds of initial consonants. If the new vocabulary for a specific lesson includes the words *ride, Tom,* and *see,* the specific phonic objective for that lesson would include having the child recognize the sounds of *r, t,* and *s,* in a wide variety of words.

The structure used to teach reading emphasizes a few general objectives during a semester, and each general objective incorporates a list of specific objectives. The structure seems to fit most elementary school subjects. We chose reading for our major effort because it seems to offer a greater variety of problems in definition and testing than most other first-grade subjects. The decision to use an area that had a variety of problems in definition and testing than most other first-grade subjects. The decision to use an area that had a variety of problems helped us build a system that can be generalized to other subject areas.

One reason why we constructed mathematics materials was to see whether this assumption about generalization was true—whether the system we developed to teach reading could be used to teach arithmetic and other subjects. We found that the system was easier to use in first-grade mathematics than in reading, for mathematics offers more limited content to be tested and a more clearly hierarchical structure than reading does. The system also seemed satisfactory to teachers who wanted to describe various courses at various grade levels.

TESTS

The tests were not standardized in large-scale trials but were improved by trying them out in small groups and revising them on the basis of the children's responses. We wrote twenty-eight reading tests— one for every three stories in the basal reading series for the first semester. Each test emphasizes the vocabulary of the three stories being tested, but also presents some vocabulary words from the previous stories and each item is associated with some specific objective. Eight reading readiness tests precede the reading tests, and sixteen tests were prepared to measure progress in mathematics. The arithmetic tests were prepared by teachers with the help of personnel from the System Development Corporation. Each test is about six pages long and requires about twenty minutes to administer. About ten formats are possible in placing items on test sheets, but the scanner limits the items to multiple choice. Many, though certainly not all, instructional objectives can be measured in a multiple-choice format.

REPORTS

The type of report most frequently provided has been described. Figure 1 presents an example. This report tells the teacher how groups and individuals achieved on general objectives and suggests remedial activities. It allows the teacher to teach lessons that remedy fairly global and recent deficiencies in the performance of a group or a child. In the beginning, teachers using the system were quite content to do little more than this, for the report provided more information than they were used to having. When the teachers became more familiar with the system, however, they were able to see its possibilities and use more information.

Several other reports or printouts were then provided. One of these is a standard weekly report that provides individual and group scores on all tests taken. With it the teacher can follow trends in the performance of groups and individuals. The standard weekly report also ranks the pupils' long-term performance and shows any sudden rise or drop in a pupil's achievement, so that the teacher can act on changes as soon as they occur.

Associated with this weekly summary are periodic individual profiles that show on a graph the trend of each child's performance. Figure 2 is an example of this type of report. The "0" base of each profile is the mean score of the child's group on each test. A series of marks above or below the "0" line shows how many standard deviations above or below the mean the child scored on each test. Often the teacher finds that a child performs above (or below) average on most tests. Sometimes changes occur that signal a need for special attention from the teacher. Figure 2 shows a change from above average performance to below average. At this point, the teacher should look for a change in the skills being tested or some prerequisite skill that the child failed to master.

Two final printouts, which are available to the teacher on request, are the most helpful for remedying the difficulties of an individual child. When the teacher wants to know what deficiency in skills is pulling down a child's score, she can request detailed individual printouts. From the more general report, she can answer such questions as: "Why doesn't this pupil read well?" "Is he having difficulty in recognizing the words, or is he having difficulty in understanding their relationship in sentences?" The printout tells the teacher how well the child has been performing on the general objectives in all his tests.

The last printout tells the teacher exactly what kinds of items the child needs practice on. For example, the child whose performance is reported in Figure 3 consistently fails to associate the letter *l* with its sound in words and should receive instruction and practice on that skill.

These reports provide information that helps the teacher make classroom decisions. A knowledge of the most recent achievement of groups

```
SCHOOL    HOLLY PARK        TEACHER   HAZEL MALLORY        DATE 04/09/68
STUDENT   ENOCH NEEDHAM     SUBJECT   MATH

TEST NO.  1   2   3   4   5   6   7   8   9  10  11  12  13  14  CUM
   3.0
   2.8
   2.6
   2.4
   2.2
   2.0
   1.8
   1.6
   1.4
   1.2
   1.0
Z  0.8          +           +
S  0.6      +   +   +   +   +
C  0.4      +   +   +   +   +
O  0.2      +   +   +   +   +
R  0.0  -+---+---+---+---+---+---+---+---+---+---+---+---+---+
E -0.2                          +   +   +   +   +   +       +
  -0.4                          +   +   +   +   +   +
  -0.6                          +   +   +   +   +   +
  -0.8                          +   +   +   +   +
  -1.0                          +           +
  -1.2                          +           +
  -1.4                          +
  -1.6
  -1.8
  -2.0
  -2.2
  -2.4
  -2.6
  -2.8
  -3.0
```

Figure 2. Individual performance profile.

and individual children makes it possible for the teacher to answer such questions about her immediate lesson plans as: "Do my pupils know their reading vocabulary well enough for me to spend the day on phonics?" The reports also suggest activities to remedy deficiencies in recent achievement and to prevent the group from moving to the next lesson faster than it should. Information on long-term trends in performance makes it possible to group pupils efficiently and alerts the teacher to sudden changes. The reports on individual pupils provide information that can be used in conferences with parents, and this information makes it possible to give any child detailed help in overcoming a specific difficulty.

At first teachers may use the system only to maintain the group-paced structure. After they become familiar with the great amount of individual information that is available, they may want to expand their use of the system so that their programs gradually assume the characteristics of individualized instruction.

PRESCRIPTIONS

The final component of the Instructional Management System is the prescription—the remedial instruction suggested on printouts when achievement is below an acceptable level. Like other components of the system, prescriptions are patterned after needs the teacher currently recognizes. Prescriptions can be improved as new and better procedures and materials are developed.

Prescriptions for the first year were developed by two cooperating

---

Building FRAZIER   Date 06/06/68
Teacher JANICE YATES
Student CATHY WILTON
Subject BI READING   Tests 9914–9928

OBJECTIVE 2 WORD RECOGNITION

Specific Objective	Possible Attainment	Student Attainment	Percent
SAME LENGTH WORDS	4	3	75
INITIAL LETTER DISTRACTOR	47	41	87
FINAL LETTER DISTRACTOR	37	33	89
MANY LETTER DISTRACTORS	30	25	83

OBJECTIVE 3 PHONICS, INITIAL SOUNDS

Specific Objective	Possible Attainment	Student Attainment	Percent
INITIAL CONSONANT F	4	4	100
INITIAL CONSONANT B	4	4	100
INITIAL CONSONANT N	4	3	75
INITIAL CONSONANT W	4	4	100
INITIAL CONSONANT P	4	3	75
INITIAL CONSONANT L	4	2	50
VARIED CONSONANTS	12	12	100

OBJECTIVE 4 PHONICS, FINAL SOUNDS

Specific Objective	Possible Attainment	Student Attainment	Percent
RHYMING WORDS	12	10	83
SINGLE CONSONANT SOUNDS	18	14	77

OBJECTIVE 5 PHONICS, MEDIAL VOWELS

Specific Objective	Possible Attainment	Student Attainment	Percent
MEDIAL VOWELS	12	9	75

Figure 3. Individual diagnostic report: specific objectives.

teachers during the summer, before school started. The prescriptions consist primarily of sheets of practice items, often borrowed from workbooks,
each keyed to the objectives being tested. When a code number appears
under "activities recommended," as in Figure 1, the appropriate sheets
are used. However, the code number could designate some other activity,
such as a group lesson, a programmed instruction sequence, or tutoring by
another child who is proficient in the skill in question. Any of these activities could be described in folders that now contain only paper-and-
pencil practice sheets. The development of alternative activities is now
receiving primary attention in the improvement of the Instructional
Management System.

CONCLUSION

The Instructional Management System, then, is a classroom management system that is being developed. The system uses the practical situation a teacher faces and offers help with information needs she recognizes.
The system accommodates the typical, group-paced classroom. At the
same time, by providing information on children's learning difficulties,
the system encourages the teacher to undertake more individualization in
her classroom. The Instructional Management System is planned to serve
the teacher who wishes to use this information to make her own program
completely flexible and appropriate for each child's individual needs.

The Instructional Management System is not a finished system. Each
semester the staff of the System Development Corporation uses the regular collection of data on pupils' performance to evaluate and revise tests,
materials, computer programs, and procedures. After such data have been
collected for several semesters and the system has been revised on the
basis of the data, plans will be made to use the system on a wider scale.

35 | The Effects of Computer Based Resource Units upon Instructional Behavior

GEORGE S. HOLDEN

Reprinted by permission from *Journal of Experimental Education*, Vol. 37, No. 3 (Spring, 1969), pp. 27–30.

Computer based resource units were developed to improve the individualization of instruction through unit teaching. Instructional behaviors of teachers were examined to see if this kind of computer aid brought about a change in the way teachers teach. A pre-post two group experimental design was used in which the data were collected by a group of trained observers using an instruction observation tool. Pre-post mean scores were tested and found to be significant in five out of seven dimensions of instructional behavior. Variety and kinds of instructional materials and methods were also examined. The data indicate that teachers who use computer-based resource units increase the number and improve the quality of many individualized instruction tasks.

The revolution which professional education has been undergoing the last few years involves changes in just about every facet of education. Included are reexamination of educational objectives, restructuring of subject matter, new practices in staff utilization and organization, originality in building design and function, diversification of instructional materials and methodology, and refinement of measuring devices. Most of the changes that are taking place seem to be related in some way to an increased awareness of the need to be in touch with the person of the individual in the classroom.

The alarming rate of change, along with the move toward the individualization of instruction, has served to complicate and confuse the decision making which must be done by elementary and secondary school personnel. Computer-based resource units, which have been given the name "Resource Guides," were developed to help the teacher make decisions in his complicated planning tasks (1, 2). Basically, in this study the computer serves as a retrieval system designed to assist the teacher in his decision making about classroom objectives, subject-matter content, instructional activities, materials, and measuring devices. The resource guide was designed primarily to help the teacher individualize instruction through unit teaching, and it was necessary to see if the instructional tasks in which teachers engage become more individualized as a result of using the computer materials. Therefore, this article reports on a study which attempted to get at the question: Does the use of resource guides cause a varied selection of teachers more nearly to individualize their instruction by (a) encouraging pupils to engage in independent thinking, (b) creating an accepting atmosphere in the classroom, (c) making appropriate selection and use of instructional materials, (d) making appropriate selection and use of teaching methods, (e) motivating pupils through challenge without threat, and (f) sensing the needs of individuals in the classroom?

To get at the question, a pre-post measure of instructional behavior was recorded so that observable differences could be noted and objectified. To discover whether or not these differences were statistically significant, the following null hypothesis was tested:

> There is no significant observable difference between the regular instructional behavior of a varied selection of teachers and the instructional behavior of the same teachers recorded at a time when they are following plans that were developed from computer based resource guides.

DESIGN AND METHODS

In an attempt to investigate the effects of computer-based resource guides upon the instructional behavior of a varied sample of classroom teachers, nineteen high school teachers and nineteen third-grade teachers were each observed four times by trained observers using Jason's Instruction Observation Record (IOR) (3). The first two observations, representing the predata of a pre-post design, were implemented under essentially the same conditions for all of the teachers.

For the postobservations, the teachers were alternately assigned to experimental and control groups. The control group was used to guard against teachers changing instructional behavior because of:

> 1. the Hawthorne effect: experimental teachers were asked to use the computer-based resource guide, while the control teachers were asked to use materials drawn from their usual sources.

2. an increased awareness of their own objectives; both experimental and control teachers were asked to identify the objectives they wished to achieve.

3. an increased awareness of individual pupil characteristics; both experimental and control teachers were asked to complete a pupil characteristics form for each pupil in his class.

A further function of the control group was to guard against biased reporting of change in instructional behavior. Observers were not told whether they were observing experimental or control group teachers.

Even though the training of the observers produced a high level of consistency among the observers in the results they achieved when they used the observation instrument, each teacher in the study had only one observer assigned to him. That is, each observer was responsible for making all four observations of each teacher assigned to him. The instructional behaviors which were observed and rated were those behaviors represented by the seven scales of the IOR.

> Scale A—Attitude to Difference
>
> Scale B—Sensitivity to Physical Setting
>
> Scale C—Attitude to Students
>
> Scale D—Use of Instructional Materials
>
> Scale E—Reaction to Student's Needs
>
> Scale F—Use of Teaching Methods
>
> Scale G—Use of Challenge

At the end of the second visit, the observers left a listing of forty to sixty objectives that might be applied to the particular unit in question and instructed each teacher to select not more than ten that he would like to have his class achieve as a whole, and any four of these ten for each pupil in the class. The observers also requested each teacher to complete one pupil characteristic check list for each pupil in the class. This check list covered the following characteristics:

1. IQ
2. Social Class
3. Reading Level
4. Sex
5. Grade Level
6. Interests
7. Vital Statistics (family information)
8. Handicap Behavior
9. Developmental Tasks

The objectives and pupil characteristics were fed into the computer, which sorted through vast amounts of coded material about the unit being studied. The result was the production of a resource guide—a reservoir of materials containing the following data relevant only to the particular class for which the resource guide was generated.

Part A—1. Subject matter outline
        2. Large group activities
           a. Introductory
           b. Developmental
           c. Culminating
        3. Small group activities
        4. Instructional materials
        5. Measuring devices

Part B—1. Individual activities per each pupil per each of four objectives
        2. Instructional materials per each pupil per each of four objectives.

Significance of difference between the pre- and postsamples and between the experimental and control mean differences were tested at the .05 level by using a t-test.

THE FINDINGS

The carefully balanced scales of the IOR provide for the heuristically useful practice of quantifying each instructional behavior in digital symbols. The symbols range from one, representing extreme avoidance of individualized instruction tasks, to twenty, representing major involvement in activities designed to further the individualization of instruction.

Table 1 reveals that all of the observed differences for the experimen-

TABLE I
Mean Scores for the Total Experimental Group

Scale	A	B	C	D	E	F	G	X
Pre	12.9	13.7	13.7	14.1	12.5	13.1	12.1	13.3
Post	14.7	15.6	15.7	16.5	13.9	15.2	14.7	15.3
Change	+1.8	+1.9	+2.0	+2.4	+1.4	+2.1	+2.6	+2.0
significant at .05 level	*		*	*		*	*	*

tal group were in the hypothesized direction of greater individualization of instruction and that six of the eight changes in instructional behaviors were statistically significant.

You will note that although scale B showed a greater mean gain score than scale A, the former was not statistically significant while the latter was. Each scale of the IOR provides for the observer to respond to "Insufficient Evidence" or "Inappropriate for this Session" as well as to the scaled behavior section. On scale B, twenty-four of the thirty-eight teachers in a sample were not given a scaled rating for either the before behavior, the after behavior, or both. So the failure to reach significance on scale B is in part a function of the number in the sample.

The failure of scale E to reach significance is another matter. It might possibly be due to the nature of the behavior rather than to an innocuous quality of the Resource Guide. Other instructional behaviors have a control-by-will quality in them. That is, it is more or less a simple matter of professional decision making to engage in the other instructional behaviors. The teacher has a more or less direct control on these; but not so with sensitivity to students' needs. Students' needs are many times represented by subtle behaviors. The teacher quality looked for here is a skill in using a silent language—a skill in FEELING communication from others. A pupil who squints his eyes, another who stares out the window, or one who talks to a classmate during a lecture—each one is telling the teacher something. More than this, a pupil who asks a question of the teacher may not be verbalizing his real question at all. His real question might go something like this: "Am I doing all right, teacher?" or "Teacher, do you like me?" The effective teacher must be capable of exercising empathy—of being sensitive to a silent language—a language that is conveyed on the vehicle of feeling and employs symbolizations of emotions, gestures, bodily movements, and facial expressions. Even time and space are important indicators of communication. Silence can indicate thought, fear, examination of a new idea, hostility, assent, agreement or disagreement, and many more qualities of communication. Teachers must be capable of sensing this "feeling" communication.

This is not the kind of ability one can call upon if he has never been sensitized to it. It is a skill that one might develop over a period of time, but does not have the control-by-will quality identified in the other instructional behaviors.

The pre-post change for the control group failed to reach significance on any of the scales except Scale B. Here again, the sample for this scale was inadequate.

It would be of no consequence if the gain scores of the experimental group registered significance and the gain scores of the control group failed to reach significance unless the difference between the gain scores were found to be significant. Nonsignificant difference between gain scores could be found if both groups registered plus charges, but the control group just missed reaching significance and the experimental group just made it. Under these conditions the postscores could be so close together that even though one was significant and the other was not, the difference between the two groups would not be a real difference. To be sure that this did not occur, the differences between the control and experimental gain scores were computed and found to be significant at the .05 level on all scales but Scale B.

The difference between the effect of the resource guide upon elementary and high school teachers was also investigated, and indications are that high school teachers are affected more. The data indicates that the reason for this seems to be that elementary teachers begin with more of an individualized instruction orientation and behavior.

A quantitative analysis of methods and materials used and of the number of pupil questions, comments and interactions supports the data reported. The experimental group postsessions used more materials, a greater variety of teaching methods, and elicited more pupil interaction.

CONCLUSIONS

The following conclusions have been drawn within the limitations of this study:

1. There is a difference between the regular instructional behavior of a varied selection of teachers and the instructional behavior of the same teachers recorded at a time when they are following plans that were developed from computer-based resource guides.

2. Resource guides significantly affect some dimensions of instructional behavior but fail to produce significant change in other dimensions of teaching. The significant changes in instructional behavior of teachers who use resource guides are changes that increase the number and improve the quality of the following individualized instruction tasks:

A. encouraging pupils to engage in independent thinking

B. creating an accepting atmosphere in the classroom

C. making appropriate selection and use of instructional materials

D. making appropriate selection and use of teaching methods

E. motivating pupils through challenge without threat

F. employing a wider variety of instructional materials

G. using a greater number of individual and small group methods of teaching and fewer large groups methods

H. encouraging more pupil involvement and interaction

3. Resource guides fail to produce significant changes in teachers' sensitivities to the needs of pupils or in their sensitivities to the effects of the physical setting.

SUMMARY

The results of the present study indicate that the development of the resource guide may contribute significantly to curriculum planning and to the improvement of individualization of instruction through unit teaching. The resource guide has been effective in causing a varied selection of elementary school and high school teachers to make observable changes in their instructional behavior, and these changes are in the direction of individualized instruction.

A persistent concern of educators has been to find ways to combat the tendency of a mass education in our conforming and success-oriented school society to dehumanize the individual. It seems paradoxical that an answer might be found in a computer, which is another object of accusation in the fight against losing sight of the individual. Yet, the computer-based resource guide seems to provide assistance in maximizing regard for the individual in the classroom.

REFERENCES

1. Eilsele, James E., "Computers In Curriculum Planning," *Educational Technology*, November 30, 1967.
2. Harnack, Robert S., "Computer-Based Resource Units," *Educational Leadership*, December 1965.
3. Jason, Hilliard, *An Analysis of Teaching Practices at Seven Selected American Medical Schools*, unpublished doctoral dissertation, State University of New York at Buffalo, 1961.

36 | Student Filmmaking: Why and How

PAUL CARRICO

Reprinted with permission from *Media and Methods*, Vol. 6, No. 3 (November 1969), pp. 41–45, 72–74.

When most people think of movie making, a dense image fallout bombards their minds: the big Hollywood feature, underground movies, news footage on TV, home movies. They rarely think of filmmaking as a part of the ordinary academic experience of thousands of students, and if they did, their response might be "So what?" or "Why?". But regardless of anyone's reaction, students assisted by sensitive teachers have discovered filmmaking as a whole new way of seeing and of telling about the world around them. Dozens of student film festivals regularly draw dozens to hundreds of youthful filmmakers, their films, and their teachers. A lot of excitement and mutual critical respect is generated by these meetings. Beyond the incandescent enthusiasm and the long sessions of looking at badly exposed and fuzzily focused images to find significant scenes or films, thoughtful educators are asking each other what it all means.

With the exception of a few schools, filmmaking is the newest baby in the media-in-education family. Like any new baby it is fawned over by some, not taken seriously by others, and the object of intense jealousy by a few. But the questions about its purpose and its parentage come and must be dealt with if progressive teachers are to avoid administrated infanticide or filmic birth control. A cynical question: "Since local TV stations have shown an interest, is filmmaking simply a device to rescue a few teachers and students from the gray world of the classroom to the grayed world of commercial TV?" A serious question: "Is it a glory-road cop-out for teachers who have failed to come up with a viable consumer rather than a creator-oriented film study program?" (After all, film study is more difficult and more valid than film production!) Two pragmatic questions: "Doesn't it take valuable study time away from the "hard" (and therefore important) subjects that students must take? Where will all the money come from?" A silly question and the one I encountered at Notre Dame High School: "What about all those kids who 'sneak back' into school to edit their films; after all, they're spending entirely too much time in the building!" My own reaction was that if schools are to have problems, this is the kind of problem they should have.

These questions remain; new ones will be invented. The best answer to them is to be found in the films themselves and in what happens in the students who make them. Heightened awareness expressed in a creative act transcends nit-picking and even serious questions. What follows here may serve as an answer or at least an approach to answers to some admittedly valid questions as well as a guide to getting started.

Even with a scant five years of production experience behind me (I am therefore a "pioneer"), I have often wondered why making films has not always been a normal part of the student experience instead of a marginal activity for a few. Hardware problems, the usual scapegoat, have never been a real no-no. Unfortunately, however, education is a conservative institution, and only recently has the establishment been able to recover from the abortive attempts at film education based on moral indignation in the forties and recognize and treat intelligently the film as an artful and occasionally artistic form of communication. The best student films I have seen have grown out of imaginatively conceived and well-executed film study programs. A friend once noted, "If you teach people to read, some of them will want to write". Teach students to "read" films and the same fortuitous problem will appear. Thus, lack of imaginative film study programs has dampened activity in filmmaking.

At first the desire to make films is amorphous and young filmmakers conceive their first efforts on the scale of something as grand and daring as the sequel to *The Ten Commandments*. But with well-sequenced exposure to the short film form, they find there the proper idiom for expressing their view of the world. Occasionally well-made student films are produced in relative cinematic isolation since some teachers are fearful that too much exposure to the work of others can be too formative and a hindrance to the purity of the individual's expression. No matter. Under the guidance of a competent teacher, either the saturation or the starvation philosophy can be successful, depending on the visual sophistication and motivation of both student and teacher.

ROLE OF THE TEACHER

The film teacher is nearly always a producer-critic, not a creator. The average teacher (even the average film teacher) has had his once glimpsed creativity either educated or "production-lined" out of his system and is "dead at the top." Despite tutorial fantasies, filmmaking is an area in which most students are clearly superior to their print-oriented teacher. Such superiority in a creative venture does not eliminate the teacher but it does modify his role.

A teacher-producer knows the creative process but rarely participates in it. His job is to assemble people and materials and to assure the proper atmosphere for creative people to work. The critic assesses the final product. Students rarely need their teacher for this role, since by the time they finish the film, it has been screened so often that they know exactly what is wrong with it. But students are not arrogant and often appreciate someone's telling them what is right with their work.

I have long been convinced that creativity and criticism are separate functions; at the end of the second semester I used to take a band of young filmmakers and their films around to other schools, PTA's, or to any group who would consent to be an audience. Such exposure provided the response and the feedback that every incipient artist needs and took care of the critical function experientially.

Creativity cannot be taught but only given a chance to grow and to be channelled. The most perennially successful film teachers try to avoid "inspiration" as such and set up as neutral a creative situation as possible. Active inspiration is "hot" and puts the teacher's trademark on student work. Unless the appeal comes from the medium itself and the student's own need for self-expression, then his movie is not worth doing in the first place and becomes the same sterile exercise as the traditional term paper or as teacher-stamped as a yearbook. The "cool" film teacher perceives himself primarily as an adult advisor, hardware expert, or the one who makes film stock, camera, editing equipment and production facilities available and leaves the student censor-free to deal with reality around him as best he can.

Freedom from censorship implies that students should also solve their own creative problems such as scripting, sound selection, movement, and pacing with the teacher refraining from any but technical advice. Students have the right to make their own mistakes. A sign of success in this "hands off" pedagogical method is not only the quality of the production (sometimes rough but really honest) but especially the fact that the name of the teacher is almost always omitted from the screen credits, so much do the students see the film as completely their own.

A few teachers, notably David McKendall, formerly at New Trier High School in Wilmette, Illinois, have employed the "apprentice" method, whereby the teacher controls every aspect of a film that is primarily his own. Students assist the teacher in the production and experience all the skills, thrills and frustrations of having participated in a well-made film. Such an approach tends to be craft-oriented but the rare creative teacher who employs it can usually deter students from a preoccupation with hardware, a problem that becomes acute in the case of some industry technicians. Such a technique is used more usually with small highly selected classes devoted almost exclusively to production.

Other teachers see themselves in the role of carefully guiding the student step by step through the maze of mechanical skills involved in successful filmmaking before permitting the student to express himself fully on film. This approach is very much like teaching grammar as a way of helping a student learn to write. Exercises in the use of the camera—the ability to choose the right lenses for a particular shooting situation, panning correctly, tracking, hand-holding a camera, photographing for texture and effect—are carefully outlined for the student. Often professional filmmakers are employed to criticize each student attempt. Other aspects of filmmaking are just as carefully organized and orchestrated to teach basic skills. The most highly publicized program of this type is a federally-financed experiment in Demarest, N.J., run by teacher, Rodney Sheratsky.

A variation was used by the author at Notre Dame High School in Niles, Ill. In an elective course for students who completed at least a semester in film criticism, young filmmakers were required to submit four projects. The first was a film made without a camera—abstract figures drawn on raw 16mm film stock with magic markers or aniline dyes. The second was a student-conceived exercise in animation using solid objects such as toys, balls, clay, etc., paper and string, or line drawings. The third was the automatic discipline of a mini-film (a film exactly one minute long) or a commercial, a form that students know well. The fourth project was a film which constituted the major work of the semester; here there were no restrictions whatever. This method put the emphasis on the medium as a self-disciplining form rather than on the teacher as guide. Students quickly discover the limitations of the medium and of themselves; rarely do they need a businessman-producer, a censor, or a teacher to tell them what they cannot do.

Other teachers such as Bob Johnson at Sir Francis Drake High School, San Anselmo, California and David Coynik at Notre Dame High School, Niles, Illinois, use a completely free-wheeling approach, adopting whatever method is suitable to the students they have. Both are competent filmmakers in their own right and know how to respect the independence of their students.

More important than the attitude that a film teacher takes toward the young filmmaker, is the attitude of the school officials and the other teachers. Outside of extracurricular activities such as sports, the school play, or an engaging music program, students rarely are involved in any experiential way in academic life. Filmmakers—especially during the editing phase—often forget to call parents, to eat, or to be overly concerned about the next morning's algebra assignment. The more creative students tend to be mercurial and forget the school structure. Ideal weather conditions sometimes lure them from the school corridor to the street, camera in hand. Authoritarian schools find such activity intolerable and respond in a repressive way; modern schools are more flexible regarding individual differences.

Worse than repression is the penchant of some administrators to exploit students (and their film teacher) to make "useful" promotional films for the school. Such films turn out to be dry, stilted, and "talky" since the subject matter is not suited to the film medium. The only exception I have seen to this is a film made by David Coynik's students, entitled *A Thousand Days*. The students were subsidized by Notre Dame High School but left free to choose "cinematic" material and to "tell it like it was." *A Thousand Days* is one of the most honest (and best) promotional films I have ever seen because it tries hard to be truthful rather than to impress.

A film can successfully be made by a class. Sister Bede Sullivan formerly at Lillis High School in Kansas City, Missouri, divided a class into teams in order to make a long film about student leisure. But for a school administration to use a film class as a self-conscious adjunct to its public relations program is downright unfair. Film production succeeds best when it is used as a free authentic vehicle of student expression.

Finally, administrators and academic counsellors who demand measurable results find the classroom film experience impossible to understand. But some of their questions are valid. Does film override or replace traditionally accepted forms of student expression? Is there a carryover of enthusiasm when a student is confronted with more pedestrian but necessary academic courses. Do ACT or CEEB test results improve? Unfortunately the only guide to answering these questions at present is human judgement.

In schools where filmmaking is a potential part of every student's experience, teachers note a proliferation, almost an explosion, in other forms of expression, especially poetry. Such a release of energy comes with discovery. Through filmmaking many students come to terms with their own vast viewing experience. Such personal "structuring" frees them from the amorphous, and hence poisonous effect of previous media intake and releases fantastic psychic energy.

There is as yet no empirical way to measure carryover but often students find information-centered classes boring after a bout with film. Modern educators agree that no course need ever be one in which "the tedium is the message." "Turned-on" students demand more of teachers; any teacher who can respond need never fear the stimulating effect of a filmmaking or film criticism course. Indeed, at many schools, teachers in sociology and religion classes are accepting the "term film" along with the traditional term paper.

Testing programs, extrinsic to the school, have not caught up to the film student as yet; tests would be geared to subject matter deemed academically respectable by college entrance committees. To date no one has suggested that students excited about learning score lower on "objective," corporation-administered tests.

THE CONTENT AND FORM OF STUDENT FILMS

Generalizations cannot be photographed and unlike research term papers, student films are made out of bits of the filmaker's own world. In inner-city schools the films tend to be about people, interacting with other people. Affluent students make more abstract films replete with alienation and protest. Although student films make general statements about human relationships, violence, or the hypocrisy of organized religion, such statements are formed out of the stuff of the photographable real world. Still shots lifted from magazines and images from TV are often incorporated into environmental and action shots to render an experience or to make a statement.

The films are rarely humorous. Heavy-handed contrast editing (a plush suburban church juxtaposed with a mangy dog in a ghetto street) suggest the blatant irony of many student films. Many are lyrical and impressionistic, evoking experiences rather than narrating them. Most narrative films demand action-matching the shots in a scene, a form of editing students find technically too sophisticated. Financial considerations demand that the films be limited to ten or fifteen minutes; a student film longer than thirty minutes is rare. Screen humor, especially purely visual humor, requires sophistication, split-second timing, and a certain emotional distance; hence it is not too surprising to find such humor almost totally absent from student films. Besides, the world they see is painfully close to Benjamin's in *The Graduate*: full of adult phoniness at home, war abroad, and ready for revolution everywhere. Student preoccupation with alienation, death, authenticity, and sober involvement may shock demure adults, but to an educator such concerns are quite understandable.

THE EQUIPMENT OF FILM PRODUCTION

Film Stock
The cost, size, and often the quality of film equipment is determined by film stock width, measured in millimeters. 16mm stock, especially

since the rise of silver prices in March 1968, has made production in this format almost prohibitively expensive for the average school. A typical price for a hundred foot roll of black-and-white 16mm film including processing is about $8.00. At "sound" speed (twenty-four frames per second) a hundred feet will last about 3.2 minutes. Good color film stock with processing varies from $12.00 to $14.00 a roll.

So it comes as no surprise that students usually stay away from 16mm film and favor much less expensive 8mm or super 8mm film stock. Black-and-white film in these sizes is hard to come by since the market demand has traditionally been for color, but most professional film laboratories stock it. Unlike the price differential in 16mm film stocks, the price of color film is very close to that of black-and-white. A typical price for fifty feet of ordinary 8mm film with processing is $3.25; $3.75 for a super 8mm cartridge of film. At "silent" speed (sixteen or eighteen frames per second) fifty feet is equivalent to 4 or 4.5 minutes of screen time. These prices can represent quite a saving over 16mm film. Often stock can be bought more cheaply than the above mentioned prices, but let the buyer beware! Sometimes bargain film is full of splices, is flawed, or overage. Our intention here is not to discuss the wide variety of film stocks available. Any reputable laboratory, camera store, or film manufacturer can supply all the technical information necessary.

The advantage of 16mm is the extremely sharp projected image. The stronger light source in 16mm projectors also permits the film to be projected under marginal blackout conditions which would "wash out" anything in 8mm. The individual frame size is also 400% larger than standard 8mm (twice as high and twice as wide). Editing is therefore easier and it is possible to recognize each frame without running it through a viewer magnifier each time, a necessity with smaller size film. The difference between standard 8mm and super 8mm film stock is not in the width of the film but in the size and spacing of the sprocket holes, which permits an image 56 percent larger than the one on 8mm film. Under similar conditions, super 8 will project a larger, less grainy picture.

The advantage of super 8 over ordinary 8mm is not only in the projected image but in the ease involved in the shooting process. Almost all super 8 film is packaged in cartridges and easily inserted in the camera, thus eliminating the need to thread the film through the camera shuttle and attach it to another reel. As soon as the film is inserted, the ASA speed of the film (a chemical speed that indicates the film's sensitivity to light) is automatically locked in with the photoelectrical mechanism in "electric eye" cameras. These features make the average super 8 camera virtually foolproof to operate.

The disadvantages are not so obvious since the industry rarely mentions them. American-made film cartridges, as pioneered by Kodak, allow the film to run in one direction only, a feature which eliminates the possibility of "in camera" addition of lap-dissolves and superimpositions, a procedure possible in many reel-to-reel cameras. Reel-to-reel super 8 cameras are made by only a few companies and are generally very expensive. Some foreign-made cartridges, particularly the Fujica, permit the film to be reversed but must be used only with the Fujica system and not in cameras designed for the American-style cartridge. While the American-style cartridge is not a disadvantage to the occasional camera user, it can be inhibiting for a student who needs dissolves or superimpositions in his movie.

Overall considerations dictate the super 8 route for most film classes. Standard 8 mm is becoming obsolete but if the production and editing equipment is available at a really low price it should not be rejected. Super 8 is here to stay, is easy for even the slowest student to use, and more economical than 16 mm. As manufacturers become more sensitive to the student market, improvements will be made in equipment and lab services. Local film labs are becoming somewhat responsive to the needs of the student filmmaker, and in general it is safer to do business with a competent local lab rather than an unknown processor in another part of the country.

Shooting Equipment

The basic hardware of filmmaking is divided into two categories: shooting (or production), and editing. Besides properly chosen film stock, a camera, lights, tripod, and a meter for measuring light intensity are basic tools for a filmmaker to get images on the film.

Cameras in every style and price range superabound. Some teachers whose schools make cameras available to students prefer having a lot of low-priced cameras to one or two expensive models. While it is true that great instruments by themselves do not make great artists, a better grade of camera can enhance young talent. Desirable qualities for any camera are: *simplicity, durability,* and *versatility.* Cameras in a school will receive rough usage, so delicate knobs and fragile bodies are not generally "student-proof." Simplicity of operation is necessary, especially for a student with a viable idea for a movie but hampered by a "hardware hangup." This seems to be especially true of female filmmakers, though not limited exclusively to them. A camera should be versatile enough to allow the advanced student to do virtually anything his imagination might suggest. Ease of maintenance is also an important consideration.

Valuable features include (1) a zoom lens, (2) a variety of speed changes (frames per second), (3) a photoelectrically operated iris or diaphragm, (4) a stop frame mechanism for animation, and (5) reflex viewing.

A *zoom lens* is a lens with a variable focal length, which in effect means that the viewing angle can be changed. If one looks through a piece of water pipe only one inch long, he can see a lot of world, but the same pipe eight inches long will narrow his view of the same world. A zoom lens has the same effect but is in addition variable over its given range. At its narrowest angle or "zoom in" position, the lens also tends to compress distance; at its widest angle or "pull back" position it tends to expand distance. At the 25 mm (one inch) stop the lens will "see" subjects in relation to each other pretty much as the eye sees them.

The zoom lens has a bad reputation because of its abuse by home movie makers. The world is a mighty disappointing place as seen through the viewfinder and the amateur filmmaker tries to compensate by excessive panning and zooming. The effect on a viewer is irritation and cinematic seasickness. If students can learn to use the infinite framing capabilities of a zoom lens and to choose details with discrimination, it will prove a valuable tool and eliminate numerous setups.

Slow motion and *accelerated motion,* too often used as gimmicks, should be available to a filmmaker. Professional cameras have a great range of speeds from just a few frames-per-second to sometimes several thousand. For students, a range close to the camera's normal speed is usually adequate. Closely related to this feature is the ability to expose one frame at a time, essential for animation.

The *photoelectrically operated iris* which controls the amount of light that reaches the sensitive film is useful where light conditions are even. But because the photoelectric cell "reads" the most intense or "hottest" light available, a device for overriding the photoelectric cell for marginal or special lighting conditions is desirable. In such an instance a light meter, either the one built into the camera or one specially designed for the purpose can be used. Good photography is the art of painting with light and a little care here can save the frustration of overexposed or underexposed footage. Light meters are inexpensive and easy to learn how to read, a sometimes necessary tool for any filmmaker.

When selecting an "electric eye" camera, the buyer should make sure it has the capability of accepting many different sensitivities as measured by ASA speeds. The cheaper cameras have a much more limited range. ASA speeds should range from 40 for Kodachrome II to at least 160 for Tri-X Reversal. New films coming out (Four-X, for example) will demand even wider ranges.

These films will allow students to shoot scenes at night, in subways, and in other areas where heretofore there just was not enough light to get an exposure.

Interior lighting is the most serious technical flaw common to almost all student-made films. Camera-mounted lights are rarely of any value, yet these are the ones—called "sun guns" or light bars—most often supplied or recommended by manufacturers. Most student "sets" can adequately be lighted with three well-placed and inexpensive photoflood lamps. Some schools find it within their budget to purchase a kit of Quartz-iodine combination flood-spotlights. Advice on lighting setups and the proper choice of bulbs of the correct color temperature (measured in degrees Kelvin) is available from film manufacturers, cinema labs, or local professionsls. Adequate lighting can be learned by anyone in a relatively short time and is as important to a good production as rhetoric is to a good theme paper.

Reflex viewing means that the camera operator sees through the camera lens itself instead of an optical system parallel to it. The photographer literally sees what the camera sees. This feature is especially valuable on close work such as titles where faulty framing is extremely annoying. Reflex viewing automatically eliminates the problem of faulty framing as well as the problems of fuzzy focus or a finger in front of the lens. The operator is enabled positively to select focus between subjects in the foreground or background. Some directors today use a shift of focus as an effective substitution for cutting.

Few people can hold a camera steady while shooting, especially if the bulk of the weight is behind the camera grip. Unsteadiness or jiggling is particularly noticeable to a viewer on long shots. Professional cameramen as a rule use a tripod whenever possible. A tripod should be chosen which is sturdy and designed specifically for a movie camera. Tripods for still cameras are generally too flimsy and do not allow the operator to pan smoothly. The camera must be held rigidly when shooting animation; there is no substitute for a tripod here.

Editing Equipment

To anyone conversant with the firm medium, it is all too obvious that editing is the most important aspect of filmmaking. On the editing table discrete scraps of film are transformed into statement; it is the part of filmmaking students find most rewarding. The necessary pieces of equipment include at least one projector, pairs of rewinds, a viewer-magnifier, and a splicing block with film cement or splicing tape. Alternate equipment might include extra takeup reels and a synchronizer complete with a pair of long-shaft rewinds (16mm only).

A projector is listed as a piece of editing equipment because every filmmaker makes his final decisions whether to cut or not to cut on the basis of how the film will look on the screen. For some filmmakers the process of editing is endless and they will nibble away at their creations long after the films are in release. This is especially true of students who change their films almost every time it is screened for a live audience. The editing projector should be one that the student loads and threads manually. Automatic or "self-threaders" and splices rarely mix. A "freeze" or "stop" frame mechanism and when possible a manually operated film advance clutch are useful for analyzing individual frames and necessary for accurate timing and sound synchronizing.

Rewinds are simple crank-operated mechanisms for transferring film from one reel to another. Motor-driven rewinding is possible on almost every projector but a separate pair mounted on the editing table or on either end of a wide board is a necessity. Between a pair of rewinds most of the actual cutting is done. A viewer-magnifier through which the film can be pulled by the rewinds is necessary, especially during the initial stages when the pieces of film are seen for the first time. Some manufacturers incorporate a pair of rewinds into the viewer mechanism itself but these tend to be fragile and unable to withstand constant use. Professional editing equipment, designed for day-after-day usage, is definitely preferable for a school.

The splicing block should, when possible, be mounted between the rewinds for easy access and for the protection of the block. Blocks employing either liquid cement or mylar splicing tape are available. Students find tape easier to use with standard 8mm or super 8mm. Applied with care it provides an adequate bond. The block should feature a straight cut parallel to the frame line of the film instead of a curved cut popular on some home movie units.

Synchronizers and their associated long-shaft rewinds are for use only with 16mm film at the present time. Using this equipment means that the student can on the editing table add fades, dissolves, and superimpositions to his film, but the equipment is relatively sophisticated for young filmmakers.

After the film has been cut into pieces, it should be labelled and stored safely while editing proceeds. The preferred way is to hang the film by one end on a "clothesline" or on a light rack built over a bin or a drum lined with a plastic bag. The soft lining along with careful handling prevents scratching. Egg crates can also be used to store the tiny rolls of film where preferred storage is not available.

After the film is edited, it can be returned to the lab for splice-free printing. If a print is not planned the film should be inspected for faulty splices and cleaned with a linen cloth moistened with film cleaner before projection. In most student productions, the many steps in the film assembly process are omitted for economic reasons and the original footage becomes the work print, the answer print, and the release print.

The most important service a school can provide the student is free and easy access to equipment, especially editing material. It is difficult for anyone to create "on cue," and school structure should not for a film class become stricture.

Sound Equipment

An apparent deprivation, the technical inability to tightly synchronize sound and picture, becomes a negative but important advantage for both teacher and student. Even with the most sophisticated equipment, adding sound is tedious. Sound, too, is so fascinating for young filmmakers that their creations might well become a series of highly verbal set pieces accompanied by pictures "in synch." At present, there are on the market several camera-tape recorder combinations which can be electronically locked together during shooting. On the surface these combinations look like an instant solution to the sound hangup but they present problems in editing. The freedom to edit film is basic to filmmaking and a freedom that a filmmaker should never relinquish. Any salesman should be required to demonstrate the advertised ease of editing. Of the two systems for interlocking—optical or magnetic—magnetic is presently preferable. The optical system now in distribution requires eleven separate meticulous steps to remove a scene. The magnetic system is also complicated, but simpler and more flexible than the optical system.

Separate recording units can be used, but nonprofessional tape recorders and projectors rarely "track" at the same speed every time, thus making simultaneous sound difficult to achieve. Sound such as music or voice-over narration is then used to underline or reinforce the visuals. During the screening the projector speed can usually be manipulated to slow down or speed up the film to permit closer synch. However, the lack of any easy way to add simultaneous sound in student films puts emphasis on the proper aspect of filmmaking, the *visual*.

An encouraging new development is a new line of super 8 projectors which permits recording directly on a magnetic strip chemically bonded to the edge of the film. This feature has long been available in 16mm but the excessive cost of the projectors and mediocre sales promotion has kept these units out of the average schools. While this system is not always suitable for the tight "lip synch" sound of the speaking face, it does assure exact "as recorded" synch during projection-playback. When audio-visual budgets are drawn up it is advisable to order one projector that can record the sound—these are relatively expensive—and one or more less expensive projection-playback units.

CONCLUSION

Why permit or even encourage students to make their own movies? If the purpose is to turn out junior size film technicians, the activity is not worth serious academic attention. Students can acquire these skills more effectively at a professional cinema school or on the job in the industry. Nor should filmmaking be used as a substitute for a film study or appreciation (a *verboten* word in academic circles) course that failed because of teacher inadequacy. But used in conjunction with such a course, it is an invaluable way to give the student a new way of seeing (that's more important than what they see) and a real feel for the medium.

Few films, even ones made by great film artists, are ever realized perfectly. Sometimes a film never gets off the ground. A group of my students—marginal kids with long hair, a beat-up convertible (jointly owned), and levis—back in the days before those things became quasi-fashionable, decided to make a film about Chicago's vertical slums, or "public housing." After dozens of interviews, runaround from politicians, and harassment from gangs, they decided that the movie was impossible to make. A teacher dedicated to education-as-product rather than process might have given them a failing mark. I gave them an "A" for all they learned about sociology, government, politics, each other, and goodness knows what else. Filmmaking courses are one of the few places students can succeed through failure.

Some final precautions: not everyone is capable of making a film, no more than everyone is capable of writing a good poem or short story. To force it on the half-willing student as an assignment is a sure way to kill its vitality and richness. A few students, too, find film such a personal medium that they almost literally pour out their souls. Such outpouring can approach psychodrama, and while there is undoubtedly a great deal to be said about the value of channeling one's amorphous subconscious into an intelligent and disciplined form, a great deal of psychological harm can result when a teacher becomes inordinately fascinated with self-revelation. Often such revelation is not apparent either to the creator or to other students; he simply feels that he has "gotten something out of his system" and an adult with critical insight will frequently find it necessary to keep such insights a professional secret. Filmmaking, like any other humanizing activity, has its prudential as well as its financial limits.

37 | The Myths of Educational Technology

ANTHONY G. OETTINGER

Reprinted with permission from *Saturday Review*, Vol. 51, No. 20 (May 18, 1968), pp. 76–77, 91. Copyright 1968 Saturday Review, Inc. This article was based on a draft of *Run, Computer, Run: The Mythology of Educational Innovation*, Harvard University Press, 1969.

Will the wonders of modern technology save our children from death at an early age? To pick up almost any current magazine or newspaper or to listen to eminent researchers and educational spokesmen is to be persuaded that, thanks to modern technology, the necessary educational revolution is just around the corner. But is it?

I share with many of my fellow computer scientists and engineers a solid faith that computers will ultimately influence the evolution of human thought as profoundly as has writing. I sympathize with hopes for programmed instruction, language laboratories, television, and film in strips, loops, or reels. Ultimately, however, is not tomorrow. Education's institutional rigidity combined with infant technology's erratic behavior preclude really significant progress in the next decade, if significant progress is interpreted as widespread and *meaningful* adoption, integration, and use of technological devices (including books and blackboards) within the schools.

But the need to convince obtuse laymen, particularly the President and Congress, of the value of basic research often leads both scientists and educators into exaggerations that begin as well intentioned rhetorical devices but may end in self-delusion. Expediency leads politicians into their own scientific or technological promises in order to help pass a bill, win an election, or sugarcoat the bitter political pill of social reform.

In early March, I attended a conference on "An Educational System for the Seventies" (ES '70) convened by the U.S. Office of Education. One preconference announcement said:

It is hoped that the conference will serve these objectives: (1) to get consultative thinking from various groups about priority goals and outcomes for ES '70 in their subject-matter area; (2) to provide practice in articulating desired student outcomes in terms of behaviors, values, attitudes, transfer to life situations, citizen role; (3) to provide cross-group communication and efforts at integrative thinking in exploring the realities of the organic curriculum; (4) to provide a limited yet critical exposure of the organic curriculum to secondary school leadership, teachers, and policymaking citizen groups.

It was quite clear on the first day of the conference that many participants believed that "ES '70" (note the noun) and "the organic curriculum" (note the noun phrase and the definite article) had a solid existence. This pervasive illusion was reinforced by a document accompanying the statement of objectives, which declared:

> This overall plan, the first phase of which is almost completed, will identify all of the activities that must be completed before the total new curriculum can become operational. These activities can roughly be classified as research, development, or demonstration.

The same document began with the claim that:

> Various elements of the educational process—such as team teaching, programmed instruction, flexible scheduling, computer-assisted teaching, and individualized curricula—have recently been examined by researchers and judged to be important additions to current practice.

A preconference report on secondary education in the United States expressed this theme as follows:

> Educational researchers have made significant findings about the learning process, curriculum innovation, and educational technology. It is distressing when one considers the tremendous time lag between the initial research findings and the implementation of these findings. Even with a rapid escalation of federal research funds for education, the return on this investment has been inconsequential. In short, it seems that a massive and radical redesign of the secondary education program is imperative. To bring this about, a coordinated planning and development effort, involving a variety of social institutions, is necessary.

Few observers of contemporary American education will quarrel with the need for reform, or with the conclusion that the educational establishment is almost ideally designed to resist change. Much depends, therefore, on whether one believes that the "important additions to current practice" or the "significant finds" are really at hand to support "a massive and radical redesign of the secondary education program."

That is why distinguishing between ultimate promise and immediate possibility becomes so vitally important. Otherwise, the conclusion that the more exotic forms of educational technology can *now* be little more than placebos for the ailing social organism will be interpreted as a denial of their potential value, thereby unwittingly reinforcing the argument against further investment for "inconsequential" returns.

The expressed distress is real enough. The President and the Congress set great store on education as a weapon of social reform. The Office of Education is consequently under great pressure to produce immediate results. But when a program must be successful by definition, the need for a good show often overwhelms scientific objectivity; after the curtain falls, little remains either of practical value or of added insight. It may be expedient politically, when poverty is "in," to seek support of educational technology on the ground that it will solve the problems of our inner cities and to use it as a Trojan horse for wheeling in needed reforms. If, however, this leads to demands for an immediate return on investment, and if failure to produce this return is both probable and verifiable, then the expedient is not really good strategy. When ideas that are promising as objects of research and honest experiment give birth, through artificial dissemination, to a brood of hysterical fads, there is the danger that angry reaction will dump out the egg with the shell.

Dealing with the mythology of systems analysis requires making a distinction as delicate as that between ultimate promise and immediate possibility. The myth of systems analysis holds that educational salvation lies in applying to education the planning and control techniques commonly believed to have been successful in the defense and aerospace industries. Advocating systems analysis as a panacea ranks with making the world safe for democracy, unconditional surrender, and massive retaliation as an experiment in delusion for political ends. Yet, not to believe in the usefulness of systems analysis is to deny the value of reason, common sense, and, indeed, the scientific method.

Systems analysis cannot be dismissed as modern gadgetry. Its best formulations are indistinguishable from descriptions of the scientific method and thus have roots reaching back through Roger Bacon to Aristotle and not, as some believe, just to the RAND Corporation. At its best, therefore, the systems approach can be used in conjunction with well developed and reliable research designs to solve problems far more satisfactorily than naked intuition. The mathematical methods of control systems theory, for example, are very effective tools for designing speed controls for engines or process controls for certain chemical plants or in finding the best trajectories for missiles.

But there is far less validity than wishful thinking in claims for the success of the systems approach in the design, management, and control of entire space and military systems, in spite of the repeated citations for these enterprises as paradigms for educational and other social systems. It is also easily demonstrable that the educational system is much more complicated than any system yet devised by the military, and that we have much less understanding of the former's component parts.

Moreover, to the extent that systems analysis is used in the Defense Department as an analytic tool rather than as an administrative club, its value depends on the possibility of doing what Charles Hitch, the man who developed it for former Secretary of Defense Robert S. McNamara, has described as "explicit, quantitative analysis, which is designed to maximize, or at least increase, the value of the objectives achieved by an organization, minus the values of the resources it uses." To this statement Dr. Hitch has added caveats that many witless disciples have apparently forgotten and which therefore bear repeating:

> However, there are risks and dangers as well as opportunities in the application of new management techniques—including the risk of discrediting the techniques, if one tries to move too far too fast. Although it did not appear easy at the time, there is no doubt in my mind that the Department of Defense, or much of it, is easier to program and to analyze quantitatively than many areas of civilian government. For example, it is certainly easier than the foreign affairs area. Quite apart from these difficulties, the substantive problems in other areas are different and new. In Defense, we had several hundred analysts at the RAND Corporation and elsewhere developing programs and systems analysis techniques for a decade before the department attempted any large-scale general application.

Although the U. S. Office of Education, among others, nowadays sets great store on the possibilities of systems analysis, a planning-programming-budgeting system (PPBS), cost effectiveness, and similar things by other names, the evidence suggests that the continuation of Hitch's comment is valid for education:

> No remotely similar preparatory effort has gone into any other governmental area, and the number of trained and skilled people is so limited that they are inevitably spread far thinner in other departments of government than they were and are in Defense.

In any case, asking *how* or *how well* is silly unless we know *what*. The "systems" label should therefore not be given too much significance: It can produce no miracles, you *can't* just feed it to the computer. Neither should it be ignored. Despite its limitations, taking the systems viewpoint—namely, agreeing in principle that it is better to think about a problem in its whole context than not—is the best available attitude toward any subject, especially one whose literature is characterized by the *idée fixe* (individualized instruction), the panacea (applying computers to education can bring a powerful new force to bear on the central-city problem), and the empty label (organic curriculum). Thoughtful and thorough engineering is always good practice.

At this point, everything required by "the instructional system" is still in the experimental stage. While classroom scheduling by computer is advertised as a *fait accompli,* this is true only in the rather restricted sense of assigning students to conventional classroom groups and insuring that the number of groups matches the number of available teachers, and that these groups and teachers fit into available classrooms. Typically, the whole operation takes place once a term. Merchandizing this unpleasant and tedious task is clearly a worthwhile and useful accomplishment, which deserves wider acceptance. It must be recognized, however, that this is a far cry from keeping track of individual students week by week, day by day, hour by hour, or minute by minute, and matching them in turn with resources themselves parceled out in smaller packages than teachers per semester or rooms per semester. Packaging individual students is more complex than packing screws for dime stores or wrapping a lamb chop in plastic for the supermarket meat counter.

The goals for education have been stated with such monumental vagueness, and yet with such colossal residues of disagreement, as to provide no useful guidance for any systematic systems design. Current educational talk and writing is all for individualized instruction. There are several plausible reasons for grasping at this straw. For instance, many psychologists now officially agree that there are individual differences in learning capabilities. There obviously is also increasing consciousness that contemporary education does not serve equally the needs and the interests of all groups in our society.

But what does "individualization" mean? Lawrence Stolurow gives his definition in terms of an interaction between students and a computer. The student's "characteristics are stored in a student data base which permits the system to interpret responses in a selective way. Responses are also related to performance expectations. On this basis, the instruction becomes individualized." This statement of a research goal (*not* a current reality) is very attractive, since there is evidence that students prefer undivided attention from a computer to neglect from a human being.

A case can also be made for a narrower notion of "individualization"—something like "personalizing" or "customizing"—namely, taking a mass-produced object and stamping it with gold initials or heaping chrome on fins to give the illusion of individual tailoring. This is the sense in which current experimental computer programs greet a pupil with "Good morning, Johnny," by filling the blank in "Good morning, ———" with the name he had to give to identify himself to the machine in the first place. This is more genteel than, "Do not fold, spindle, or mutilate!"; "Hey, you!"; or "Good to see you, 367-A-45096!" It is, however, just as superficial, even when randomly selected variations heighten the effect of spontaneity.

A more charitable interpretation says that individualizing means giving full scope to idiosyncrasy. Harold Benjamin, in his witty but profound lecture *The Cultivation of Idiosyncrasy*, points out that this interpretation raises a question "which a democratic society may ignore only at its deadly peril." The question is double-barreled: (1) How much uniformity does this society need for safety? and (2) how much deviation does this society require for progress?

Yet the proponents of individualization pay only the scantiest attention to the fundamental goal-setting and policy decisions inherent in Benjamin's query. They often ignore even the most elementary systems-design consequences of their belief in individualization.

If—as is true of all present computerized systems of "individualized" instruction, as well as of many others based on explicit definitions of "behavioral objectives" (BO's)—the intent is to instruct students in such a manner that all will achieve a final level of competency which meets (or surpasses) the same set of minimally acceptable performance criteria, the objective cannot be the cultivation of idiosyncrasy. It is, rather, what an industrial engineer might call mass production to narrow specifications with rigid quality control. Each pupil is free to go more or less rapidly exactly where he is told to go.

Our present and most pressing problem is the lack of an empirically validated theory of teaching, and, in fact, we even lack a useful set of empirically validated principles of instruction that could form the primatives of a theory of teaching. This is not to say that we lack teaching practices that are widely used. Rather, it is to say that choice among existing practices cannot be made from data demonstrating the greater effectiveness of one over another. This problem, combined with the cost of computer systems, makes it more likely that we will reject a useful idea than it is that we will accept a useless one.

Semantic perversion, therefore, tends to mask the fact that the techniques now being developed may have great value in training to very narrow and specific "behavioral objectives," but do not address themselves to the many broader but just as basic problems of education. Training to minimal competence in well-defined skills is very important in a variety of military, industrial, and school settings. It is not, however, the whole of what the educational process should be.

What conclusions can one draw about a desirable course of action? There is a strong temptation, reinforced by the accepted ritual of constructive criticism, to end a critical essay with an upbeat note, a ray of hope, and, preferably, the proposal of a favorite scheme of one's own. The systems analyst, however, like the doctor or lawyer, owes it to the ideal of professional integrity to tell his client the truth as he sees it, not as the client would like to hear it. He may or may not have a useful prescription. Polio has been conquered, a mumps vaccine has just come out, but the common cold and cancer are still with us.

However wasteful in appearance, it fits my prejudices best to encourage as much diversity as possible—as many different paths, as many different outlooks, as many different experiments, as many different initiatives as we can afford once the demands of education have been balanced against those of other needs of our society. We should plan for the encouragement of pluralism and diversity, at least in technique.

Advocating diversity in goals raises even deeper questions, although the two are linked. If, for example, we were to supply individual tutors to children (the expense is currently comparable to that of computer consoles), how much freedom of action would it be "safe" to give to tutors? The computer at least can lend itself to safe, guaranteed uniformity in its individualization.

This point of view argues, for example, toward channeling educational resources through pupils and their parents rather than through the educational establishment, federal or local. It seems vital to encourage greater freedom of choice in a situation which, however diverse in appearance because of the existence of 27,000 school districts, in fact has a dreary monotony.

Vesting all educational authority in the federal government makes no sense, but letting our schools continue as local monopolies perpetuates on the local level a crime we would not and do not tolerate nationally. One could visualize under such circumstances a situation where various public or private organizations might create national school systems operating local schools as branch offices or as franchises under contract with the local school board. Giving pupils the option to go to a town-operated school, a school operated by a neighboring town, a school operated in the given town by one company or another, could encourage competitive initiative. Unfortunately, this kind of approach also raises the specters of support to parochial schools, and of racial or economic segregation.

There may be other alternatives that could provide a kind of large-scale evolutionary effect with enough units at stake to create a fair probability that lots of different paths will be taken, and that illuminating controversy will rage. A miracle may make this happen with the seventeen schools participating in the ES '70 venture. Whatever the setting for educational experimentation, it is vital in our still profound ignorance to shy away from rigid prescriptions of either goal or technique. There is too much rigidity even in the present innovation fad which, ironically, diverts human and financial resources from both basic research and sustained application and evaluation efforts into the most visible quickie approaches that can sustain the illusion of progress.

PART EIGHT

The Total Scene Concerning Change and Innovation in the Educative Process

The several articles that are included in this part attempt to bring about a confluence of ideas relative to the total scene concerning change and innovation in the educative process. A careful reading of each may lead the reader to the point that was made earlier in this volume, that to talk about innovation as if it were an isolable, one-dimensional thing is almost an impossibility. There tend to be "spill-overs" or complementary innovations that are inclusively and mutually supportive in developing new climates or formats for learning. The educative process can hardly be called a one dimensional process. It is multiphasic, almost amoebalike in the manner that it pushes out to encompass many things that surround it and that nurture it in its continuous growth and expansion. It is almost impossible to speak about one innovation, such as continuous progress education, and not also talk about the whole area of cooperative educational endeavors, for the two frequently coalesce and are thought of as representing a new form of education. It is equally difficult to discuss the move toward educational innovation without at the same time discussing the organizational climate that prevails in any given educational institution. The manner in which people view themselves and administration views the educative change process is very carefully tied up with the direction and the activities of innovation. Also, no text or collection of readings on innovation could ever be really complete without some of the names that appear in the section that follows. The opening statement by Robert H. Anderson and the closing statement by John I. Goodlad serve as the two boundaries of this section. Both are extremely well-known for the major contributions they have made in the realm of educational innovation. The name of Harold Gores is always present in any discussion on change and innovation in the educational process, and the facilities that house them. This part is an attempt to bring together and place in the context of the school the multiphasic changes and innovations that mark the educational process and reflect and are reflected in the combination of ideas that frequently come together to establish a new kind of education.

Anderson orients his particular statement toward the planning and execution of a program in early childhood education. Dr. Anderson has been a long-time advocate of first-rate early educational programs. In this article he deals not only with those concepts relative to the many aspects of early childhood education, but also with some of the physical settings necessary for bringing about a better preprimary educational program. He attempts to aid people in understanding the preprimary educational approach or approaches in order that there will be a greater successful implementation of these programs. The considerations that he deals with to enable administrators to have a greater understanding hopefully will prove helpful in developing significant educational activities appropriate for the very young child.

The article by James Cass on the Beloit-Turner school is one that shows in action many of the innovations that are described in this book. The Beloit-Turner middle school is one that was clearly conceived as a place for children. It is an open-design school that is calculated actively to enhance the program functions of youngsters in the preadolescent years. Cass indicates that it will take more time to get a final reading on this particular school because the program is still evolving and its eventual success will depend on the skill and dedication of the teachers who implement it; he indicates, however, that it is the most interesting place in town and that all teachers seem firmly committed to the concept of the school—their only reservations being how best they can employ their professional skills in this kind of environment. The immediate concepts that come through in these activities are the humanistic features that abound. As Herbert Jackson, principal of the Beloit-Turner School, indicates, "The most important characteristic for teachers at our school is that they like kids."

This humanistic theme is carried through in the article on one of the most significant experiments in secondary education in America today—the Parkway Program. While the Beloit-Turner experience turns inward to the setting within the school, the Parkway Experimental High School turns outward to incorporate all of the elements of community, involvement, and participation that are calculated to create a relevant educational experience. It is open not only in design but also in embracing concepts concerning learning. Philadelphia itself is the classroom and the life of the city is the school's curriculum. Buttressed by tutorial groups, faculty selection by committee, real student involvement in decisions, and unusual curriculum offerings of faculty interest, it is a beacon of innovative practices that could well be copied by many educators.

The congenial school discussed by Harold Gores shows how facilities are calculated to create the kinds of settings that lead to innovative and changed processes of education. From his vantage point with respect to facilities and programs, Gores contends that schools must be designed as community resources so that they can serve not only the children but also the totality of the educational endeavor. He believes strongly in a systems approach to the development of schools in general so that the result will be both buildings of beauty and buildings of service as well.

The next three articles should be taken as a core. Regardless of what the setting or the organizational change is, if there is not a change in the role of the teacher then the setting will only house conventional programs. Hyman, Hoy and Appleberry, and Burns are all concerned with the change of teacher behavior. Hyman offers six frameworks that we can employ as we observe teaching. From them we can establish vantage

points to create the opportunity for change. Hoy and Appleberry talk about the two kinds of climate: custodial and humanistic. Humanistic schools have more open organizational
climates. The research clearly points to the change that needs
to take place because they find most schools to be custodial
institutions and hence less innovative. Burns gives a list of
twenty-two suggestions that could lead all those who would
innovate into the program of involvement that could result in
educational redefinition. The points are precise and serve as
guidelines for getting more humanistic, open schools discussed
by Hoy and Appleberry.

Finally, Goodlad closes this part by offering us reasons why
the lag in making our ideas and innovations work exists. He
makes some dynamic suggestions for updating skills and for
training future teachers. This serves as the final statement on
how we go about creating the total changes and innovations
necessary if the educative process is to keep pace with this
rapidly changing world.

38 | Schools for Young Children: Organizational and Administrative Considerations

ROBERT H. ANDERSON

Reprinted with permission from *Phi Delta Kappan,* Vol. 50, No. 7 (March 1969), pp. 381–385.

In a new policy statement [1] by its Research and Policy Committee dated July 1968, the influential Committee for Economic Development has issued a strong appeal for the fundamental improvement of American education. The document includes these passages:

> We . . . recommend extensive experimental activity in preschooling, not only in the substance and process of instruction but also in organization, administration, and finance. [2]

> We are convinced that reconstruction of instructional staffs, instructional patterns, and school organization must lie at the heart of any meaningful effort to improve the quality of schooling in this country. [3]

That advances in teaching techniques, materials, and technology depend ultimately on ways the staff is trained and organized is another theme in the report.

Accepting the committee's conclusions, at least to the extent that organization does matter, let us turn to a discussion of some ways programs for educating young children might be set up.

---

[1] Committee for Economic Development, *Innovation in Education: New Directions for the American School.* A Statement on National Policy by the Research and Policy Committee, 477 Madison Avenue, New York 10022: CED, July 1968. 75 pp.

[2] *Ibid.,* p. 15.

[3] *Ibid.,* p. 14.

GENERAL ORGANIZATION

There is no automatic supposition in this discussion concerning *where* the education of children ages two through five will be located or in what manner it will be administered and financed. The Committee for Economic Development, it may be noted, favors a "mixed" system including both public and private preschools, with nonprofit schools serving as demonstration units. At present, virtually all programs for children below age five are under the sponsorship of private groups or public agencies other than the local public school district. Head Start, for example, is only rarely affiliated with a public school. There are only a few school districts that sponsor "junior kindergarten" (or equivalent) for four-year-olds, and even tax-supported kindergarten services for five-year-olds have, until very recently, been available to less than half of American children. Where such services have not been offered, private and church-related groups have provided them on a fee basis. Meanwhile, the public schools have faced an evergrowing problem of how to finance classroom construction and other operating costs when and if kindergarten services are added.

The few existing school programs for two-year-olds are usually intended to cope with special problems and to equalize developmental opportunities for the culturally deprived. Though most such programs are now independent of the public school, it can be argued that all so-called preschool programs ought to have ties with a public school district. This might provide a small measure of needed guidance; at least it would enable the school district to begin building a record of the child's developmental history. Various community agencies, especially those concerned with health, should also be closely involved.

Harold and June Shane[4] have envisioned what they call a "minischool" for three-year-olds, emphasizing experiences designed to increase the sensory input which is so essential if children are to develop their full intellectual potential. These small units might exist in housing projects, store fronts, or even in regular schools. Next the Shanes envision a two-year preprimary continuum for the four- and five-year-olds, to replace the present kindergartens. Following this flexible unit would be a "seamless" primary unit, succeeded in turn by the middle school and the secondary continuum. Implicit in the Shane predictions, as indeed in most current writing about school unit organization, is that the successive units of the school should overlap and "flow into" each other in ways that greatly reduce the painful historic problems of unit articulation.

The size of the preprimary school program, whether in separate units

---

[4] Harold G. Shane and June Grant Shane, "Forest for the 70's," *Today's Education*, January 1969, pp. 29–32.

or all under one tent, will of course vary from place to place. Ideally, for reasons that are documented in other articles of this issue, each group of children should be a heterogeneous mixture within which occasional homogeneous subgroupings are possible. It should be in the care of a team of adults, including professionals and nonprofessional aides. The professional staff should include one or more teachers who coordinate and supervise the work of aides, tutors, resource persons, and other personnel, plus health workers, guidance specialists, and others who assist in the various functions of pupil diagnosis, program planning, instruction, and evaluation. Depending in part on the maturity of the children, the program itself should add, to the "regular" class experience of a group of young children, such other experiences as individual exploration, small-group or individual interaction with an adult, small-group activity with a considerable degree of independence, and larger-group situations in which stories, TV, and other presentations are involved.

Much of what happens will be in the context of play situations, but, especially for some children at the upper age levels, there may be relatively structured lessons. Obviously, such a program requires the close coinvolvement of several adults whose professional talents, personalities, interests, and styles are sufficiently diverse so that they are capable, collectively, of appropriate response to a wide range of pupil needs. It also requires that time, space, and resources be organized and utilized very flexibly.

The needs and characteristics of younger children call for a somewhat different and presumably less "open" pattern of staffing and organization than those appropriate for children in middle and later childhood. The young child is obviously less ready to cope with complicated instructional machinery, with a great many types of social situations, with an extensive and varied physical environment, and with a large number of adults each of whom presents different opportunities and challenges to him. Therefore various organizational and instructional trends now gaining in acceptance in upper-elementary and secondary levels, especially cooperative staffing patterns and mechanized instruction, will necessarily be used in preprimary schools with a degree of caution.

Of interest in passing is that nursery school teachers have in the past often worked within an informal, collegial pattern of staff organization. Over the past decade many elementary schools have been experimenting with a variety of new ways of utilizing teachers and aggregating pupils for instruction. It is not yet clear which of these emerging staffing and grouping patterns will work best in preprimary schools with different kinds of people, but it seems no longer in much doubt that the autonomous teacher working continuously with only one class of children will in the future be an exception rather than the rule in all levels of schooling.

Apart from the inherent advantages for teachers as they work, share, and study together, it is good for the children to live in the same family with a group of adults whose behavior offers a constructive model for their own. By being themselves, by fulfilling different roles, by exhibiting different interests and views, and especially by living and working together in reasonable harmony, the teachers help the children to understand and appreciate important truths about human interaction.

That the teachers are a heterogeneous lot stands to benefit children in yet another way. One of the chief aims of the school serving young children should be to collect, analyze, and act upon a vast array of data concerning each child's life history (short though it has been!), the out-of-school environmental situation in which he lives, the present state of his intellectual and social development, and other clues to his needs and potential. This implies that the school staff must therefore include a variety of persons whose training and personality equip them to examine and understand many different dimensions of the child's world, including his health and medical history, his views of himself and others, his verbal competency, and even the aesthetics of his life and environment. It also implies, by the way, that this broadly talented school staff must devote large blocs of time to the functions of interviewing, advising, and assisting parents and other significant adults in each child's life. Ideally, the home-school relationship should be nurtured in ways that insure complete two-way communication and also a maximum of mutual assistance.

The child will reveal his interests, predispositions, and needs through the way he responds to the various stimuli the school situation presents, including the personalities and offerings of several different children and adults he encounters. By observing these responses and the conditions under which a particular child seems best to function and to learn, the staff can then deploy itself and groups of children in ways that exploit and capitalize the insights in hand.

SCHOOL LINKAGES

When the early childhood program is included within or as a part of a regular elementary school building, the organization plan of the school should provide at least three lines of communication reaching out from the preprimary unit. One of these would be to other units and services within the school, and would seek links not only with adults but with the older children. Another would be to outside agencies and resources, important examples being the public library, social service departments, and church-sponsored or private pre-schools with which functional linkages might be arranged. A third would be the school's community, including especially the parents of enrolled pupils but also resource people from the neighborhood. Other linkages are possible, notably with television workers if plans for educational programs beamed at preprimary children and their families are successful.

Within the school, the most obvious ties of the preprimary people are with the primary unit itself. Hopefully, the relationship can be so close that barriers ordinarily separating kindergarten from "first grade" will cease to exist. More mature preprimary children might spend part of their day in primary classrooms, and some primary children might similarly spend part of *their* day in the more relaxed environment of the preprimary. Teachers could, likewise, move freely between the units; it would even be desirable, each September, for one or more of the preprimary teachers to "move up" with the six-year-olds into the primary, while a former primary teacher reclassifies herself as a preprimary teacher for a year or more. This practice would not only foster continuity in the teacher-pupil relationships that develop and ensure a smooth transition for each class, but it would greatly improve inner-staff relations and also stimulate professional growth. As Gorman [5] contends, the occasional reassignment of teachers is a stimulant to new learning experiences and also facilitates the development of new structures such as nongrading.

A new and promising trend is in linking older children, not only the "star pupils" but also those of average or below-average attainment, with those in the lower classes in a tutorial or other helping role. It will be remembered that in the little red schoolhouse, in historical plans using prefects or monitors, and in developing countries where "each-one-teach-one" has been practiced, more advanced students served in effect as teachers and often gained a great deal in the process. Evidence mounts to support this contention; and it seems highly desirable to provide even greater opportunities for older pupils to "teach" younger children, to play a big-brother role, or to have some other responsibility which will help themselves as well as the younger children to grow in various ways.

Parents and other community adults (and teen-agers) can also play a significant role in the daily school life of the young children. Many small cooperative nursery schools operate regularly with unpaid parents doing not only housekeeping chores but also the work of "assistant teachers" under the director's supervision. The use of parents and others as resource people is also quite common, as is the use of college students (some of these being older women) who are in early stages of teacher training. These practices ought to be continued and expanded; and in addition there should be a closer tie-in between the school and the home, especially in cases where tutoring and other forms of compensatory assistance can be provided to children in underpriviged families. Recent

[5] Charles J. Gorman, "Annual Reassignment of Teachers: An Important Ingredient of Nongrading," *Elementary School Journal*, January 1969, pp. 192–97.

studies at Catholic University, Syracuse University Medical School, and elsewhere have shown that it is possible to raise the intellectual effectiveness of infants quite dramatically through tutoring which consists of play activities, reading and talking to the children, the taking of walks and trips, and other experiences some children miss: the crucial element evidently being the one-to-one relationship in which the adult's attention is focused on the child. Continuation of special help of this sort will be necessary for some children as well as adults can assist in such programs.

LAUNCHING NEW PROGRAMS

It seems altogether likely that American education is making ready for some fairly radical changes, among them being the long-overdue inclusion of preprimary offerings in the regular school program. Granted that the cost will be high and problems of launching and housing this new service will be enormous, it nevertheless seems that parents and politicians alike will soon be persuaded that this next step is necessary.

In many ways such a development will cause headaches among schoolmen. For one thing, there is a flimsy foundation of experience on which to build. That the provision of high-quality preprimary education is a relatively new cause among educators, however, has certain advantages worth noting. In most communities, habit-ridden teachers and fossilized preprimary curricula are not yet on the early childhood scene, nor are inflexible classroom spaces and outdated educational equipment. Even where these already exist, the prospect of significant expansion means that new teachers, new spaces, new equipment, and (let us pray) new approaches and content in instruction will be entering the picture. As a result, and despite the many problems in tooling up for the "golden age" that hopefully lies ahead, there is a real opportunity to launch fresh, imaginative, and sound programs in physical settings that are truly appropriate. It is, of course, important to implement the expansion only as adequate resources become available. Headlong expansion without good planning could be disastrous.

But reckless expansion seems very unlikely. The catch-up cost of providing classrooms to meet the actual need for kindergarten space alone (much less the total preprimary requirement) will reach billions of dollars. A significant increase in operating costs, particularly salaries, will also be necessary and most communities will find it expedient to absorb these costs by stages. Furthermore, recruitment and training of sufficient professional personnel will prove a demanding task for the colleges.

Lest we be overwhelmed by these practical limitations, and as a way of gaining experience and momentum, why not move toward full-scale programs one step at a time? Our priorities can go, first, to the provision of kindergarten services where they have not existed. Next, heeding Esther Edward's advice that "kindergarten is too late," [6] we can move to extend the kindergarten program by adding the four-year-olds. Finally, the "mini-school" can be incorporated. The master timetable can extend over any given number of years, although obviously the fewer the better.

One potential hang-up is the extent of the service to be provided. Some may argue that the program should be five (full or half-) days per week within the school environment, especially for the older children. Until housing and financing for a full program became available, however, it would seem reasonable to offer a *modified* program which brings each child into the school (or whatever other space is being used) at least one or two half-days per week. A hard-pressed community could begin, for example, with a once-per-week arrangement while it is constructing new classrooms and building up its staff and program. In a year or two, the offering could be increased to twice per week, and then to three days per week, and so on.

Especially during the growth period but perhaps as a permanent feature, the basic in-school program could be augmented by television offerings (to help parents as well as children), by parent-directed activities for groups of children in homes and churches, and by such additional activities as may be possible with the cooperation of local libraries, museums, and community centers.

HOUSING THE PREPRIMARY

With respect to facilities, the profession now has the benefit of over 10 years' experience in developing architectural and engineering solutions to the space problems posed by current educational innovations. At the elementary level, experience with team teaching, nongrading, teacher aides, programmed learning, flexible scheduling, educational television, and a wide range of electronic and mechanical resources, with instructional materials centers, independent study, new curricula, clinical teacher education programs, and other "new" or newly important arrangements has helped educators to appreciate how the school plant can contribute to the growth and effectiveness of both children and teachers. It is no longer unusual for new buildings to be flexible and functional. Even the taxpayer now seems persuaded that beauty, comfort, and even excitement are legitimate considerations in school planning. This acceptance of the creative role of the physical environment must be brought into play for the youngest children as well.

[6] Esther P. Edwards, "Kindergarten Is Too Late," *Saturday Review*, June 15, 1968, pp. 68–70, 76–79.

Very timely are three excellent new publications which describe the kinds of facilities modern preprimary programs require. One of these is *Designing the Child Development Center*,[7] a U.S. Office of Education booklet outlining the physical properties of a Head Start center. Its comments on personnel, site, the outdoor playscape, a range of interior environments for the children, and space provisions for community people as well as school staff can prove useful not only to Head Start leaders but to educators in general. Also exciting and informative is a new Educational Facilities Laboratories report, *Educational Change and Architectural Consequences*.[8] Though it deals with all school levels, its discussions of current innovations and of "the instructional encounter" in varying-sized groups are informed and perceptive and contain, in each instance, examples from early childhood education. A section on the preprimary school describes and illustrates a kindergarten facility. It includes a testing center which resembles a very small nursery school and which has an adjacent observation room and a nursery play yard. Near this center are the school's chief instructional spaces: one room and outdoor play area for the less mature children and another for more sophisticated activities, many of which center around learning to read. The outdoor play areas, similarly, are designed for both less advanced and more advanced pupils. A small projection arena, called a "theaterette," is shared by and linked with the two classroom areas.

A third booklet, *The Prepared Environment*,[9] examines and discusses school and equipment design implications of certain concepts, for each of which an educational rationale is presented, followed by architectural interpretations. There are five such discussions: dependence, independence-interdependence; early stimulation and learning; manageable complexity; the play of young children; and the role of the teacher.

PASSING THE ROADBLOCKS

In the EFL booklet, as in most of the current literature in support of structural and educational reforms, it is acknowledged that the new approaches have yet to take hold on any significant scale. That they are consistent with, and supportive of, the goal of providing truly individualized instructional opportunities to many different types of children makes

[7] Ronald W. Haase and Dwayne Gardner, *Designing the Child Development Center*. Washington, D. C.: Office of Economic Opportunity, 1968, 24 pp.

[8] Ronald Gross, Judith Murphy, *et al.*, *Educational Change and Architectural Consequences: A Report on Facilities for Individualized Instruction*. 477 Madison Avenue, New York 10022: Educational Facilities Laboratories, Inc., 1968, 88 pp.

[9] Margaret Howard Loeffler, *The Prepared Environment and Its Relationship to Learning*. Oklahoma City: Casady School, 1967, 32 pp.

it all the more urgent that their full-scale adoption become widespread. Most of the theoretical roadblocks to organizational reform, particularly the mythology surrounding self-contained classrooms, have eroded in the face of recent evidence and experience. Roadblocks that remain, however, include the lack of flexible or even adequate facilities and the failure of school administrators to provide real leadership in helping teachers to understand and to implement the newer options in pupil grouping, scheduling, use of resources, and deployment of adult personnel.

These general observations obtain at all levels of schooling. From the viewpoint of early childhood education, the problem is exacerbated by the failure of most school administrators (including college deans and department heads) to comprehend and to sympathize with the functions and importance of nursery school and kindergarten offerings. The great majority of administrators are men, and unfortunately preprimary education and for that matter elementary education generally have tended to be a woman's world. In addition, most superintendents and deans were themselves secondary school teachers in their early careers and, except perhaps later as parents, they have had little exposure to preprimary teaching. We may hope that recently, as a result of forces reviewed in the KAPPAN issue, the necessity for redressing this situation is becoming apparent to school officers generally.

One fact that has often inhibited the educational administrator, and which must ultimately be accepted by taxpayers, is that appropriate school offerings for young children are necessarily more expensive than those for older children. Ratios of adults to pupils must be more favorable, and unsupervised individual work is more rare, in preprimary classrooms. However, evidence now exists to support the argument that in the long run there is a significant saving to the society when priceless human resources are recognized and developed before it is too late. It is, to put it more directly, even probable that appropriate and well-financed preprimary and elementary school programs can lead to radical changes and significant economies in the presently wasteful enterprises of secondary and higher education.

It would seem, then, that the successful implementation of downward school expansion depends to a significant extent upon the understanding, the skill, and the *zeal* with which superintendents of schools, deans of education, and other key leaders accept this new challenge. Badgered as they are by political and financial problems, they will need all the support and encouragement that the other friends of early education can muster.

39 | A School Designed for Kids

JAMES CASS

Reprinted with permission from *Saturday Review*, Vol. 53, No. 12 (March 21, 1970), pp. 65–67, 75. Copyright 1970 Saturday Review, Inc.

Most schools are designed for adults, for the comfort and convenience of faculty and administration. The Beloit-Turner Middle School in Wisconsin, by contrast, was clearly conceived as a place for kids—or, more accurately, it was artfully designed to house a program based on the special nature and needs of early adolescents.

The visitor's first impression of the school is one of openness—of wide-open, visually attractive space. His second impression is one of almost constant movement, relatively quiet, purposeful, and relaxed, but unceasing. Only later in the day does he realize that he has heard no bells ringing to signal the end of class periods, and that classes of various sizes have met for differing lengths of time, and then have dissolved and reformed with a minimum of disturbance.

The heart of the school consists of three large classrooms—or pods, as they are called—each serving as a homeroom for 125 to 150 students, and as a classroom for varying numbers of students throughout the day. These pods are arranged in a U-shape around a central core of administrative and special service offices, and a large, open instructional materials center. The remainder of this central core consists of an ingeniously tiered cafeteria/commons, which connects the two side pods at the open end of the U, and doubles as a classroom for either large or small groups, as well as a "socializing center" for students. Divisions between the various open areas are marked only by the different colors of carpeting that covers virtually all the floors in the school—including the cafeteria. Adjacent areas house the auditorium, gymnasium, and facilities for music, art, home economics, and industrial arts.

Designed by architect Jack Reif of John J. Flad & Associates (Madi-

"The most important characteristic for teachers at our school is that they like kids. It's nice if they know a little English or math or science, but that's not half as important as how they feel about kids."

—HERBERT JACKSON, Principal, Beloit-Turner Middle School

son, Wisconsin), the school incorporates elements of open design that are by no means new, but are employed with a sensitivity that not only makes it possible for an unusual educational program to function, but actively supplements and enhances it.

The program itself is based on the assumption that sixth-, seventh-, and eighth-graders have special interests, needs, and objectives—and that the school should work with these special qualities rather than against them. Conceived by Professor Rolland Callaway of the University of Wisconsin, Milwaukee, the program specifically assumes that these early adolescents need an active, social school environment, because they are deeply involved in questioning who they are and in exploring the nature of their relationship to everyone and everything. Consequently, this is not the age at which a child is ready to confine his study to the separate, highly organized disciplines. Rather, his study should draw upon the disciplines, and he should begin to develop varied academic skills, but the emphasis should be placed on the exploration of social issues and problems, with particular attention to the development of individual interests, values, and attitudes.

To keep the program as flexible as possible, the day is divided into three large blocks of broad objectives. One half of the day is allotted to "Developing Social Sensitivity and Understanding" (which draws on the social studies, English, and foreign languages), one quarter of the day to the "Physical Environment" (which focuses on science and math), and the remainder of the day to "Developing Creative Interests and Abilities" (which offers students freedom to develop their own interests in art, music, home economics, and industrial arts). Each large group of students works with a team of teachers, teaching assistants, student teachers, and interns, as well as with specialists. The instructional program itself is not predetermined, but is "relegated to on-the spot, day-by-day, week-by-week planning of the teaching team and the students." The part of the day devoted to the creative arts leaves the student free to choose his own area of interest—and to change it at will.

The school was opened just last September, and all facilities were not completed until early December, but both the school and its program appear to enjoy substantial community support. Although located in a typical Midwestern rural-suburban area that is far from affluent, no federal, state, or foundation funds were involved. It was purely a community effort that has, perhaps, been characterized best by former board of education president William D. Behling, executive director of the Beloit *Daily News*. "The Turner Middle School," Mr. Behling says, "is the remarkably successful result of an uninhibited effort by an improbable group of people who sought only to find a better way of meeting the educational needs of the early adolescent."

It is far too early to assess the ultimate success of the school, but teachers and students are enthusiastic. The teachers, to be sure, are rather more restrained in their adjustments—not least, perhaps, because they find it less easy to adjust to the openness and the constant movement, and because their responsibility for developing an effective instructional program is so much greater than it would be in a traditional school. Yet nearly all are firmly committed to the concept of the school and seem to have reservations primarily about whether they have discovered how best to employ their professional skills in the unfamiliar environment.

But the children have no doubts. "It's the freedom that's so great," they say, "you can do what you want." And they add: "Yes, we learn just as much as we did last year—we learn more. Sure, we still have to study science and math, but it's different." The ways in which it differs may vary for individuals, but they have a common theme that echoes Professor Callaway's assertion that, when we enforce rules of quiet conformity on students, we "foist behavior patterns on youngsters in our schools which we, as adults, would not live with."

"The teachers don't push you into learning," a diminutive sixth-grader explains, "they let you come in by yourself and do it the way you want. We learn more because we want to—and it's so great because after you've done your work nobody cares if you visit with your friends." Three eighth-grade girls, alternately studying and talking in a little corner formed by movable tables with low tack-board backs, agree with their sixth-grade colleague. "It's better when you get the latest gossip while you study," they say. And one adds: "You only really learn when you

---

"Doors lock a kid's mind. The moment he walks into a classroom he has about eighteen by thirty feet, and that's it. He's shafted. He can't move. If we're going to give kids the right to think and explore, and discover, they have to be in a building where they have freedom to move, freedom to think. Movement and thinking go hand in hand."

—HERBERT JACKSON

"The typical school is organized on the assumption that if one child talks to another he is either out of order or he's cheating. At Beloit-Turner, however, the school building is designed to encourage social activities and relationships. For example, the cafeteria is used by the children for a variety of purposes. Besides eating lunch and socializing here, they may come at any time of the day to work in small groups or merely to take a 'Coke break' from their studies."

—DR. ROLLAND CALLAWAY, Professor of Education, University of Wisconsin-Milwaukee

"Should a student or a group of students become inspired to engage in role-playing or the construction of a model or set, he is allowed to proceed to the Creative Interests and Abilities area to take advantage of his momentary inspiration. The same holds true if a student feels that he wishes to listen to music, or paint a picture, or work out an experiment in the physical environment area. Although it is absolutely necessary to have some sort of schedule structure, whenever possible, it is ignored."

—CARL STRASSBURG, Superintendent, Beloit-Turner Joint School District No. 1.

want to." A seventh-grader is entranced by the freedom allowed him to go play chess when he has finished his math lesson. And others clearly share his pleasure—two or three chess games are in progress at almost any time of the day, a dozen during the noon hour.

But Danny, a bright, articulate eighth-grader who has been a serious discipline problem in the past, sums it up: "You can't help but learn more, there are so many things to do—and in the afternoon [during the time allotted to creative interests] you can do anything you want." However, Danny's friend, who has a similar history, has had more difficulty in adjusting to freedom—and provides the counterpoint. "Last year when you did something you weren't supposed to do, and got away with it, you had a feeling of accomplishment. This year nobody cares. Take gum. They say go ahead and chew gum in class—so I lost my taste for it. Nobody chews gum any more—maybe two or three guys in the whole school."

It will take much more time to get a final reading on the Beloit-Turner Middle School. The program is still evolving, and its eventual success will depend in large measure on the skill and the dedication of the teachers who implement it. But perhaps the best interim assessment has already been made by the students themselves. As a result of their demand, the school is open seven days a week. It's the most interesting place in town.

40 High School with No Walls— It's a Happening in Philadelphia

HENRY S. RESNIK

Reprinted with permission from *THINK Magazine* published by IBM, Vol. XXXV (November–December 1969), pp. 33–36. Copyright © 1969 by International Business Machines Corporation.

In the great jungle of public education, the high schools are open game these days, and the onslaughts of the critics, from respected academics to long-haired student activists, are having a devastating effect. The severest criticisms define the typical American high school as a prison-and-factory, but even establishment insiders have admitted that most high schools are several generations behind the times. Everybody, it seems, is looking for alternatives, and the school system of Philadelphia has found what many educational reformers consider a truly exciting possibility: an experimental high school called the Parkway Program.

A year-round happening, the program is a school without grades, marks, arbitrary rules, authority figures, a building—or, its advocates claim, boredom.

The locale is in and around central Philadelphia: in offices, museums, science centers, hospitals, theaters, department stores; in luncheonettes, in the Automat, on street corners, and stairways. Students can opt for such courses as: law enforcement at the administration building of the Police Department, library science at the public library, and biology at the Academy of Natural Sciences. In fact, with all of Philadelphia as a resource, Parkway students are free to study just about anything that may interest them.

When most administrators want to boast about a new high school, they produce drawings of a $14-million edifice that took three years to build; the best picture of the Parkway Program is an aerial view of Philadelphia's Center City. The program is named after the Benjamin Franklin Parkway, a mile-long boulevard lined with cultural institutions that begins at City Hall and culminates in the Greek-revival Museum of Art on a hill overlooking the Schuylkill River. The Parkway Program brushes aside the traditional notion that learning must be acquired within four-walled boxes called classrooms and acknowledges that life and learning are all part of the same ongoing process. The city itself is the classroom, and the life of the city is the curriculum.

NO LID TO BLOW

There are no dropouts here. Parkway students linger long after scheduled classes are over and often volunteer to come in for various weekend activities. As far as the program is concerned, no administrators are worried that "the lid will blow." There *is* no lid.

Perhaps most important, the program is structured to acknowledge the value and uniqueness of every individual. For most of the people the program serves—teachers and students as well—school has become a portal to self-fulfillment.

Philadelphia's "school without walls" began as a brilliant gimmick for decreasing overcrowding—at virtually no cost to the school system—and publicizing the climate of innovation that a new Board of Education had been trying to establish since the beginning of 1966.

According to local legend, a board official looked out his office window in the board's Parkway headquarters one day, saw the huge palaces of culture—the Free Library, the Franklin Institute, the Art Museum and dozens of others—that line the Parkway for most of its length, and said, "Why not use all this as the campus of a high school?" When the proposal was announced in February 1968, it was the talk of Philadelphia—the combination of economy and novelty lent the idea an almost irresistible magic. Several leaders of Parkway institutions complained that they had not been consulted and that their participation was far from guaranteed, but these objections were lost amid the general din of rosy publicity.

Old guard administrators at the Philadelphia Board of Education still maintain, as they did at the beginning, that the program is no more than a good job of public relations on the part of the reformist board and the liberal administration of Superintendent of Schools Mark Shedd. It is indeed good copy, but, more than any other single experiment in Philadelphia's huge reform movement, the Parkway Program delivers the basic educational changes that Shedd promised when the Board hired him early in 1966. Although the program has a good deal of surface glitter and seems so much a merely slick idea, it questions basic assumptions about the structure of schools. Its supporters believe that its potential for effecting change is virtually unlimited.

"THE RIGHT MAN"

In retrospect, it is clear that the possibilities of the proposal might never have been realized if it had fallen into the wrong hands. For months after the board's announcement, traditionalists within the school system limited their reaction to questions about how administrators could ever coordinate the activities of so vast and sprawling a campus. For them, the proposed "Parkway High School" was merely a difficult exercise in scheduling, a nightmare vision of shuttle buses jamming the parkway, and harried vice principals imploring systems analysts to help them out of the mess. If this attitude had prevailed, the program could easily have amounted to a bizarre variation on the usual humdrum theme.

But then, in June 1968, the board announced the appointment of 42-year-old John Bremer as the program's director. An Englishman and a born rebel, Bremer had roughly twenty years of educational experimentation to his credit. Nine of these he had spent in England, principally in connection with the Leicestershire Schools, which are now being widely hailed as models for reform in elementary education throughout the United States. Most recently, after emigrating to America and teaching education at the university level, Bremer had been unit administrator of New York's Two Bridges district, a tempest-torn effort at decentralization and community control. Bremer was so soft-spoken and mild-mannered that some observers within the central administration wondered in the beginning whether he could handle the politics of the job. Soon, however, their fears were set firmly to rest, for it became clear as time went on that, in the words of an educational consultant close to the program, Bremer has been "the right man in the right place at the right time."

Typical of Bremer's approach was his insistence, from the earliest days of his appointment, that, contrary to popular belief, there would be no shuttle buses connecting the various parkway institutions—students would have to find their own way of getting from one place to another, no matter what the distance. The decision reflects a philosophy that has come to dominate the program and to determine its basic shape and style: Bremer is committed to individual growth, creativity, and autonomy; he is an enemy of bureaucracies that tell people exactly what to do and think (or how to get to a destination); he delights in public criticism of the educational establishment. At the opening of the summer session in July 1969, he told a group of students entering the program for the first time, "In terms of behavior and attitudes, you're going to have to unlearn everything you've learned in your public school education so far, as quickly as possible."

The pilot "unit" of the Parkway Program opened in February 1968, with approximately 140 students, among whom half were black and 20 were from Philadelphia suburbs; nine full-time teachers; another ten or so student-teachers or undergraduate interns; and a huge second-story loft headquarters two blocks from City Hall. A second unit was opened, in rented office space five blocks from the first, at the beginning of the summer session, enrolling another 130 students. In September 1969, a third unit, about ten blocks from the first, was opened in an old school building. This consists of an elementary school for 130 children in kindergarten through fourth grade, modeled on the libertarian British infant schools that Bremer helped to pioneer, and a high school for 130 students who participate in and study, among other things, the entire operation of the elementary school. A fourth unit, again with 130 high school students, has just opened. The original plan called for a high school of 2,-400 students, and although Bremer has considered such modifications of the plan as a "nongeographical school district" encompassing much larger numbers of students throughout the city, each unit in the growing program has been modeled on the same basic pattern.

One of the greatest attractions of the Parkway Program for students is the tremendous freedom it allows—some observers believe that the program is merely chaotic. Bremer insists, however, that he has provided a tight "internal" structure. While each unit has taken on a distinct character of its own, at any rate, certain structural elements are common to the entire program:

LIKE A FAMILY

Tutorial Groups

These groups of about fifteen students and two teachers are the principal base, rather like a family, of each student's Parkway career. In the tutorial group, which meets for two hours four days a week, the student plans his schedule, receives personal counseling, and makes up deficiencies in such basic skills as reading and math. Some tutorial groups plan parties and outings; others organize informal athletic events; others agree to study a subject of mutual interest. The tutorials are also responsible for the extensive written evaluations of both students' and teachers' work that take the place of grades.

Selection by Lottery

One of Bremer's educational axioms is, "Anything that can be measured is educationally worthless." Consequently, the Parkway Program bypasses standardized tests as a basis for admission and favors the totally random method of drawing names from a hat. There were 10,000 applications for the 130 places in the second unit; some teenagers burst into tears when they missed their chance at the public drawing.

HOW TEACHERS ARE CHOSEN

Faculty Selection by Committee

Most teachers in the Parkway Program are selected by committees consisting of university students, parents from the community, visiting teachers, and students and teachers from other units. After the initial interviews, a few dozen of the most promising applicants are assigned the task of deciding what process of elimination they should use in filling the limited number of openings, and are then observed by Bremer and key advisers as they thrash out the problem.

Institutional Offerings

Each unit is responsible for enlisting the aid of the various downtown institutions, both public and private, in the form of courses and other projects, which range from discussion and planning groups to paid employment. So far, each unit has managed to line up more than thirty offerings. The Parkway catalog lists 90 "cooperating institutions."

Faculty Offerings

Since the program operates only within general requirements for the high school diploma in the State of Pennsylvania, the permanent faculty members have been able to explore many subjects and courses of study that the traditional high school would never allow. During the first session, for example, students could choose from such unusual fare as: "Psychology and Personal Problems," "Multi-media Journalism," "Filmmaking," "Vagabond Sketching," "Kite-flying," numerous workshops in creative writing, and courses in 10 languages.

Town Meetings

Sometimes shouting sessions, sometimes orderly public debates, the program's weekly town meetings have emerged as the principal form of government in each unit. Discussions range from such basic questions as what kinds of rules and philosophies the unit should adopt to such mundane matters as the filling out of forms, but the emphasis throughout is on total participatory democracy.

"EVERYBODY'S YOUR FRIEND"

What may be the most important factor in the program's success, however, is the emphasis on community that has come to motivate the behavior of most participants as if it were a religious force. The various structural elements have certainly encouraged this sense of community, but it seems to derive as much from Bremer's inspiring, almost charismatic vision as any other single factor. According to Mario Fantini, the program's liaison with its initial sponsor, the Ford Foundation, "John Bremer made the program *human*." Most teachers are known, at any rate, by their first names only, and students usually describe the warmth and intimacy of the program as if they can scarcely believe they have found such things in a place called school. "Here you get the feeling that everybody's your friend" is a typical reaction.

Bremer insists that the almost random selection of students and faculty has neutralized his power to create a private fiefdom; nevertheless, it is clear to any visitor that he has set the tone for the entire operation and that this tone is almost always informal and spontaneous. Members of the first unit were so friendly and drew so close, in fact, that they may have inadvertently perpetuated a certain anti-establishment cliquishness.

"The first day of the program," reports one teacher who had had more than a decade in the traditional system, "one of the students said 'What do you want to be called? Some of the teachers are called "Mr." or "Mrs." Some are called by their first names.' I said "You call me 'Mrs.' After 10 days' time I didn't want anybody calling me 'Mrs.' again."

Another teacher defines what seems to be the most important factor in the self-education of everyone in the Parkway community: "One of the things I've gotten," he observes, "is a sense of power. In the regular school situation you have it within the confines of the classroom, but here I'm really in control of myself and the program as it affects me and the people I'm working with. There's always the sense that the kids are teaching you and you're teaching the kids."

"My kid had already dropped out, even though he was still going to school," says the father of a Parkway student. "They discouraged him at his old school; they discouraged his musical talent, one of his main interests. He's a much different person now—he's interacting with the other kids and the faculty to a far greater extent. . . ."

Constantly attracting such testimonials from throughout the city, the Parkway Program flaunts its own inability to be evaluated in traditional terms.

"It's founded on a new principle of what education is," says Mario Fantini, who is also one of Ford's leading educational theorists. "The existing system isn't working. If you look at the student unrest as a symptom of the inability of the educational system, forged in another century, to be responsive to the concerns of this generation, it seems that many of those concerns would be addressed in a Parkway-like school."

MORE PARKWAY PROGRAMS

Some educators across the country seem to agree. By the fall of 1969, similar programs were under way in at least four major cities; several community groups in Philadelphia were eager to align themselves with Bremer and his philosophy; the Board of Education had voted to increase the size of the student body in 1969 to 700; and Bremer had a pledge of $500,000 from the school system's operating budget. For once, it seemed, a school had managed to please just about everybody.

There have been critics, of course. The program has been attacked as just another of the board's fancy experiments and there have been threats to block city funding. Yet the Parkway Program costs no more than what the board would need to educate the Parkway students in regular high schools.

Some observers argue that despite his emphasis on individual initiative, Bremer has often been hypocritically, arbitrarily authoritarian. A few teachers contend, moreover, that the most important advantage of the program is not its structure but the intimacy provided by a smaller teacher-student ratio—an intimacy that Bremer may have trouble maintaining as the program grows.

Though riding the crest of a wave, Bremer appreciates what he often refers to as the "messiness" of learning. He is almost proud to admit that the first sessions were not without their problems. Principally, too many students have not received the training in basic skills which is supposed to be a primary function of the tutorials. He is confident, however, that the problems will be solved—solving educational problems, is, after all, what the program is about.

41 | The Congenial School

HAROLD B. GORES

Reprinted with permission from the March 1969 issue of *Educate*, © MCMLXIX, Gellert Publishing Corporation, Vol. 2, No. 2 (March 1969), pp. 24–30.

I direct a small foundation whose mission is to help schools and colleges with their physical problems—anything in education you can, with impunity, kick with your foot.

We deal with the solids of education, as distinguished from its liquids —the people who flow in and flow out—and its gases, the curriculum.

Let me begin by inviting you to take a walk through the typical American school, with special reference to the schools of the inner-city.

First of all, the inner-city school is usually a fortress, a great masonry lump afloat on a sea of blacktop surrounded by a chain-link fence and sporting two basketball hoops. If it were the national intention to eject the middle-class families, both white and black, from the central city, this is the ideal device.

It's a big box filled with little boxes called classrooms. Let's walk up to the front door and, if you have the strength to swing it open, let's go down the bowling alley corridor—a long ceramic echo-cavern, slick and slippery if the janitor is good. If he is not so good, the corridor is not so dangerous.

On either side of this traffic chute, and connected like the coaches of a train, are the classrooms—each 24 feet long, 32 feet wide, 9 feet high, or whatever happens to be the local mystique as to how big a classroom should be.

The classroom is a great ceramic vault that looks much like a kitchen. It has a kitchen floor, kitchen furniture, and hard, clammy, bolt-of-lightning cracked, painted cement block walls. The only thing that yields to the body or to the touch, or nourishes the eye, is the acoustic ceiling without which the place would be uninhabitable—but you can't reach it.

Into this great, self-contained, self-contaminated classroom is deposited one teacher for one year with 25 children if the district is rich, 35 if it is poor, 50 if very poor. And in these boxes, like minnows in a net, are schooled the annual crop of small fry: the six-year-olds in one box, the seven-year-olds in the next box, and so on. Chronology and the seasons determine who gets together in education.

We ask, "Is there a library in the school?" In half the elementary schools there will not be. If there is a library and it is a large school, the chances are it is two classrooms big, created by leaving out the partitions separating two of the boxes. A library tends to be two boxes big, just as a kindergarten is one-and-a-half boxes big. We don't know how big a classroom should be, but we do know that a kindergarten should be one-and-one-half times as big as that.

LIBRARY VERSUS AV: DON'T LOOK FOR HARMONY HERE

Going into the library, you see it is mostly a place for books, as it should be, but where are the other carriers of information? The audiovisual section, if it is a fairly good-sized school, will probably be in the basement. Unlike the library, it is presided over by a man. These two people frequently do not like each other. The audiovisual arrived late in education, and there being no place for it, it was relegated to the basement under the supervision of a man since it took a man to lift the heavy stuff in the early years.

Is there an auditorium? Maybe. Ten years ago the auditorium was disappearing from the American high school because it was being utilized only about 10 percent of the time. But now the divisible auditoriums are at hand—over 100 since the first one in 1960 in Boulder City, Nevada. Being divisible, the utilization can now approach 100 percent.

When we go to the gymnasium, we see a very large box whose dimensions are determined by the rules of basketball. Tell me how many youngsters are in a high school in Portland, Oregon, or Portland, Maine, and I'll tell you the dimensions of the gymnasium: I will simply calculate how many basketball floors would be dealt out to schools of that size. Basketball has its vocational uses, of course—for anyone who has a pituitary derangement—but what can it do for girls who constitute one-half the student body? Fortunately, the old gymnasium is giving way to the field house, a great cavity of interior space in which the field sports can be played by students in all seasons.

The Goodyear Rubber Company is working right now on a membrane that will eventually cover four acres of land. Its target cost is $1.50 a square foot, its annual maintenance cost, $.05 a square foot. Here, for the first time within the grasp of education, is what one might call the poor man's Astrodome. In that great cavity of space, people—the whole community—can indulge in sports, games, physical education, recreation, day and night, the year 'round.

Last week, in Texas, I visited one of the superb schools of this country. It is a huge, loft building in which the teachers, children and the curriculum cut their own pathways through the airconditioned space. It is an acre of June.

IS THIS AN ENVIRONMENT FOR FIVE-YEAR-OLDS?

While at this great school, I asked to see the kindergarten. And there the little kindergartners sat at their little miniaturized tables in little miniaturized chairs like a group of shrunken businessmen—little five-year-olds sitting in this austere, steel and plastic environment. The only thing that yielded was the floor, which was carpeted—it was the only touch that saved the place from being totally inhumane. Though one of the best (designed) schools in America, the kindergarten bore little relation to the nature of a five-year-old child.

Typically, the kindergarten's furniture and equipment are miniaturizations of the first grade's, and the first grade's are for shrunken second-graders, and so on, ad infinitum, all the way to college. Must we keep shrinking everything down as the legs shrink, until we finally get this antiseptic, indestructible environment for soft, little, five-year-old children?

I suggested that somebody ought to dare to splash some color around the place. . . . One of the great decisions of early childhood occurs at the carnival when the child comes to the carousel and has to choose which horse to ride on the merry-go-round. A big decision. Why shouldn't chairs teach? Why shouldn't there be a decal of a lion on the back of one chair, a tiger on another, a rose, or whatever a girl might like on a third? It wouldn't cost much money. Let's have the same excitement in choosing a school chair that the child has at a carousel.

Do all tables have to be stamped-out kitchen furniture? For four-year-olds couldn't we have at least one table that looks like a turtle? It wouldn't cost a great deal, and maybe it would start to bring some excitement into the education of the very young.

So much for school. If it reminds some of you of the school you left last Friday, I can only say, "It's typical." And the typical suburban schools aren't a great deal better. Most school buildings—egg-crate, cookie-cutter, stamped-out, two-classroom-wide arrangements, assembled in linear fashion—do nothing to acknowledge the change in psychology that has come to undergird education in recent years.

But now, with the coming of air conditioning, we can have great zones of space. We don't need all the partitions and walls anymore if we dampen the environment acoustically, especially by carpeting the floor.

To show how fast acoustic floor covering is being accepted, in 1956 the sale of carpeting to education, schools and colleges, was in the order of $50,000. In 1966, it was $99 million. We are winning the battle for carpeting, and we're winning the battle for air conditioning.

A LIVING SPACE FOR LEARNING

Now we can design great zones of space, rather than, as McLuhan would say, "linear space." Now we can have great zones of space, acknowledging the organismic psychology and the gestalt we use when we describe a whole child, or a whole group, or a whole school, or a whole society. Stimulus-response, Pavlov and his dog, no longer dominate school design.

Let's visit a couple of schools that are striving to create a new environment to support sensitive learning.

If you are in New York City, go see P.S. 219, an early childhood facility. It's a great dome of space, 7,850 square feet of beautiful, malleable, universal space uninterrupted by posts, walls, or other barriers that would have to be forever walked around. About 180 children—nursery, kindergarten, first- and second-graders—are in this little satellite school.

See the options open to the teachers in this school to rearrange themselves, each to the other and to the children, according to changes in program. Here's a school that won't grow obsolete, that won't be a Procrustean bed for education, that was designed with less arrogance than some schools which are designed as though everything else in the world will be changing except education.

If you are in the Chicago area, look at the Barrington Middle School. Here's a school built of pre-engineered components, giving the school a chance to change its mind through the years as to its organization and arrangement.

If you are in Clarksville, Tennessee, visit the new high school. It's air conditioned, carpeted, and has great zones of space.

"TRUST" CAN CREATE A HUMANE ENVIRONMENT

Again, in New York City, look at Harlem Prep, a converted supermarket of 20,000 square feet. Harlem Prep is for youngsters who have failed and dropped out of regular schools. In planning the school, Mother Dowd told me that Harlem Prep, to fulfill its mission, must be

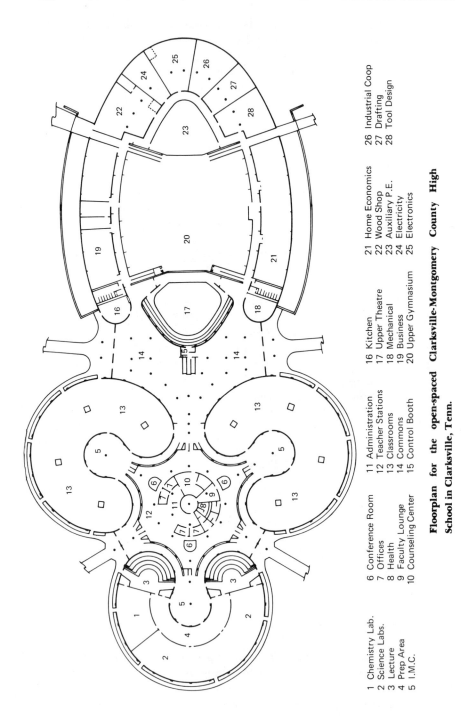

Floorplan for the open-spaced Clarksville-Montgomery County High School in Clarksville, Tenn.

1 Chemistry Lab.
2 Science Labs.
3 Lecture
4 Prep Area
5 I.M.C.

6 Conference Room
7 Offices
8 Health
9 Faculty Lounge
10 Counseling Center

11 Administration
12 Teacher Stations
13 Classrooms
14 Commons
15 Control Booth

16 Kitchen
17 Upper Theatre
18 Mechanical
19 Business
20 Upper Gymnasium

21 Home Economics
22 Wood Shop
23 Auxiliary P.E.
24 Electricity
25 Electronics

26 Industrial Coop
27 Drafting
28 Tool Design

designed around "Trust." "We will have furnishings in here that will yield to the body, that will delight the eye."

Now the notion of designing around trust rather than around maintenance, custody, and indestructibility, is both fresh and hazardous. Errant scholars, jackknife in hand, can destroy a humane environment. Mother Dowd bets they won't. And I bet she's right.

. . . AND REDUCE THE NUMBER
OF RUDE INSCRIPTIONS

(Incidentally, the quickest way to cut down graffiti in a boys' laboratory is to put in a mirror. The poetry on the walls just disappears—to the loss of American letters, maybe—as the boy's improved image of himself and the school raises the level of his response.)

This school in a supermarket provides humane space, supportive of the occupant's image of himself and the institution. It could turn out to be the best space for education in New York City.

If you are around Cleveland, go to the GE factory, a school which doesn't have a principal (he's called the manager), and whose students go automatically onto a payroll the minute they register. The school is for potential dropouts. Most of these young people want immediate reward; they don't subscribe to the Puritan ethnic of studying now to be rewarded later. They want "walking-around" money; they want it now.

Next, if you are near Cherry Creek, a suburb of Denver, look at a school there in which there will be practically no conventional school furniture. Much of the furniture will have come from the home furnishings market. The school is saying, in effect, that when children and teachers get together, it shall be in a space that has the quality of the living room, not the kitchen.

While at Cherry Creek see, too, the school being remodeled, though built originally in 1965! It is, of course, relatively easy to finance the remodeling of schools built in 1900—and the 15 largest cities in the country have 600 of these old bastions still running. But here is a 1965 school, deemed now to be obsolete and frustrating to the faculty and the program.

If we could visit the kind of school that will be emerging, what will be some of its characteristics?

THINK OF A SCHOOL AS A COMMUNITY RESOURCE

First of all, it will be designed not just for children. A school designed just for children deprives the community of a resource it should have. To be sure, it should serve children well, but it should also serve all people. Such a school, though, requires a higher quality in design, especially of space. Children don't vote, so they get whatever municipal cruelty doles out to them. But if the space is also to be congenial to people of all ages, it has to be better.

The library eventually will be the biggest space in the school. Those of you who are in the audiovisual hardware business should focus on the library rather than the classroom. The word "library" is a good, honest word, which I hate to see replaced by things like IMC (Instructional Materials Center).

The man in the street will vote for a library. He trusts one; he knows what it is; but an IMC sounds like the Space Program, and he knows that's expensive. Why take on the additional burden of changing the public nomenclature? Why can't a good, honest word like "library" be the label to cover the place for all the carriers of information?

Place the library so it can absorb the surrounding cells, so it can grow within the school, especially as the school gets more and more vivid materials from the private sector.

MACHINES WILL FREE TEACHERS
TO TEACH VALUES

When these vivid materials do come, less and less of the teacher's time will be employed in dispensing facts. Machines, whether the medium is paper, celluloid, tape, or tube, can vividly and ever patiently give the facts, thus freeing the faculty to deal with values and the meaning of it all.

Schools that intend to strap the child into an astronaut carrel and pump his head full of information are not really in education; they are in training. They may turn out scholars who are smart, but not wise. And this is why the machine is not a threat to the teacher. The teacher, and only the teacher, can deal with education; the machine is for training.

Much of the instructional technology coming into the school has purported to be a replacement of the teacher, an answer to the teacher shortage, a money-saver. So far, to my knowledge, none has fulfilled these early claims.

My observation and belief is that those machines that will survive in education and prosper, that will serve as well as make money, will be those that are teacher-extenders as distinguished from teacher-substitutes. As the machine extends the teacher's capability by taking over the burden of fact-transmission, the teacher is freed to return to his ancient trade —philosophy—the meaning of it all—what's true, what's false, what's moral, what's immoral, what's amoral. And no machine can take that person's position. So, in a sense, the machine is the way to freedom for the teacher to teach, unencumbered by the need to train.

SYSTEMS APPROACH TO BUILDING

As you build schools, be sure to consider the systems approach now emerging in this country and in Canada, and employing pre-engineered components. Watch Toronto, watch the Montreal Catholic School System. Watch Pittsburgh's Great High Schools which will be modular to achieve speed of erection and flexibility.

If you are in the inner city, look at the plans for a new college in Brooklyn's Bedford-Stuyvesant, a college which in effect will lace its way through the community without reducing the density of population or displacing it.

Well, there are so many things to say, but I would conclude only by saying a school teacher named Katherine Lee Bates, author of *America the Beautiful,* gave us the theme for today. In line with the theme of this conference, if someone asks, "What do we do?" I would suggest we turn to *America the Beautiful* to find the phrase that best describes the nation's greatest domestic challenge and objective: "Thine alabaster cities gleam, undimmed by human tears."

42 | Frameworks for Observing Teaching*

RONALD T. HYMAN

Reprinted with permission from *Journal of Secondary Education*, Vol. 43, No. 7 (November 1968), pp. 313–319.

There is one stubborn fact that a principal cannot deny; one duty critical to the principal's job that he must perform—the principal must evaluate his teachers. Now in actual practice it makes little difference whether this duty is required by state law or whether it arises from a regulation set by the school board and superintendent. The net result is the same—the principal must make a judgment about the teachers in his charge. Judge he must. That's the way it is.

Hopefully, the judgment the principal makes is based on a matching between: (a) some criteria he has established or accepted which outline effective teaching, *and* (b) data he has gathered about the teachers. But which criteria and which data? I will not dwell here upon criteria since the search for generalized notions about good teaching has been less than fruitful. I will touch on this matter later. Philip Jackson, a noted researcher on teaching, writing on this topic put it this way:

> "There is the lamentable, but undeniable, fact that our search for the good just doesn't seem to have paid off. Almost all of the noble crusades that have set out in search of the best teacher and the best method—or even the better teacher and the better method—have returned empty-handed. The few discoveries to date (it would be unfair—and, in front of this audience, imprudent as well—to deny that there have been any) are pitifully small in proportion to their cost in time and energy (5:8-9)."

Therefore, let us turn to the second question, namely, what data might a principal, or researcher, gather about his teachers.

*Author's Note: *Adapted from a speech delivered at the Opening Session of the Eleventh Annual Mid-Winter Meetings of the Connecticut Association of Secondary Schools, Hamden, Connecticut, January 18, 1968.*

If I were to ask ten principals to describe a particular teacher, there is little doubt that we would get disagreement. The ten principals would probably disagree simply because they would focus on different things. And this brings us to the heart of our concern. When we observe—visually and/or auditorily—we do so from a particular vantage point. We have no choice. We all know that observation is selective and the first step is the selection of our framework, whether we are aware of it or not, whether we admit it or not. Frameworks are "windows through which we see the world and our own transactions with the world, and they make that world meaningful to us in their own terms. No man ever sees the world other than through some conceptual system, whether he is aware of this or not (3:61)."

Thus, our ten principals are bound to disagree since they have not decided on which framework to use—which window they will look through to see teaching. "To see teaching" here means "to understand teaching." And this brings me to another main point. We get meaning out of our sense data only as they are interpreted within a framework. Events are meaningless unless *they* fit together—or, better yet, unless *we* fit them together in a framework of our choosing.

Let me quickly turn this around before we go too far. Not only is the framework necessary to give us meaning for our data but it is also necessary as a guide to the collection of data. That is, we do not even know what data to gather about teaching unless we get guidance from our framework. We know what data to collect only as the concepts we hold guide us. This our students are now learning in the "new curriculum" courses. J. J. Schwab, a leader in the reform of the "new biology," has written eloquently on this point. He tells about the study of small aquatic animals at the turn of the century. The biologist's knowledge of the dartings, play, and other movements of tadpoles and small fish was meager indeed. Even when a biologist wanted to know more he did not know what to look for—what to inquire about, as Schwab would say. But the frustration about inquiry disappeared when the biologists took the framework of the simple machine. "This idea of a simple machine was applied to the study of behavior by supposing that every movement through space of an animal was a response to some single, specific, stimulating factor in the environment." The biologists later discarded this naive conception but it did give them at the time questions to ask. It guided them in their collection of data (9:25–26) and this is the point.

SIX FRAMEWORKS

Having said this about the importance and necessity of frameworks, let me identify six that a principal might employ as he observes his teachers.

1. The Communications framework—this involves such concepts as feedback, messages, input, output, redundancy, selectivity, channel, and media. For example, the principal would do well to look for feedback in the classroom. That is, how does the teacher provide for getting feedback for it if he is the key person and the one who will use it? Does the flow of teaching look like this?

Teacher ⟶ Teacher's ⟶ Pupil ⟶ Pupil's
                Performance   Performance

Or does it look like this? (7)

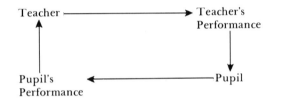

Now feedback is something every communications system needs because it influences the nature and amount of input that goes into it. Take the common occurrence of a teacher who, in explaining an intricate issue in mathematics, fails to get feedback. That is, he fails to find out if the students are meaningfully following his train of thought. Without feedback after the first few minutes, the teacher may spend the rest of the hour talking to ears that cannot decode his message.

In addition to focusing on feedback, the principal can gather data about the channels used to communicate, e.g., language, gestures, pictures. Further, what mixture of media does the teacher use? Tape recordings? ETV.? Written words? Talk—does he always talk? If the teacher mainly uses one channel and one medium, the principal will get clues as to the type of messages transmitted by the teacher.

One more point needs to be stressed. Whenever we communicate— whenever we transmit messages—as I am doing now, we always send more than one message. This is especially true when we speak face-to-face for then there are tone qualities, facial expressions, and hand gestures that vary in meaning from person to person. Accordingly, the communicator must consider not the message he is sending but the *set of messages*. The pupil listening to the teacher may pick up, due to his own peculiar receiving system and due to interference on the channel, a different message from the one intended by the teacher. The principal would do well to ask about the set of messages being transmitted in the classroom— what the teacher thinks he is transmitting and what he is indeed transmitting to the pupils.

2. The Sociological framework—this involves such concepts as au-

thority, power, influence, role, leadership, and group. You are all familiar, I am sure, with the work of Kurt Lewin who in the 1930s worked with different styles of leadership in youth groups: democratic, authoritarian, and laissezfaire. Lewin showed that a change in leadership style significantly affected the action of group members. Parallel studies in connection with teaching show similar results.

This sociological perspective perhaps has been the favorite one used by researchers and principals as well. The literature on teaching is replete with studies examining the relationship between achievement in learning and leadership style. At this point one can only safely say that though most of us prefer a more democratic classroom, the evidence is inconclusive as to the relative effectiveness (1). This, it seems to me, is due to the complexity of the issue and the vagueness of the criterion called "learning."

I offer here only one brief suggestion. If the principal uses this framework, he would do well to look for the interplay among three related notions: being in authority, being an authority, and being authoritarian (8).

3. The Games framework—this involves such concepts as competition, excitement, win/lose, penalty, referee, coach, and strategy. At this point in the twentieth century it would be difficult to deny the position of sports, games, athletics in American life. Also, consider for a minute how games have influenced our classroom speech, and it will be apparent why I include Games as a vantage point for observing teaching. It is not just that these are expressions but that people do see teaching as a game. That is why they use these expressions in the first place. Two illustrations: (a) "O.K., since Joe is absent, Jonathan will pinch-hit for him on the panel"; (b) "Charles, it's your turn to carry the ball."

The principal may well focus on what rules have been established and whether the players know—and understand—those rules. It may well be that some pupils are penalized when they do not even know the rules or when the rules are vague or arbitrary. Consider the fact that in the classrooms the teacher often turns out to be the rules committee and the referee. That is, he makes the rules *and* decides on infractions of the rules. Is this fair play?

The principal would do well to focus on the rules of the game that are actually played by the class though they are necessarily stated explicitly. For example, though they are found in no rules book students generally abide by these two rules: (a) Don't ask a question that requires a long answer near the end of the period; (b) Don't argue with the teacher. If you win, you really lose anyhow since he's the referee and scorekeeper. What rules are in effect when Mr. Jones teaches? Are they the same in Mr. Smith's classes? By a searching observation the principal will be able to identify the rules which are in effect but are never explicit.

The principal would do well to look for the games teachers play.

James Macdonald recently identified and briefly described six games: the information-giving game, the mastery game, the problem-solving game, the discovery or inquiry game, the dialogue game, and the clarification game. The principal might ask such questions as: (a) Do the teacher and pupils know what game is being played? (b) Are their roles in the game clear? (c) Does everyone know and understand the rules of the game (6)?

Before leaving this vantage point it is necessary to deal further with one crucial point—the element of competition in the classroom. Now in athletic games there is the idea that if, for example, Yale plays Harvard and Yale wins, then Harvard must lose. When Yale competes with Harvard, someone wins and someone loses. Is this true in teaching also? Some teachers and some pupils may think it is. Some teachers and pupils may be competing with each other—Yale/Harvard style. Some teachers may teach in such a manner as to be in competition with their pupils— all the time teaching with a thought which says, "If Johnny wins, I lose." This means that Mr. Jones must arrange it so he will win and Johnny will lose. Many students hold the converse view. Obviously, however, this win/lose notion is inappropriate. Only if the pupil wins, so to speak, does the teacher win. If the pupil loses, the teacher most surely loses. The principal, then, can meaningfully look for data about the ideas teachers and pupils hold related to the competitive win/lose concept. Their behavior will manifest their viewpoints.

4. The Aesthetics framework—this involves such concepts as rhythm, balance, harmony, creative expressiveness, and beauty. Of all the frameworks I include here, this one by far is the least common and most neglected. The principal might well focus on the way the teacher moves from point to point so as to build up to a climax. How does the teacher utilize the concept of personal satisfaction so as to help bring about a feeling of joy? How does the teacher employ such techniques as "comic relief" to break the tension and excitement that often builds up in a class? In what ways is there expression of individuality within a context of order and equilibrium that fosters emotional satisfaction? The principal might do well to focus on the rhythm of the class. Is the rhythm one of routine, which encumbers both teacher and pupil? Is the rhythm one that keeps everyone alert and alive? How well does the teacher play-it-by-ear, to use an appropriate metaphor?

5. The Psychological framework—this involves such concepts as interpersonal relations between teacher and pupil, personality, emotions, anxiety, acceptance, rejection, security, and the like. Here we ask such questions as: (a) Does the teacher show positive regard for the pupil? (b) Does the teacher reject the pupil? (c) Does the emotional tone of the classroom threaten the pupil? and (d) Do the teacher and pupil manifest empathy for each other?

This framework, I am sure, is quite familiar to you all. For this reason I shall not dwell on it any further.

6. The Cognitive framework—this involves such concepts as thinking operations, knowledge, content, subject matter, and intelligence. It guides us to ask such questions as: (a) What content is it that teachers and pupils talk about? (b) To what aspect of the topic at hand do teachers and pupils devote their discourse? (c) What are the various types of logical thinking processes manifested in classrooms? (d) How can we empirically specify examples of the operations of the intellect? (e) What types and examples of creative, productive thinking can we locate in classroom discourse? (f) When we say, "This teacher really teaches the pupils how to think," what is it that he teaches the pupils to do? and (g) What are the cognitive skills that teachers and pupils perform in their verbal behavior?

In our book, *The Language of the Classroom* (2), based on a three-year research grant from the U.S. Office of Education, we created and used an instrument to analyze the verbal behavior of the classroom within this cognitive framework. We were interested in several of the questions cited above. For example, in studying a unit on international trade we were interested in knowing how much time the 15 classes we tape recorded each spent on such topics as Import/Exports, Barriers to Trade, Promoting Free Trade (European Common Market), and Factors of Production. But that was not enough, for it was obvious that classes that spent time connotatively defining an import (i.e., a good coming into our country) and denotatively defining an import (i.e., Volkswagen, rubber, banana) were doing quite different things from classes that explained the processes of importing and exporting and showed why they are necessary to our American life. Also, these classes were different from those evaluating the President's import policy, e.g., the gold flow to Europe. We thus analyzed the class sessions according to the topics discussed *and* the logical operations performed. Let me quickly add that there are several other recent studies that also analyze teaching from this vantage point but they do so with different schemas.

So far, then, I have identified these six frameworks: Communications; Sociological; Games; Aesthetics; Psychological; and Cognitive. Needless to say, there are more.

APPLICATIONS

What then does all this mean? How can the principal make use of these frameworks? Let me now make some points about applications.

1. The principal as observer must take a vantage point. It may well

be one of the six I have identified. Whatever it is, however, the principal in his discussions with the teacher—for supervision without feedback discussions with the teacher is hardly worthy of the label "supervision"—must make his perspective clear to the teacher. And vice versa. This is a first step to fruitfully working toward improvement of teaching. If the principal and the teacher are aware of each other's framework, then the road is clear for further work. If they are not, the feedback discussions may easily lead to confusion. They must be talking on the same wave length, so to speak.

2. The principal should seek to fully and clearly understand the perspective of the teacher if he is to help the teacher to improve. The principal may himself favor a psychological approach. But he will have a tough time working with a teacher unless he clearly understands how the teacher views the class for it is the teacher who is directing the pupils. If the principal wants to understand Mr. Smith's lesson, then he needs to understand how Mr. Smith views teaching. Winch says it in this way:

> It is clear that men decide how they shall behave on the basis of their view of what is the case in the world around them . . . If O wants to predict how N is going to act, he must familiarize himself in terms of which N is viewing the situation (10:21,91).

Let me give a concrete example. We at Rutgers recently surveyed all the teachers in the South Brunswick, New Jersey, school system. We asked them about the definition of teaching and what perspective they use in viewing teaching. We found that those who responded to our instrument held different views on teaching. One interesting difference involved the elementary school staff and the senior high school staff. We asked them to rank five vantage points in order of correspondence with their own views. The results were as follows:

Elementary (K–8)	Senior High (9–12)
1. Psychological	Cognitive
2. Aesthetics	Psychological
3. Sociological	Communications
4. Cognitive	Aesthetics
5. Communications	Sociological

Now, not only are the two groups different, but the elementary faculty were stronger in their views than the senior high faculty. I use this empirical data to point up the idea that the principal must understand how his teachers view teaching if he is to work meaningfully with them.

3. The principal, whatever framework he uses, should in gathering his data look for patterns in the teacher's activity. A principal who is able to discuss patterning with a teacher is able to broaden the teacher's view

of his own activity. It is a way of seeing the flow of classroom discourse that might otherwise go unnoticed.

4. The principal might well use a different framework or specific focus within a framework for the various types of lessons he observes. If the principal observes a class discussing Teen-age Drug Addiction in a twelfth-grade Problems of American History Class, it is a good idea to look for the evaluative or divergent thinking operations as a clue to how current issues are handled. If the principal finds that only the teacher gives personal evaluations while the students restrict their statements to definitions and facts, he has a right to be disappointed.

Now if the principal observes a small group discussion set up as part of a team approach and multiple groupings, he might choose to focus on the interpersonal relations the teacher establishes with the pupils. This might be particularly apropos if the group is discussing a book like *The Catcher in the Rye* or *Lord of the Flies*.

5. The principal by employing a particular framework with a teacher may use it as a base for establishing criteria for judging good teaching. That is, in their discussions the principal and teacher can together work on what they believe constitutes "good" teaching. This step will further future supervisory work. "When supervision takes place in an atmosphere where both parties know what is expected of them and know what is being examined with evaluative criteria openly stated, then improvement can occur. Supervision within a framework eliminates concentrating on trivia and fosters sharp, sensitive organization of data. Supervision under such conditions leads to better relations between supervisor and teacher. Subsequently, the sensitized teacher will be able to work better with his pupils and this, I submit, is what we are all supporting. Supervision can become the opportunity for growth. More than that, observation can become the opportunity for emphasizing the 'vision' half of the 'supervision' relationship between supervisor and teacher (4:112)."

CONCLUSION

I conclude by saying that I have presented six frameworks for observing teaching—six frameworks for gathering data about the teachers a principal supervises. I am now proposing to you that, in order to get a balanced picture of a teacher, a principal should use a variety of frameworks as he supervises. For just as a teacher needs variety to spark and balance his teaching, so does a supervisor need variety. Indeed, by varying his framework, the supervisor in effect demonstrates to his teachers the merit of variety and balance. The characteristics of good supervisory relationship are quite similar—if not the same—as a good teaching relationship. The principal in his own way can help improve teaching. And this is what, I believe, we are all interested in. I ask you to consider what I have said and move from framework to framework. I trust that you can use this idea of multiple vantage points in your work with teachers. Try looking through different windows; see how teaching looks from various perspectives. You may find some frameworks suit you personally more than others. But in any case try a variety—broaden your own vision.

REFERENCES

1. Anderson, R. C., "Learning in Discussion: A Resumé of Authoritarian-Democratic Studies." *Harvard Educational Review,* 29:201–215, Summer, 1959.
2. Bellack, Arno A., Herbert M. Kliebard, Ronald T. Hyman, and Frank L. Smith, Jr., *The Language of the Classroom.* New York, Teachers College Press, 1966. p. 274.
3. Belth, Marc. *Education as a Discipline: A Study of the Role of Models in Thinking.* Boston, Allyn and Bacon, 1965, p. 317.
4. Hyman, Ronald T. "The Language of the Classroom: Implications for Supervisors and Teachers." *Journal of Secondary Education,* 42:106–113, March, 1967.
5. Jackson, Philip W. "The Way Teaching Is." *The Way Teaching Is.* Washington, D.C., National Education Association, 1966. pp. 7–27.
6. Macdonald, James B. "Gamesmanship in the Classroom." *Bulletin of the National Association of Secondary School Principals,* 50:51–68, December, 1966.
7. Packer, C. Kyle and Toni Packer. "Cybernetics, Information Theory and the Educative Process." *Teachers College Record,* 61:134–142, December, 1959.
8. Peters, R. S. *Ethics and Education.* Glenview, Ill., Scott, Foresman and Company, 1967.
9. Schwab, Joseph J. "Structure of the Disciplines: Meanings and Significances." *The Structure of Knowledge and the Curriculum.* Ed. by G. W. Ford and Lawrence Pugno, Skokie, Ill., Rand McNally, 1964. pp. 6–30.
10. Winch, Peter. *The Idea of a Social Science.* New York, Humanities Press, 1958, p. 143.

43 "Openness" in the Organizational Climate of "Humanistic" and "Custodial" Elementary Schools

WAYNE K. HOY
JAMES APPLEBERRY

Reprinted with permission from *Research Bulletin*, Vol. 14, No. 1 (Fall 1969), pp. 12–15.

The emphasis on pupil control in the organizational life of schools is not new nor surprising to teachers and administrators. Indeed, recent studies of public schools have emphasized the saliency of pupil control in the school culture.[1] In the study of one school, for example, pupil control was described as the dominant motif of the school social system—the "integrative theme" of the school which gave meaning to teacher-teacher and teacher-administrator relations.[2]

Control is a problem faced by all organizations, but it is especially important in certain types of organizations such as schools. Schools are service organizations which have no choice in the selection of clients (students) and the clients must (in the legal sense) participate in the

---

[1] Donald J. Willower and Ronald G. Jones, "Control in an Educational Organization," in *Studying Teaching*, ed. J. D. Raths and others. Englewood Cliffs, N. J.: Prentice-Hall, Inc., 1967. See also D. J. Willower, T. L. Eidell, and W. K. Hoy, *The School and Pupil Control Ideology*. University Park, Pa.: Penn State Monograph No. 24, 1967; and Wayne K. Hoy, "The influence of Experience on the Beginning Teacher," *The School Review*, LXXXVI (September 1968) 312–23.

[2] Willower and Jones, *op. cit.*

organization. These organizations seem likely to be confronted with some clients who have little or no desire for the services of the organization, a factor which accentuates the problem of client control in such organizations.[3]

Schools, however, differ in terms of the nature of their educational viewpoints and policies concerning control of students. Some schools are characterized by stress on maintenance of order, impersonality, distrust of students and, in general, a punishment-centered orientation toward students. Other schools are marked by an accepting, trustful view of students and confidence in students to be self-disciplining and responsible. To what extent are these kinds of differences in pupil control orientation related to other important characteristics of schools? More specifically, this paper will focus on the "openness" of the elementary school climate as it relates to the pupil control orientation of schools.

"CUSTODIALISM" AND "HUMANISM"

Following the lead of earlier research on pupil control, we adopted the concepts of "humanism" and "custodialism" to refer to contrasting types of individual ideology and the types of school organization that they seek to rationalize.[4]

The prototype of the custodial orientation is the traditional school which provides a rigid and highly controlled setting concerned primarily with the maintenance of order. Students are stereotyped in terms of their appearance, behavior, and parents' social status. Teachers who hold a custodial orientation conceive of the school as an autocratic organization with a rigid pupil-teacher status hierarchy; the flow of power and communication is unilateral downward. Students must accept the decisions of teachers without question. Student misbehavior is viewed as a personal affront; students are perceived as irresponsible and undisciplined persons who must be controlled through punitive sanctions. Impersonality, pessimism and "watchful mistrust" imbue the atmosphere of the custodial school.

The model for the humanistic orientation, on the other hand, is the school conceived as an educational community in which students learn

---

[3] Richard O. Carlson, "Environmental Constraints and Organizational Consequences: The Public School and Its Clients," in *Behavioral Science and Educational Administration*, ed. D. E. Griffiths. Chicago: University of Chicago Press, 1964, pp. 262–76.

[4] For a more complete discussion of the conceptualization of pupil control ideology and the development of an operational measure for pupil control ideology, see D. J. Willower, T. L. Eidell, and W. K. Hoy, *The School and Public Control Ideology*. University Park, Pa.: Penn State Studies Monograph No. 24, 1967.

through cooperative interaction and experience. Learning and behavior are viewed in psychological and sociological terms rather than moralistic ones. Self-discipline is substituted for strict teacher control. The humanistic orientation leads teachers to desire a democratic atmosphere with its attendant flexibility in status and rules, sensitivity to others, open communication, and increased student self-determination. Both teachers and pupils are willing to act on their own volition and to accept responsibility for their actions.

"OPENNESS" OF SCHOOL CLIMATE

Openness of organizational climate refers to teacher-teacher and teacher-administrator interactions which are genuine or authentic; i.e., behavior emerges freely and without constraint. A school with a great deal of openness is a dynamic organization which is moving toward its goals while simultaneously providing satisfaction for the teachers' social needs. Leadership acts emerge easily and appropriately as they become needed. The open school is not preoccupied exclusively with either task-achievement or social needs satisfaction, but satisfaction from both emerges freely. On the other hand, limited openness in the climate of a school indicates that there seems to be little going on in the organization. Although some attempts may be made to move the organization, they are met with teacher apathy and really are not taken seriously. In brief, morale in this type of school is low and the organization appears stagnant.[5]

DESIGN AND METHOD

As part of a larger study, 15 relatively "custodial" and 15 relatively "humanistic" elementary schools were identified from an original group of forty-five Oklahoma elementary schools drawn from varying sizes and types of communities.

Schools were classified as humanistic or custodial on the basis of the mean school scores on the Pupil Control Orientation Form, PCI Form. This scale, consisting of 20 Likert-type items, was developed to measure the control orientation of educators toward students in terms of "humanism" and "custodialism". Responses are scored from 5 (strongly agree) to 1 (strongly disagree); the higher the over all score on the instrument, the more custodial the ideology. Examples of items used include: "A few pupils are just young hoodlums and should be treated accordingly." "It is

[5] Andrew W. Halpin, *Theory and Research in Administration*. New York: The Macmillan Company, 1966, pp. 189–90.

often necessary to remind pupils that their status in schools differs from that of teachers." "Pupils can be trusted to work together without supervision" (score reversed). The 15 schools with the highest mean PCI scores designated custodial schools (Range=55.2−61.8) while the 15 schools with the lowest PCI scores were termed humanistic schools (Range=45.7–52.5).

To obtain a measure of the "openness" of the climate of these elementary schools, the Organizational Climate Description Questionnaire (OCDQ) was personally administered to the faculty in each school. Virtually all of the faculty in each school responded to *both* instruments. The OCDQ was developed by Halpin and Croft [6] in a major study of the organizational climate of 71 elementary schools. The instrument consists of a series of subtests. An "openness" score for each school can be computed by summing the school's score on the Esprit and Thrust subtests and then subtracting the school's score on the Disengagement subtest.

RESULTS

Elementary schools with a humanistic pupil control orientation had significantly more *open* organizational climates than those with a custodial pupil control orientation ($F=18.77$, $p<.01$). The average openness score for humanistic schools was 51.47 compared to a mean of 33.67 for custodial schools. The relevant data are summarized in Table 1.

TABLE I

The Openness of the School Climate of Humanistic and Custodial Elementary Schools: Summary Data and Analysis of Variance Data

	Humanistic Schools	Custodial Schools
Number	15	15
Mean Openness Scores	51.47	33.67
S.D.	13.27	8.79

Variance Source	df	ss	ms	f
Between Groups	1	2376.30	2376.30	18.77*
Within Groups	28	3545.06	126.61	
Total	29	5921.36		

* $p < .01$.

[6] Andrew W. Halpin and Don B. Croft, *The Organizational Climate of Schools.* Chicago: Midwest Administration Center, 1963.

DISCUSSION

The significance of pupil control orientation as an important aspect of the organizational life of elementary schools was supported by the findings of this study. The behavior of teachers and principals in humanistic elementary schools was, in general, marked by more openness, acceptance, and authenticity than the behavior of educators in custodial schools. Authenticity and openness in organizational behavior seem highly compatible with a humanistic pupil control orientation and incompatible with a custodial orientation.

The importance of the concept of openness in the organizational climate of schools has been discussed in detail by Halpin and Croft; they imply that perhaps openness of the school climate might actually constitute a better criterion of a school's effectiveness than many measures that already have entered the field of educational administration and now masquerade as criteria.[7] If the openness of the school climate is a valid criterion of school effectiveness, then schools with a humanistic pupil control orientation appear to be significantly more effective than those with a custodial orientation.

Moreover, to the extent that elementary schools attempt to communicate values as well as to communicate knowledge, a humanistic pupil control ideology seems to us, highly functional. A positive and strong commitment of students to the school seems required to communicate values effectively.[8] It also appears unlikely that such commitment can be effectively attained in the custodial school; in fact, the custodial atmosphere in the school is more likely to produce alienation of students rather than commitment.

Many elementary schools are custodial institutions.[9] Changes in these schools toward a more humanistic orientation may be sluggish, painful, and in many instances unsuccessful. There are no simple approaches. For example, recent research findings suggest that the pupil control ideology of beginning teachers (who in general were relatively humanistic) become significantly more custodial as they become socialized by the teacher subculture, a subculture described by the vast majority of new teachers as one in which good teaching and good control were equated.[10] More research is necessary for exploring various strategies for changing the cli-

[7] Halpin and Croft, *op. cit.*, pp. 82–83.

[8] For an excellent analysis of commitment and values, see Amitai Etzioni, *A Comparative Analysis of Complex Organizations*. New York: The Free Press, 1961, p. 83.

[9] See Jonathan Kozol, *Death at an Early Age*. Boston: Houghton Mifflin Company, 1967.

[10] Wayne K. Hoy, "The Influence of Experience on the Beginning Teacher," *The School Review*, LXXXVI (September 1968) 312–23; and Wayne K. Hoy, "Pupil Control Ideology and Organizational Socialization: A Further Examination of the Influence of Experience on the Beginning Teacher," *The School Review* (September 1969).

mates of schools. In the meantime, enlightened administrators with an understanding of the social characteristics of the school and its personnel may begin to design and experiment with strategies for changing the atmosphere of schools. However, humanistic changes will almost certainly face considerable resistance from many teachers and will probably be accompanied by unintended consequences; therefore, considerable individual and organizational patience and realism will be necessary to achieve even partial success.

44 | Suggestions for Involving Teachers in Innovation

RICHARD W. BURNS

Reprinted with permission from *Educational Technology*, Vol. 9, No. 1 (January 1969), pp. 27–28. Copyrighted by *Educational Technology* Magazine, Englewood Cliffs, New Jersey.

Through the mail I have received several inquiries pertaining to the problem of how to involve school personnel, especially teachers, in tasks associated with new instructional programs. Schools introducing dial-retrieval systems, learning laboratories, programmed instruction, CAI, video systems, and other such innovations find it difficult to involve the classroom teachers—but unless they are involved, new programs are unlikely to succeed.

Unfortunately, there is no magic wand to wave nor an "abracadabra" to use to solve this problem. At best there are generalizations, some of which may apply in a given situation. The following suggestions are offered—perhaps some may serve as guidelines for your school or project. No order of importance is intended in the listing.

1. Work initially with a small, select staff.
2. Try to select a staff of young, eager, interested, innovative persons who are eager to get ahead.
3. Select a problem that is generally recognized as such so that the idea of change will be more readily accepted.
4. Select a project that can be handled easily. Often a small pilot project should be a first step.
5. Pick an area of instruction that is easily structured. Let the staff members choose the area they feel needs work.

6. Provide your staff with a library of handy reference material relating to all aspects of the problem.

7. Hold planning sessions as necessary but keep them short.

8. Hold frequent, but short, staff meetings. Only require those to attend who are directly involved in the agenda. Frequent meetings insure progress and provide for all phases of the project to come under observation. This prevents minor problems from growing into major problems and also insures that all problems receive immediate attention.

9. Do not "nit pick"—keep the major problems in focus, and many of the minor irritations will cure themselves.

10. Reward the staff involved—build into the project a system of incentives such as released time or extra compensation.

11. Give credit as often as possible, preferably publicly, to those involved.

12. Fix responsibility—everyone should be clear about their share of the responsibility and the goals they are to reach.

13. Set definite time limits—it is too easy to delay and procrastinate when time is open-ended.

14. Short-term goals and short-term time limits, sequentially assigned, are preferrable to complex goals and long time limits.

15. Do not rush the project—start early and have a lead in time which will allow for the education of all personnel involved.

16. Do not burden the staff with clerical work, trivial chores, nonessential reports, and tasks that less expert persons can do. Furnish your expert staff with total administrative and clerical support.

17. Encourage the staff to elect or select areas of responsibility, whenever possible, as such areas (tasks) of interest are more readily pursued than are arbitrarily assigned tasks.

18. Encourage all types of communication between members and between levels. Encourage suggestions and permit free, constructive criticism. Get all the "feedback" possible.

19. Training of a staff can be accomplished best by face-to-face or crosstable communication with "experts" and "advisors," rather than a more formal teacher-structured or academic approach.

20. Be flexible, and when errors occur, correct them. The best plans are not perfect; so, change plans when necessary. Dead-end roads will occur; and when they do, do not hesitate to scrap one idea in favor of another.

21. Encourage production. Whether it is plans, idea lists, outlines, drafts of software (instructional materials), tests, or other materials which are being developed, always get something written as soon as possible. It is easier to correct, change, and proof imperfect drafts of all sorts of material than it is to wait and produce only

when the production is likely to be perfect. Many people have a hesitancy to produce, and as a result they delay to the point of non-production and only worry about the enormity of the problem.

22. Provide for helpful supervision. Supervisors should be resource persons rather than merely overseers.

Anyone initiating or involved in a project applying modern technology to an instructional problem would benefit from reading *Developing Vocational Instruction* by Robert F. Mager and Kenneth M. Beach, Jr.; Fearon Publishers, 2165 Park Boulevard, Palo Alto, California 94306. Do not let the term "Vocational" distract you, as what the authors have to say is as applicable to nonvocational as it is to vocational instruction. It is a condensed guide to a systematic approach wherever an instructional system is being developed.

Of prime importance in any project of software development is to first establish a feeling of real need. A school district which is currently going through this type of project (Bethlehem Area School District, Bethlehem, Pennsylvania) under the direction of Roy A. Brown, assistant superintendent in charge of instruction, expressed this point well in a letter: "Simply, we were asking ourselves how can the subject which is taught be taught more effectively." They are utilizing teachers and staff who are creative and change-minded and who want to develop better ways of instructing learners.

A second area of great importance is the development of instructional objectives. This topic, although not extensively documented, has recently received attention.

45 | Lag on Making Ideas Work

JOHN I. GOODLAD

In the decade of the sixties, innovation was the name of the education game. Schools were to be nongraded and team-taught. Curriculums were to be infused with new content and method. And students were to have tailor-made lessons, individually scheduled and even taught by computers.

Starry-eyed innovators predicted that these and more would be widespread by 1970.

The year 1970 has come. These innovations and more are, indeed, here—but only at the periphery. The task of the seventies is to get reforms out of the clouds and into tens of thousands of classrooms.

It is now clear that the central thrust of the educational reform movement of the sixties has been blunted on school and classroom. A recent study in which I participated reveals that nongraded, team-taught, computer-scheduled schools are hard to find. Telling and questioning by teachers, not active dialogue and inquiry by students, constitute the teaching-learning mode.

Much of the intent of new instructional materials is lost because teachers have not learned the methodology to go with them. Students tend to be taught in class-size groups with little attention to individual differences among them. The textbook dominates as the prime medium of instruction.

EVERYONE'S BUSY

Our most sobering finding is that only a scattering of schools— perhaps 5 or 6 percent at best—has anything resembling a critical mass of people seriously at work on the problems principals and teachers say they have.

Almost everyone is very busy—with daily problems of managing school and classroom, with evening classes in self-improvement, with districtwide projects of one kind or another, and with the myriad details of keeping school.

The ship must be kept afloat, so there is a great deal of activity on deck. But the real problems lie deep in the hull.

The problems for the seventies are staggering. No single innovation or collection of innovation, tacked on to what exists, will solve them. A process of fundamental reconstruction is called for, a process that strikes simultaneously at three critical points: the context of schooling (materials, content, organization, and so on), personnel on the job, and personnel in training.

Teachers on the job are quite impotent in seeking to effect change unless the setting in which they work is oriented toward change. The norm must be change: on the job, for the school, and for the teacher-preparing institution.

Changing teachers and the schools in which they work calls first for decentralizing to them much of the authority and responsibility for decision making which now resides in the central office. The same principle of individuality which we seek to apply in the instruction of children must be applied to local schools.

The principal, teachers, parents and pupils in each school are the ones closest to the data and therefore most able to build a vital program for a particular school. The single school is the largest organic unit for educational change.

If the school is to become the dynamic, self-renewing unit it should be, the energies of its personnel must be focused on its needs and problems. The in-service education of teachers should arise out of the demand placed upon them by these needs and problems.

It should be provided on "company time" and at "company expense." Public schooling is one of the largest enterprises in the country that does not provide for systematic updating of skills of its employees and for payment of the costs involved.

It is in changing schools that future teachers must be trained.

Teacher-training programs must get off the college campuses into schools serving as teacher-education centers. On entry into such programs, future teachers must become members of teacher teams in collaborating schools and receive ascending stipends as they progress from minimal responsibility as aides to maximal responsibility as resident teachers.

JOINT EFFORTS NEEDED

Their work must be under the joint supervision of academic personnel from the colleges and clinical personnel from the schools. Teacher education courses should be broken up into varying lengths and the training period should culminate in a terminal, professional degree.

No courses should be required for and protected by state-certification requirements. Only the institutional arrangements of collaborating schools and colleges would be reviewed and accredited by the state. The candidate is to be judged on performance.

I believe that, during the seventies, there will be a renaissance in teacher education and schooling along the lines of what is briefly sketched here. But efforts concentrated on only one critical point of attack will not suffice.

We will be successful in markedly upgrading the quality of education only if we take full account of the fact that preservice teacher education, in-service teacher education and the schools themselves are dependent interrelated and interacting components of one social system.

INDEX

Ability, 163, 186
Academic assistant, 132
Academic gains, 167–177
Academic senate, 133
Acceleration, 75–77
Achievement, 60, 66, 76–79, 80, 86, 177, 194
Administrator, 135
Adolescent, 386–390
Adviser, house, 239
Age, 62, 86, 189
Age-grading, 62–63
Aides, 29
Aims, of instruction, 16–17, 25, 68
  See also Goals
Air-conditioning, 400–401
American tradition of individualism, 238
Anderson, Robert, 109, 374
Arithmetic, 76, 330–332
Audiovisual section, inadequacy of, 399

Baden, Walter, 40
Barcus, Del, 312, 314
Behavior, 419–420
Bell, Andrew, 107
Biology, 407
Bjelke, Joan, 109
Boys, and independent study, 250–255
  nonpromotion rate of, 51–52
  and team teaching, 152–153
Bremer, John, 393–397
Britain, education in, 184–190
Budget, 99

Buildings (*see* School, buildings; Facilities, instructional)

CAI (*see* Instruction, computer-based systems of)
California Achievement Tests, 50, 167–169
California Reading Test, 139, 140, 141, 142, 145
California Short Form Test of Mental Maturity, 137, 139, 140, 141
Canada, schools in, 5
Carpeting, 400–401
Carrico, Paul, 296
Cass, James, 2, 374–375
Change, 1–5, 128–130, 373–426
  avoidance of, 134
  how to introduce, 24–31
  See also Innovation
Chatelaine, 7–11
Cheating, 233
Chekhov, Anton, 223
Claremont High School, 287–292
Class(es)
  in graded schools, 41
  social, 164, 189
  structure of, 268
Classification, 50
Classroom, 115, 158, 234–235
Clerical aide, 120
Colleges, 334
Communication, 408
Computer, 278, 284, 295–296, 328–329, 368–371

Concept approach, 101

Conference, 365–366

Content, 99–106, 193, 218, 222

Continuous progress education, 33–40, 55–67, 99, 103–105, 211, 214, 218

    See also Nongraded programs

Cooperative teaching (*see* Teaching, team)

Costs, 335

Courses, 91, 98

CPE (*see* Continuous progress education)

Creativity, 3, 170, 172–173, 226, 354–357

Crowder, Norman A., 307–308

Cultural electives, 211

Curriculum, 8, 13, 37, 57, 64, 69–70, 72, 130, 132, 221, 226, 242–243, 247, 284

    in Beloit-Turner Middle School, 387

    and CAI programs, 324–333

    in Canada, 10

    content, 18

    development, 121

    diversity, 288

    in nongraded secondary, 94–105

    in Parkway Program, 391–392, 394–396

    planning by computer, 346–351

    redesign, 225

Cycling system, 99–101

Dalton Plan grouping, 206

Deceleration, 75–77

Democracy, 213

Designing the Child Development Center (R. Haase and D. Gardner), 384

Development, 9, 50–52, 62, 74, 129, 222–223

Differential Aptitude Test, 139–141

Discipline, 389

    academic, 16

Discontinuity, 63, 64

Dual Progress Plan, The, 211

Dufay, R. R., 70–71

Durrell, Donald D., 12, 18, 22

Education, 1–2, 5

    British, 184–190

    and the larger learnings, 221–228

    for the seventies, 365–371

    versus training, 404

    weapon of social reform, 367

Educational Change and Architectural Consequences (Gross, R., *et al.*), 384

Educational technician, 132–133

Educational technology, 293–371

Electives, 99, 101–103

Elementary and Secondary Education Act of 1965, 2

Elementary schools (*see* Schools, elementary)

ENTELEK, 327

Endurance, 226–228

English, 310

    and independent study, 251, 252

    in nongraded high school, 100–103

    preparation of teachers, 299–300

    teachers, 210

    and team teaching, 136–148

English, Fenwick, 109

English 2600, 311–312

Enrichment, 162

Environment, 224

Equipment, filmmaking, 357–363

ESEA (*see* Elementary and Secondary Education Act of 1965)

Evaluation, 124, 220, 222, 231–232

    English achievement, 136–148

    immediate, with CAI, 325–335

    IPI, 244–245

    of modular scheduling, 280

    and reporting, 73

    of teachers, 406–414

    of team teaching, 157

Examinations, 184, 185, 189

Excellence, 21–22

Expenses, preprimary, 385

Experiment(s), 137–148

    with computer-based resource units, 346–351

    in health, 149–153

    with programmed instruction, 311–315

    with teaching machine, 317–318

Experiment(s) (*cont.*)
  television, 302–303
  with underachievers, 166–177

Facilities, instructional, 159
Failure, 80
  attitude in streaming, 188
  not used as threat, 96–97
  of team teaching, 154–160
Feldhusen, John, 295
Filmmaking, 352–364
Flanders' Interaction Analysis, 193, 198
Flexibility, 59, 69–71, 85, 157, 172–173
Ford Foundation, 111
Foreign language, 104, 310
Form (grouping), 92–94
Frameworks for evaluating teachers, 408–414
Franklin School Project, 111–121
Frazier, Alexander, 214, 297

Games, 409
Gary plan, 108, 206
Gates Advanced Primary Reading Tests, 50
Gayfer, Margaret, 5
Geddes, Cleone, 295
Gehret, Kenneth G., 264
Georgiades, William, 109
Gifted students (*see* Students, gifted)
Girls, in independent study, 250–255
  and team teaching, 152–153
Goals, 8, 27, 28, 218, 222, 339–340, 371
  cognitive, 96, 193–194
  of individual instruction, 219, 229, 259
  middle-class orientation of, 63–64
  in team teaching, 156
Goldstein, William, 109
Goodlad, John I., 374, 376
Gores, Harold, 375
Grade, definition of, 41
Graded schools (*see* Schools, graded)
Grading (*see* Reporting)
Grouping, 4, 71–73, 87–89, 92–99, 161–212, 220

Grouping (*cont.*)
  ability, 20, 75–77
    in Britain, 184–190
    evaluation of, 161–165, 179–183
    evaluation of teaching, 191–198
    summary of research in, 200–203
  departmental, 205
  experiment with underachievers, 166–177
  heterogeneous, 162–164, 166–177, 188, 191–198, 200–204, 379
  homogeneous, 23, 61–62, 72, 188, 205, 239
  in modular scheduling, 279
  multiage, 35–36, 72
  nongraded, 21
  plans, 204–211
  and team teaching, 112, 117–119
Group(s), 114, 154, 156, 157
  tutorial, 394
Guidance, 94
Gymnasium, 399

Hagstrom, Ellis A., 109
Harris, W. T., 42
Harvard University, 111
Headmaster, 185
Head Start, 3, 4, 19, 378
Health, 149–153
Heathers, Glen, 4, 5
Hedges, William, 214
Heinich, Robert, 294
Henmon-Nelson Test of Mental Abilities, 151, 250
Hillson, Maurie, 39–40, 214
History, 251
Holden, George S., 296
Hosic's Cooperative Group Plan, 205
Housego, B. E. J., 39
Hoy, Wayne, 375, 376
Hyman, Ronald T., 375

IMS (*see* Instructional Management System)
Independent study, 17, 19–20, 22, 154, 213, 219, 232–234, 246–255
Individual, differences in, 64, 236
Individually Prescribed Instruction Project, 215

Industry, 334
Information retrieval systems, 235
Innovation, 1, 3, 5, 10, 12–21, 271, 421–423
    See also Change
Instruction, 19–21, 63, 124, 188, 256–261
    computer-based systems of, 295–296, 316–318, 324–335, 346–351
    evaluation of, 157
    fundamentals of, 26
    and IMS, 336–344
    individual, 4, 17, 72, 182, 191–192, 206, 213–261, 329–330, 392, 394
        characteristics of, 230–235
        computer aids, 325–326, 346–351
        defined, 214, 369–371
        elements of, 217–220
        for the nonpromoted, 49
        and organizational arrangements, 22–24
        results of experiments in, 315–316
    individually prescribed, 23, 215, 241–245
    mediated, 294, 298–323
    programmed, 295–296, 305–323, 329–330
    and team planning, 123
    and television, 300–303
    tutorial, 326–327, 381, 394
    See also Teaching
Instructional Management System, 336–344
Intelligence, 170
Interaction Analysis, 197–198
Invention, 226
Iowa Tests of Educational Development, 280
IPI (*see* instruction, individually prescribed)
IQ, 170, 186–187
    See also Tests, IQ

Jackson, Brian, 186–187
Jason's Instructional Observation Record, 346–350

Jerman, Max, 295–296
Johnson, Howard M., 264

Karnes, Merle, 164
Kindergarten, 209, 378, 400–401
Kooi, Beverly, 295

Lancaster, Joseph, 107
Language arts, 76
Language of the Classroom (Bellach, Kliebard, Hyman, and Smith), 411
Leadership, 27, 158–159
Learner, 35, 63, 218, 222, 226
Learning, 3, 57
    cultural differences in, 63–64
    development of skills in, 19, 20
    discovery method, 70
    emphasis on process of, 70
    failure-free, 218, 227
    in free environment, 388–390
    larger aspects of, 214, 221, 222–228
    resource centers, 234
    by teaching, 234
Learning Research and Development Center, 241, 243
Learning theory, 27–28, 305, 319–321
Library, 9, 10, 399, 404
Library Orientation Test for College Freshmen, A, 250, 253

Machines, teaching (*see* Teaching machines)
Management, classroom, 336–344
Marking (*see* Reporting)
Mastery, 17, 21–22, 28–29, 163, 214, 218, 230
Materials, 3, 70, 122, 219, 222, 243, 305–306, 310
Math, 95–96, 104, 310
Maurer, David, 40
Merit pay, 128
Methodology, 219, 222
Methods of inquiry, 16–18, 27–28
Metropolitan Achievement Tests, 250, 251

Michigan State General Self-Concept of Ability Scale, 280
"Mini-school", 378
Modular scheduling (see Scheduling)
Module, 263–264
Montessori, Maria, 305
Moore, O. K., 317–318
Motivation, 8, 10, 97

National Foundation for Educational Research (Britain), 189
Newton Plan, 210
Nongraded programs, 14, 20, 22, 28–29, 33–35, 41, 204, 207, 209
  defined, 55
  elementary school, 68–78
  evaluated, 79–84
  reporting, 73–75
  secondary school, 85–106
  See also Continuous progress education
Nonprofessional, 113–114
Nonpromotion (see Promotion)

Obsolescence, 315
Oettinger, Anthony, 296–297
Olsen, Jim, 164
Olson, Carl O., 109
Ontario Institute for Studies in Education (Toronto), 5, 7
Organization, 12–13, 15, 20, 222
  changes in, to foster excellence, 21
  at elementary level, 18
  questionnaire, 8
  in relation to aims, 5–6
  selecting new patterns of, 26
  See also Grouping; Nongraded programs
Organizational Climate Description Questionnaire, 418
Originality, 172–173

PACE (see Projects to Advance Creativity in Education)
Paraprofessional, 132
Parents, 74, 159, 163, 280–281, 381
Parkway Program, 391–397

Pask, Gordon, 316–317
Perceived Parents Attitude Scale, 169
Perceived Peer Relationships Scale, 170
Personality, 186
Pfeiffer, Isobel L., 164
Philadelphia Parkway Program, 391–397
Physical being, 223–224
PI (see Instruction, programmed)
Placement, 36, 57
Planning, 56–57, 122–126, 155, 268, 346–351
Plans, 204–211, 267–274, 287–292
Plowden Report, 185, 187–189
Poet, 217, 223, 227
Polos, Nicholas C., 264
Prepared Environment, The (M. H. Loeffler), 384
Pressey, Sidney L., 306–307, 370
Primary schools (see Schools, elementary)
Principal, 116, 133, 159, 406–414
Problem-solving, 16–17
Programmed instruction (see Instruction, programmed)
Programs, 2, 63, 91, 214, 247–248, 319
  for Beloit-Turner Middle School, 387
  computer, 324–327, 330–333
  evaluation of, 16
  Parkway, 391–397
  preschool, 378–383
  tutorial, 326–327
  Winnetka, 22
Projects To Advance Creativity in Education, 3
Promotion, 10, 35, 44, 53, 58
  in nongraded schools, 42–43
  and nonpromotion, 39, 49, 60–61
Pupil (see Student)
Pupil Control Orientation Form, 417
Psychology, 410

Questionnaires, 7–11, 250–253

Rand, M. John, 109
Rate of advancement, 22

Readiness, 58–59
Reading, 76
  experiment, 318
  goals, 339–340
  retardation, 19
  tests, 50
Reform, 384–385, 424–426
Release time, 157
Remedial prescription, 343–344
Reporting, 21, 38, 73–75, 105
Reports by computer, 41–44, 338
Research, 3, 112, 129
  on ability grouping, 162, 201–203
  budget, 99
  federal, 366–367
  on independent study, 249–255
  lack of, 162
  on teaching, 299
Research worker in education, 114
Richardson, Don H., 215
Robinson, Wade M., 109
Rudd, W. G. A., 189
Rutgers Plan, The, 210
Russian schools, 182

Saettler, Paul, 295
SAKI (see Self-organizing Automatic
    Keyboard Instruction)
Salary, 116, 128
Scheduling, 96–97, 263–292
Schlaadt, Richard G., 109
School and University Program for
    Research and Development,
    111–112
School(s), 16, 63
  buildings, 121
    freedom to explore, 388
    new concepts in, 398–405
    for preprimary schools, 383–384
  and business functions, 133
  child-centered versus subject-cen-
    tered, 68
  climate in, 415–420
  for continuous progress education,
    64–66
  decentralization of, 425

School(s) (cont.)
  elementary, 68–78
    aim of, 70
    and change, 134
    climate in, 415–420
    grouping plans, 204–211
    and IMS program, 337–344
    nongraded, 68–78
    study of instruction in, 256–261
    teachers in, 412
    team teaching in, 111–121
    Winnetka program, 22
  graded, 34–35, 41–43, 56, 239
  grammar, British, 184
  infant, British, 185
  junior, British, 185
  level of authority, 371
  manager, 133
  middle, 386–390
  physical structure of, 10
  preschool, 377–385
  and scheduling, 265
  secondary, 97
    in Britain, 189–190
    differentiated staffing in, 134
    experiments in, 136–153
    failure to teach learning skills
      in, 19–20
    flexible scheduling in, 266–275
    fostering excellence in, 22
    grouping plans, 205–211
    and independent study, 246–255
    nongraded, 85–106
    and programmed instruction, 314–
      315
    Parkway Program in, 391–397
    research implemented in, 366
    study of English achievement in,
      136–148
    study of teaching in, 149–153
    team teaching in, 109
  task of, 19, 21
  use of programmed instruction in,
    309–316
  year, length of, 106
Schwab, J. J., 407
Science, 13, 76, 310
Segregation, 180

Self-organizing Automatic Keyboard Instruction, 317
Sensibility, 224–225
Shane, Harold, 165, 378
Shane, June, 378
Shaw Health Knowledge Test, 149, 151
Shorthand, 104
Skills, 19–21, 28–29, 74, 76, 243, 253, 339, 340
Skinner, B. F., 308–309, 320–321
Snobbery, 188
Social issues, 387
Social sciences, 310
Social studies, 76
Sociology, 408–409
Spanish, 312–313
Spelling, 310
Staff, 185
    differentiated, 127–135
    and flexible scheduling, 268, 274–275
    and planning changes, 22–27
    preschool, 379–380
    reeducation, 14, 30
    specialization, 29
    in team teaching, 116, 120
    See also Teachers
Standards, 17, 87, 96, 184
Stanford-Binet Test (1937), 167
Stoddard dual progress plan, 22
Strands computer program, 330–333
Streaming, 185–190
    See also Grouping
Student(s), 70, 145, 158, 179, 181–182, 188, 193–194, 341–344, 416–417
    and ability grouping, 200–203
    able, 185, 200–201, 210, 273–274, 312
    attitudes of, 76–77, 170, 173–175, 177
    average, 76–77, 152–153, 162–163, 312
    in Beloit-Turner Middle School, 387
    British, 184
    and Computer-Assisted Instruction, 325–333

Student(s) (cont.)
    in continuous progress education, 57–58
    and filmmaking, 352–364
    gifted, 9, 76–77, 164, 166–177, 209
    and independent study, 232–234, 247–255
    and individual instruction, 182, 232–234
    and mediated instruction, 301
    and modular scheduling, 279–281
    nonacademic, 97
    and nongraded organization, 82–84
    in Parkway Program, 393–395
    redeployment, 118, 121
    and schedules, 267, 269–271, 283–285
    slow, 22, 64, 76–77, 95–96, 193–194, 201, 209–210
        and ability grouping, 162–163
        grouping of, 209
        in health experiment, 152–153
        and learning by teaching, 234
        and programmed instruction, 312
        and promotion study, 44–53
        and streaming, 186–189
    superior, 152–153, 162–163, 180
Studies, 3
    of ability grouping, 75–77, 200–203
    of age grading, 62–63
    of behavior, 3
    of Canadian schools, 7–11
    of climate in elementary schools, 417–420
    of computers and planning, 346–351
    of continuous progress education, 39–40
    of flexible scheduling, 266–275
    of independent study, 246–255
    of instruction, 257–261
    of modular scheduling, 276–282
    of nongraded organization, 79–84
    of promotion, 44–53
    of secondary English achievement, 136–148

Studies (*cont.*)
    of secondary teaching, 149–153
    of teaching behavior, 191–198
    of team teaching, 150
    of underachievers, 166–177
Supervision, 413
Suppes, Patrick, 295–296
Systems analysis, 235, 367–371
Szabo, Michael, 295

Taxonomy of Educational Objectives
    (*1956*) (Bloom), 193, 197–198
Teacher(s), 24, 29, 36, 74, 76, 89, 103,
    106, 113, 146, 158, 164–165, 172,
    180–181, 193–194, 201, 237, 316,
    388, 404, 412, 425
    and computer resource guides, 346–
        351
    English, 210, 299–301
    and individual instruction, 182, 232
    and innovation, 421–423
    and Instructional Management Sys-
        tem, 337–338, 341–344
    observation of, 400–414
    in Parkway Program, 395
    preschool, 379–381
    role in classroom, 134
    role in filmmaking, 353–357
    role in independent study, 248–249
    role in modular scheduling, 279–
        281
    sample of flexible schedule for, 271–
        273
    senior, 111, 115, 132
    specialists, 18, 135
    in team teaching, 115, 157–158
    and television, 300–301
    and various groups, 188, 192–198,
        257–261
Teaching, 192–198
    differences evaluated, 256–261
    effectiveness of, 149–153
    of homogeneous classes, 191–198
    improvement of, through planning,
        122–126
    lack of validated theory of, 370–371
    of large groups, 114

Teaching (*cont.*)
    low attraction of, 112
    observation of, 406–414
    problem of evaluating, 298–299
    team, 14, 15, 18, 107–160, 210–211
        and advancement, 23
        defined, 108, 115
        demands of, 156–159
        evaluation of, 123, 136–148
        experiment in health, 149–153
        flexible schedule in, 137–139
        Franklin School Project, 111–121
        literature on, 29
        nature of, 155–156
        reasons for failure of, 154–160
        in secondary schools, 109
        staff, 115–121
    and television, 299–301
    See also Instruction
Teaching machines, 306, 308–309, 317–
    318, 319
Technology, 293–371
Television, 300
Temple City Plan, 128–135
Tests, 180, 181, 186, 194, 196–198
    achievement, 171–172
    Brown-Holtzman Survey of Study
        Habits and Attitudes, 250, 280
    California Achievement, 167, 169
    of creative ability, 170
    of Critical Thinking, 250
    Flanders' Interaction Analysis, 193
    in individually prescribed instruc-
        tion, 243
    and Instructional Management Sys-
        tem, 337–338, 340–342
    IQ, 161–162, 180, 182, 185
    Organizational Climate Description
        Questionnaire, 418
    Perceived Parents Attitude Scale,
        169
    Perceived Peer Relationships Scale,
        170
    Pupil Control Orientation, 417
    reading, 50
    Scholastic High School Placement,
        280
    School Inventory, The, 250, 252

Tests (*cont.*)
  Stanford-Binet (1937), 167
  used in studies, 137–153
Thelen, Herbert A., 320, 323
Title III (*see* Elementary and Secondary Education Act of 1965)
Tradition, role of, 114
Training, teacher, 18, 425
Transfer system, 186–187, 189
Trump Plan, 23, 210

Underachievers, 164, 166–177
UNESCO Report, 186–187
Ungraded schools (*see* Nongraded; Continuous progress education)
Unit, 124, 243
United States Government, 333

United States Government (*cont.*)
  Office of Education, 3, 265–266, 367–368
University, in Britain, 184–185, 190
Unstreamed schools, 184–190
Uses for Things Test, 250, 252

Visual arts, 225
Vocabulary, 76

Winnetka Plan grouping, 205–206
Winnetka program, 22
Woodring Proposal, the, 210
Worth, Walter, 39

Zahorik, John A., 215